THE STORY OF
JUDAS PRIEST
Defenders of the faith

MW00578940

THE STORY OF
JUDAS PRIEST
Defenders of the faith

NEIL DANIELS

OMNIBUS PRESS
London • New York • Paris • Sydney • Copenhagen • Berlin • Madrid • Tokyo

Copyright © 2008 Omnibus Press
(A Division of Music Sales Limited)

ISBN 13: 978.0.8256.3605.9
Order No: OP52536

The Author hereby asserts his/her right to be identified as the author of this work in accordance with Sections 77 to 78 of the Copyright, Designs and Patents Act 1988.

All rights reserved. No part of this book may be reproduced in any form or by any electronic or mechanical means, including information storage or retrieval systems, without permission in writing from the publisher, except by a reviewer who may quote brief passages.

Exclusive Distributors
Music Sales Limited,
14/15 Berners Street,
London, W1T 3LJ.

Music Sales Corporation,
257 Park Avenue South,
New York, NY 10010, USA.

Macmillan Distribution Services,
53 Park West Drive,
Derrimut, Vic 3030,
Australia.

Every effort has been made to trace the copyright holders of the photographs in this book but one or two were unreachable. We would be grateful if the photographers concerned would contact us.

Printed in the United States of America by Quebecor World

A catalog record for this book is available from the British Library.
Visit Omnibus Press on the web at www.omnibuspress.com

Dedicated to my grandparents
Joseph Brian Daniels
and
Rita May Daniels
R.I.P.

CONTENTS

FOREWORD BY AL ATKINS

1969 brings back many fond memories for me. One particular memory that stands out is of the greatest rock'n'roll band ever – The Beatles. 1969 saw their last live public performance on the roof of Apple Records in London and the release of their penultimate album, which was the magnificent *Abbey Road*. The Beatles have always been a major influence on me as a musician, singer and songwriter. It was because of them and the Sixties Merseybeat sound that I wanted to get into the rock'n'roll business in the first place, and I'm bloody glad I did. I have no regrets at all about that.

One other memory from 1969 is of my old friend Robert Plant, who is also from my home town of West Bromwich in the heart of the Black Country. Along with Jimmy Page, John Bonham and John Paul Jones in Led Zeppelin, he and the band released their first album, titled *Led Zeppelin*, in January of that year. A new benchmark for heavy rock was set and the history of rock would change its course forever. I can remember when I first listened to songs like 'Babe, I'm Gonna Leave You', 'Black Mountain Side' and 'Dazed And Confused'. Zeppelin entwined so many musical influences, from rock'n'roll to folk to blues and even classical. I was mostly interested in the heavier rock sound of Zeppelin. I knew where I wanted to go from then onwards.

In 1969 I formed a small local heavy rock band influenced by the likes of Cream, Led Zeppelin and Jimi Hendrix. The band was called Judas Priest. The name for the band was decided by my bass player and best mate Bruno Stapenhill, who took it from the Bob Dylan song 'The Ballad Of Frankie Lee And Judas Priest'.

Who would have thought back then that they too would become a major part of rock'n'roll music history? I certainly didn't! I would have laughed at the idea and thought it was some sort of wind-up.

Although I was only a part of Judas Priest for four years, I nevertheless feel that I left my mark by writing classic songs such as 'Winter' and 'Never Satisfied' on *Rocka Rolla*, which was the band's first album in 1974 for Gull Records. I also helped to write 'Dreamer Deceiver' and 'Victim Of Changes', which were recorded for their second album, *Sad Wings Of*

Destiny. Actually, 'Victim of Changes' is an absolute gem of a song and I have recorded it twice myself; on the album of the same name and for my latest release *Demon Deceiver*. The lyrics are an amalgamation of Rob Halford's song 'Red Light Lady' and my own song 'Whisky Woman'. I am proud to say it is one of the all-time great heavy metal songs.

I have followed Judas Priest's every move from day one and have collected their albums over the years. If I am to be completely honest with myself and the band's fans, I'll admit that I do have regrets about leaving Judas Priest back in May, 1973. But, on the other hand, I don't think they would have taken the same direction if I had stayed with them. We all make decisions that we feel are the right things to do at that particular point in time and have to live with the consequences in later years. I needed to leave Judas Priest for a number of reasons, primarily to look after my family and to provide for them financially, which Judas Priest was not doing at that time. Being in the band was a tough slog even though we did have some fun. In the end, I had to leave. I didn't really have much choice.

I have many fond memories of being in Judas Priest – and some not quite so fond – but one thing is for sure – I formed the band in 1969 and without me and Bruno, there would be no Judas Priest, and for that I am immensely proud.

Rob Halford's dynamic, powerful and uniquely high-octave voice and phenomenal stage presence is a force to be reckoned with and those heavy, twin-guitar harmonies, courtesy of the great guitar duo Glenn Tipton and K.K. Downing, are something I could only dream about in those early years. Ian Hill's thumping bass and Scott Travis, who is the only American drummer to have played in the band, have also added enormous strength to Judas Priest's sound, which is something I am also envious of.

I still keep in touch with Judas Priest when they are in town and have the utmost respect for a band that have worked so hard over all these years and still come up with more and more classic metal songs.

In actual fact, I had the chance to meet up with them not too long ago on their recent tour of the UK in 2005. I met the lads backstage at the NEC show in Birmingham and we shared a few beers and had a few laughs about the old days. It was good. My friend who came along with me to watch the gig was in total awe when he shook their hands for the first time, but to me they are still a bunch of old mates who made good. I was particularly pleased to see them play 'Victim Of Changes' during the set.

I have often been asked: 'How did it all begin?' So when Neil contacted me about an interview for this book I was more than happy to take part. Talking to Neil via email and over the phone for several months during 2006 and 2007 brought back a lot of memories for me, and I am more than pleased to share them with him and everybody else who cares to listen. I have tried my best to explain my role in the history of Judas Priest and have put lots of photos and memories on my website (http://www.alatkins.com) for fans to learn about the years before Rob came along.

One thing is certain though – Judas Priest are the true Heavy Metal Gods. No band comes close to their sheer power and amount of classic metal songs. I hope they carry on making more great music for the future . . .

Al Atkins
January, 2007

INTRODUCTION

". . . Priest are 'defenders of the faith' . . . the faith being heavy metal music. And we're defending it against every aspect . . . it's a statement for everybody."

– Rob Halford speaking to *Sounds* magazine in 1983 whilst promoting *Defenders Of The Faith*

IN October, 2005, while Judas Priest were on tour in America, their manager Jayne Andrews collected the 'Metal Guru' award on the band's behalf at *Classic Rock* magazine's 'Roll Of Honour' ceremony in London. *Classic Rock* created the award for those artists "who have shaped the world of metal". It was an incredible and fitting achievement for a band that had over the course of so many years constructed, defined, typified and even experimented with the genre. Fast forward to Las Vegas in May, 2006 and Judas Priest, along with Queen, Def Leppard and Kiss, were recognised at the initial *VH1 Rock Honours* awards ceremony, which was being televised around the globe. Bands such as Foo Fighters, Anthrax and the All-American Rejects paid homage to their childhood idols. However it was the Boston-based metal band Godsmack who paid tribute to Priest with a soaring medley of 'The Hellion', 'Electric Eye', 'Victim Of Changes' and 'Hell Bent For Leather'. Although hardly at the end of their career, such acknowledgements proved that Judas Priest's hard work and effort had not been without merit. It was almost as if the award – and others like it – was created especially for them.

The Hollywood film *Rock Star* is often considered to be the (partly) true story of Judas Priest. Their history does seem like some Tinseltown rockumentary, as lived out by a bunch of penniless English working-class rockers with boundless talent and determination. Even Rob Halford agrees that the Judas Priest story is pure Hollywood, although he certainly wasn't thinking of a film like *Rock Star* when he spoke to *Hard Rock* magazine in 1986: "If you want to go out and see a movie about the band, go and see something like . . . *Spinal Tap* . . . As a matter of fact, our story has a better ending than that." Indeed it has.

Judas Priest suffered years of poverty, neglect and depression only to rise to the top of their game with record sales of over 30 million and legions of fans, admirers and imitators. Above all else – and because of their rich and creatively diverse back catalogue – they gained respect from their peers. As such, they will go down in heavy rock's history as originators.

There have been various line-up and image changes over four decades of Judas Priest. They began in the late Sixties as a pseudo blues-rock outfit dressed in ordinary working attire. In the early Seventies, they looked and sounded much like a progressive rock band, implausibly dressed in coloured satin, chiffon, frilly costumes and overly large Stetson hats. In the late Seventies, they finally settled on the more familiar black leather and chains. It seemed as if Judas Priest were on a mission to deliver heavy metal to the world, although it took them several years to discover this.

Heavy metal is the one true form for Judas Priest, who established the blueprint for every sub-genre that has followed. Yet it is often derided by puritanical writers and conservatives. The band were involved in an infamous court action in America when they were accused of inciting two young men from Reno, Nevada to commit suicide in 1985; the case was finally resolved in 1990 but it continues to have a lasting affect on the band. One of the young men was killed instantly but the other lived for a further three years with horrendous injuries. Priest were also targeted by the Parents Music Resource Center (PMRC) throughout much of the Eighties. 'Eat Me Alive' was listed third in the "Filthy Fifteen" – a list of songs that the PMRC deemed should be banned because of their lyrical content. Controversy also followed Priest into the 21st century when their ex-drummer Dave Holland, who played on the albums *British Steel* and *Screaming For Vengeance*, was convicted and imprisoned in 2004 for sexual abuse and attempted rape of a 17-year-old special needs boy. He received an eight-year sentence and a large fine. It's enough to say that Holland's career is well and truly over.

Equally newsworthy was Rob Halford's decision to 'come out' as a gay man on the MTV show *Superrock* in February, 1998. In the macho world of heavy metal, this was a particularly brave move.

"We represent British heavy metal and we want to take it around the world," Rob Halford told *Kerrang!* in 1982. No other metal band on the planet, whether it be Black Sabbath, Iron Maiden or Def Leppard, has persevered with this conviction as consistently as Judas Priest.

In keeping with the Spinal Tap theme, an unbelievable nine drummers (John Partridge, John Ellis, Alan Moore, Chris 'Congo' Campbell, John Hinch, Simon Phillips, Les 'Feathertouch' Binks, Dave Holland and Scott Travis) have graced the Judas Priest drum stool. However, it does seem as though they have finally settled on the formidable talents of American Scott Travis, who joined the Priest fold at the tail end of the Eighties.

There have been several changes in the vocals department, too. Before Rob Halford's arrival in 1973, there was singer and co-founder Al Atkins, who lacked the drive and determination of his successor. A few years after Halford's abrupt and highly publicised departure in May, 1992, American Tim 'Ripper' Owens lent his vocal talents to two unremarkable studio albums, one of which, 2000's *Demolition*, arguably becoming the biggest miscalculation of their career. As was the case with Iron Maiden, Judas Priest hit the doldrums in the Nineties and early Noughties, often playing to small crowds who barely even noticed the new singer. It was embarrassing to see the band sink to such depths.

This is not to say that Priest never made a wrong move during Halford's reign; there was the terrible *Ram It Down* album and the controversial *Turbo*, which relied entirely on synthesizer guitars. Although in hindsight the latter is not nearly as poor as it was initially made out to be, and it has recently, and quite rightly, achieved cult status. Their debut set *Rocka Rolla* has much to offer compared to later, more significant albums.

Priest also failed miserably at adopting a new image during the mid Eighties, mimicking the hair-metal look of bands like Mötley Crüe and Poison, who were dominating MTV. Although Priest were among the first metal bands to produce music videos in the early Eighties, they have made some truly horrendous clips over the years. Those early examples should perhaps act as a guide on how music videos should *not* look.

Priest fans breathed a sigh of relief when Halford returned to the band in July, 2003, which, to date, appears to be permanent.

Despite all the gold records, sold-out tours and awards, at the time of writing there is not one book available on the history of Judas Priest. The long out-of-print 1984 book *Heavy Duty* by Steve Gett was an authorised account of the band's rise to success. Although entertaining and passionately written, it is far too slim and reads like a press release, neglecting much of the pre-Halford history, which seems to have been disregarded by the band and their management, whether deliberately or otherwise.

When researching this book, an approach was made to Judas Priest's management. It soon became clear that they were less than enthusiastic about the prospect and declined to co-operate, which is probably just as well considering how their involvement in *Heavy Duty* made that book so sanitised. I received an email to the effect that Judas Priest ". . . do not want an 'official' book on themselves and are not prepared to put time and effort into it – they feel they need to put all their time and effort into their music just now."

In a separate email to the author in 2006, Jayne Andrews stated their position: "It has come to our attention that you are trying to get various contact details for producers and musicians who have worked with Judas Priest in the past – I should reiterate that the band do NOT condone this book, as I informed you – it is not an *official* book on the band and we will make that clear to anyone who asks."

While making some great music over the years the band also made more than a handful of questionable decisions, and this book addresses such matters.

Judas Priest's rise to prominence and notoriety has been written about in a whole wealth of magazines, fanzines, rock encyclopaedias and biographies on other heavy metal bands. Moreover, the struggle to re-establish themselves with a new singer during the Nineties (akin to fellow British metal legends Iron Maiden with Blaze Bayley) has also been well publicised. The tale of how Tim Owens got the singer's job with Priest was even partially immortalised in the 2001 Hollywood film *Rock Star* starting Mark Wahlberg as a tribute-band singer plucked from obscurity and flung into the international spotlight. Priest's renewed success and critical acclaim culminated in them co-headlining the 2004 Ozzfest tour of America with Black Sabbath – their first tour with Halford since 1991.

Though it is the Halford-fronted line-up that has received (and continues to receive) the most attention, *Defenders Of The Faith* endeavours to delve further into the band's past, beginning with the groups that preceded the first line-up (Mark I) formed by Al Atkins and his best friend, bassist Brian 'Bruno' Stapenhill in 1969. Together, the pair had previously been in and out of many West Bromwich-based bands before they eventually formed and named Judas Priest. The importance of Atkins to Judas Priest has long been overshadowed by the success that followed his departure.

At various points, you will notice that the narrative drifts off on a tangent, discussing various solo projects of current and former band members, and other musical but not specifically Judas Priest-related endeavours. One way or another such tales all form part of the Judas Priest legend. Allied to this, several appendices at the end of the book are intended as a reference tool for Priest fans.

Rock hard and ride free, people – this is the complete and headbanging story of Judas 'fucking' Priest . . .

Neil Daniels
February, 2007

PART 1

THE BLACK COUNTRY: BRITISH STEEL, COAL MINES AND THE INDUSTRIES

ONE

Before The Dawn

". . . Walsall and West Bromwich were pretty bleak parts . . . We could all relate to the need and the want of trying to break out of an unpleasant cycle."

– Rob Halford speaking to *Classic Rock* magazine in early 2006

THERE is probably no more appropriate place in Great Britain to create heavy metal rock music than in the Midlands or, to be more precise, the vast area of the West Midlands known as the Black Country.

It's inconceivable that Black Sabbath and Judas Priest – both in their own ways archetypal British heavy metal bands – would have created the music they have spent the past 30 years of their lives making if they had come from, say, the sprawling green acres of Sussex or the rocky peninsulas of Cornwall. If the saying is true that great originals have to suffer for their art, during the earlier part of their career, Judas Priest, in each of their incarnations, certainly did: financially, creatively and personally. This was due, in part, to the hardships of their origins.

To understand Judas Priest and the genre they helped construct and define, it's important to put their home region in some sort of historical and social context as it continues to influence Priest's music to this day, even though they have never actually recorded an entire album there. The lyrics to 'Deal With The Devil' from 2005's comeback album *Angel Of Retribution* is an accurate if brief portrayal of how the band survived working in the industrial provinces. Halford's anthemic 'Made In Hell' (from *Resurrection*) tells a similar story. Like the original members of Black Sabbath, Judas Priest have never forgotten their roots; their upbringing remains indelible.

It is widely acknowledged among music historians that Black Sabbath made the first 'proper' heavy metal album in 1970. In his extensive Sabbath biography, *Sabbath Bloody Sabbath*, Joel McIver writes: "Did Black Sabbath invent heavy metal and if so how the hell did they do it? Heavy metal wasn't planned: it came about thanks to a set of fortuitous coincidences that placed the vital amount of pressure at a key point in musical evolution, and the whole flow of history was altered as a result."

This book does not examine the evolution of heavy metal, although it can be argued that Judas Priest considerably furthered the genre's progression from the hard blues-rock of Led Zeppelin and Deep Purple to the screaming, roaring metal chords of the 21st century. "We didn't call our stuff heavy metal then," K.K. Downing told *Metal Hammer* in the late Eighties. "It was progressive blues, which became progressive rock." Once the term heavy metal became widespread in the Seventies, Judas Priest were the first band to fully embrace and develop the identity and sound.

McIver correctly acknowledges that the almost identical backgrounds of Priest and Sabbath infused their heavy, dark approach: "They didn't suddenly choose to join a band in order to play heavy music: they played heavy music because they wanted to, and because they *needed* to – to be noticed and to let out the pressure they felt inside them. And where did it come from? From their surroundings."

Priest's surroundings were imperative to their sound, although they did not know it at the time. Whereas Black Sabbath, who started out as the Polka Tulk Blues Band, formed in Birmingham in 1968, Judas Priest's genesis was in the Black Country. When writers lazily refer to Judas Priest as a "Birmingham-based Band" or "the heavy metal band from Birmingham", they are emphatically wrong. Judas Priest is a heavy metal band that formed in the *Black Country*. Because they no longer specifically work there (except at home), it is erroneous to use words such as 'based'.

Over the years, there has been much controversy and debate as to what exactly the Black Country is in terms of its regional scope and breadth.[*] Like the city of London and elsewhere, the Black Country expanded over the years, eating away at neighbouring towns and villages, especially during the industrial revolution when market towns were much smaller and more localised. Historians claim that by the late 12th century, Wolverhampton was a diminutive market town but, according to W.G. Hoskins in his book *Local History In England*, "The town underwent a radical transformation during the course of the 19th century, by 1901 its population was over eight times larger than it had been in 1801." Hoskins provides another example of mass growth in the Midlands when he writes

---

[*] Local governments claiming parts of the Black Country include Dudley, Sandwell, Walsall, West Bromwich, Blackheath, Stourbridge and Wolverhampton, although there has been some confusion on the issue.

about how Heath Town in Staffordshire started out as a "squatter settlement" for workers in the metal industry in the 18th century, "but by the time the First World War happened it had become part of the conurbation that linked Wolverhampton to Walsall, Dudley, West Bromwich and Birmingham."

The 2006 edition of the *Collins English Dictionary & Thesaurus* defines 'conurbation' as "a large densely populated sprawl formed by the growth and coalescence of individual towns and cities." The Black Country most definitely fits this description, lying several miles outside of Birmingham in the county known as the West Midlands and parts of Worcestershire, Warwickshire and Staffordshire.* The area is bound by its gritty, industrial past, its name a consequence of the soot, pollution and general grimness that shrouded the region from the factory chimneys that turned the skies a darker shade of grey. Certainly, the atmosphere had a profound impact on Judas Priest's early albums *Sin After Sin* and *Stained Class*. This same dark landscape is widely believed to have influenced J.R.R. Tolkien while he was writing the *Lord Of The Rings* saga, specifically the bleak landscape known as 'Mordor'.

Tolkien himself was born in South Africa but spent part of his childhood in Birmingham and a small village in Worcestershire. His grandparents on his mother's side lived in Birmingham and actually owned a shop in the centre of the city. The depressing atmosphere and scenery that he saw during the early part of his life, which had a profound impact on him and his work, certainly influenced heavy metal and hard rock. Halford admitted the Tolkein influence to *Classic Rock* in 2006. "*Lord Of The Rings* is *de rigueur* for me because it's so metal."

Al Atkins, K.K. Downing and Ian Hill were all born in West Bromwich, while Glenn Tipton was born in Blackheath and Rob Halford grew up in Walsall. The fathers of Tipton and Halford both worked in the steel and metal industries. The metal trade in the Black Country dated back to the 16th century although, like much of the UK, the industry there had dwindled since the Sixties and Seventies. With the decline of the mining and manufacturing industries, the Black Country is no longer the industrial heart of the UK but a typical multicultural area with similar urban problems to elsewhere in Britain. The housing areas built in the post-war years in and around the Black Country provided homes for the families of

* Although the region has no formal centre, Dudley is considered by many to be the unofficial capital.

Downing, Hill and ex-drummer John Ellis, who all grew up on the rough Yew Tree council estate in West Bromwich.

The thick local dialect that characterises Midlands people has at times been the butt of (sometimes harsh) jokes for comedians. In many ways, the distinctive accent divides the inhabitants from the perceived wealthy upper classes of the South and the poor working classes of the North. They just don't seem to fit at either end. Dudley-born TV comedian Lenny Henry has prospered using his accent as the butt of his jokes, although more often than not they are aimed at himself. Each member of Judas Priest (with the obvious exception of American Scott Travis) has retained their broad Brummie (a colloquial word used to describe people from the Midlands area) brogue,* as do the members of Black Sabbath and Slade.

Unemployment was a key concern for the members of Judas Priest during the Al Atkins-fronted years. Rob Halford also struggled to find employment, hence the antisocial lyrics of 'Running Wild' and the anger of 'Breaking The Law'. Albums like *British Steel* indicated these early years of hardships stayed with them, and would influence the band's unique brand of heavy metal.

---

* Most evident in Rob Halford's voice on some of the slower Judas Priest tracks and particularly the album *Priest . . . Live!*

TWO

1963–1968

". . . The only thing they didn't like was calling the band Judas Priest."
   – Al Atkins, on his parents' opposition to his newly formed band
                              having a name with religious connotations

ALLAN JOHN ATKINS, more popularly known as Al, was born
on Tuesday, October 14, 1947 in West Bromwich. Like the rest of
Britain, the area was recovering from the devastating results of Nazi bombing during World War II and derelict sites lay everywhere. It was a grim
experience but families stuck together through the hardships. Atkins' childhood was strict. "I was brought up in a very religious family," he says. "My
father always wanted to be a priest; my mother was a Roman Catholic and
was very uneducated, being taught by nuns all through her schooling."

Despite this religious background, Atkins' home life seemed to be
similar to that of any other child in West Bromwich. He had an older
brother, Brian, and elder sister Valerie. The Atkins' fourth child, a girl
named Shiela, died of pneumonia aged four. Atkins was particularly close
to his brother, although he admits that they were vastly different. "My
brother and I were like chalk and cheese," he says. "He chose God. I stole
cars and took drugs."*

The Atkins' house in Stone Cross was small, like most of the other
homes in the neighbourhood. The family struggled to get by but still
managed to make ends meet.

Like most children in his borough, the young Atkins wasn't brilliant
academically, attending Charlemont School – from infants to senior –
simply because he had to. Perhaps surprisingly, Al's parents were supportive when he decided, upon leaving school, that music would be his
destiny. The Midlands was a thriving place for young, enthusiastic musicians. "Oh, in the Sixties . . . bands like The Beatles . . . we had the Liverpool beat boom and then we had the Birmingham beat boom. There were

_____
* Brian is now the pastor of a small church.

loads of bands coming out then and that's when I first started . . . it was a great scene in those times, you know. The music was great . . ."

In the very early days of his musical youth, Atkins was actually a drummer. "In the early Sixties, pop bands were starting up everywhere in Britain and playing in every pub and club across the country, all copying their idols like The Beatles and the Stones, myself included. I was obsessed by this new beat music and started my own band playing drums. It was in 1963 and my first band struggled alongside some of the older boys from Birmingham, and we split up after just a short time together.

"My parents were quite happy when I started to take up music seriously because I hung around with people like Bruno [future Judas Priest bassist and founding member, Brian Stapenhill], who was a big gentle giant and kept me away from a bunch of kids who were always getting into trouble . . . [He] lived just around the corner from me and things started to feel more confident."

Stapenhill remembers the first time he met his lifelong friend Atkins: "I used to play along to all The Shadows' and The Beatles' records, the old R&B numbers and that, and [there was this] chap named John Powney. His brother played bass and had a guitar and Allan lived in the next road down. We both went to the same school but I think he was a year in front of me. I think he must have heard us rehearsing and practising and he was starting a band up at the time . . . playing drums. We started having a rehearsal together and it sounded OK for the time. We got Bri (Brian) Powney on bass and Colin Matthews was on air rhythm guitar. I played lead and Al was on the drums and vocals.

"Bruno and I teamed up with a little 'mod' guitarist called Albert Hinton, also from West Bromwich," says Atkins, "and called ourselves The Reaction."

Bruno Stapenhill: "[Our] first booking was a neighbour's wedding at a place in West Bromwich up by the All Saints called The Coral Hall. It's gone now. It was an old corrugated tin shed. I was only 15."

As a simple trio, the band didn't immediately gel and it seemed obvious from the start that things would change fairly quickly. While still The Reaction, Atkins, Stapenhill and Hinton decided to switch roles. Al Atkins: "We were gigging quite a lot by now and everyone said I was a better vocalist than a drummer, so I switched to being a front man. Bruno changed over to bass guitar and I took over the vocals."

Bruno Stapenhill: "[The role switching] affected our sound because it freed Al up from playing the drums while trying to sing. It gave him more scope to concentrate on his vocals."

With the inclusion of rhythm guitarist Brian Fieldhouse and drummer Lawrence Farley, the group changed their name to The Bitta Sweet in 1965. Bruno Stapenhill: "I grew up with all The Shadows sort of stuff. We were doing Shadows and early R&B, like 'I'm A King Bee', and that sort of stuff. A few people told me it was more like pop stuff [so] from then on we branched into more blues-based stuff like the [Clapton-era] Blues Breakers, the early type blues . . . 'Smokestack Lightning' with a rock feel to it."

This change in the band's musical direction strengthened the sound and helped Atkins find his footing in a band environment. Fielding helped to create the heavier sound that Atkins and Stapenhill were striving for.

Work picked up as word of mouth spread around the local music scene. Their manager Ken Ford started putting them into bigger clubs and among the better known acts that The Bitta Sweet opened for were David Bowie, Dave Dee, Dozy, Beaky, Mick & Tich, and Long John Baldry & The Steam Packet, featuring Rod Stewart and Julie Driscoll on backing vocals.

Stapenhill reminisces fondly about the period: "Baldry was well known on the blues circuit. I mean, he'd got Rod Stewart with him. We did the Plaza Ballroom at Handsworth, The Ritz and Old Hill in Birmingham, Rialto, Adelphi and Gala Hall in West Bromwich and the Plaza at Old Hill. We always used to like playing the Old Hill because it had a revolving stage."

The Bitta Sweet split up at some point in 1965, though Stapenhill is unsure exactly when.[*] "We never secured a record deal," he says. "But this band was a first big stepping stone in my career. We split up when Albert got married and moved to Australia."

The mid Sixties was a hugely creative period for rock'n'roll, with blues influences beginning to heavily feature in British pop music. The Kinks' 1964 hit 'You Really Got Me' grabbed an entire generation with its repeated guitar riff, which is where some observers argue that heavy metal originated from.

The Who's 1965 debut album *My Generation,* featuring 'The Kids Are Alright' and its stunning title track, was an example of the hard rhythm

---

[*] On the Al Atkins website, *http://www.alatkins.com* there is a black and white photograph of the five-piece Bitta Sweet: Brian Fieldhouse, Al Atkins, Albert Hinton, Bruno Stapenhill and Lawrence Farley. The photo states 1966–68, although Atkins too believes the group actually split in 1965.

and blues sound that young Brits were striving to create, inspired by the grit and intelligent playing of the legendary American blues masters and the home-grown success and lyrical genius of The Beatles. The combination of sturdy vocals by Roger Daltrey, the dominant guitar of Pete Townshend, the floridness of John Entwistle's bass playing and the dynamic drumming of Keith Moon was earth shattering. "We always leaned towards The Small Faces, The Who and heavy rock stuff like that," says Atkins. "We were always listening to those sorts of heavier bands." He and Stapenhill were also particularly fond of the blues-rock trio Cream – guitarist Eric Clapton, bassist Jack Bruce and drummer Ginger Baker – who formed in mid-1966. The band's name derived from the term 'cream of the crop', as each musician was already well-respected in the UK jazz and blues scene.

In 1966, Atkins was asked to join the unfortunately named Sugar Stack, who were already established before The Bitta Sweet's demise. Atkins recalls that the band, which comprised local lads Geoff Furnival and Mick Reeves on guitars and drummer John Partridge, had heard The Bitta Sweet and invited he and Stapenhill to join them. With nothing else on offer, the pair immediately agreed.

Sugar Stack offered Atkins and Stapenhill their first opportunity to play the heavy blues-rock music they enjoyed listening to so much. Al Atkins: "It was a really, really good band. It was a five-piece and [John Partridge] was very influenced by Ginger Baker. We had a long, tall guy [Mick Reeves] who had a twin-necked Gibson like Jimmy Page had later on. And so we did a lot of heavy blues music and Cream stuff as well."

Stapenhill also speaks positively of the band's music but admits that it was an odd sound. "That was a strange mix of material. As odd as it might sound, it was like blues and Tamla, really. We were doing all the Tamla-Motown stuff but played with a rock blues guitarist – it sounded all right. It was quite a good mix of stuff . . ."

Sugar Stack gigged around the area extensively during the course of 1966, playing in pubs and working men's clubs. While providing a good opportunity for Atkins and Stapenhill to play the blues-rock they admired, there was a demand on the circuit for softer, pop material, which neither cared for at all. Al Atkins: "After about a year Bruno, John and myself started to hate the pop side of the band and decided to leave."

Cream's second album, *Disraeli Gears*, released in November 1967, inspired Atkins and Stapenhill to form a heavier blues band. One song in particular, 'Blue Condition', struck a chord with Atkins and Stapenhill and they decided it was an appropriate name for their next venture. "We were very influenced by that sort of band . . . Cream, Deep Purple, any bands like that really," Atkins recalls. "Pink Floyd were also coming on the scene, being progressive and heavy . . . you think, 'This is what we wanna do next.' It was always about listening to the next thing that was happening."

Stapenhill confirms Blue Condition's main influences: "We did Cream and Jimi Hendrix stuff. I think it was round about then that Al probably started writing. We started to throw material of our own together."

To complete the line-up, Atkins and Stapenhill recruited Dave Goodman on guitar and drummer Pete Boot, later of metal acts Budgie, Bullion and Lion.

Pete Boot: "It was around about 1967, I used to practise in the rooms above my parents' café [the Spot Café, Darlaston in the West Midlands]. One night, there came a heavy banging on the door. I thought that someone had come to the door to complain about the noise I was making. On opening the door I was confronted by a huge figure of a man [and] he introduced himself as Bruno Stapenhill. He immediately stepped into the café closely followed by two others, one of whom was Allan Atkins. They had plans to form a new band and asked me if I would join them, [which] I accepted."

Boot, Atkins and Stapenhill have remained friends ever since that moment. "Back in those early days, everybody knew everybody and nobody knew anybody," Boot recalls, "but they all knew somebody who played in a band, just friends making music. Throughout my teenage years I played in many good local bands." Boot recalls both Goodman and Stapenhill's musicianship as being of a high standard even back then, when they were not particularly experienced.

From the end of 1967 into 1968 Blue Condition spent much of their time gigging, although Boot recalls only that they played live "together for about six months at venues such as The Ship and Rainbow in Wolverhampton". "It was excellent!" he says enthusiastically. "I was breaking new ground, with musicians whose standards I struggled to reach but they had great patience . . . and most importantly I owned the group van – a Ford Thames."

Boot remembers an occasion when Blue Condition made a brief trip south to audition for Ron King Management, which managed Amen Corner, among others.

Pete Boot: "We travelled all the way down to Essex, and were told to set up in a corner and play three songs. We opened with a Hendrix song and Bruno broke a string, but we struggled through. At the end of the three songs the silence was broken by the comment: 'You're too fucking progressive'. We have always believed that Mr. King made the comment. But for the record he did spend time with us giving advice, he came across as a sincere person . . . We may have been progressive, but we were PROUD!"

"It was a fiasco," admits Stapenhill. "We went down there and there were a few bands doing this showcase or audition. It was in some hall in Romford. It was right in the middle of this bloody market stall and we had to carry all the gear over the bloody cabbages and veg, they were stuck in the gutter and that. We got in there and set up. I think we were doing a Hendrix thing. We'd just started off, I just went to start to play and one of my bloody strings went. And of course, you've only got about three numbers to play, so you haven't got time to fart about changing strings. I played as best I could, and Ron turned round and said the band's too progressive for what we're looking for. I remember that."

As with later bands in Atkins and Stapenhill's careers, there was little in the way of rock'n'roll hedonism to distract them. A decent pint of beer was about all that was on offer. Boot says there was no real drug scene back then: "Bruno had some ointments for piles, does that qualify? Oh, and yes, we drank tea."

Stapenhill agrees that the band had few excesses. "We used to have the odd smoke but I like me pint more than anything else and I still do. We used to go to parties but nothing like what you hear about [John] Bonham and Ozzy Osbourne. We was quite level-headed really, I suppose."

Despite such fun and excitement, after a year, Blue Condition split, though no one can seem to recall for what reason. Al Atkins: "It was like everything else, you know. You play for just a while and then, I don't know, you fall out or whatever. It was a good little band though."

Boot says the demise of Blue Condition came about because, "Al left the room! We were all young and had a whole life ahead of us. Socially, we have spent little time together. Al Atkins must be one of the most dedicated musicians I have worked with. He helped me change my style from pop to rock . . . I have always had respect for Allan. He stood in the many doorways of the rock world, but for some reason never entered the room and shut the door behind him."

After Blue Condition split in 1968, Atkins wound up in another band with Stapenhill called The Jug Blues Band, featuring Barry Civil and John Perry on guitars and the latter's sibling, Jim Perry, on drums. They began life as Halfbreed and then changed to Chapters Of Life, but their agency at the time thought the names were too progressive and thus not marketable.

12

"It was labelled a blues band, and again, it probably was but we was doing sort of rocky-stuff as well," says Bruno Stapenhill.

Their agency intended on promoting The Jug Blues Band as blues-rockers along the lines of Cream, Ten Years After or Love Sculpture. Though delighted at the prospect, Atkins recalls that they were not too keen on the name. "It was nothing to do with us really; we didn't even like the name. But, you know, that's what we was called . . . and we thought, well, 'If we're gonna get work we've gotta stick with the promoter and management,' that was the main thing."

Like Atkins and Stapenill's previous bands, Jug lasted for roughly one year, from 1968 to 1969 (Civil left to join another local outfit called Froot and Jim Perry became a member of blues band F.B.I. before moving on to Stallion, Lion and Bodie & Jinx), although they had their share of memorable gigs, one supporting fellow Midlands band Slade and Spooky Tooth at the Wolverhampton Civic Hall. Allan Atkins remembers this night vividly because of an offer that was made. "Adrian Ingram was a brilliant guitarist. He was really noted locally and he asked me to sing for his band, who were called Evolution at the time. I joined up with 'em but I never actually played any gigs with them. We rehearsed a little bit together but they went up to Morocco for three or four months and I never went with 'em. That was it really. Adrian is now one of the UK's top jazz players."

As Atkins remembers it, he left Jug that very night at the Wolverhampton Civic Hall, but it turned out that Evolution only wanted him to drive their tour bus around Morocco for the few months they were there. Atkins told them to "stick it". Evolution were managed by a Midlands-based promoter, Jim Simpson, who at one point was also the manager (and a member) of The Locomotive. Pete Boot knew them well: "The band's keyboard player used a Hammond organ on stage. Well, one day they had been rehearsing in his mother's front room in preparation for the evening's booking, and later on in the afternoon they packed all of the equipment that had been used in the mother's house, including the Hammond organ, into the back of the van, totally unaware that the family's pet cat had crept into the back of the keyboards. Well, you can imagine the scene when halfway through their first number out of the back of the organ emerged the poor cat as confused as everyone else; the crowd was in uproar as it was possibly the best part of the whole act."

To try and keep some sort of blues/progressive scene alive in Birmingham that was also within reach of other Midlands-based acts, Simpson had set up a blues night called Henry's Blues House at a pub called The

Crown, on the corner of Station Street and Hill Street. It not only played host for the acts Simpson managed like The Bakerloo Blues Line but for other blues and rock artists such as the American blues pianist Champion Jack Dupree and Earth, who later became, more famously, Black Sabbath.

Jim Simpson: "I rented this pub every Tuesday just as a showcase for [The] Bakerloo Blues Line. I rented the upstairs room of the pub and I put the band on, looked at the door take and paid the band and marketed it . . . they didn't use words like that in those days. And that's how it started. There was no place for work at all . . . we were the first progressive club outside of London. I don't know how true it was because I was sure it was happening elsewhere . . . so there wasn't that much work around in those days."

Simpson maintains Henry's was a fundamental part of the late Sixties Midlands blues-rock scene: "In those days . . . we had bands there like Status Quo, Taste [featuring Rory Gallagher] and [Arthur] Big Boy Crudup who wrote 'That's All Right [Mama]', which was his hit originally . . . Henry's Blues House was great . . . not just because Black Sabbath came out of it . . . It was named after a dog; Henry was a dog . . . a very glamorous Afghan hound."

Atkins' memories of Simpson are far from positive. "Adrian Ingram, who was a brilliant guitarist, chose me as a vocalist in two of his bands, Evolution and The Bakerloo Blues Line, which eventually changed its name to Hannibal. Both were managed by Jim Simpson, who kicked me out of both bands. He probably can't remember me with my long hair and beard but I'm glad he did [kick me out] because I went on to create my own project [Judas Priest]." Simpson, for his part, can barely even recall Atkins' name let alone his brief involvement in these bands. Ingram admitted to the author that he is equally baffled.

Whatever the specifics of Atkins' involvement in Ingram's bands, he says he left Evolution and wanted to go back to The Jug Blues Band but his reinstatement was declined. "They turned their backs on me, they said, 'Look, we've worked hard, now you've just pissed off and now you wanna come back?' I was always one for tryin' . . . you know, this ain't working; let's do something else, you know. Or if a chance comes along, take it. I still believe that now. You don't get many chances in this business, you know, and that's the way I've always felt."

THREE

1969–1970

"He was listening to a Bob Dylan album of his . . . It was Dylan's album John Wesley Harding *and a track come on called 'The Ballad Of Frankie Lee And Judas Priest'."*

– Al Atkins

IN 1989, K.K. Downing told *Metal Hammer* writer Chris Welch: "I started Judas Priest with myself on guitar, Ian [Hill] and another singer, Allan Atkins." He was wrong.

The true story of Judas Priest actually began *without* K.K. Downing – who was turned down at his first audition for the band – or any of the current band members for that matter. In 1969, the original line-up was singer Al Atkins, bassist Bruno Stapenhill, guitarist Ernie Chataway and drummer John Partridge. The setting was West Bromwich.

Stapenhill and John Perry had left Jug and reunited with Al Atkins, who was looking to get a band back together with their help.

Al Atkins: "There was me and Bruno, there was Johnny Perry out of the Jug Band and there was John Partridge out of the Sugar Stack band. So I'd picked up different players from different bands and made a little bit of a 'mini-local supergroup'."

Unfortunately, it seemed as though the gods were against them as, within days of their first rehearsal, John Perry died in somewhat mysterious circumstances, fatally injured in a road accident that some believe he orchestrated deliberately in order to commit suicide. "He actually committed suicide in the group's van," says one source close to the group. "I think it was a bit of drugs and over what happened with his girlfriend or something like that. He was a nice guy and he could have been really good. He reminded me very much of a young Gary Moore-type player."

The remaining trio were devastated. Atkins recalls, "It was a real good shock to us. I said . . . 'Let's just not keep mourning, let's just get another guitarist in. That's what Johnny would have liked us to do.' Within a week or so we were auditioning for somebody to take his place."

15

Auditions to replace the deceased guitarist took place in September and among those who attended was one Kenneth Downing, though he failed to impress Atkins, Stapenhill and Partridge. His playing was all over the place, with little focus or creativity. He mimicked Jimi Hendrix while churning out poor versions of Cream songs. In past interviews, Downing has admitted that he had been playing the guitar for less than two weeks before the audition, hence his inept performance.

Stapenhill recalls that Downing was auditioned in the front room of his parents' house: "I used to have this little Dallas amp beside the fireplace. He came and looked and Al said he seemed like an up-and-coming guitarist. And we said, 'Oh, you know, just have a browse through a 12-bar, a blues or a rock thing or something . . . just anything really,' and he said, 'What's a 12-bar?' He hadn't got a clue! He really hadn't got a clue what he was doing. He just wasn't up to our standards then. And we said, 'Sorry, you just ain't up to it Ken . . .' He was a nice enough chap. And I think we advertised and that's when Ernie [Ernest Chataway] cropped up. He just slotted in perfectly, straight away. He was really the co-founder of Priest."

"K.K. Downing came for one of the auditions," confirms Atkins. "He never got the job. Ernie got the job . . . He was about the same age as K.K. He was only young, about 17. He was a very natural musician. He played guitar, keyboards and harmonica. Name it, he'd do it. He was just a really, really good player from Birmingham."

Not only did Chataway's guitar playing impress the trio of Atkins, Stapenhill and Partridge, but his ability on keyboards and harmonica made him far and away the best choice. The teenage guitar player was signed to the Randells Replacement Agency in Birmingham, which found work for musicians looking to join bands. When the agency pointed Chataway in the direction of Atkins, the band did not shy away from talking about Perry's suicide in front of him. "I knew all about [John Perry] and it was a bit uncanny because I think he was 16 when he killed himself, he was a bit older than me and . . . we kind of looked a bit similar-ish, you know. It was talked about a lot . . . I suppose it was quite a big deal really but I was never, you know, it wasn't a thing I was worried about. Or, 'I've got to fill his boots' or do this or that. It was just a totally different thing. Again, you see, I'd never met the guy . . ."

What appealed most to Atkins and Stapenhill about Chataway's playing was that he reminded them of Gary Moore, then with Irish blues band Skid Row.

Ernie Chataway: "I was obviously into the blues guys. Brian [Stapenhill] was the musicologist of the band. He had a radiogram and bought the records. I was always into Jeff Beck but they got me into the *Truth* album and the *Beck-Ola* album, with Rod Stewart and Ron Wood. And that was it for me. Brian got a reel-to-reel tape player and we set it up in the bedroom and we recorded loads. There used to be a magazine called *Beat Instrumental*, and I borrowed some for the Peter Green chords from a guy in Worcester who owned a guitar shop."

It has been suggested that Chataway had previously played in Earth, the band that would become Black Sabbath. Atkins believes he jammed with them somewhere in Birmingham and was once in a band that was signed to the same agency. Either way, they were impressed with the name Black Sabbath.

Al Atkins: "We all said that's a cracking name, you know, and wondered what sort of music they played. It was really loud, heavy music and I said we ought to lean more towards that heavy sound. We thought that was the next thing that was gonna happen round here."

Atkins was aware that Robert Plant was now the singer with Led Zeppelin. He went to see this relatively new band on March 22 at Mothers Club in Birmingham, in a support slot to ex-Jethro Tull guitarist Mick Abraham's Blodwyn Pig. "They got paid £75 that night. I said, 'This is great.' It's a crossover . . . you know Cream was a loud, blues band type of thing but this was more into getting a heavy and loud type of thing."

Atkins & co. rehearsed in the back bedroom upstairs at Stapenhill's house at Stone Cross, West Bromwich. With a new guitarist, the line-up was settled and all they now needed was a band name.

Al Atkins: "Bruno came up with the name. I asked him to try and think of a name similar to Black Sabbath. And he came up with one in a couple of days. He was listening to a Bob Dylan album of his, something I was never into but Bruno was. It was Dylan's album *John Wesley Harding* and a track came on called 'The Ballad Of Frankie Lee And Judas Priest'."

Bruno Stapenhill: "I thought that seems like a nice name for a band, you know? 'The Ballad Of Frankie Lee And Judas Priest' from *John Wesley Harding*. I remember telling Al, 'What do you think of that for a name?' I mean, he was never really into Bob Dylan and he says, 'Oh, that's great, that's a great name.' And that's how it came about."

'The Ballad Of Frankie Lee And Judas Priest' is a quasi-autobiographical tale, generally assumed to be an allegory about Dylan's relationship with his then manager Albert Grossman. The pair were growing apart professionally and personally when the song was written in 1967, not least because Dylan believed Grossman had duped him into signing unpropitious contracts. Infamously, of course, Judas was the biblical traitor to Jesus Christ, and Dylan felt betrayed by Grossman in the same way that Judas had betrayed Christ. By the end of the song, Frankie Lee – as quoted in *Bob Dylan Anthology: 20 Years Of Isis* by Derek Barker – "died of thirst, as though he had neglected his basic needs in the pursuit of many pleasures from Judas". Frankie Lee's own death allowed Dylan to shed his skin and be reborn, thus, "It is about the end of an era and the need for a new beginning."

Atkins states that the band hadn't come up with the name when John Perry committed suicide, so it's safe to assume they called themselves Judas Priest at the very end of 1969 or, at the latest, the start of 1970. "The name was decided in Brain Stapenhill's front room," Chataway claims.

Despite their fondness for blues-rock, the newly named Judas Priest rather unwisely dubbed themselves a progressive band, a label from which they could not escape and in the end decided to stick with. Though they rehearsed U.S. West Coast covers by the likes of Quicksilver Messenger Service and Spirit, Atkins began writing songs of his own in the hope that one day they would record them under the Judas Priest moniker. "We did Quatermass* stuff, and we did some of my own," he says. "I started writing songs all the way through the Sixties and I was always throwing one in the list every now and then. We kicked off with a tour of Scotland in the winter, which was unbelievable."

The group's first tour, of Scotland in either late 1969 or January 1970, is recalled with something approaching horror by all involved. Atkins, Chataway and Stapenhill all speak bitterly of an experience that would probably have put many weaker bands out of action.

Ernie Chataway: "The heater broke in the van and we spent the night freezing."

Al Atkins: "That's when I wrote the lyrics to 'Winter'. It was a nightmare mini-tour where everything went wrong. 'Magnet' [John Ward], our roadie, broke his arm but still drove all the way to Scotland.† John [Partridge], the drummer, came down with flu so I had to play drums and sing. The clutch broke on the bus so Magnet, Bruno and myself had to fit a new one. The nearside door window jammed so we had to hang up an old army blanket to keep out the cold. We got stuck in a snowstorm up the

---

* A late Sixties progressive outfit signed to Harvest Records, featuring Pete Robinson (keyboards), bassist John Gustafson and drummer Mick Underwood.
† Ward, the band's only roadie, went on to work for Ian Paice from Deep Purple.

Shap Fell, so missed the first gig. These were just a few things that went wrong. I would have called this 'The Winter Of My Discontent Tour'."

Bruno Stapenhill: "The clutch went on the van the night before we were supposed to go up there. And we'd gone round to Ernie's house . . . just up the road from the prison, in a little terrace house . . . I mean it was in the middle of bloody winter. Luckily, the van had got timber floor-boards in the back, which we could get up to get to the gearbox. In the old Thames vans the engine was under the board, in between the two seats at the front. It was this bloody horrible bump. And our roadie Johnny Ward was a mechanic. We changed the clutch and that was at about 10 o'clock at night. Fezza [John Partridge] had phoned up earlier on in the evening and says he weren't gonna go. We says, 'Oh, you've gotta go. We can't cancel it now.' And he phoned up again at Ernie's about nine o'clock and says, 'No, I'm definitely not going.' And Al said, 'Well, I'm taking your kit.' We got all the gear back in the van again. So Al took his kit and played the drums. It was all right, it was great, we had a good laugh, but I remember getting bloody snowed in on the way up there before the motorway had opened up. There was a well-known transport café up there, the Jungle café; it's probably still there, on the old A-road. And we had to spend the night there; the road was just blocked off with lorries, like. It was all good fun."

Despite the harshness of the weather, the gigs made the whole tour worth the hassles. Ernie Chataway: "The only actual real tour that I can remember in all honesty was that Scottish one, it was horrendous [but] the gigs were great. It went down a storm you know . . . I played drums on that, and sang! And I played mouth organ on one, Al jumped on guitar and we did like a Sonny Terry thing and they loved it."

Atkins, whose memory is a little more reliable than the ex-guitarist's, supports Chataway's story: "Bruno broke one of his bass strings and walked off stage to mend it. Ernie put down his guitar and started to sing and play harmonica to a Sonny Terry and Brownie McGhee blues song that he knew, so I picked up his guitar and accompanied him. It was in one of those Locarno ballrooms."

On the surface, Judas Priest Mark I appeared to have a steady line-up. They had played live, toured and acquainted themselves with each other, but their efforts were largely fruitless without the help of a manager who knew how to organise the business side of things, which the band certainly did not. The decision was taken to advertise in the local papers for the services of a manager.

Al Atkins: "We advertised in the local paper saying, 'We've got this band together,' this unusual band, heavy rock band or whatever, and we need some management. And a guy called Alan Eade came on the scene and says, 'Can I have a listen to you?' We auditioned for him and he said, 'You're absolutely brilliant.' He had a lot of pop, sort of poppy bands on his list but he said, 'I love this sort of rock music.'"

Bruno Stapenhill: "We got on all right with him. I think he talked a bit more than he was, but he was all right. He weren't very tall – stocky chap."

Chataway remembers Eade as being helpful to the band's cause and understanding that they wanted to break out of the local circuit, but it would take hard work. "He seemed like a really nice guy," he says.

With Eade's encouragement and assertiveness, Judas Priest went into the studio to record two tracks to send to record companies in the hope of a record deal. The songs were 'Good Time Woman' and 'We'll Stay Together' and took just a few hours to record. "Probably about four hours, maybe a bit less than that," says Stapenhill.

"I know I played a blinding solo," says Chataway. "You couldn't use any overdrive and stuff then, you know, you could only play it loud and it was like, 'Woahhhh!'"

With two recorded songs under their belt and a manager to propel them to another level, they were feeling justifiably confident. The demo was sent out to prospective labels and met with interest, primarily from Harvest, an EMI offshoot, and Immediate, the maverick independent run by former Rolling Stones manager Andrew Oldham. On November 25 the band put on a showcase gig at The George pub in Walsall, and in the audience was Robert Plant, just back from Led Zeppelin's third US tour, during which they had headlined Carnegie Hall in New York.

Stapenhill has vivid memories of Plant, less so of the gig: "Oh, we knew Planty from before that . . . his mum and dad kicked him out because they wanted him to follow an academic career and he wanted to get into music, and he moved in with an Asian girl from West Brom. We all used the same pub in West Brom above Woolworths, the Duke Bar. Bonham used to go in and Planty, you'd sort of exchange what was happening in the music world and that. It was only a small room and it was always full of musos."

Of the showcase at The George, Chataway says: "That would be the one where Planty was, I remember Planty there now. He'd got a purple velvet coat on and these big fur boots. He hasn't changed much, has he? And he got a load of people around him I remember . . . I didn't like him! I thought he was a big-head . . . because we all thought he'd copied The Jeff Beck Group, which I still maintain to this day. I never did like him, we never did get on, but I did some recording with him. In fact, one of the first bands I got together was when I came to Worcester. It was . . . Ian Jennings and Ian Wilson, Maureen's [Robert Plant's first wife] little brother you know. I was trying to get a bit of an R&B/B.B. King-type thing. And with anybody who joined the band [Wilson] was like, 'I'm Robert Plant's brother-in-law,' you know what I mean?"

Aside from this encounter with Robert Plant, The George pub looms in Chataway's memory for another reason. "I remember it because I fell off the stage in front of my mum and dad and my sisters and everybody. I think I rolled off with Allan. We used to beat guitars up because I had a Gibson 330 or 335, which I hated with a vengeance because it kept feeding back . . . we used to beat the guitar up with the mic stand and I remember rolling around on it and looking up at my parents."

After playing their set for the record companies, the band were introduced to the men from Immediate Records, who seemed keen on this young band called Judas Priest. A three-year contract was proffered and, to celebrate, they held a champagne party at Eade's house. It comes as no surprise that none of them have any memories of it.

On a high, Judas Priest began preparations for the recording of their first album, but their euphoria was premature. Within two months of signing their first record deal, Immediate went into liquidation, and the band were back to square one.

Al Atkins: "We got a deal within six months and went into the studio to re-record 'Good Time Woman' and 'We'll Stay Together'. We were asked to try and write something more commercial, so we did. It was a bit more commercial but we actually liked it. They were gonna sign us for four years so we was quite chuffed with that . . . then we started writing some more stuff for an album, and the company actually folded. I don't know what went wrong." The mood in the Judas Priest camp shifted dramatically. Stapenhill says, "We got this and thought, 'Oh, this is great like, this is brilliant.' And it just fizzled out, like."

The band dealt with the arduous Scottish tour and quick demise of Immediate by packing up their gear and going back on the road. In the meantime there were drummers coming and going and the relationship between Chataway, Stapenhill and Atkins soured as they became divided over the band's musical direction. Atkins grew increasingly tired of the blues influence and wanted to lean more towards the dark, heavy sound pioneered by Black Sabbath on their 1970 debut album.

Al Atkins: "After [Immediate] folded, I said, 'Let's just release this . . . let's just get on the road and start playing again' . . . [but] the band had got a slight problem with Ernie. He was a great player but he leaned very much towards the . . . very bluesy style. And I said we needed to get into heavier stuff, like what Sabbath was doing and all this stuff. At the end of the year, like '69, '70, we sort of spilt up . . ."

Black Sabbath, Led Zeppelin and the like were just too heavy for Stapenhill, who still enjoyed listening to bands like The Shadows. It seemed that for Atkins and Stapenhill the vicious circle of joining or forming short-lived bands would never cease. Judas Priest Mark I came to an abrupt end during the spring of 1970. Their last gig was at the Youth Centre in Cannock on April 20.

Bruno Stapenhill: "It seemed like we weren't going anywhere at the time. I think it was just an amicable sort of split."

Al Atkins: "Bruno had an offer from another band to go to Denmark, where they'd played for months. It was a soul band, The Roy Gee Explosion. I think Ernie went to London and John [Partridge] moved out of town to Stourbridge. And I sort of . . . settled down and got married with my girlfriend and I decided I'm gonna form another band, and that's when I sort of teamed up with K.K., you know."

After the demise of Judas Priest Mark I, the going wasn't quite so easy for the group members, with each one moving from band to band, never seeming to settle in one musical environment. In 1970, Bruno Stapenhill was offered a gig with a soul band. "I went over to Denmark for three months. It was all right. They wanted a bass player and a drummer [but] it started to go a bit stale, I mean, we used to do all the nightclubs in Brum [Birmingham] and it was bloody soul-destroying – get there at four o'clock, set your gear up and you've gotta bloody hang around then until about one o'clock in the morning. It was horrible. Anyway, I says, 'Oh, I've had enough of this.' "

Stapenhill moved back into the heavy rock live circuit with back-to-basics bands like Suicide and Bullion, where he teamed up again with Pete Boot and Ernie Chataway. Bullion shared the same management agency as Judas Priest Mark IV in the early Seventies.

Bruno Stapenhill: "Bullion and Priest and The Flying Hat Band, Glenn Tipton's band, we were all working for the same agency in Birmingham. We used to gig together. Bullion was the last band to play the Cavern before it was pulled down! We played there on the Friday night and then there was a big party on the Saturday with the bands from Liverpool, and then the bulldozers went in on the Monday and knocked it down. So we were actually the last paid band to play on the actual Cavern space!" Stapenhill and Boot finally re-joined Atkins in the Seventies cult band Lion.

During the second half of 1970, between bands and bored, Atkins took on a mundane job, which at least kept him outdoors. "I was a gardener for West Bromwich Council," he says, "and it lasted one year until I stopped to concentrate on the band."

Tired and depressed with both work and his domestic life, he decided to get another band together. One particular night in October 1970, Atkins took a stroll down to 'Holy Joe's', a school building belonging to an old church, St. James, in Wednesbury, a small town a few miles outside of West Bromwich. The vicar, nicknamed 'Holy Joe', allowed local bands to use parts of the school for rehearsals.

John Ellis: "I think there were eight or 10 rooms or something. He [the vicar] used to nip up to the old pub just on the top of the road on the corner. And he used to come back worse for wear. Sometimes he used to let people practise in his front room to earn extra cash." It was famous in the area according to Atkins. "There was loads of bands that used to rehearse there, there was Trapeze, Slade, Robert Plant, there was me . . . it was a local rehearsal room." More than three decades later, Atkins recalls the evening he met his future bandmates: "I went down there and I thought I'd have a listen to see who was playing, you know. You could go down there and meet bands and have a chat. I thought I'd go down to see if there were any new bands."

Atkins heard something he liked coming from one of the rooms, took a look inside and saw "three young head-banging crazy longhairs, amps full up."

As soon as Atkins heard the noise he knew he had to approach them. "I could hear this band playing away . . . I couldn't hear no vocals, just a really loud band, giving it all," he says. "I thought it sounded pretty good, it sounded really heavy. So I popped me head round the corner . . ."

The guitarist was K.K. Downing, who had auditioned the previous year and whom Atkins had knocked back for his musical inadequacy. The bassist was Ian 'Skull' Hill and the drummer John Ellis. There was also a fourth person present, Trevor Lunn, who acted as the trio's unofficial roadie. The three musicians had been friends for years.

John Ellis: "Me, Ian and Kenny grew up together . . . I attended Yew Tree Primary and Junior Schools prior to Churchfields . . . and I think both Ken and Ian went there but I didn't know them then. When I left school I became a mod and bought a scooter. Ian had one as well, so we was in our own little scooter gang. We lost contact with Kenny . . . Kenny had friends on the other side of the estate. Me and Ian were listening to this sort of brilliant music that was around at the time. We just couldn't help ourselves but try and get into it. So a friend called Trevor Lunn, he bought a guitar and Ian started to play a little bit. I got to play a little bit and then they got to hear about Kenny, and Kenny got to play a little bit. So the three of us sort of emerged from that and Trevor became our roadie."

Al Atkins: "There was K.K. I remembered him from the year before because of his long blond hair, and he was a very enthusiastic kid. He wanted to learn all the while and I thought he sounded better than he used to. Why he failed the audition with us before was because I think he liked his wild metal a bit too much. You couldn't really tell what he was actually playing. I thought, 'Oh, he still likes his wild playing but you can actually hear some of the stuff he is playing now.' I'd never met Ian or John Ellis before. They were his old friends from school. I says to 'em, 'How you doing Ken?' and we had a chat and I said, 'This sounds good.' I told them I wanted to reform Judas Priest again if I could. I told them about the tour we did of Scotland and how we did get a record deal but the company went bust. We were on the verge of just doing something in the first year . . . we went in the right direction you know. And I asked, 'Do you want to team up with me?' And they said, 'Yeah, bloody hell.' "

Downing, Hill and Ellis wanted to use the name Freight for their band but Atkins suggested using the name Judas Priest again because it had already acquired a small reputation and would thus save them a bit of time, while they tried to become established in the area.

Ellis doesn't recall any second thoughts or arguments with Atkins about the name change. "Freight was a bit of a nonentity at that time," he says. "Black Sabbath were making their mark as a heavy rock band. We thought, 'Yeah, that sounds like we could do something with that,' so we adopted the name." With the others in agreement, the next incarnation of Judas Priest was conceived.

While Atkins had been roaming around West Bromwich looking for a new band, Stapenhill was in Denmark but, when the bassist returned home, he was pleased that his friend had found something new. "They was all right, you know? I mean it was basic sort of riffy stuff, it was OK. Of course, I mean, it was Al who nurtured 'em . . . that got them where they were in the early days."

K.K. Downing[*] was born Kenneth Downing Jr. on October 27, 1951 in

[*] The story goes that his name was abbreviated to 'K.K.' because a Danish girl he knew could not pronounce Kenneth and called him K.K. instead.

West Bromwich. That same month, a Mexican chemist by the name of Luis E. Miramontes invented the first oral contraceptive for women, an appropriate coincidence considering the number of girls with whom Downing would allegedly share a bed with.

K.K. attended Yew Tree Junior School before moving up to Churchfields High School, aged 11. He was raised on the Yew Tree Housing Estate, an extensive council-housing project for underprivileged working-class families. John Ellis and Ian Hill were raised on the same estate.

John Ellis: "The Yew Tree Estate was a huge council house/flats sprawl with its own shops, community centre, and two public houses, one Labour club, of which my father was an original member, doctors, dentists, etc., and the nearest towns were West Bromwich or Walsall. Both had bus routes and took about half-an-hour each. [It was] a great place to be as it was designed to take families out of the terraces and give them all three-bedroom houses with gardens, hot and cold water, and inside toilets – just the job in post-war Britain.

"The Yew Tree was full of families, so there was an abundance of kids of all ages to play with – huge areas to get football games going, canals nearby to explore and new building sites to get up to no good in. I had a great time. There were a few trouble families and a few bullies, but you just got on with it. By and large, times were good."

K.K.'s father, Kenneth Downing Sr., worked infrequently as a general labourer while his mother, Margaret, raised the family – Kenneth Jr., brother Adrian, and sisters Margaret and Linda. Like many unambitious children who grew up in Britain as the Fifties became the Sixties, K.K. left school at 15 but found no work. "Ken had a very troubled family life," says John Ellis. "His dad never worked and was always at the dogs or the bookies. His mum was sweet but he used to get into trouble with his folks because he was always staying out without letting them know, and he had no money for his board. So, yes, eventually he walked or was thrown out. He didn't have much contact with his mother or his sisters after that I think."

From what is commonly understood, Downing had very little, if any, communication with his parents after he was asked to leave the family home. He never spoke about his family to anyone when he was younger. Some reports have suggested that Downing has lost all contact with his mother. Speaking to *Kerrang!* at the time of the release of *Priest . . . Live!*, Downing admitted he was from a troubled family: "A lot of kids out there have problems with their parents. I know I did. I got kicked out of the house when I was 16 and I haven't spoken to my folks since."* It would seem that it took many years for mother and son to repair their turbulent relationship. Whatever happened to repair those broken bridges is a closely guarded family secret.

Downing started to play guitar at 16, attempting at first to emulate his hero Jimi Hendrix. His parents resented this and thought he should "get his act together", commonly understood to mean "get a job and look after yourself like an adult." Downing decided otherwise, growing his hair and absorbing the music played by guitarists like Eric Clapton, Peter Green and Jeff Beck. Suddenly the adolescent had new meaning in his life.

John Ellis: "Ken was very good with the ladies because of his striking, natural blond hair and piercing blue eyes. We used to hunt in pairs then, and I always ended up with the less pretty one of the girls we used to get."

Al Atkins: "Kenny was very outgoing and loved the ladies, but he had a steady girlfriend for a long time named Carol. He loved playing snooker and you would always find him at West Bromwich Snooker Hall if you wanted him. Both Ian and John were very laid-back guys."

Beverley Stone, who was a childhood friend of both K.K. Downing and Ian Hill and then the girlfriend of Priest roadie Keith Evans, says, "They never got into trouble but they didn't seem to be interested in school, they were always just into music. We were all Hendrix fans except for Trevor Lunn and John Ellis, who were into Eric Clapton. I've got a picture of us at the Isle of Wight pop festival."

Stone can vividly recall the reaction Downing had on his face when he heard his childhood hero, Jimi Hendrix, had died on September 18, 1970. "We use to meet at a pub called the Halfway House," she says, "and once when Kenny turned up, it was the day Jimi Hendrix died and I remember him being absolutely devastated. We couldn't believe it."

Downing did not like to work, being too preoccupied with ideas about becoming a rock star to care about menial jobs. Ellis remembers, "Ken only served a very small amount of time as an apprentice chef in a hotel in Worcester."

Al Atkins: "I can't ever remember Ken working, but John worked at K and J's paper mill and Ian was working at a car component company."

Mick Owen: "At the time [K.K.] was a great guy [but] he suffered from asthma and he was always making a funny noise. I pulled him [up] about it

---

* Yet when the author spoke to Downing in October, 2006 about work on the latest Priest album, he let slip: "In fact, I'm just gonna do a little bit of work now before I go to me mum's – I haven't seen her for two months."

once and he said it was asthma . . . He was talking about taking an injection for it or something."

As well as being a skilled chess player, Downing spent most of his time fishing, which was his favourite hobby when he was young, as Owen remembers. "He used to go fishing with just a little old woman's black umbrella as a fishing brolly. That's how bad it was. He was destitute . . ."

Graham Walker also knew the blond guitarist at a young age: "I was introduced to the band by a lad named Keith 'Evvo' Evans, who was their roadie. I met K.K. in the local billiard hall − over Burtons − through a mutual friend and later, when this hall was shut, we transferred our custom to the rival 'Willie Holt'."

Evans, whose present whereabouts are unknown, was integral to the Mark II line-up in late 1970 as their roadie, best mate and probably their biggest fan. "Keith Evans was very close to the band in those early days and he went on to be the sound engineer for Black Sabbath and AC/DC, living in Los Angeles for some years," says Walker. "He came back to the UK and was a pub manager. I saw him some four/five years ago when he was jointly running a music-orientated pub in Brierley Hill, Dudley called The Rock."*

Ian Hill was born Ian Frank Hill on January 20, 1951 in West Bromwich. "[Ian] was bright," according to Colin Roberts, "and was good at sports and he liked the girls. He did a little bit of playing up."

Despite growing up on a harsh housing estate, life for Hill was not nearly as depressing as it was for Downing. The three of them grew up on a section of the estate called Bermuda Mansions, which Roberts says, "is flattened now. It's a private housing estate. [However] Ken lived on the other half of the estate . . . on the top end, which is still there."

Despite his seemingly ordinary childhood, Hill, an only child, was devastated by the death of his father, a jazz musician who played double bass in a successful local trio. It traumatised him and perhaps goes some way to explaining his reserved manner. Hill was certainly reticent to talk about his father's death among his circle of friends. "He never spoke about it to anyone," says Beverley Stone. "I think he died just as I met Ian."

It helped that Hill had a strong mother figure, as Roberts can attest. "His mother was a brilliant person as I can remember," he says, "very stable."

Despite Hill's reputation as the quiet member of the band, Roberts

---

* The Rock has since closed down and is now a supermarket.

27

remembers that, like Downing, Hill was not at all shy in female company. "[He had] plenty of women. Three of 'em had got girlfriends, and I hadn't got one but they always took me with 'em for some unknown reason . . . I thought [Ian] was very outgoing. He was a ladies' man. Everything else was always the best. He got the best scooter in the street or on the estate. I think he got the record for the most mirrors on a scooter . . . a 180SS."

Hill worked briefly at Regent Spring, a car accessory shop, and his nickname 'Skull' derived from when he was quite young. Beverley Stone remembers, "He was called that because he was very hollow-cheeked, with high cheekbones, and his face just looked like a skull. He's a big fella now but when you look at old photos you'll understand why he was called that." Indeed, Hill's current size – looking like a retired rugby player with bulging arms and chest – belies his nickname.

Hill first learned the rudiments of bass playing on his dad's double bass. "He messed with that and decided to get into the guitar," says Roberts. "We were all Cream fans as kids and Hendrix too."

Unlike Rob Halford and Glenn Tipton, Downing and Hill have rarely spoken about the bands they played in before Judas Priest. However, Colin Roberts has vague memories of one that featured both Hill and Downing and "this other bloke". "It was his band," says Roberts. "They were called Spider's Web and they said, 'Do you wanna be a roadie and we'll do this, this and this?' . . . and I said, 'It'll be no good.'"

Even before becoming Judas Priest, Downing, Hill and Ellis had formed a special bond, but it was often the case that John Ellis was left out of the fold. Many childhood friends and former acquaintances of the guitarist and bass player refer to Downing and Hill in the same breath as if they were a comedy duo. John Ellis: "Kenny was out of work for a long, long time. I got a job at the time at a printer's in the high street, and we became the closest friends you'd ever wish to be. I looked after K.K. I gave him money when he needed it, paid his board, fed him when he needed it and all that kind of thing. We became extremely close. We had our moments . . . we enjoyed our trips now and again."

John Ellis, born at his grandmother's house in Dora Road, West Bromwich on September 19, 1951, soon moved to the Yew Tree Estate. His passion for drums began at a young age. "I started playing drums while still at Churchfields," he says. "A mate of mine called Derek Wood, who later went on to play bass for another local band called White Rabbit, had a huge house in a run-down part of Wednesbury. His father used to be a jazz drummer and had a home-made drum kit, which I used to play, while Derek used to pretend to play guitar and sing along to all the hit records at the time. His dad was impressed with me and even came down my house on the Yew Tree Estate to tell my father that if I ever showed interest in playing drums, he should encourage me."

When Ellis met Al Atkins, the second line-up of Judas Priest was off the starting blocks by October, 1970.

FOUR

1971–1973

"We were just learning the ropes . . . The quality of the music, I didn't think was that good. And we used to cannibalise other people's music to make something out of it."

— Ex-Judas Priest drummer, John Ellis

FROM around October, 1970 to March, 1971 the Mark II Judas Priest rehearsed tirelessly, concentrating fully on the music – girlfriends were banned from the rehearsals – and it was several months before the band felt comfortable enough to play in front of a live audience.

Al Atkins: "Our first gig was on March 16 at Essington Working Men's Club . . . we went on to play with Status Quo [and] Supertramp, there was loads and loads of bands we used to open up for at the time."

John Ellis: "We did the colleges and the universities. We played with people like Slade, Thin Lizzy, Trapeze, Strife and The Flying Hat Band . . . loads of 'em."

Atkins has particularly fond memories of Welsh rockers Budgie. "There was a little bit of rivalry because we always thought we were as good if not better than Budgie. When we played with them on their home ground, they were always better than us because they got their home crowd. When we played live in Birmingham, we always got our own home crowd. And we always went down better than them."

Even though they played to a bigger band's decent-sized crowds, when it came to a gig under their own steam Judas Priest found it difficult to attract a sizeable audience. Graham Walker recalls seeing them at The Farcroft Hotel in Handsworth, Birmingham: "I remember there being just six or seven of us in the audience."

Other bands might have folded under the strain but Atkins and his team players were certainly persistent. Like most bands of the era they succumbed to certain temptations. "I think we all dabbled with LSD at some time but I was the main druggy in Priest," he says. "There was nothing like coke, just weed and uppers and sleepers." Atkins was partial to

Mandrax, which was particularly dangerous when taken with alcohol.

In Atkins' words, the band "stripped the Judas Priest Mark I song list back to the bare bones and [while] this may have taken a while, I started writing a lot of new songs as well . . ." One of the first songs he wrote for the second line-up, 'Mind Conception', was slipped into the live set straight away. As time went on, Atkins became more confident of his writing capabilities and began to add more of his songs to the band's repertoire.

Al Atkins: "I was writing a lot of the stuff at the time. 'Whiskey Woman' was one, which became 'Victim Of Changes' when Rob came into the band. He added the slow bit . . . 'red light lady'. And they called it 'Victim Of Changes'. We kept a Quatermass song in there and we used to kick off with a Jimi Hendrix number because Kenny was absolutely mad on Hendrix."

From 1971 onwards, Priest opened with 'Spanish Castle Magic' (from Hendrix's 1967 album *Axis: Bold As Love*.) This was generally followed by 'Winter', 'Holy Is The Man', 'Voodoo Rag', 'Black Sheep', 'Never Satisfied', 'Whiskey Woman', 'Joey', 'Mind Conception' and 'Caviar And Meths', a lengthy number used as the band's dramatic encore. About half of these were written by Atkins during 1971/2 when the possibility of making an album did not seem too remote.

John Ellis: "At that time, I didn't think we were particularly good. We were just learning the ropes. I mean we weren't crap; we got a bit more professional than the start-up bands. The quality of the music, I didn't think was that good. And we used to cannibalise other people's music to make something out of it. We did two tracks by Quatermass . . . Alan did most of the writing. He was a jack-of-all-trades. I mean he could play a bit of guitar, a bit of drums, a bit of bass and he could sing. He actually came up with the material. We were just glad to follow really. He'd been playing a bit longer than we had."

Their progress accelerated when a friend, Dave Corke, stepped in as manager. Atkins: "He said, 'I can't play a bloody thing but I love music, can I be an agent or a manager in some of the bands? Can I help you?' I said, 'If you get us the work, you're the manager.' He was lugging the phone book everywhere, 'I've got a gig lined up here and there,' he said. 'Come on, let's get on the road.' We had a couple of roadies – one was Trevor Lunn, who was also friends with K.K. And suddenly by the end of the year [1971] it was picking up again."

Like the rest of them, Dave Corke, or 'Corky' to his friends, grew up in West Bromwich. John Ellis: "David Corke was a Churchfields lad with huge thick glasses and a shock of black curly hair. He also had chest scars from when he was scalded as a child, which I think he was a bit self-conscious about. He was a good laugh though, with a wicked sense of humour. He was in our scooter gang too. He was fascinated by music and bands although he was not musically talented in any way as far as I can remember. He got his kicks out of listening and going to loads of gigs."

Al Atkins: "He was a big mate of Ian's from school and hung around with the band from the start."

Corke's talent lay in the managerial and administrative area of the music business. He would use a number of pseudonyms, including Eric Smith, when phoning up record companies and PR people. If they turned Judas Priest down, he'd ring them up again, giving a fake name. The oddest thing about Corke was that his office was in a telephone box. Al Atkins: "[It] was at the bottom of his street but he soon moved on . . . He became like another member of the band." Atkins is still loosely in contact with the elusive Corke and has nothing but respect for his workaholic ex-manager. He says that it was because of Corke's eagerness and intelligence that the band got their first gigs.

Corke decided it was time for Judas Priest to go into a recording studio and in July, 1971, after practising and refining their sound, the Mark II line-up went in to record their first couple of tracks. "We did a couple of my songs, 'Holy Is The Man' and 'Mind Conception'," says Atkins.

John Ellis: "They were recorded at Zella Records. By today's standards, the recording was pretty poor. It was obviously very novel because we'd never been in a recording studio before. I really enjoyed it . . . the end result was a dozen or so demo discs, which were all right, but it wasn't as good as it could have been, especially the drums. I didn't think the drums cut through as much as I would like, even though everything was mic'd up and everything."

Atkins was not in the best condition and admits that he had "a sore throat" in the studio and was "stoned out of my head". The recording process was certainly an eye opener for the band, who paid scant attention to the advice and opinions of the sound engineers present. With no overdubs and copious sound overspill, the experience was treated as a learning curve.*

Priest carried on gigging towards the end of 1971, but just when it looked as if they could actually go somewhere, John Ellis, the only

---

* Al Atkins believes he has the only copy of that very rare Zella studios demo from July, 1971.

member of the group to have stayed in regular employment, working as a commercial apprentice for Kenrick & Jefferson, a printing firm in West Bromwich, was having problems. "I suffered a nervous breakdown," he says. "I think it was maybe doing too much of the old acid. I started to have flashbacks and stuff and it just undermined my confidence and I became a bit of a wreck. So that was after about two years, so I left. I mean, there were lots and lots of great moments. When you play on your own and get an encore, and stuff like that . . ."

It came to a point where Ellis was so exhausted and nervous that he would vomit before going on stage and could barely look at an audience, even when he found the strength and confidence to play in front of them. For the sake of his health and sanity he felt he had to leave the band.

Al Atkins: "John left after about, I think, nine or 10 months. We was under pressure because we started getting a lot of work . . . I wasn't working, K.K. wasn't working, Ian had packed his job up and we just wanted to play. John wasn't like that, he wanted to hold onto his job and he was under pressure from work, [plus] his dad had just died. He just wasn't concentrating fully on the band. John tried to hold down his job and play and rehearse every week with us until he finally cracked up and went for the stable life."

The last gig John Ellis performed as drummer for Judas Priest was at The Yeoman, Derby on October 6, 1971, playing alongside Slade, who later that month would have their first number one hit with 'Coz I Luv You'. Atkins remembers receiving the news before going onstage: "He said, 'I'm packing up', and he was having a bit of a breakdown . . . he said he was packing it up for good."

Ellis advised his bandmates to get a replacement as soon as possible, and was anxious to get the gig over and done with. "I think I was suffering with nerves . . . I started to get stage fright and a lack of self-confidence. My girlfriend, who later became my wife, had to walk around outside with me to try and calm me down."

"The gig was a disaster," Ellis adds. "There were three bands, with Slade topping the bill, we were due on second but Slade had to go on to another gig after this one, so insisted on going on second. The first problem was reorganising all the equipment, as we had already set up. The second problem was it was Derby College end-of-term bash and was full of crazy students all wanting to dance. Well, Slade went down really well in view of their style of music and power. When we went on it all fell a bit flat, as our music was a bit more serious and certainly not to dance to."

Al Atkins: "I believe Priest were to top the bill over Slade, although they had a record in the charts and there was a bit of a row over it with Dave Hill and the promoter."

In hindsight, Ellis does have slight regrets about leaving when he did. "In retrospect, I wish I had stayed on. I remember after a week or so going to the local mental hospital as an outpatient and taking some anti-anxiety drugs, everything came back to me . . . I became normal again. But it was too late then, they had secured the service of Chris ['Congo'] Campbell. It wouldn't have been easy to try and work my way back into the band, so I didn't. I just played with a few locals at working men's clubs, playing 'The Anniversary Waltz' and that kind of thing. But it didn't last very long, it wasn't the same, and I was a bit too busy and loud for most working men's clubs."

After leaving Priest, Ellis set about reorganising his life, eventually becoming a salesman in the print industry. He followed the band's career, reading about them in the music press and occasionally keeping up to date with their musical output, although he has only stayed in sporadic touch over the years. "I still see Ian Hill. He's a lifelong West Bromwich Albion supporter and he still takes his son up to the Albion. I still see him every now and again just to say hello."

At Ellis' suggestion, the band replaced their drummer almost immediately, firstly with Alan Moore, who made his first appearance on October 13 at Walsall's Yew Tree Centre. The Mark III line-up played a couple of dates in Wales before driving back to England to finish off the year in Derby.

Al Atkins: "Nothing against John but Alan was a more experienced drummer. He had a bit of drive . . . lovely kid . . . He fitted in with the band right away. It made us sound even better than we had before."

The hastily hired Moore left after only a few months, probably at the very end of '71. Al Atkins: "Alan had a better offer from a band called Sundance from Birmingham, which I don't blame him for taking. They were doing a lot of country-rock, blues stuff. They got a record deal and were after a good drummer. So they asked Alan and he took the job. If you get a better chance always take it, you'll regret it later."

Next in the drum seat was Chris 'Congo' Campbell. "He wasn't as good as Alan but he was very photogenic with the rest of the band," says Atkins. "He was a Jamaican with a big Afro haircut. He looked really good."

With Campbell on board, 1972 kicked off with a gig in Nottingham. In April, Priest supported touring American band Spirit for one date at the Wellington Hall, Shropshire. The story goes that Judas Priest generously lent the Californian psychedelic rock band some of their stage equipment after Spirit had had their equipment van stolen only days before. Consequently, the Americans had to travel to the gig by train. They thanked Priest onstage although the venue was hardly packed.

Al Atkins recalls a slightly different version of events: "I made this gig April 29 but I may be wrong. The story was that Spirit turned up at the wrong Wellington down south [in Taunton, Somerset] and not in Shropshire, so they had to speed up there without their gear. They made it just in time but had to borrow Priest's back line-up." Atkins also remembers that the guys in Spirit bought the band a few pints as a gesture of thanks.

By the end of 1972, financial problems were taking their toll. Atkins, who had a wife and child, was finding life particularly strenuous. Although they were playing continually all over the length and breadth of Britain, money was tight and the rock'n'roll lifestyle was far from glamorous. Judas Priest opened for the likes of UFO, The Flying Hat Band, Budgie, Doctor Ross, The Wild Angels, Curved Air and The Sensational Alex Harvey Band, and headlined a gig above fellow Midlands band Magnum, which furthered their reputation in the area, yet they were still not good enough to make any kind of dent in the national music scene.

However, their fortunes started to change in 1973 when they signed with IMA, a new Birmingham-based management agency. After the hard touring schedule of the previous year, the new contract brought some welcome support for the band. IMA, previously based in Lichfield in Staffordshire, was formed by Norman Hood and Black Sabbath guitarist Tony Iommi.

Hood remembers the formation of the company: "I eventually joined forces with Jim Simpson through our shared interest in American blues, and we found and toured US bluesmen in this country alongside Jim's UK bands, often backed by bands like The Idle Race. These tours gradually expanded into the 'American Blues Legends' packages. During this period, Sabbath split from Jim, but I retained contact and a friendship with Tony Iommi. Tony told me about a band from Cumbria he had an interest in and we decided to form an agency specifically to promote his band – Necromandus. The Agency was formed in 1972 and was called Tramp Entertainment.

"Around the end of the year, I met up with Dave Corke, who had been a casual acquaintance, and he joined the agency – ostensibly to work with Necromandus but in actual fact he spent far more time plugging his own pet band, Judas Priest. I remembered seeing an incarnation of Priest some time earlier and had not been too impressed. I was happy to have them on the books, though, as Corky was passionate about them.

"In late 1972, Tony and I decided to up the profile of the agency, and with a third director in Ten Years After drummer Ric Lee, we moved into central Birmingham. Tony signed a lease on Robert House, Hurst Street on December 12, 1972. We registered a Limited Company – Pactmoor Limited – on January 10, 1973, and the business name IMA on February 26. Though still trading as Tramp, we thought IMA was a bit posher! The initials stood for International Management Agency and not Iommi Management Associates or anything like that.

"On January 19, 1973 we had signed a management agreement with Judas Priest (Downing, Atkins, Campbell and Hill) so they were actually signed before we became IMA."

Of course, Priest milked their association with Iommi. Al Atkins: "Sometimes I'd slip and say Tony Iommi was our manager, but he weren't really. It was just a company he financed . . . his pet band was Necromandus from up north. I mean he absolutely loved them. They were like a very jazzy, progressive-rock band. But they were a good band. And another band was The Flying Hat Band, which was Glenn [Tipton's] band. Bruno and Pete Boot, the two I'd played with before, were in the same agency with their new band Bullion. The Steve Gibbons Band was on there. It was a good agency. It was a good thing that they started looking around and giving work to all these bands."

IMA started to get the band more work and it seemed that each month was filled with plenty of gigs, even though they were making little money. "[They were] always very pleasant," says Hood, "rarely complained – to me, anyway – about the workload. Ken and Ian were always fairly quiet around me, but any problems always came via Dave Corke, of course."

Hood remembers Judas Priest as hard working, one of the more consistent bands in the area. "I was initially not too impressed but as the band got more and more experience on the road, they got tighter and far more professional. Really, they came as a package with Corky, though as the band got better, we got them working really hard and Tony became more interested in them. They soon became our hardest-working band, due in no small measure to Corky's interest."

A record deal was still proving an elusive entity. Atkins was fatigued and bored with all the hard work and having nothing to show for it except lost time and a drained bank account. Downing and Hill were younger, less experienced and weren't as concerned at this prospect.

Al Atkins: "The problem is the bigger you get the more overheads you get. When Priest made it in America, they were still in debt . . . I mean we didn't have a record deal in them days. When we was playing live, our PA system was actually hired by a company at the time called Green Goblin and, by the time you've looked at your finances, you've got no money. The bigger we was getting the more roadies we was taking on, the more transport, the show was getting bigger and more costly. And we just ended up with no money . . ."

With a wife and baby girl to provide for, Atkins decided to call it a day. Judas Priest's final tour with Atkins as lead singer was called The Heavy Thoughts Tour, after a song he'd penned for what IMA hoped would be the band's debut album. The circumstances surrounding his departure were far from amicable.

Al Atkins: "We were supposed to play this gig in Morecombe and when we got there it was a tiny venue on the sea front and I refused to play. Kenny then said if we didn't play he would walk out the band – and he did. Ian, Congo and myself walked into Tramp Management's office the next day and had a big row over putting us in these tiny venues. I said, 'I know I need the money, but we are going backwards by playing this sort of gig.' I told them Kenny had left the band and we needed to come off the road, get a new guitarist and Tramp had to finance us while we did this. They refused, so I decided to disband Judas Priest."

Atkins waved goodbye to Judas Priest for the second and final time in May, 1973. He remembers his last gig was at the Hippodrome in Birmingham on April 15 as support to Family. Other reports suggest it was on April 29 at the Wellington Hall, Shropshire, where Priest had played exactly a year before.

Having joined in early 1972, Chris 'Congo' Campbell had managed to stay in Judas Priest for a little over a year, longer than any other drummer to date.[*] The band's faithful roadie and closest friend Keith Evans also waved goodbye to Judas Priest in 1973.[†]

Atkins temporarily abandoned rock'n'roll to nervously re-join the world of regular employment. "I worked in a cost office at Sutton Coldfield when I left Priest. A cost office is where you price up vehicle repairs at a garage. It just sounds good." Despite vowing never to return, in hindsight, Atkins says that he did actually intend to resurrect the Judas Priest name again with a new line-up after he took time out to care for his

* The author was unable to locate Campbell, who has since faded into obscurity.
† Evans got a job with AC/DC as a roadie and technician to Angus Young. Moving to LA, he worked for Black Sabbath before returning to England to manage a rock pub. Sadly, he has also proved unreachable.

family. But in 1973 he was under the financial cosh, so any notions of this were put on hold.

He eventually grew bored of the day job and formed Lion with Pete Boot, Bruno Stapenhill and former Stallion and Jug Blues Band guitarist Harry Tonks. Lion came close to signing a record deal in 1974 with major label EMI, and supported punk legends The Sex Pistols and The Stranglers and toured Europe with The Heavy Metal Kids before disbanding at some point in 1978. Atkins remembers, "Lion recorded two demos written by myself and Harry Tonks at Zella in Birmingham. The tracks are titled 'Reminiscence' parts one and two. Then we recorded two songs at Gentle Giant's studios in Leeds. The first was again an Atkins/Tonks song, 'On The Wheel', and the second was my own composition 'Journey'. This was released by an independent label up north, I believe, but I never got a copy."*

After the demise of Lion, Atkins released several solo albums; the first, *Judgement Day*, appearing in 1991, included his version of 'Victim Of Changes', which by that point had attained legendary status in heavy metal circles. The following year saw the release of *Dreams Of Avalon*, which reunited Stapenhill and Atkins for the first time in many years. In the mid Nineties, while preparing a third solo album for Priest's label Gull Records, Atkins was rooting through his personal collection of mementos and found, to his surprise, a rough demo of 'Heavy Thoughts'. He decided to complete the long-lost song and, for the *Heavy Thoughts* album, he teamed up with Budgie guitarist Simon Lees, who still continues a professional relationship with Atkins to this day.

It was initially hoped K.K. Downing would collaborate with Atkins to mix *Heavy Thoughts* but this never happened, although according to Atkins' liner notes, Downing was actually "in the studio giving a helping hand". In the end, the album was produced in 1994 by John Parr and Paul Hodson, and contained 'Caviar And Meths' in a version that was closer to the original eight-minute Priest live encore from the early Seventies.

Heavy Thoughts was initially scheduled for release in 1995 but didn't reach the record shelves until 2003, on the London-based Market Square Records label.† In the interim, Atkins' fourth solo offering *Victim Of*

---

* A very rare 1976 Lion demo track called 'On The Wheel', which was a live fan favourite, can be heard on a Budgie fan album called *Hole In The Head Gang*.
† A rare black and white poster of Judas Priest Mark II appeared within the sleeve artwork. Al Atkins: "I have the only original one left and, if I get it signed by the band, I was offered £2,000 by the Hard Rock Cafe."

Changes was released in 1998. For this album he teamed up with ex-Priest drummer Dave Holland for a collection of re-recorded, Atkins-connected Priest songs such as 'Holy Is The Man', 'Mind Conception', 'Winter' and 'Never Satisfied'. Because of this, Atkins justifiably came under fire for using his role as former lead singer and co-founder of Judas Priest as a means for a career.

After *Victim Of Changes*, Atkins flirted with other musical projects. Thanks to his reputation as Priest's collaborating founder and ex-singer/songwriter, he was now a cult figure in metal circles. In 2004 he played at the Metal Meltdown Festival in New Jersey on a bill headlined 'The New Wave of British Heavy Metal All Stars Band', where he met ex-Iron Maiden axe man Dennis Stratton. The two formed The Denial but "after months of trying to secure a deal and not getting the gigs we wanted – i.e. big festivals – we called it a day," says Atkins.

Despite it taking over a year to make, Atkins is more than comfortable with his fifth studio album, *Demon Deceiver*, released in late 2006 on Swedish label Diesel & Glory after a six-month delay. Promotional duties included a couple of gigs at JB's in Dudley, where, to his surprise, Atkins was reunited with Ernie Chataway and Priest's old roadie, Trevor Lunn.

Atkins continues to receive occasional royalty cheques for his Judas Priest lyrics. When asked if he harbours any regrets about leaving the band in light of what followed, Atkins is ambivalent. "Yes and no . . . yeah, obviously I regret it but who knows what fate's gonna be. If I had stayed in the band, they might not have made it . . ."

PART 2

HEAVY METAL:
A MIDLANDS SOUND UNFOLDS

FIVE

1973–1976

". . . On the bill was a band called Judas Priest . . . and they were horrible. They were bad, hated them. Didn't really take any great notice other than they were bad!"

– Ex-Judas Priest drummer John Hinch

HAVING temporarily disbanded for the second time in their short but tumultuous career, Judas Priest reached a turning point in 1973. Although left in limbo, K.K. Downing and Ian Hill were unwilling to abandon the rock'n'roll lifestyle in the way Atkins had. Indeed, the idea of going back to a regular job was nothing short of inconceivable, so they decided to look for a new singer and drummer.

"Some time later, Kenny and Ian came to my house," Atkins recalls. "I had to give 'em the name Judas Priest. They said, *'We're* gonna use the name.' I said, 'Well, *I* was gonna use [it].' I said I had been approached by Chris Campbell, his younger brother, a guitarist and a bass player and asked, 'Do you wanna join us and form Judas Priest again?' That would be strange – a white guy with these black dudes as Judas Priest! But it's funny how things happen in life. I said, 'No, I don't want to do it.' I teamed up with Bruno and Booty [Pete Boot], my old mate out of Budgie – he left Budgie and came back with us again – and we decided to form another band."

By the time Downing and Hill approached Atkins, they had a new drummer in John Hinch and a vocalist named Robert Halford. Atkins wasn't bothered. He had no reason to believe Judas Priest would progress any further than where they had got to.

Hinch was initially reluctant to join Judas Priest after having seen them live in April, 1973. "I never actually met them," says Hinch. "Whether Rob did or not, I don't know. But I think I might have met Al Atkins at some subsequent time . . . I think they'd already made their plans to do whatever they were doing and, when we joined the band, our memories of seeing them at the Food Hall [Birmingham College of Food and

43

Art] were just like, 'Oh, fucking hell, we don't wanna join . . .'"

However, the prospect of joining Priest was made more attractive to Hinch and Halford by an arranged support slot on Budgie's next UK tour. Priest also had a Ford Transit tour van and a better PA system than Hiroshima, the band the two were in at the time.

John Hinch: "So we had a couple of rehearsals and me and Rob said, 'Well, if they've got a tour we might as well join them just for the sake of doing the tour and getting some work, but don't worry, because we'll soon change the name because it's a shit name! But that never came round . . .'"

Hinch and Halford knew Ian Hill through Hill's relationship with Halford's sister. "He put a word in to Rob that they were looking for a vocalist and also a drummer," says Hinch.

Downing and Hill were at Halford's Walsall house, waiting for his sister to get ready for a night out, when they overheard Halford singing along to a Doris Day song on the radio. Liking what they heard, Downing and Hill asked Halford to audition.

After seeing the new Halford/Downing/Hill/Hinch Mark V line-up of Judas Priest when they started gigging in July, 1973[*], Atkins wasn't taken aback by their new singer, and this re-affirmed his belief that he had made the right decision by giving up on the name.

Al Atkins: "It was really strange because I went to see 'em playing and I thought, 'Hang on, they're still doing the same set!' It was very strange. But I didn't like Rob's voice at all. I thought [he] sounded like he was trying to copy Robert Plant or something. He had a very high voice. I'm into really meaty vocals, gritty and macho. I was brought up listening to Paul Rodgers, whose style I like very much. And then it was Robert Plant and later, David Coverdale, but I don't think I sound like any of them. Rob's completely different from that, and he sang the songs completely different from when I was in Judas Priest, it was bizarre. I thought this was quite weird." It would take him several years to get used to Halford's unique vocals.

Rob Halford was born Robert John Arthur Halford in Sutton Coldfield, Birmingham on August 25, 1951. He spent his childhood growing up on Lichfield Street in Walsall, northwest of Birmingham. The Beechdale Estate was a tough working-class environment, at odds with the young Halford, who knew he was different from every other boy in the area. He has often been quoted in interviews as saying he was the product of a very

---

[*] The first gig is reported to have been at Bolton Town Hall on July 17.

ordinary, typically British working-class family. They had little money and lived in grim surroundings but were tightly knit. His father worked in the British steel industry and the sounds of the metalworks and local industries would have a major impact on Halford's music in later years, though he was unaware of it at the time. Unlike the majority of post-war British children, especially those who were working class and Northern, Halford had a desire to break away from these mundane, stifling trappings.

While a member of his school choir, Halford discovered he could sing. His first band, Thark, led by a much older guitar-playing schoolteacher, played songs by the big rock bands of the era. Halford told *Metal Hammer*: "A bunch of us guys would get together and do Stones, Hendrix, Cream – stuff like that, just fooling around."

After leaving school, he quit the band and, through an advertisement in a local paper, took a job working as an apprentice theatrical lighting engineer and amateur actor for a couple of years at Wolverhampton's Grand Theatre. He imagined that working in a theatre would help him achieve his dream of becoming an actor, or at least someone who would be recognised by an audience.*

Regardless of the low pay and long hours, Halford's time at the Grand Theatre was character building. However, he had a change of heart when he realised the road to becoming an actor was arduous and time-consuming. He told *Metal Hammer* in the late Eighties: "Around 16 or 17, I realised the only way to get on stage quickly in front of an audience, which was my big ambition, was to do it through music."

Next Halford joined a band called Lord Lucifer. "I was in a few local semi-professional bands in and around my hometown," he told *Hard Rock* magazine in 1986. "I look back at them with a great deal of fondness." Lord Lucifer was followed by Hiroshima, and it was here that Halford truly discovered his desire for music, singing and audience attraction.

Halford's best friend in Hiroshima was drummer John Hinch, born in Lichfield on July 19, 1947. By the age of 16 he had lived in Cornwall, Twickenham, Ghana and Sierra Leone. He settled back in Lichfield in his late teens, which is when he started playing in bands.

John Hinch: "I also attended Hampton Grammar School and was in the

---

* As with similar types of low-paid employment, the turnover of staff was high and there is currently no information available at the Grand Theatre on ex-employee Robert Halford. According to the Marketing Officer there, the chief electrician during the Sixties and Seventies only "has a recollection of a Robert who lived in Walsall who was on the electrics crew when he was chief".

same year as Brian May who, believe it or not, shares exactly the same birth date. Then one more for luck, another budding guitarist at Hampton . . . Jimmy Page – though he was a little older."

While at the King Edward VI Grammar School in his hometown, Hinch was a close friend of Jeremy Spencer, who later found success in Fleetwood Mac. Hinch remembers that Spencer "was stunning as a pianist even at the age of 15 or 16 – classically trained. This was my first introduction to music and drums thanks to him."

Local legendary blues guitarist Dave 'Clem' Clempson also had a major creative impact on Hinch as a musician. "The first band I was in was a band called This Generation, which then spawned The Pinch, which was me and Clem . . . but eventually it ended as Bakerloo Blues, which was me, Clem and a guy called Terry Poole."

In many ways it was odd for a drummer like John Hinch, never a 'heavy' player, to go from being a member of jazz/blues band The Bakerloo Blues Line to the harder style of Judas Priest. "I was really surprised to see him go to a heavy band," says Jim Simpson. "He wasn't a bad drummer, but he wasn't a natural musician." Hinch maintains that The Bakerloo Blues Line went for a completely guerrilla style of playing, which had an impact on Judas Priest while he was in the band.

After leaving Hiroshima to join Downing and Hill in the latest incarnation of Judas Priest, the new singer and drummer realised there would be much hard work involved in re-igniting the band – not just creatively but also with book-keeping and general management issues, even though the management services of Dave Corke had been retained.

John Hinch: "My forte has always been to actually look after the band management, agency and all the business side of things. Needless to say, the band was nowhere. I mean, they'd sort of done gigs, got the money, split the money, paid the costs or not paid the costs as the case may be. So that's when I created a set of books, got the whole thing running properly, and found work for the band."

It soon became apparent that Halford was the most creative member of the new-look Judas Priest, and it was his confidence that engineered a belief that the band could go beyond the endless treadmill of pubs and clubs. The grim faces of audience members in working men's venues like the British Legion or Miners' Clubs could be dispiriting, but Halford's enthusiasm, as well as his songwriting ability, kept the band's ambitions alive.

John Hinch: "Rob is excellent at creating words out of nothing. I mean, just give him a tune and within a flash of lightning he's mumbling out any old words, and obviously it's the basic formula to fit the words to the songs. So, yeah, obviously we were doing [old] Judas Priest tracks and then slowly but surely Rob started to write . . . we used to rehearse, rehearse, rehearse, then lots of new songs came out."

Like John Ellis before him, Hinch was the only member of the band with a regular job, which led to some friction. "I never actually gave up work, so I was never a full-time professional [drummer]. In those days I did roof tiling, wall tiling, floor tiling, you name it. So I was always earning money outside of the group. The likes of Kenny and Ian particularly . . . were just lazy bastards who never had a job in their life. So it was quite upsetting, of course, because, dare I say little things like on the motorway, 'Oh, well, I'm gonna have sausage, egg and chips!', but we can't afford anything!

"As the band progressed and became bigger, Rob, in particular, would always wanna stop in a bed and breakfast, which in those days dare I say was £1.50 or £2.50 a night! But when you're only earning £25, it's quite a substantial amount. Because I bought the truck – a Mercedes truck – for the band, besides the PA and god knows what else, I just thought, 'Well sod this, I'll save my £1.50 and I'll sleep in the truck with the crew guys', but I still wanted my £1.50! They always went into hotels . . . they couldn't get over the cost of actually running a band.

"I was effectively managing the band. I was on two-and-a-half per cent of the gross, not 10 per cent [and] not 20 per cent, as my fee for doing the books. We were [also] registering VAT and the Inland Revenue and all the rest of it, so it was all proper."

In early 1974, aside from a few UK dates, including a gig at London's Marquee club, Judas Priest set off for their first European jaunt from February 19 to April 7 with gigs in Germany, Holland and Norway. Playing just one date in each country, it was a long drive from the German show on February 19 to Holland on March 4 before the band headed back to England in their damp van for a solitary appearance on March 15. The band then returned to Norway for more gigs on March 25 and April 7. Like the Scottish tour of 1970, they chose the coldest time of the year to travel, with temperatures dropping to minus 28 as they journeyed through Stuttgart. The bad weather persisted when they played in Scandinavia, with the eventful Norwegian 'tour' looming large in Judas Priest history.

All the costs were kept to a bare minimum, primarily for petrol and maintaining the band's sound equipment. At one point even Halford, or the "prima donna" as John Hinch referred to him, had to clean his teeth in the snow because money was so scarce.

Speaking with hindsight about the hardships endured in Norway, Downing could afford to laugh when looking back. "It was somewhere fucking freezing cold," he told the author during an interview for *Fireworks Melodic Rock* magazine. "The diesel froze up on the freeway the one night. I mean literally, there was me and one of the roadies volunteering to get out and this is like with two-inch heels on? [We had] boots on, walking back to the nearest lodge in the blizzard and the other guys were just left there until the morning. We wondered if they were still gonna be alive!

"We played places where, well, you can imagine what it was like," he continued. "And every night it was – 'Can you turn it down?' We would tour in the van and sleep in the van with the gear, brush your teeth in the snow. To me the most rewarding thing I've got is the memories of those early days and a few photographs here and there, and band members, mentioning no names, taking a shit in an envelope in the back of a van – in the back seat is what I'm saying! It's too fucking cold and there ain't no toilet nowhere in the middle of a blizzard I can tell you."

After the brief European sojourn, Judas Priest spent the rest of the year playing up and down the UK with Budgie. As well as cover versions they continued to play several Atkins-penned songs even though the new line-up had been developing their own material since the previous year. For their first serious demo, the band laid down 'Ladies', 'Run Of The Mill' and 'Caviar And Meths'. With the help of Corke, the demo ended up in the hands of London-based label Gull Records.

Gull, a subsidiary of Decca Records, was launched by David Howells and his partner Derek Everett. The pair had worked together for a number of years before forming the label, as Howells explains it: "Derek Everett and I first teamed up at CBS in the mid Sixties when he took over as head of A&R. He was a brilliant spotter of pop acts and I looked after the American acts and signed contemporary British artists. Between us, on the British side, we signed and developed The Tremeloes, Georgie Fame, Marmalade, Al Stewart, Soft Machine, Robert Wyatt, The Zombies, Argent, The Love Affair and Fleetwood Mac, amongst many others. It was a magic period and a very special record company.

"Then in 1970 we left to face the new challenge of rebuilding MCA in the UK and we had a great run there, with acts such as The Average White Band, Budgie, Wishbone Ash, Neil Diamond, Osibisa, Camel, Tony Christie and The Chi-Lites, [before] leaving in 1974 to start our own label."

Primarily, it was Judas Priest's gig at the Marquee Club in London on February 11 and another gig in Fulham that clinched their deal with Gull.

David Howells: "I first saw Judas Priest live at the [Fulham] Greyhound at Dave Corke's invitation in 1974 and thought they were terrific. Unlike most new bands, they had a strong set of songs that complemented their sound. What marked them out from their competitors and peers at that time, in addition to the vocal prowess of Rob Halford, was the remarkable balance in their songs and the set as a whole.

"I thought [Rob] was special. I never heard Al sing with Priest, I only heard him later on his solo stuff, but they were very different kinds of vocalists."

Whether the original demo still exists is not known, but on the strength of it Priest drove down to London to sign the contract with Gull on April 16. The occasion was sandwiched between more gigs throughout the country, but touring didn't seem half as strenuous now they had something positive to show for their hard work.

A tour of the British Isles began in St. Albans, Hertfordshire, on April 13 and carried on throughout the summer in clubs and pubs in cities such as Doncaster, Leeds, Scarborough, Newcastle, Sheffield, Manchester, Derby and Blackburn.

David Howells: "Priest worked around 20 days a month at the time, extraordinary for an unknown act. Mind you, the itinerary was varied to say the least, covering the whole of the UK, not necessarily in any logical order. The benefit of course was the closeness of the band, the honing of their skills and the tightness of the set."

Howells was struck by the band's determination. "My memories are of a band that had accepted that it takes a lot of hard work to convince people that you are worth listening to and just got on with it. After all, they'd been on the circuit, in one form or another, for years."

Surprisingly, Judas Priest were considered out of touch by contemporary standards. "They were not playing fashionable music and if anything were out of step with the mainstream," says Howells, "which is probably one of the reasons that they took so long to get signed."

Fortunately, their unfashionable attire, including Downing's Stetson and Halford's frills, was of no immediate concern to Howells. "It was about their sound and potential, especially Rob Halford's voice and the songs."

Howells recommended adding a second guitarist to the line-up. Others claim it was Corke's or (*Rocka Rolla*) producer Roger Bain's idea but Howells says, adamantly, "The one thing I felt could improve their act would be the addition of a second lead guitar. At MCA I'd worked with

Wishbone Ash, and it seemed to me that the adoption of their twin guitar signature to Judas Priest's heavier, fatter sound would beautifully underpin Rob's extraordinary voice."

In terms of incorporating twin guitarists, Wishbone Ash helped to set a trend and many that followed, such as Iron Maiden and Judas Priest, went on to copy this style with greater success. Ash's Martin Turner cites Peter Green's Fleetwood Mac and the obscure late Sixties British psychedelic group Blossom Toes as having influenced them, as well as The Allman Brothers Band from Macon, Georgia.

It was a wise move for Priest in hindsight, though Downing took some convincing, believing at first that it reflected badly on his playing. Al Atkins: "I think [David Howells] thought K.K. was a little bit weak at first but he had great stage presence . . . he may have thought the guitar needed beefing up."

Downing soon came round to the idea, not least because, after years of struggle, a record contract might depend on it. Howells, however, doesn't recall Downing baulking at having a guitar partner: "I've always admired Ken Downing for the fact that he not only embraced the idea of a second lead guitar, but he went out and found the strongest possible guitarist partner in Glenn Tipton, who was in fellow Birmingham group The Flying Hat Band."

Al Atkins disputes this, claiming Dave Corke suggested Glenn Tipton. Whatever the truth behind his recruitment, Tipton would prove to be a vital component, the driving force that the band needed.

Glenn Raymond Tipton was born in Blackheath, Sandwell on October 25, 1948, and raised in Halesowen, Dudley. The family's semi-detached house on Newlands Drive, Hurst Green was close by the junction with Narrow Lane, not far from where Robert Plant also grew up. Tipton attended Hill Top Secondary School in Long Lane, Halesowen, which was then in an area known as Hill and Cakemore. As a child he enjoyed music and sport, initially football and cricket then golf and tennis. "Glenn was part of a group of lads who played football and cricket on a spare field belonging to Quinton Cemetery bordering Narrow Lane," says childhood friend Morris Walker.

Tipton undoubtedly acquired his musical talent from his mother, a professionally trained pianist and former teacher. Like many other schooled musicians, Tipton's mother made him learn piano. However, he was not nearly as attentive or patient as he should have been, and turned his attention to the guitar that his elder brother Gary was learning to play. Walker recalls that Gary played in a band called The Rocking Atlantics, "or even maybe just The Atlantics".

Tipton stuck at the piano until he was around nine, and this groundwork stood him in good stead when he finally picked up a guitar at the age of 18 – fairly late by most standards. "I never took a lesson until I was 20," he says. Walker remembers Tipton playing guitar with another friend called Martin Berry, who lived a few streets away on the same housing estate.

In the beginning, Tipton played a Hofner semi-acoustic before he went through a series of electric guitars including a Fender Stratocaster, a Gibson SG and a short-scale Rickenbacker, all played through a 100-watt Marshall stack. Like Downing, Tipton loved the late Sixties heavy blues-rock sound and visited local clubs to see his idols on stage. He told *Classic Rock* in 2006: "I used to go to a club in Birmingham called Mother's. I'd see bands there like Taste with Rory Gallagher."

Before joining Judas Priest, Tipton played in a number of unimpressive local bands. From 1970, he was with a four-piece outfit called Shave And Dry with vocalist Pete Hughes, drummer Barry Scrannage and bass player David Shelton, and from 1971–72 he played in Merlin, again with singer Hughes, as well as drummer Trevor Foster and bassist Frank Walker. At one point Andy Wheeler, who also had a short-lived tenure in The Flying Hat Band with Tipton, played bass for Merlin.

Tipton's first serious group was three-piece outfit The Flying Hat Band, formed in 1972 with bass player Mars Crowling (who years later joined the Pat Travers Band) and drummer Steve Palmer (brother of ELP's Carl Palmer). They recorded an album for Vertigo Records, who had signed Black Sabbath, but the label deemed it insufficiently commercial.* As with so many other Midlands-based musicians, Tipton's first live gig was at Henry's Blues House in Birmingham. The Flying Hat Band had a degree of success there and former IMA boss Norman Hood remembers them as, "[A] cracking blues-rock band. Glenn was a really hard-working front man, and listening now to a cassette of a club gig they did, he worked a crowd brilliantly, even in those days."

When Tipton joined Judas Priest in the first half of 1974, The Flying Hat Band had pretty much ceased to exist, although they had toured Europe with Deep Purple that same year, which Tipton told *Hard Rock* "was a scary experience at the time." Tipton's departure was the final nail in the coffin.

---

* A series of bootlegs and unreleased demos have been in circulation for some years.

It was David Howells' suggestion that the band work with producer Roger Bain, who had helped to develop heavy metal through his ground-breaking work with Black Sabbath on their first three albums, *Black Sabbath, Paranoid* and *Master Of Reality*. Bain had also worked with Howells at MCA, producing Budgie's albums.

John Hinch: "Roger Bain came up to see the band and the first thing he said was that he just wasn't happy with Kenny and his guitar . . . After playing with Clem Clempson and various others, I was not a Judas Priest fan from the point of view of the quality of the playing."

With a confirmed record deal, a second guitarist, and an established rock producer, Judas Priest recorded their debut album during the summer of 1974. "The album was recorded over three weeks at Island, Trident and Olympic studios in London," recalls Howells. "I seem to remember they met The Rolling Stones and Supertramp, amongst others, all in their first visit to recording studios. Heady times . . ."

Howells does not remember any serious arguments between band and producer in the studio, although they did have their occasional spats. "The song selection was easy," he says. "It was the basic live set. One of the reasons so many first albums are so good is simply a repertoire developed and perfected over a long period of time, plus the lack of expectation.

"The first demos I'd heard, I seem to remember, were 'Run Of The Mill', 'Whiskey Woman' and 'Caviar And Meths'. To this, they added amongst other tracks, 'Never Satisfied', 'One For The Road', 'Dying To Meet You' and 'Cheater'.

"The original Al Atkins compositions remained and in some cases evolved. The newcomers put their mark on the songs and developed new ideas. 'Whiskey Woman' grew into the classic 'Victim Of Changes' once Glenn and Rob were on board."

Indeed, 'Victim Of Changes' emerged from an amalgamation of the Atkins song 'Whiskey Woman' and 'Red Light Lady' (written by Halford), and was recorded as a demo during the time of *Rocka Rolla*. Neither Howells nor Atkins can recall why the band merged the lyrics.

John Hinch: "Literally, I used to have tears in my eyes when I used to do ['Victim Of Changes']. Loved it, absolutely loved it. I've got two original demos of 'Whiskey Woman' because we used to always open with that, and then of course it grew when Glenn joined the band and they did the twin guitars."

It's curious why producer and band decided to exclude would-be classics like 'Victim Of Changes', 'Tyrant', 'Genocide' and 'The Ripper' from the final cut (although all would feature on the follow-up, *Sad Wings Of Destiny*). 'Caviar And Meths' was reduced from its eight-minute stage encore version to a brief studio instrumental.

David Howells: "That would have been a band decision to edit ['Caviar And Meths'] and there was almost an embarrassment of riches when it came to the choice of songs for *Rocka Rolla*. Again Judas Priest and Roger Bain would have made decisions of what to use and what to hold back for the next album, for a variety of reasons."[*]

Al Atkins: "'Caviar And Meths' never actually got recorded properly. There just was a little bit, a snippet out of the middle that was changed, I don't know why." His outlook on the record could not have been improved by Downing and Hill being credited as chief songwriters, including some of the Atkins-penned songs. "They recorded my song 'Winter', which I think K.K. put his name to."

Hinch was also unhappy with the writing credits. "One of the main issues with me was that on the songwriting side it was a pretty close shot between Rob and Kenny. And then, of course, Glenn, obviously being a guitarist and maybe a little bit more proficient than Ken, started to write stuff and was, if you like, pushed to actually get his songs accepted. So it was always one of those typical group scenarios where, 'Oh, yes we're all writers of the music' but of course when it actually came to the nitty-gritty and the record crops up . . . then suddenly [it's], 'Oh, I wrote that' [and] 'Oh no, that was me.' So that, if you like, put my nose out of joint . . .

"You didn't get any credit for it, it all came down to who wrote the words and who wrote the music – fuck the drums and fuck the bass, you know. A typical band! It was effectively 50/50, i.e. Rob used to do all the lyrics, i.e. 50 per cent, and whether it be Glenn or Ken or both of them for the other 50 per cent of the music. No doubt Glenn thought, 'I'll be on a little bit of an earner here if I add a few words into them' because as I say, there are quite a few songs that were recorded."[†]

With just a week shy of a full month to record the album, Priest had constructed something they had spent long years aspiring to make – an incredible achievement by any standards. However, the band felt that Bain and the label heads at Gull had manipulated them like chess figures. Judas Priest would look back on the whole recording process of *Rocka Rolla* as a

[*] Nowadays Roger Bain refuses to talk about his past and his career in the music business.
[†] Tipton is credited as a co-writer on only two songs, 'Rocka Rolla' and 'Run Of The Mill'.

learning curve, and for future albums they would be much more forward when it came to making decisions and offering ideas and suggestions.

David Howells disagrees with Priest's attitude. "No band should be happy with its first album. In retrospect, every artist I'm sure feels they could have done better on their first one but the whole point is to be constantly challenging yourself and trying to improve.

"A first album is also something of a statement of intent. There are instances of debut albums being blockbusters straight out, but usually it's more a case of setting out your stall . . . Perhaps that's just where they were at that time. I still think it was a good debut album and pointed to where the act was going."

Al Atkins: "I didn't like *Rocka Rolla* that much. I never liked the drumming and I didn't like the production at all."

John Hinch: "I will criticise the production. In fact, one of the things that I've thought of actually doing was just to contact Dave Howells and see if I could go back into a studio to redo the drums, old as I am, because I'm pretty well ashamed of the very stiff, crappy sound. On the internet I read something about all sorts of mad, different mixes of the original, and apparently the German one is the best. It's got the thickest, heaviest sound. But I'm not impressed [with *Rocka Rolla*] whatsoever!"

Regardless of what anybody thought of *Rocka Rolla*, the Judas Priest sound of 1974 was still in the early stages of development. "It was a mix really, I mean, yes, it was different," says John Hinch. "You were playing with bands that were doing anything from soul to pop to whatever. So there weren't that many that you can call heavy metal. I don't even think we used to call it heavy metal. There was this – if you can call it – Judas Priest riff-type [music], which Kenny was totally into, Kenny and Ian."

David Howells: "As well as a record label and music publishing company, Gull also had a design division, Gull Graphics. My partner was John Pasche, who incidentally, designed the memorable Rolling Stones' 'Lips & Tongue' logo. Our other clients included The Average White Band, The Bay City Rollers, Isotope, *The Rocky Horror Show* movie and The Who."

John Pasche: "I had been doing a considerable amount of freelance work in the music business in the early Seventies while working as an art director for an advertising agency. Notably work for The Rolling Stones but also sleeves for David Howells, who was working at MCA Records. When he decided to leave and set up Gull Records, I was asked to work alongside him at their offices in South Molton Street, effectively as a freelance designer, which is where Gull Graphics was born. David ran the record company and I did the graphics, not just for Gull but also for many of my own clients in the entertainment industry."

David Howells: "Around this time one of John's designs was rejected by Mick Jagger for the Stones' *Goats Head Soup* album, an airbrushed image of a bottle top with 'Rolla Rolla' written on it. This struck me as being in keeping with Priest and a great title for their album. So I showed it to the band and suggested they write a song around it, and they came up with one of the strongest tracks on the album."

John Pasche: "As far as I can remember, David certainly did champion the band and I was unaware of any subsequent ill-feeling between them. *Rocka Rolla* was just a concept for a sleeve/album title that I had for no particular band at the time, so I decided to go ahead and photograph the image. I showed it to David and everyone was happy to use it for Judas Priest's first album. As they later developed their music and image, Priest went on to use imagery more fitting to the genre and style of heavy rock/metal bands. Looking back at all of their various sleeves, it certainly looks the 'odd man out', but then maybe being different and standing out from the crowd is not necessarily a bad thing."

John Hinch: "I do remember everybody going, 'Well, that's different.' 'Oh, yeah, the Coke thing . . . it might create a bit of an upset with Coca-Cola . . . big people, Coca-Cola.' You've gotta remember we were all naive novices but, at the time, there wasn't such a thing as a heavy metal album cover. There wasn't any dragons and swords and, if you like, heavy metal hadn't really been invented. But once again, if it wasn't accepted, how's it there? They seem to have this wonderful ability in hindsight to blame everybody for what's gone wrong in their career . . . it's a little bit juvenile."

Rocka Rolla was released on August 23, 1974[*] to a low-key reception, especially from the mainstream music press, who hardly gave it a mention. The album lacked the heaviness and doom-laden riffs of the succeeding albums and, although an important part of Priest's history in showing them struggling to find their creative voice, it suffered in comparison with other contemporary heavy rock albums. Whatever merits can be bestowed on *Rocka Rolla*, the band has never spoken keenly about it. In 1989, K.K. Downing told *Metal Hammer*, "We thought we had arrived but it was a big disillusionment . . . We heard the final cut and the pressing wasn't any good. That was tough."

---

[*] Some sources suggest it came out in early September.

While the late Sixties had brought a wave of British rock bands who took classic American blues and threw it right back at them with a heavier sound, the Seventies saw an even harder and louder (almost unbearably so for some) brand of rock. Black Sabbath and their peers Deep Purple were not solely responsible for the creation of heavy metal: Led Zeppelin had released five albums by 1974 and songs like 'Communication Breakdown', from their 1969 self-titled debut album, 'Whole Lotta Love' from 1969's *Led Zeppelin II* and 'Rock And Roll' from 1971's *Led Zeppelin IV* were benchmark songs in terms of 'heaviness'.

Glenn Tipton told *Metal Hammer*'s Chris Welch in 1990: "Heavy metal stemmed from the blues . . . That turned into heavy rock and then heavy metal in the days of Deep Purple and Black Sabbath. There were a whole bunch of bands in that era springing from people like Cream and Jimi Hendrix."

So when *Rocka Rolla* is stacked up against albums by Zeppelin, Sabbath and Purple, it's understandable how the members of Judas Priest virtually shunned their debut album on its release and have barely spoken about it since. Opener 'One For The Road' – a progressive song that could have easily fitted onto a Blue Oyster Cult record – doesn't really show Priest, as we know them now, in a hard-rock light, although it has a catchy rhythm juxtaposed with a decent guitar solo in the middle. 'Rocka Rolla' is notable for Hill's bass line, which would unfortunately get lost under the heavy guitars of Tipton/Downing on later recordings. Sounding more like Status Quo than a Priest effort because of its anthemic chorus, 'Rocka Rolla' was played live for the next few years and was released as an unsuccessful single off the album.

A couple of the better songs, 'Winter' and 'Deep Freeze', fit seamlessly together and could now easily slot into Priest's contemporary live set. 'Winter', a Sabbath-inspired track, begins with Halford's eerie vocals and a gloom-filled riff. The overwrought 'Winter Retreat' doesn't quite fit the bill, with Halford's flirtatious vocals lacking his usual power. 'Cheater' is a nifty little blues number featuring some tight twin-guitar work and even harmonica. 'Never Satisfied' starts off in the right mood, deep and brooding, before finishing with Halford's trademark falsetto.

'Run Of The Mill' is fairly dull and joyless and appears to be a lot longer than it actually is. With a running time of just over eight minutes, that's saying something. 'Dying To Meet You' is another dirge that plods along at a snail's pace, although it's more interesting than the former song largely because Halford's low-key vocals offer intrigue – the song coming to life just as the listener nods off. As already discussed, the closing instrumental

'Caviar And Meths' was sliced to last only a couple of minutes and as such is uneventful.

The last gig Judas Priest had played prior to the recording and release of *Rocka Rolla* was at the Mayfair Ballroom, Newcastle-upon-Tyne in the middle of June, and after a break for rehearsals, the Rocka Rolla tour began at the Huddersfield Arts Theatre on September 10, supported by Jailbait.

It was during this exhaustive tour around the British Isles that Hinch became even more frustrated and annoyed with the other members. Hinch, in hindsight, may not have been the best drummer to grace Judas Priest's drum stool but, to his credit, he was a hard worker and cared about the band. Yet he felt his dedication was being ignored.

John Hinch: "I bought the truck by borrowing a couple of thousand quid off one of my uncles. And that had to be repaid, so of course every now and then I would have to grab 20 quid out of the kitty to keep him happy and so on. As it progressed, we bought a car, so the band were turning up in style but I carried on in the truck. That's when I started to grow apart from the others to be honest because I was effectively travelling with our two crew guys, setting the equipment up. If anything broke down, I was the guy that mended it. The other two guys couldn't drive so I was doing all of this, looking after the contracts for the gigs, the recording stuff and Christ knows what [else]. And really drumming to me just became secondary, it was like, 'OK, here we go we're on stage' and then invariably you'd get an argument just for the sake of an argument . . ."

Hinch recalls one particularly argumentative night when Priest played at the Penthouse, Scarborough on September 27. "There'd be interviews to do and there'd be a huge argument between Rob and Kenny, 'I'm doing that,' and, 'No, you did the last one,' and all the rest of it. Ian's a nice guy, very, very quiet and all the rest of it. Then with Glenn . . . it just got into a situation where there were just bloody arguments and arguments and arguments . . . we were doing a gig in Scarborough. And we went into about the second number and the PA just packed in. You've gotta remember in those days it's not like it is now. You could be playing, say, 20 or 25 nights out of a month, night after night after night, and it didn't follow any particular pattern.

"So from there I drove everybody home because I used to have to drop everybody off and then the next day, [at] a football ground somewhere or a club within a football ground, I got all the truck unloaded to get the PA out. [I] set up the PA, mended the PA and put it all back in the truck, picked everybody up to do the gig and it was not a good day – Rob went absolutely berserk . . . It was a bit of a sour situation . . .

"When we used to do St. George's up in Liverpool, we stopped at Ian's mum's house and there was a double bed in one of the rooms, so I used to sleep with Rob . . . crazy world."

Despite the turbulent atmosphere, Hinch continued to drum for Judas Priest over the coming months. The band gigged right up until December 28 with a show at the Royal Links Pavilion in Norfolk. Despite the month's festivities there was little time to relax as, sandwiched in between more physically draining UK dates, Priest were due back on the Continent, playing Holland in March of '75.

In the author's interview with K.K. Downing for *Fireworks Melodic Rock* the guitarist was justifiably proud of how hard the band worked on the road to promote themselves. "We cut our teeth grinding up and down the country, and that's what we thought was the way forward to becoming a good live band and then hope somebody would spot us and go, 'Oh yeah, can we record your music?' "

In April, Judas Priest recorded an appearance on the BBC2 TV series *The Old Grey Whistle Test*, presented by Bob Harris, performing 'Rocka Rolla', 'Dreamer Deceiver' and 'Deceiver'.

Brian Ross, of NWOBHM* bands Blitzkrieg and Satan, recalls seeing this appearance. "They just played such powerful music that they stood out when music in general was beginning to go a little stale and jaded."

As a result of the many appearances Priest had made in London (primarily at the Marquee) during 1974 and '75, they were invited to play the Reading Festival on August 23, their first major event. It proved a potentially vital career move that helped attract both new converts and major press attention. As David Howells tells it, "The big breakthrough was their support appearance at the Reading Festival, which won them a rapturous reception from an initially hostile crowd. Not a foregone conclusion prior to their entrance, as the previous act had, I believe, been bottled off the stage!"

Priest's set at Reading included an obscurity called 'Mother Son', which is believed to have been recorded during an acoustic performance for Gull, although it was never finished and has never seen the light of day. John Hinch describes it as: "A very long song that was written by Glenn, very, very complicated but at the same time, it was reasonably good." The set also included 'Island Of Domination', 'Dreamer Deceiver', 'Deceiver' and

---

* New Wave Of British Heavy Metal

lengthy versions of 'Mother Son', 'The Ripper' and 'Rocka Rolla', the latter oddly featuring backing singers.

The Reading Festival turned out to be John Hinch's swansong with Judas Priest. The reasons given for his departure are contentious, to say the least. The band have claimed in interviews that he was fired for a lack of skill, while other reports suggested he quit because of an injury caused during a fight that prevented him from playing. John Hinch believes there was more to it than just his drumming ability. "What happened was the train of events got extremely nasty, after the PA broke down two nights in a row [in Scarborough]. Glenn came round one day and there were a few things that had gone wrong – he was not happy, and that's when I just thought enough is enough, and they agreed and that was it, I left!

"I wouldn't say it was amicable because I was owed a lot of money, but in all honesty with the guys . . . I got, say, 75 per cent of whatever I was owed for my quarter share of this, that and whatever else. And then from there, I just sort of launched myself into . . . a normal life."

David Howells: "I had a lot of time for John. He worked hard for the act, not only as the drummer but, as I remember it, he used to drive them, put up and break down the equipment with the roadies, and if my memory serves me right, he did the bookkeeping as well.

"It's hard to say what really happens with relationships in a band, unless you are in there at the time. Most people find it difficult enough in a relationship with a partner; multiply that by four or five and it gets interesting, I guess."

With a vacant drum chair, for reasons that are largely unknown, Alan Moore was re-enlisted for the *Sad Wings Of Destiny* recording sessions. Hinch did not receive a credit on the album – even though he laid down the drums on the initial versions of such songs as 'Tyrant', 'Victim Of Changes', 'The Ripper' and 'Genocide' – his original drum parts being replaced by Moore.

John Hinch: "That upset me to be honest with you. Having played all of those songs and practised them and refined them, as songs do evolve over a long period of time, it was a real bit of a pisser. I left and wasn't on that album."

The album recording sessions commenced at Rockfield Studios, Wales, lasting about a fortnight from November into December, with the mixing taking a week at Morgan Studios, north London, in January, 1976.

David Howells: "For *Sad Wings Of Destiny*, I felt that Priest had developed to a point where we could change the production approach, so I commissioned two young studio geeks from Morgan Studios, Jeffrey Calvert and Geraint Hughes to work with the band. Priest knew where they were going musically, so I was looking to capture their distinctive sound, and that's where Jeff and Geraint came into the picture. It wasn't an easy relationship call as Jeff and 'Max' [as Geraint Hughes was professionally known] had recently delivered Gull's first number one single, 'Barbados', under the name Typically Tropical.

"Not the most obvious people to record a metal act, but for me they had a great sonic understanding, having spent so much time at Morgan, which at that point in the Seventies was one of the leading European studio set-ups with Rod Stewart, Cat Stevens, Yes and most of the leading players of the time there at one point or another."

Chris Tsangarides, who would become a behind-the-scenes figure in the Judas Priest camp over years to come, acted as co-engineer along with Calvert and Dave Charles. Geraint Hughes took many shots during the sessions. "Well, firstly I wasn't the photographer, I was the co-producer of the album along with Jeff Calvert and the band. There has been some confusion in the past as I used to use a pseudonym of Max West. The photos were purely for fun and personal documentation . . . There was never a formal shoot, I simply snapped randomly."*

Hughes had actually worked with Judas Priest prior to the recording of *Sad Wings Of Destiny*. "We recorded a single at Morgan Studios earlier that year," he says, "a cover of the Joan Baez song 'Diamonds And Rust'.

David Howells: "'Diamonds And Rust' was I believe the only time I suggested Judas Priest record someone else's song. After all, they weren't short of good songs themselves. It was just that I thought that Joan Baez's 'Diamonds And Rust' would complement their own material and make a good single. Incidentally, my memory tells me that it was the last track recorded by the band for Gull, rather than coming before *Sad Wings Of Destiny*."

Whatever the true origins of the recording, 'Diamonds And Rust' was an odd choice for a band like Judas Priest to cover.

David Howells: "I always believe if you are going to cover songs it's a good idea to go in the opposite direction, i.e. male version of female song, heavy version of folk song. It's more surprising that way, and it's

---

* When asked in 2006 what happened to the photos, Hughes replies, "Nothing really, they remained in a box and then ended up on my website. I have passed a few of them on to a guy from BBC Wales who is writing a book on Rockfield."

something I've had some fun with over the years with various artists. Part of the role of A&R is to give the artist stimulus and to challenge them to grow. Needless to say this is often misinterpreted. I thought it worked out well, but initially the act did not agree, so we didn't use it at the time."*

Rockfield was then one of Britain's foremost recording studios. Queen had recently recorded parts of their legendary epic 'Bohemian Rhapsody' there, while Black Sabbath, Rush and Motörhead later recorded at the country facility. Howells admits that there were some difficulties at Rockfield, probably because the band felt that, having made an album, they had a better understanding of the recording process. David Howells: "I don't think it was necessarily easy, given the difference in personalities, but the challenge produced the magic and a great album, *Sad Wings Of Destiny*, came out of it."

Hughes described Glenn Tipton as "sometimes very serious, sometimes a prankster. Took his guitar playing very seriously and took the band very seriously. Probably the main driving force behind the band. Oddly enough he liked fishing, a most rock'n'roll thing . . . [K.K. Downing] was a some-what warmer guy than Glenn, a bit mischievous, also took the band and his playing very seriously. A peacemaker in disputes."

Hughes remembers Ian Hill as "shy, never said much, always in the background, but always very pleasant," while Alan Moore was a "very nice guy, became a good friend, a real prankster – shaving foam on the pillows! A very talented craftsman. [He] supplemented his drumming career as an HGV driver for Edwin Shirley Trucking." Hughes admits he found Rob Halford an enigma, "a somewhat unfathomable and compli-cated guy, prone to mood swings, hard worker at his vocals. I never felt I knew him or that he was a friend." Certainly, Halford never spoke about his sexuality, as Howell asks, "Would it have mattered? I doubt it."

At Rockfield, the hours were long but the band stayed focused. "None of them did any drugs to my knowledge; they would always decline my spliff," according to Hughes. "Work would start around 3 p.m. and after an evening meal, it would continue to about 3 a.m. The only woman present for a few days was Viki, Alan Moore's girlfriend." Hughes did not hang out with the band except "in the pub at Rockfield sometimes." It's no wonder he admits to not having any outstanding memories from the sessions. "They all seemed to get on very well, no rows at all. Jeff and I knew that there were gripes they had about Gull, but they were careful to

---

* Import editions and reissues of *Rocka Rolla* included 'Diamonds And Rust' as a bonus track. It was first officially released on 1977's *Sin After Sin*.

keep that to themselves because, I guess, they knew that we were also signed to Gull as artists. We never probed at all."

It was at this time that other changes started to make slight rumbles. "I think the leather image was in its early stage of development . . ." Hughes observed.

Priest's idea for their second album was to make it progressive but not experimental or overblown, to be within reach of the progressive rock fan without distancing the typical hard rock fans who favoured simple riffs and catchy arrangements.

Geraint Hughes: "All in all, myself and Jeff Calvert were pleased. We would have liked to have been a bit more experimental, but they were purists. Glenn reacted quite strongly at me feeding his guitar through a synth to create some unusual filtering effect, K.K. cooled things down and we arrived at a compromise. At the end of the day, my impression was that the band were pleased with the production, however, not pleased enough to use mine and Jeff's services again."

Neither were they satisfied enough to re-engage the services of John Pasche. David Howell says, "This time for the cover design I commissioned Patrick Woodroffe to come up with an illustration and that worked out too." Pasche's recollections about the cover sleeve for Priest's second album, which features a fallen angel in a gothic fantasy world, differ slightly from Howells' version of events.

John Pasche: "My involvement in *Sad Wings Of Destiny* was the art direction of the illustration, the design of the logo on the front and the layout and type on the rest of the package. Patrick Woodroffe did the illustration to my brief and then I put the whole artwork package together."

Pasche has some lasting memories of Judas Priest: "The band often came in to see me in my studio and chatted about their exploits on the road – it sounded really tough for them touring at the time, living/sleeping in a van up and down Europe. I was really pleased for them that it all came good for them in the end, as I really liked their albums and them as individuals. Once when they came in, they asked me if I wanted to join the band, but it was probably a bit of a wind-up! I often saw them live and, as in the case when they did showcase gigs at the Marquee, I was there putting up the displays for their current album in the window and foyer. It was all very hands-on – first design the sleeve and the poster, then go and stick the stuff on the wall. But that was all the fun of it!"

Sad Wings Of Destiny, released March 26, 1976, is generally considered by many, not least the band, to be the first true Judas Priest recording, containing all the now familiar Priest trademarks, not least the powerful gothic fantasy sleeve that later became associated with heavy metal. The iconic Priest symbol (jokingly referred to as "the Devil's tuning fork" by the band) hangs from the chain around the angel's neck on the cover artwork.

Sad Wings Of Destiny showed signs of many influences from the likes of Sabbath to Queen – the latter one of Halford's main musical inspirations, with *Queen II* ranking among his all-time favourite albums. The most effective part of lengthy opener 'Victim Of Changes', aside from the opening riff, fell roughly halfway through the song when it broke down to a beautifully orchestrated interlude, while Halford's falsetto at the climax was among his finest vocal moments. 'The Ripper', another Priest classic that has been played off and on over the years, concerned the infamous Victorian serial killer, a precursor to the type of daring subject matter the band were willing to explore. 'Dreamer Deceiver' was held together with classical influences. 'Deceiver' revved things up again while 'Prelude' was an odd but effective two-minute instrumental written by Tipton. 'Tyrant' was another typical slice of Seventies heavy metal (resurrected in 2001 for Rob Halford's double live CD *Live Insurrection), as was 'Genocide', lasting over five minutes and perfectly encapsulating the twin-guitar attack of Tipton and Downing, while 'Epitaph' bore the Queen influence – an eccentric, peculiar anomaly that showed their emotional edge. 'Island Of Domination', a beastly, distinctively hard-edged metal beast, rounded off proceedings.

With a second album in the shops, a UK tour began on April 6 at the Plaza in Truro and concluded at the Roundhouse in London on June 20. However, due to major financial problems, each band member was forced to seek employment to keep the band going, as an approach to Gull for extra supporting funds – thought to have been around £25 each per week – had been rejected.

K.K. Downing told *Metal Hammer*: "We all had to take part-time jobs. Ian was driving a van and I was working in a factory, Glenn was painting the local garage. We thought this was hopeless. We couldn't concentrate on our career . . ."

The band's dire financial straits led Alan Moore to leave for the second and final time. The last anybody heard of Moore he was driving a tour truck on a Rolling Stones tour in the Eighties. Judas Priest Mark VII's line-up had ended.

Needless to say, Priest were upset and angry with Gull, so when they were approached by CBS Records (whilst still under contract) they showed no remorse about moving elsewhere. CBS were impressed enough with the *Sad Wings Of Destiny* album and the success of the subsequent UK tour that A&R man Paul Atkinson signed the band to the label in 1976, offering them a £60,000 advance as part of a worldwide record deal.

When asked about Priest's actions after Gull's treatment of the band, David Howells is phlegmatic. "We signed, developed and helped them become the Judas Priest the world has known for 30 years," he explains. "It's never easy to lose an act like that. In retrospect, of course, it's easy for me to say, 'It was only a question of time before they made the breakthrough.' But, all the signs were there after *Sad Wings Of Destiny* came out. The groundwork had been done. This was no overnight success. People were taking notice, at last, particularly the media."*

By mutual decision, despite all the hard work he had poured into the band, Priest also sacked David Corke, their manager since 1970. Taking the advice of CBS, Priest signed with Arnakata Management, Inc. and Jim Dawson became their new manager. Former drummer John Hinch has some strong words about the way Judas Priest treated their ex-manager Dave Corke.

John Hinch: "Even though effectively it was me that drew a contract up to sack him, he was still a part of Judas Priest. Dave is the most generous bloke in the world. He has worked bloody hard for a thousand groups and back in those days – I don't know about now because, to be honest, I haven't spoken to him in a couple of years – he could talk to anybody . . . He could actually, for the sake of argument, phone up and get put through to the main man of CBS or the head of EMI . . . Dave was a gem. He could see a band and know that it was gonna happen, including Judas Priest. But basically they shat over the poor guy and he's very, very bitter about it. The number of times that it happened to him, he should have been a multi-multi-multi millionaire as opposed to penniless. Very sad, you know."

With a strong second album and a new record contract on an internationally renowned label, things were definitely looking up for Judas Priest. But for most rock/metal bands a change was coming . . .

---

* Howells continued with Gull Records throughout the Seventies and is now involved in the London-based company Darah Music.

SIX

1977–1979

". . . I bought Sin After Sin *and that was the thing that really got me . . . After* Sin After Sin *I was hooked!"*
— Jeff Waters, founder of Canadian thrash metal band Annihilator

WITH the explosion of punk rock at the tail end of 1976, those with long hair and a liking for traditional rock music were in danger of being eclipsed. In an interview (dated July 4, 1987) K.K. Downing told *Sounds* writer Mary Anne Hobbs how "punk arrived and everybody started calling Ritchie Blackmore an old fart. There were only two metal bands who toured that year, us and UFO. We didn't give a shit about the press; we just went out for the kids."

Each succeeding year seemed to bring a further leap in Priest's career in terms of music, image, popularity and confidence, whether playing live or recording. At the start of 1977 the band began rehearsing for their third album, their first under the CBS agreement. Replacing Alan Moore was Simon Phillips, who recounts, "I had been professional for eight years prior – four years with my father's Dixieland band, then the London show *Jesus Christ Superstar*, and during my time there I started playing sessions. I worked in New York for a brief time in '74, then back to London and was playing on all sorts of albums – Robert Palmer, Phil Manzanera, Murray Head, Gary Boyle, Jack Bruce and countless other sessions."

Indeed, by 1977, when CBS employed Phillips for the *Sin After Sin* sessions, he was rapidly earning a revered reputation as a session drummer. In addition to the above acts, his exemplary curriculum vitae included Steve Ashley, Martyn Ford, 801, Big Jim Sullivan Band, Chopyn, Dana Gillespie, Gordan Giltrap, Dave Greenslade, Albert Hammond, Nazareth, Brain Protheroe, Veronique Sanson and The Walker Brothers.

The band also roped in the services of Deep Purple bassist and producer Roger Glover. "I believe someone from their record company approached my managers at the time," says Glover. "I seem to recall that I was considered as a producer after they had listened to 'This Flight Tonight' by Nazareth, a production of mine. It has a similar feel. As to why they wanted to cover it, I don't know."

Simon Phillips: "After finding out they did not have a full-time drummer at that time [Glover] recommended that I should play on the album. I had worked with Roger on his solo album *Elements* in the summer of 1976 and also the *Whitesnake* album later the same year, so I had got used to his way of working and we obviously had a great rapport."

However, according to Glover, it was the band who approached Phillips, not himself. Glover was aware that they had lost their drummer before recording commenced but he admits he "knew very little" about the band before working with them: "I have no idea how Gull Records treated them. As far as I know, they were not particularly excited about anyone producing them – they believed in their own abilities and direction and wanted to do it by themselves. This became apparent after our first meeting in the rehearsal studio – they did not warm to my presence at all. At the end of an uncomfortable day of listening to them playing the songs that they intended to record, I called for a meeting in the local pub, and I told them that I sensed their discomfort and was not interested in producing any band that didn't want me. They seemed relieved to be able to speak freely and told me that they were unhappy with the record company forcing them to have any producer, not just me. We parted company on friendly terms and I assumed that that was the end of it.

"They started the album on their own and I became involved only later on, when things started to go wrong for them. They had lost their drummer by this time and had only six days of studio time left. They told me that they had approached Simon Phillips to do the sessions and I was pleased with that, since I had worked with him previously and knew that he worked fast. I agreed to help them out and, after abandoning all their previously recorded efforts, we really got down to business and managed to get the album done very quickly."

Phillips was also unfamiliar with either *Rocka Rolla* or *Sad Wings Of Destiny* prior to recording. "At that time I knew nothing of their business – I was just there to concentrate on making a great record."

After rehearsing at Pinewood Studios, the album was recorded from January through to February at Ramport Studios in Battersea[*] – The

---

[*] While recording at Ramport, the band stayed at a local bed and breakfast, which, ironically for a band named Judas Priest working on an album to be called *Sin After Sin,* was located in – of all places – a convent.

Who's studio – and mixed at Wessex Studios, north London.

Simon Phillips: "[Ramport was] very popular at that time for rock projects. I was there from February 1 to 5 – just five days. I don't know how long it took to do vocals, overdubs and mixing – I was not there for that part of the process.

"I think all [the songs had] been written. All I remember was one rehearsal where we just played – no demos to listen to, just sat down and played – great!"

Despite a tight recording schedule, Phillips vaguely remembers going back into the studio on February 16 to lay down more drum parts. The band's confidence shined through during the making of the album, helped by a lack of interference from the record label. "It was not stressful," says Glover, when he thinks back to early 1977, "intense would be a better word, mainly due to the lack of time. They were very professional and worked well . . . [Rob Halford] was a man who vocally had a very individual and original passion. He believed in himself and I respected that a lot."

While both Glover and Phillips insist there were no high jinks in the studio during the making of *Sin After Sin*, several widely circulated anecdotes concern a poisonous fish kept in an aquarium in the studio reception area and the band getting legless in a local hostelry on a lethal alcoholic brew known as 'The Hosepipe'. Phillips has next to no memories of either of these stories. "I do remember something about the fish – I think they told everyone they were piranhas or something . . . Don't remember 'The Hosepipe'. I think I just used to roll a fatty and get high at the end of the day and listen back to the rough [mixes] at deafening levels.

"During the sessions, it seemed as though Glenn was the leader – guiding the rest of the guys. K.K. spent most of the time in the control room, with Roger listening and giving his thoughts and input. Rob was fairly passive but still with ideas and input – in fact, I seem to remember he was really enjoying it and very encouraging. Ian was the quiet one – just like John Entwistle was with The Who."

Neither Phillips nor Glover has kept in touch with the band since the completion of the album. Roger Glover: "Of course I am aware of their career and [we do] meet occasionally, and have even played on the same stage – Monsters of Rock, Donington in 1980 and more recently at Tommy Vance's Memorial Concert at the Albert Hall [in] 2006 – and it has always been friendly."

Simon Phillips: "We didn't have long enough together so other than being friendly it never went further. Also, they lived in Birmingham at that time – I seem to remember – and I was living in London, so it was not the easiest thing to do to hang out with them . . . I did bump into them again in Los Angeles in 1990 at SIR. I was rehearsing with Joe Walsh, John Entwistle and Keith Emerson – and they were in the next room."

Despite hiring him purely as a session drummer, Priest were so impressed with Phillips that they offered him the touring job, but he declined due to other professional obligations.

Simon Phillips: "I had just joined Jack Bruce's band. We had made a record in '76 and I was on a royalty with that band – so I had already made a commitment to someone else."*

The legendary Mark VIII phase of Judas Priest's career started in March 1977 when, at Glover's suggestion, the band hired ex-Fancy drummer Les 'Feathertouch' Binks for the pending Sin After Sin tour.

Roger Glover: "I knew Les Binks very well having worked with him on several projects including [Glover's solo album] *The Butterfly Ball (And The Grasshopper's Feast)* in 1974. He was a member of Fancy, along with Ray Fenwick and Mo Foster."

Les Binks was born James Leslie Binks in Northamptonshire on April 5, 1948. While Binks was in Fancy, the band enjoyed two Top 10 hit singles in 1974, a cover of The Troggs' 1966 classic 'Wild Thing' and 'Touch Me'. The drummer had not only worked with Glover but also with legendary vocalist Eric Burdon.

Sin After Sin was released on May 14 and spent six weeks in the UK charts, peaking at number 23 – a different story from their first two releases.[†] The album began with 'Sinner' – a six-and-a-half-minute metal onslaught. 'Diamonds And Rust', included from the previous recording session, was a far cry from the folk-based Joan Baez original. Later, Priest went back to basics with the song, slowing it down to a semi-acoustic version using electric-acoustic guitars. Akin to 'Sinner', 'Starbreaker' became a heavily played song in the band's late Seventies and early Eighties live set before it was eventually dropped in favour of newer material. 'Last Rose Of Summer' was a surprising curiosity – a delightfully tender tune with Halford demonstrating how his high-octane vocals were suited to passionate ballads as well as heavy metal. Opening with a short set

---

[*] Phillips continued to work for other artists such as The Who, Michael Schenker, Mick Jagger and Gary Moore, and has been drumming for AOR legends Toto since 1992.

[†] The 2001/02 Sony CD reissue includes a live version of 'Jawbreaker' and a previously unreleased cover of The Gun's 1968 UK hit 'Race With The Devil'. The latter was the product of a jam session during the recording of the *Stained Class* album in 1978 but was discarded.

of vocal melodies, 'Let Us Prey/Call For The Priest' kicked into force. Phillips' drumming ran at an intense pace, matched by Downing and Tipton's duelling guitars.

'Raw Deal' purportedly made reference to Fire Island, located in New York State, a popular gay holiday playground. Another ballad, 'Here Come The Tears' was more up-tempo than 'Last Rose Of Summer', increasing in speed and depth as it progressed. 'Dissident Aggressor' could easily lay claim to founding the various genres of metal that were to follow in the Eighties, especially thrash.

Although Priest strove for something heavier than *Sad Wings Of Destiny*, they could not have predicted how much of an influence their early albums, including *Sin After Sin*, would have in shaping the future of heavy metal. "Whenever you are in the studio there is never a feeling that you are doing anything more than trying to capture the moment," says Glover, "the future of what you are doing is of the least concern."

Some of the heavier songs, such as 'Dissident Aggressor', have a Sabbath-esque menace and ambience. However, Glover says that Black Sabbath was "not to my knowledge" an influence on the album.[*]

The cover of *Sin After Sin* featured a gothic temple with the silhouette of a woman sitting by the temple's doorway. With dark lyrics, a sinister sleeve and overall sound, the album was a logical stepping stone for the progression of the band's individual sound and of heavy metal itself.

Simon Phillips: "I know that now – but not then. I just played the way I felt it. Really, I was bringing in styles from other music like – believe it or not – funk and fusion, but played with a rock'n'roll sensibility. Also, I brought a different sound to the records of that time – using a large drum kit tuned in my particular way I guess . . . I've had many young heavy metal drummers come up to me and list that record as one of the main influences for them, and also the beginning of heavy metal as it is today."

One musician who counts himself as a fan is Venom's bassist and singer Cronos. "I remember when *Sin After Sin* came out and it was nicknamed 'Riff After Riff'," he says. "There was just so many cool riffs on that album, listening to early Judas Priest takes me right back to my latter teenage years."

Simon Phillips: "I just recently downloaded [*Sin After Sin*] from iTunes and I really enjoyed hearing it again after all this time. It was a great album."

---

[*] The thrash metal band Slayer covered 'Dissident Aggressor' on their 1988 album *South Of Heaven*.

The Sin After Sin tour commenced in Scandinavia – which remains a stronghold for Priest – including a date at the Kuusrock Festival in Oulu, Finland. The British leg – a triumphant success in terms of attendances and reactions from fans and critics – commenced on April 22 at Cambridge's Corn Exchange and finished in London with a blistering gig at the Victoria Theatre on May 22. Brummie prog-rockers Magnum were the support band.

While the band were on great form, the London gig was marred by a riot breaking out between brutish bouncers and fans who were disgruntled by their treatment. Among the audience was Priest fan Derek Oliver, who later wrote for *Kerrang!* and other significant metal magazines. "I was just amazed that the bouncers were literally kicking the shit out of people in full public view. It was a pretty horrific event all in all."

One of the advantages Priest had under the auspices of their new, larger record company was the opportunity to go to America. Judas Priest first played the United States on June 17, 1977 at the Civic Centre in Amarillo, Texas. Like other British kids who grew up in the grim, deprived, post-war years, America seemed like a distant paradise. Rob Halford in particular was affected by the idiosyncrasies and laid-back pace of the American way of life. For a gay man having grown up in the stifling environment of the Black Country, it must have seemed like a release.

The tour of the US finished in July, by which time Priest had played in cities such as New York and Chicago, supported AOR acts Foreigner and REO Speedwagon on a few dates in large arenas holding up to 10,000 people and, most prestigious of all, supported Led Zeppelin for two dates at the Day On The Green Festival at Oakland Coliseum, California on July 23 and 24 – Zeppelin's last shows in the US.*

Halford later commented on Zeppelin's performance to *Kerrang!* in the mid Eighties: ". . . I saw Led Zep at a Day On The Green show . . . and you could tell they were bored shitless playing 'Stairway To Heaven' for the millionth time!"

Priest's last British gig in 1977 was a random show at the Blue Lagoon Ballroom, Cornwall on August 29, before they finished off the Sin After Sin tour supporting AC/DC in Europe. Binks had comfortably settled on the drum stool and it appeared that he had become more than just a drummer for hire. Priest fans were ecstatic because Binks was steadily building up his reputation as a brilliant drummer.

---

* Their remaining tour dates were cancelled when singer Robert Plant was told that his five-year-old son, Karac, had died due to serious respiratory problems.

The recording of fourth album *Stained Class* took place in October and November, 1977, at Chipping Norton Studios in the picturesque setting of the Cotswolds – a markedly different environment from the urban London studios they'd previously used (although the album's mixing was done at Advision and Trident). This time CBS hired the expertise of Dennis MacKay to produce. After the album was completed, the company decided that the band should record a cover version as a potential hit single, something that had thus far eluded them. Because previous album sleeves depicted fallen angels, fantasy worlds, gothic temples and lyrics about death, existence, outer space and existentialism, CBS thought Priest were too dark and cheerless for chart success.

However, with MacKay not available, the band had to go through the hassle of finding a new producer just for one song. They ended up with James Guthrie, who had previously worked with Pink Floyd as an engineer. After spending hours throwing around various ideas of what to record, Guthrie and Priest chose to cover late Sixties English blues-rock band Spooky Tooth's 'Better By You, Better Than Me' (written by organist and singer Gary Wright). It was recorded at Utopia Studios in London. Little did anyone know it would become the most controversial song in Priest's canon.

Released on February 25, 1978, *Stained Class* reached number 27 in the UK, spending a healthy five weeks in the charts. The main surprise was that the album jumped into the US *Billboard* Top 200 Albums, Priest's first chart success in the States.[*]

What marked a difference in turn from the album's predecessor was the heavy influence of science-fiction themes, particularly of a Forties and Fifties pulp paperback vein – a theme that would grow stronger with the albums that followed. Specifically, 'Invader' and 'Savage' illustrated these other-worldly concepts. The album sleeve depicted a metallic cyborg with a laser or iron bar right through its head. Also, the artwork was notable because it featured the now iconic Priest logo.

Stained Class began with 'Exciter', an influential precursor to the speed metal of the Eighties. John Ricci, guitarist with Canadian band Exciter, says, "We were called Hell Razor from '78–'80, During that time, we were a local band playing cover tunes and we grew tired of the name. We wanted a fresh start and to write original material. One day on the

---

[*] The 2001/02 reissue contains the out-take 'Fire Burns Below' and a live version of 'Better By You, Better Than Me'.

way to rehearsal, one of our road crew suggested the name Exciter. The Judas Priest song would be a great name for the band and we all agreed . . . Priest are our biggest influence because they seem to have the right balance of power, speed, and heaviness, and that's the formula that guides Exciter."

'White Heat, Red Hot' fired up with a deadly chorus and Priest's supremely tight rhythm section in full force. The cover version of 'Better By You, Better Than Me' retained Spooky Tooth's blues feel while the title track, about mankind's destruction of the Earth, was an instantly memorable, grinding slice of metal – deadly in its execution. 'Invader' began with the sound of a UFO approaching, typical of a black and white Fifties B-movie, before the usual Priest traits kick in. The simplistic but infectious chorus on 'Invader' was followed by the tribal feel of 'Saints In Hell', with Hill's pounding bass and Binks' sturdy drumming. 'Savage', a screaming, blood-curdling demon, was about relations between the American Indians and the ignorant settlers who destroyed their tribes. 'Beyond The Realms Of Death', co-written by Halford and Binks, was an anti-power statement of intent and remains among Halford's best lyrical endeavours, demonstrated through its longevity. A lengthy song that built up before breaking down, it displayed Tipton's classically trained ear working with Downing's more aggressive attitude towards the guitar. Like much of the album, the lyrics for 'Heroes End', credited as being penned solely by Tipton, was Priest at their most serious, concerning the concepts of aging and death.

The 68-date Stained Class world tour began at Cramer Links Park, West Runton, on January 19, 1978. The UK leg, finishing in Guildford at the end of February, included their first gig at London's famed Hammersmith Odeon (now the Apollo) – a venue Priest would return to numerous times over the years. Halford, who was now carrying his infamous bullwhip, lashing it at the unsuspecting audience, upset one fan who took offence to being lashed. When the guy grabbed the whip, a fuming Halford retaliated by walking off stage, grabbing a fire extinguisher and taking his revenge on the front members of the audience.

By the time Priest hit America for their second US tour from March through until July 7, their image had drastically changed. Gone were the pompous coloured satins, French nylons, cheap flares and chiffon, large Stetsons and the outdated glam spandex; Halford now dressed in blue denim with a black leather biker's jacket and hat, with the rest of the band wearing leather adorned with silver studs and chains.

Although verging on the ridiculous, Priest added to the aura of heavy metal by adopting a style, that would rapidly become familiar. Soon, metal bands worldwide (especially in the UK and US) would copy and mimic this image change.

Priest were less than happy with headlining act Foghat's inhospitable attitude towards them. This was only made bearable by the cheers and screams Priest received from eager audiences during their short half-hour set. After the discomfort of touring with Foghat, from then on, Priest vowed to treat their own support acts with generosity and kinship.

After finishing off their American tour duties, Priest commenced a brief tour of Japan for the first time. Japan, along with the US, would form the core of Judas Priest's international fan base. Playing Tokyo, Nagoyo and Osaka from July 25 to August 5, the tour was rapturously received by young Japanese fans; in interviews, members of the band compared it to their own version of 'Beatlemania'.*

After finishing the Far East tour, Priest headed straight back to Britain to begin work on their next studio album. Recording commenced in August and ran into September at Utopia Studios, with extra work done at Basing Street and CBS Studios, London. Priest had enjoyed such a creative relationship with James Guthrie during the recording of 'Better By You, Better Than Me' that they retained him for the album.

By this point, having recorded four albums to date, Priest had more than a basic knowledge and understanding of recording studio applications. They became more technically minded and, as such, more creatively controlling in their opinions during the recording process.

The controversially titled *Killing Machine* album was released in Britain on November 11, 1978. Peaking at number 32 in the UK top 40, its chart position was not as high as the previous two albums for CBS although it remained for nine weeks in the charts.

Again, the science-fiction fantasy themes so prevalent on *Sin After Sin* were fully explored on *Killing Machine,* and the futuristic sleeve gave critics strong hints as to which direction Priest were keen to explore. Not only that, but the album also explored the subjects of urban violence and social decay.

Like 'Dissident Aggressor' from the previous album, 'Delivering The Goods' was a screeching, energetic, fully fuelled opener and by far one of Priest's better, yet frustratingly underplayed, songs. 'Rock Forever' had a

---

* What marked this tour out from previous road jaunts was how readily fans bootlegged it; concert recordings are still available to buy on the internet and in selected stores around the world.

live anthemic appeal while 'Evening Star' (released as a single) broke down during the chorus before building up again with a set of vocal falsettos. 'Hell Bent For Leather' became a renowned metal anthem and one of the most widely played Priest songs. As with 'Evening Star', 'Take On The World' was not one of the album's better moments but it had a basic, catchy, repetitive rhythm and sing-along chorus – akin to Queen's 'We Will Rock You' – although not as technically simplistic.

'Burnin' Up' was followed by the title track, 'Killing Machine', a sinister piece of work featuring dark lyrics and a butch attitude. The anti-social 'Running Wild' (written by Tipton) reflected the increasing anger and depth in the band's music and has proved its worth among Priest classics by its inclusion on various compilations. 'Before The Dawn' flowed smoothly, with Halford's melodious vocals working alongside Downing's subtle chords and having a surprising effect. The album ended with the croaky, macho and seemingly effortless 'Evil Fantasies'.*

To promote the new album, the X-Certificate Tour started in Blackburn at King George's on October 24, with support coming from Lea Heart. Priest's newly honed image was the subject of much press attention. Halford, in biker's jacket, black sunglasses and cap, posed with bullwhip in hand, handcuffs dangling from his black leather trousers. On other occasions, Tipton wore all red leather. Tipton, Downing, Hill and Binks also dressed in black leather, although their image was not nearly as camp.

Years later, in defence of Priest's drastic change of image, Halford told *Sounds*: "People don't realise it, they think we're copies of some other forerunner. But it just came naturally in our music. To look at yourself in the mirror before you go onstage an' to see yourself in leather certainly does give you that eagerness to get on and do it, rather than if I'd got a pair of blue shorts [and] spotted socks on."

"We've taken the metal all over the world and it's happening *everywhere*," Downing told *Soundcheck!* in the mid Eighties. "Everybody's wearing now what we've been wearing for years, leather and studs."

As far as concert attendances went, Priest were now playing decent-sized venues such as the similarly named Apollo theatres in Glasgow, Manchester and Birmingham, as well as another night at the Hammersmith Odeon. The tour thrived with sold-out nights before reaching completion in November at Peterborough's Wirrina Stadium. The year ended with

---

* The recent 2001/02 reissue included the previously unheard out-take 'Fight For Your Life' (the song's main rhythm was used years later for the more familiar 'Rock Hard, Ride Free') as well as a live version of 'Riding On The Wind'.

some early pre-release US promotion for *Killing Machine* via a couple of December gigs in New York State.

On January 25, 1979, Priest performed the chest-thumping 'Take On The World' (released January 20 with a live version of 'Starbreaker') on BBC TV's *Top Of The Pops*. The song reached number 14 in the UK singles chart, proving that as a metal band Priest were attaining a larger audience. The programme's producers told Halford that it was inappropriate to display his handcuffs and bullwhip before the cameras because it might disturb youngsters while upsetting more conservative older viewers. Needing as much exposure as possible, the vocalist complied. The pious Mormon family collective, The Osmonds, performed their latest single on the same programme – an ironic combination of acts.

CBS deemed *Killing Machine* to be inappropriately titled for American tastes, fearing its violent and alienating connotations might harm the album's chart success. When released there at the start of 1979 the name was changed to the less controversial *Hell Bent For Leather*. Priest did not uphold their creative convictions, going along with this advice in a further effort to crack the American mainstream. The release delay in the US gave the commercially minded record company the idea of adding an extra track. It was decided that the band should cover Fleetwood Mac's 1970 rock classic, 'The Green Manalishi (With The Two-Pronged Crown)'. As with 'Better By You, Better Than Me', Priest held little opposition as long as they could stamp their own individuality on the recording, making it an authentic Judas Priest song. Because it became an almost permanent fixture in the band's live set over the years, many Priest followers were unaware that it was not an original song.[*]

Touring in 1979 began with a return to Japan on February 10. Because there was only a gap of several months since their last tour there, the reaction they received was less than stunning. There was a more major problem in that Halford was suffering from laryngitis (although some sources claim it was a mere cold), which affected his vocal capabilities. After listening to the live tapes, recorded at Koseinenkin Hall and Nakano Sunplaza Hall in Tokyo on February 10 and 15, respectively, various overdubbing was allegedly done on certain tracks, which is why the album *Unleashed In The East* was referred to in some quarters as 'Unleashed In The Studio'. The band rigorously denied that the entire album was overdubbed, although they admitted that Halford's vocal problems had

---

* The track was added to later reissues of the original UK album.

to be addressed. The mixing was done at Startling Studio in Ascot, Berkshire.*

Released on October 6, 1979, *Unleashed In The East* was Judas Priest's highest-charting album to date in the UK, reaching number 10 and staying in the charts for eight weeks. In the States it made the *Billboard* Top 200 Albums, peaking at 70.†

Like all great live rock and metal albums such as AC/DC's *If You Want Blood You've Got It* (1978), Black Sabbath's *Live Evil* and Saxon's *The Eagle Has Landed* (both 1982), the original nine-track *Unleashed In The East* was a fast and finely played set containing most of Priest's killer cuts such as 'Victim Of Changes', 'Diamonds And Rust', and soaring opening track 'Exciter'.

In *Classic Rock* magazine's 2003 poll of the '50 Greatest Live Albums Ever!', *Unleashed In The East* – ranking at number 16 between Rush's *All The World's A Stage* (17) and The Clash's *From Here To Eternity* (15) – was described as "a formidable demonstration of Priest's live power."‡

Two years later, tennis player Pat Cash confessed in a *Classic Rock* article headed 'Every Home Should Have One: Albums You Should Own', that he was a major Judas Priest fan because of *Unleashed In The East*. "I knew absolutely nothing about heavy metal at all, but one day while flicking through the racks at my local record store I saw the cover of *Unleashed In The East* . . . buying the album that day completely transformed the life of that 16-year-old . . . I bought the reunion album *Angel Of Retribution* and enjoyed it a lot, but *Unleashed In The East* is still my ultimate desert island disc. Even now I work out to it in my garage."

Unleashed In The East marked the first of eight album collaborations with 'Colonel' Tom Allom who had been a co-engineer on Black Sabbath's first two groundbreaking albums. "Actually, when we joined

---

* The studio was part of Tittenhurst Park, an estate owned by Ringo Starr (and previously, John Lennon) who was living as a tax exile in France at the time.
† As was often the case with East Asian metal releases, the Japanese version of *Unleashed In The East*, changed to the less imaginative *Priest In The East*, had several live bonus tracks added, namely, 'Rock Forever', 'Delivering The Goods', 'Hell Bent For Leather' and 'Starbreaker'. Those bonus cuts were later used as selective B-sides on various UK single releases in the early Eighties and appeared on the 2001/02 CD reissue.
‡ Coincidentally, Priest's second live album, *Priest . . . Live!* just scraped into the *Classic Rock* poll at number 48. *Unleashed In The East* ranked as one of 'The Best 25 Heavy Metal Albums Of All Time' in Ian Christie's book *Sound Of The Beast: The Complete Headbanging History Of Heavy Metal* while, more controversially, it was also named the number one 'Best Faked Live Record'.

CBS, Tom came to rehearsals to see if we wanted him to produce our first album on the label," Glenn Tipton told *Sounds* in 1982.

Oddly enough, Priest were wary of working with Allom because of a potential clash in backgrounds. "We didn't register him because he looked the perfect English gentleman, an' we thought he'd be a bit out of place," Tipton told *Sounds*, "but as soon as we worked with him on *Unleashed* . . ."

After the Japanese dates, in February, the band headed back to the US where, during the song 'Hell Bent For Leather', Halford rode on stage astride a Harley-Davidson motorbike for the first time. The famed motorbike company was reportedly suffering a slump, so Halford's endorsement was welcomed. After the contracts were signed, he received the initial bike (which was later given away in a competition) for the sum of just $1! Like the bullwhip, the motorbike soon became fixed as part of Halford's iconography in the minds of heavy metal fans around the world, and inspired many imitators.

The first of two US tours that year started in the southern states on February 27 and ran through until May 6 – including a show in Toronto, Canada – finishing up in Milwaukee. Priest played support to such acts as UFO, Angel and Pat Travers. A UK stint immediately followed in May, supported by the Liverpool rock band Marseille. On the back of a hit single ('Take On The World') and the just-released 'Evening Star', it was Priest's most successful UK tour to date, sometimes playing two consecutive nights in cities such as Sheffield, Newcastle, Birmingham and London (at the Hammersmith Odeon, a venue they had become attached to). The same night as the second show at Birmingham Odeon (on May 17), the band recorded a *Top Of The Pops* appearance to plug 'Evening Star'.[*] Consequently, they were late on stage, much to the vocal annoyance of those who had travelled long distances to attend.

By way of compensation, a third night at the venue on May 31 was added to the end of the tour's itinerary. The gig proved to be Les Binks' last with Judas Priest and the drummer left rather hastily in July, 1979.[†] It's generally assumed that the other band members believed that Binks was too technical for the more simplistic, arena-charged metal they now

---

[*] Released as a single on May 12, 'Evening Star' would only peak at number 53. Nevertheless the band were pleased with the attention the single – which included 'Beyond The Realms Of Death' as an extra track – attracted in the music press.
[†] Binks had left by the time of the cover shoot for *Unleashed In The East*. An examination of the sleeve reveals Halford's stance in front of the drums cleverly concealing his absence.

wanted to play. After leaving Priest, Binks was briefly on loan to the short-lived Lionheart for a few gigs while still in fellow NWOBHM band Tytan in 1982/83, since when he has spent much of his time in cover bands in and around the London area.*

Binks' replacement David Holland was born in Northamptonshire on April 5, 1948. Similarly to Glenn Tipton, Holland took piano lessons during his pre-teenage years. He soon developed an affinity for drumming and it was after constantly pestering his parents that his first drum kit was purchased. On the one hand, they were keen for him to pursue his obvious musical talent, but on the other they also wanted him to concentrate on his schoolwork. As Holland grew older, his tastes changed from the pop music of the time to the harder blues-rock sounds of Cream, Free and Led Zeppelin. He also had a keen interest in US psychedelia and funk, buying imported American releases.

From his first group The Drumbeats to Rugby-based The Liberators, Holland took his time in trying to find a secure base, moving from one band to the other, much like any other young musician. A former work colleague of Holland's, Michael Gadsden, remembers the drummer as quiet when they worked together at the Co-op, a large department store in Northampton, in the Sixties. "I think [Holland] was only 16 or 17 – and he worked in the shirt department. I sat at the canteen one day and he told me he played in a local band, I can't remember the name of the band but I think it was the Johnny Dave Five . . . but [then] he had an offer to play with a band called Pinkerton's Assorted Colours."

This little-known group (who progressed from The Liberators) had a number 8 hit in 1966 with 'Mirror Mirror'. It was Holland's first taste of success, but he decided to move on to another band. After leaving Pinkerton's Assorted Colours during the second half of 1968, as well as doing session work for other bands in the Midlands, Holland joined Finders Keepers, featuring guitarist Mel Galley and bassist Glenn Hughes.†

In March, 1969, Finders Keepers evolved into the five-piece Trapeze with the inclusion of singer John Jones and keyboardist Terry Rowley. The band were confident enough to decline an offer to join The Beatles'

---

* The author endeavoured to contact Binks (who has become something of a cult figure among older Priest fans) but because the drummer allegedly receives the odd royalty cheque from Priest he declined to be interviewed.
† Of the group's few obscure singles, 'Sadie, The Cleaning Lady' in 1968 was the most popular.

London-based label Apple; instead, they joined Threshold, The Moody Blues-owned label, believing that this would give them more creative freedom to record the blues-rock they admired. Trapeze's self-titled debut was released in 1970 but, shortly afterwards, Rowley and Jones quit (they went back to their previous band the Montanas) reducing Hughes, Galley and Holland to a new-look 'power trio'. When Hughes replaced Roger Glover in Deep Purple in 1973, Trapeze soldiered on with further line-up changes until Holland's departure in August, 1979 to join Judas Priest.

Due to the success and reception that greeted *Unleashed In The East*, Priest supported New York shock-rockers Kiss on a second tour of America that was arranged for October through November. By the end of the tour, Holland was fitting comfortably into his new role and felt more relaxed with his playing. Starting in Belgium on November 11, a European tour supporting AC/DC led them through Scandinavia, Germany, Switzerland and France until the final date on December 15.

The Seventies had ended on a high note for Judas Priest. Armed with a genre-defining album, Priest were poised, in 1980, to go even further.

A press shot of Judas Priest Mark V in 1974, when the band were promoting their debut album *Rocka Rolla* for Gull Records; left to right: Ian Hill, John Hinch, K.K. Downing, Rob Halford and Glenn Tipton. (GERED MANKOWITZ)

A grainy shot of K.K. Downing (right) and friends outside West Bromwich Registry Office for a friend's wedding sometime around 1970-1971; left to right: roadies Keith Evans and Trevor Lunn, Judas Priest Mark II drummer John Ellis and KK. (COURTESY OF BEVERLEY STONE)

Another grainy shot at the wedding: left to right: Keith Evans, Trevor Lunn, Nicky Bowbanks (Rob Halford's partner when Halford first joined the band in 1974, who died in a car crash in 1992), John Ellis and K.K. Downing. (COURTESY OF BEVERLEY STONE)

In the Scott Arms pub in West Bromwich; left to right: Dave Foster, a friend of the band in the early pre-Rob Halford days, Judas Priest Mark II drummer John Ellis and Keith Evans, Judas Priest's roadie from the early seventies. (COURTESY OF BEVERLEY STONE)

Judas Priest Mark IV circa 1973 when the band were signed to Tramp Entertainments / I.M.A. (co-owned by Tony Iommi) in Birmingham; left to right: Ian Hill, K.K. Downing, Chris 'Congo' Campbell and Al Atkins.
(COURTESY OF NORMAN HOOD, www.normanhood.co.uk)

Artist John Pasche, who designed the album cover for Judas Priest's 1974 debut *Rocka Rolla*. (COURTESY OF JOHN PASCHE)

A contemplative Rob Halford in 1974 when the band was signed to Gull Records.(GERED MANKOWITZ)

A barely recognizable image of Judas Priest Mark V from 1974. In those days K.K. Downing was rarely seen without his famous Chiffon hat. (GERED MANKOWITZ)

Flying solo – Glenn Tipton in a true rock star stance during the *Rocka Rolla* days in 1974. (LORENTZ GULLACHSEN)

Before the leather and studs days – Rob Halford screamin' like a banshee on stage, promoting the band's first album, 1974's *Rocka Rolla*. (LORENTZ GULLACHSEN)

K.K. Downing looking more like a male model than a heavy metal guitarist in this publicity shot from the *Rocka Rolla* days. (GERED MANKOWITZ)

A shot of Glenn Tipton at Rockfield Studios in Wales in late 1975. Those recording sessions gave birth to the ground-breaking *Sad Wings Of Destiny* album, released in 1976 via Gull Records. (GERAINT HUGHES, COURTESY OF GERAINT HUGHES AND DAVID HOWELLS)

A frustrated Rob Halford in a recording booth at Rockfield Studios at the end of 1975. (GERAINT HUGHES, COURTESY OF GERAINT HUGHES AND DAVID HOWELLS)

Judas Priest Mark VII; left to right: Ian Hill, producer Jeffery Calvert, K.K. Downing, Glenn Tipton, Rob Halford, unidentified friend, unidentified friend, Vicky (Alan Moore's girlfriend) and drummer Alan Moore on the right. This was taken at Rockfield Studios during the recording sessions for *Sad Wings Of Destiny* at the end of 1975. (GERAINT HUGHES, COURTESY OF GERAINT HUGHES AND DAVID HOWELLS)

PART 3

RUNNIN' WILD:
UNLEASHED IN AMERICA

SEVEN

1980–1984

"Judas Priest were the first band to properly embrace the whole leather and studs image . . . It was a fantastic image, sharp and dangerous . . ."
— Venom bassist and singer Conrad 'Cronos' Lant.

THE New Wave Of British Heavy Metal (aka NWOBHM) covered a period from around 1979 to 1981 when a new generation of longhaired bands emerged to perform the type of heavy rock that punk rock had tried to sweep under the carpet. In his superlative book *Suzie Smiled . . . The New Wave Of British Heavy Metal*, John Tucker says, "In basic terms, the NWOBHM was a time and a place in the history of rock music, influenced by what came before and influencing what came after. The term 'New Wave Of British Heavy Metal' itself is attributed to Alan Lewis, editor of *Sounds*, in 1979."

Of the most iconic and ultimately successful exponents, there were Def Leppard from Sheffield, Iron Maiden from the East End of London, Saxon from Yorkshire, and Venom from Newcastle. There were others of course: Diamond Head, Bitches Sin, Avenger, Raven, Girlschool, Satan, Blitzkrieg, Trespass, Tygers Of Pan Tang, Witchfynde, Aragron, Atomkraft, Angel Witch, Hellanbach – the list goes on.

Inspired by such Seventies heavyweights as UFO, Motörhead, Rainbow, Scorpions and Judas Priest, these young, feisty bands set a new benchmark for heavy rock. Consequently, the NWOBHM groups themselves would influence other generations of bands, primarily the Eighties thrash era in America that included Metallica, Slayer, Megadeth, Anthrax and Testament.

Yet K.K. Downing was dubious regarding the NWOBHM, telling *Sounds* in 1982 that "UFO, Scorpions an' Priest, they were totally aware of not ripping each other off, everybody was totally dedicated to having their *own* show, their *own* image."

There are many debates as to the importance of the era and which bands could accurately be termed 'NWOBHM'. As Tucker rightly argues, Judas Priest had an impact on the period but were definitely not part of it: ". . . if nothing else, Judas Priest's big break came at the time of the NWOBHM, with the release of *British Steel* in 1980. Rob Halford's *Sad Wings Of Destiny*-era kaftan-wearing days certainly didn't inspire much apart from hysterical laughter." However, they were a profound influence on the new movement, including Venom – who laid the blueprint for the controversial sub-genre black metal with their second album named, appropriately enough, *Black Metal*. Another fan of Priest from the NWOBHM-era was Blitzkrieg's Brian Ross. "I think that Priest were the main influence on the New Wave bands," he says. "They set the standard that we all tried to reach."

In January and February 1980, Judas Priest began work on the follow-up to *Killing Machine*. After discovering a rapport since their first meeting at the Royal Oak pub in London's York Street, the band decided Tom Allom – who had recently made a name for himself producing Def Leppard's *On Through The Night* – would be the best choice to produce. Having already worked on the live *Unleashed In The East*, *British Steel* marked the first studio album in their creative partnership, taking just under a month's work at Startling Studios, Ascot, with engineer Louis Austin.

Soon after beginning work, the band felt the studio was too small and claustrophobic. Because they were so closely confined they decided to wander around the large house to experiment with sounds. What they set out to capture was a sense of the industrial working class; the noise of factories, steelworks and clashing hot metal. In the documentary *Classic Albums: British Steel*, Glenn Tipton confirms, "A lot of character in Judas Priest stems from . . . the upbringing in the Midlands."

During the mid Seventies, British Steel only had factories in five areas of the country as a plan to curb costs. With massive financial losses, factories in the Midlands closed down and workers went on strike. Under the Conservative government, which came in power in 1979, job losses were as high as 11,000 by the early Eighties. The idea for the album's title was generally thought to have come from Halford, whose father had worked for the company, after seeing a razor blade with the name 'Sheffield Steel' on it. Other sources cite Hill as the originator after he saw the mass television and press coverage being given to the striking steel workers. Either way, each of them agreed it represented both contemporary working-class Britain and the raw sound of British heavy metal music.

In a sense, the jarring sounds the band captured were designed in the same way a filmmaker used cinema as a storytelling medium. For 'Breaking The Law' the band used recordings of milk bottles being smashed against marble walls. Police sirens could also be heard, but in actual fact the noise came from Downing's guitar, which was heavily compressed to give the song's antisocial theme authenticity.

To achieve other effects on the album, trays of cutlery were toppled over, guitar straps were whipped against tables, billiard cues were bashed against the kitchen floor and microphones were thrown from the first floor balcony onto the expensive marble floor. Even the drums were recorded in the Georgian mansion's marble entrance.

Prior to the album's UK release, band publicist Tony Brainsby devised a publicity stunt involving the master tapes being stolen from New York's Coronet Studios and put up for a $50,000 ransom demand. Tipton told *Sounds*: "Well, the first we knew about it was when we read about it in the papers. It was blown out of all proportion – that 50 grand ransom thing was nothing to do with the band whatsoever. We phoned up the management and said, 'What the hell's going on? Is this a publicity stunt? If it is, kill it. We don't need this press.' Honestly, when we saw that story in the papers, we were sick."

British Steel was released on April 19, 1980 and attained Judas Priest their highest ever UK album chart position of number 4 (34 in the States), lasting a lengthy 17 weeks in the UK chart. A minor controversy blew up because of the album cover, designed by CBS sleeve artist Roslav Szaybo, depicting a hand firmly gripping a razor blade that boldly states 'British Steel'. Some countries found it to be offensive and approached the record label asking for the cover to be airbrushed, so the hand held the razor blade without it slicing through the fingers. This time, the band held firm, correctly believing it would dampen the image's hard-hitting impact. K.K. Downing told *Classic Rock* in its December, 2006 issue: ". . . the way it was portrayed, with the razor blade going into the fingers, but no blood; what it's saying is that it's a safe thing to be into this [metal] music." In so doing, Priest took the razor blade – most notably a symbol of punk rock fashions – and co-opted it as an emblem for longhaired metal fans.

At the time of the album's release, Tipton told *Sounds*: "Well . . . [the sleeve] could have been better I admit, but I quite like it. I'm a bit disappointed with the back sleeve though, I'm not too keen on the group photos."

British Steel spawned three hit singles, the first of which, 'Living After Midnight', went to number 12 upon its release on May 29. 'Breaking The

Law' followed on June 7 (the same chart position of 12) while 'United', released on August 23, got to 26. A testament to the enduring appeal and mainstream success of *British Steel* was that by 1989 it had reached sales of over one million. When reissued in 2001 after the *Classic Albums* television special, it got to number 17 in the Swedish charts. *British Steel* has proven to be one of the most enduring and popular heavy metal albums ever.

Priest started to appear in front of the cameras more often. When performing 'United' on the August 28 edition of *Top Of The Pops*, it was rare to see the band lip-synching. The accompanying promotional videos for the singles 'Living After Midnight' and 'Breaking The Law' were directed by Julien Temple, who has since made his name as a music video director, most recently with the acclaimed 2006 film *Glastonbury*.

The video for 'Living After Midnight' was a recorded live performance of the band playing at Sheffield's City Hall, showing heavy metal fans eagerly playing air guitar to the song. The energetic Halford posed for the camera at every given opportunity.

The video to 'Breaking The Law' was a barely watchable piece of dross, yet it has become one of the most-seen heavy metal clips. Posing as vicars and using their guitars as weapons, the band played a group of criminals who break into a bank to steal a gold record. The acting was hammy, the poses they made were laughable and, by the end of it, the security guard was singing and playing along. Both song and video have become legendary – albeit for different reasons entirely!

These early videos illustrated how Priest eagerly embraced pop culture and were quick to latch on to the vehicle of music videos. In order to sell more albums it was important to appeal to MTV – the all-music cable station launched in 1981 – as Halford told *Classic Rock* (April, 2006): "MTV was just about to become enormous, and we understood that enough to make use of it."

British Steel opened with the skull-crushing, thrash metal-precursor 'Rapid Fire'.* Halford's love of adjectives was at its most adventurous in 'Rapid Fire'; among the song's lyrics, the word 'desolisating', he presumably derived from 'desolation'. 'Metal Gods' was, as the title suggested, a sturdy, metallic monster; what made it stand out was how the guitars echoed the vocal line during the chorus. 'Breaking The Law' became not only an anthem for a host of metal bands who originally bought *British*

---

* In some countries (including the US), the album kicked off with 'Breaking The Law'. Thanks to the latter song being a hit single at the time, the record label changed the track order.

Steel in 1980, but also a generation since. Northern Ireland metal band
Therapy? and German metal goddess Doro have both recorded versions of
the song.

Doro Pesch: "We did a record that was called *Classic Diamonds* with a
symphony orchestra. Actually, I always wanted to cover a real Judas Priest
song and, on this record, I thought maybe that's a great challenge to do it.
Then we did 'Breaking The Law' and . . . I thought 'Wow! 'Breaking The
Law' came out so good!' and even the orchestra people, they all turned
into metal heads."

'Grinder' was a metal furnace of sounds with fiery guitars, chest-beating
drums and unrelenting vocals. 'United', which *Sounds* described as "an
unqualified dirge" in one review and a ". . . camp football chant" in a
separate appraisal, took some getting used to after such an intense start. As
a single, it commenced well enough but ended up moving off into rather
kitsch territory (although it was suitably apt for the band's 2004 'Reunited'
festivals tour). 'You Don't Have To Be Old To Be Wise' featured a finely
crafted lead riff and solo. The creation of metal classic 'Living After
Midnight' occurred when the band, along with Tom Allom, worked on
the song's rhythm late into the night while Halford was trying to sleep.
While subconsciously paying attention to the riffs he had a momentary
brainwave for a lead lyric, hence the title 'Living After Midnight'. The
fatigued and grumpy singer delivered his lyrics to the band the following
morning.

'The Rage' was a curiosity, starting off with a reggae bass line (a rare
moment to shine for Ian Hill) before the heavy rhythm kicked in. 'Steeler',
not as focused as most tracks on the album, borrowed Motörhead's feel –
fast, gritty and loud.[*]

From March 7 into April, Judas Priest toured the UK with support act
Iron Maiden. There was a degree of rivalry between the old guard and the
NWOBHM heroes, sparked primarily by Maiden's then singer Paul
Di'Anno telling *Sounds* writer Gary Bushell that Maiden would definitely
"blow the bollocks off Priest." That was not to say Di'Anno was unim-
pressed, telling writer Mick Wall in his authorised Maiden biography *Run
To The Hills*: "Couldn't believe our luck, mate! . . . It was weird, too,
'cause I actually remember going to see them play the old Hammy Odeon
on their previous tour. If anybody had said to me then, 'Next time Priest

[*] The 2001/02 reissue added the trite 'Red, White And Blue', penned years before it was
finally recorded at Compass Point Studios, Nassau, in July, 1985, and a live version of
'Grinder' closed the album.

play here, you'll be up here, too,' I'd have said they were taking the piss, you know?"

As a consequence of Di'Anno's tongue-in-cheek words, Priest acted bitterly towards Maiden, as bassist Steve Harris confirmed in *Run To The Hills*: "They [Priest] made it difficult for us . . . Their soundman, Nigel, started mucking us around. It was bloody annoying, but, if anything, it just made us that more determined to deliver."

As told in Wall's biography, on the day the tour began, Maiden – at the invitation of Priest's then-manager Jim Dawson – turned up to watch Halford and his colleagues rehearse at Willesden, north London. However, the uptight Priest took this as an arrogant insult. The fact that Dawson failed to inform them of Maiden's visit only caused even more animosity in the Priest camp. Downing told Wall: "I just thought they were taking the piss . . . But they were just lads. They didn't know any better. And these days we're all great mates, you know?"

One of the things that seemed to annoy Priest most about Iron Maiden was how much they had copied their image. "It's disappointing when you tour one year with Maiden in support and they come out and wear all your clothes," Downing told *Soundcheck!* writer Neil Jeffries. "I have to look at some pictures twice to see if Dave Murray is really *me*!" Other observers also spotted the likenesses in leather attire between Di'Anno and Halford.

John Jackson, a booking agent at Cowbell Agency who had both Priest and Maiden on his books, asked EMI to foot the money for Maiden to support Priest on the tour. After Priest fired Jackson for supposedly showing a bias towards Maiden, Jackson consequently set up his own company, Fair Warning, with Maiden as the first act on his books. Iron Maiden went on to achieve more fame and fortune than any other metal band including Judas Priest.

A one-off gig at north London's Rainbow Theatre on April Fool's Day was included in the tour itinerary as part of Levi's Jeans' 50th anniversary. A minor controversy occurred when, while onstage, Halford dropped his trousers and let himself hang loose in front of a baffled crowd. *Sounds* printed a photo the following week, blanking out Halford's private parts, joking, "Mr Halford is prone to wearing Y-fronts beneath his leotard! Where will it end?"

Priest's set list on the British tour included the opener 'Hell Bent For Leather', 'Beyond The Realms Of Death', 'Victim Of Changes', 'Starbreaker' and 'Take On The World'. They decided to drop 'Exciter', claiming that it had run its course. Surprisingly, there was a lot of press coverage in heavy metal circles about the decision to drop the song, spark-ing rumours that Dave Holland could not handle the speed and intricate technicalities of the song. In his defence, Tipton spoke to *Sounds*: "Dave gives us such a massive amount of feel, he makes us really deliver . . . I'd like to squash the rumour that he can't play 'Exciter'. Listen to 'Rapid Fire' on the album . . . it's much faster than 'Exciter' . . ."

Fans and critics were more surprised by the complete exclusion of songs from *British Steel*. Tipton also cleared that up when speaking to *Sounds* after the tour: "We were going to do 'Grinder' and 'Steeler', but in the end we decided to do one final tour playing material from and promoting *Unleashed In The East* . . .We hadn't toured the UK with that album, so we thought we'd drop the new tracks." The gigs were adjudged to have been a roaring success, with a *Sounds* reviewer proclaiming: "So ended the best concert that I and, judging by the comments of fans afterwards, many others had been to in a long, long time."

Priest toured parts of Europe such as Germany, Belgium and France in April followed by an extensive summer tour of America from June to August, with rising stars Def Leppard and co-headliners the Scorpions. Americans immediately warmed to songs such as 'Living After Midnight' and 'Breaking The Law', thus making *British Steel* Judas Priest's first gold album in the US. Ticket sales for dates in the big cities sold out, while for the Grand Slam Super Jam, held at the Busch Stadium, St. Louis, Missouri, Priest played alongside Sammy Hagar, April Wine and Shooting Star.

Lifelong fan Maria Ferrero of the New York-based firm Adrenaline PR recalls enthusiastically: "Jesus! I could never forget the first time I ever saw Judas Priest live. It was on the *British Steel* tour and I saw them at the Palladium in New York City. A band called The Playmates opened up for them but they were no competition for the Priest. I remember, very vividly, that 'Living After Midnight' was the song that got us jumping off of our seats . . . My friends and I are from the south Jersey suburbs and we took the bus into New York. At 15 years of age that was a big deal. Anyway, I remember sitting in the very last row of the venue and being so excited to hear their incredible songs and being completely blown away by Rob Halford's voice and the duelling guitars of K.K. Downing and Glenn Tipton – who I had a crush on. So at the end of the show, I tore down the fabric on the wall to keep as a memento. I kept it under my bed but it stunk, and you could smell it from outside my bedroom. My dad screamed for weeks at me to throw it away."

After an exhaustive but exhilarating American tour, Judas Priest played the first ever Monsters Of Rock Festival in the now hallowed grounds of

Donington Park on August 16, 1980, headlined by Ritchie Blackmore's Rainbow. Joining them on the bill were Saxon, Riot, Touch and April Wine, with Judas Priest performing after the Scorpions, although peculiarly Priest were the only band not to feature on the *Monsters Of Rock* compilation. In the foreword to a special one-off *Monsters Of Rock* issue (a collaboration between *Classic Rock*, *Metal Hammer*, *Guitarist* and *Total Guitar* magazines), Glenn Tipton said, "At the time Donington was one of the most important shows Priest had ever played in Europe. It's a shame we never did the festival again after that. We probably could've headlined. But Rob left, and that took a big chunk out of our career."*

Halford's memories of Priest's 1980 appearance also appeared in the special: "On the day, I thought it was cracking. It was especially good for us because they were our home crowd, if you like, and we felt very comfortable." Halford admitted soothing his nerves with "about a dozen pints of Bank's ale."

Aside from a one-off German show in August, Priest began work on their next album but, after penning new material in September, they were dissatisfied with the results. After a complete rethink, the band decided to write and record their next album outside of Britain for the first time. Oddly, their choice of location was Ibiza, in an old farmhouse that had been converted into a studio.† The primary reason for this was financially motivated. Now that the band were beginning to make money, the UK's tax laws meant they would not gain much from their earnings. Many British recording artists, such as The Rolling Stones, Rod Stewart, Black Sabbath and Queen, had moved abroad to escape their homeland's tax system.

"Tax! I know it's ridiculous but if we record out of the country we get a 25 per cent rebate, so it makes sense," Downing told *Sounds* in 1982. "The British tax laws are so stupid that they penalise the people who are making money for the country!"

Many Priest fans questioned whether the band could deliver the goods in such a sunny, exotic location as opposed to rainswept England. "There was a time when if you were gonna write an HM (heavy metal) album you had to do it in the city, in some grimy, heavy, doom-laden, gloomy, soot-covered place!" Halford told *Kerrang!* in 1983. "There's no reason to do that."

---

* Judas Priest were invited back to play at the festival in 1987 but as Downing told *Metal Hammer*, "They asked us if we wanted to do it but who the fuck wants to support Bon Jovi?"
† The building burnt down toward the end of the Eighties.

Much to the band's annoyance, upon their arrival, the studio was barely ready for recording. Aside from working on the album, again with producer Tom Allom and engineer Lou Austin, Priest spent much of their time boozing. The band have remained tight-lipped about their Spanish antics during the Eighties, but a story that crept out was the police paying a visit to the studio because the owner was allegedly in dire straits financially. The police took the master tapes back to the station as collateral before the problem was finally sorted out.

Regarding the recording of *Point Of Entry*, Downing confessed to *Kerrang!* that "[Glenn and I] couldn't decide how to split [the solos], so we sat down and timed every available solo space and divided it that way. Occasionally I'll fancy doing one particular solo or Glenn'll fancy another, and we just decide what's best for that song."

In the same interview, Tipton had a similar view about the difficulties of having two lead players. "You are often faced with situations where both of you might want to take a lead break and both of us have had to make concessions. It can lead to arguments if you let it."

After returning from Ibiza, *Point Of Entry* was mixed at Startling Studios. When the album was released in Britain on February 26, 1981, fans were bitterly divided in their opinions. "I suppose it didn't have the correct ingredients for what you need to gain major recognition . . ." Halford confessed to *Kerrang!* in 1982. "Some people told me that they reckoned the album was a bit self-indulgent and that we did things just for ourselves."

Others were more willing to accept the changes. Future vocalist Tim 'Ripper' Owens says, ". . . I fell in love with Judas Priest because they changed with every record. Someone said that doesn't sound like classic Judas Priest and I said, 'Well, what does?' 'Painkiller' wasn't 'Screaming For Vengeance', it's Glenn playing arpeggios for God's sake." It was around this time that budding musicians such as Annihilator's Jeff Waters started getting into Judas Priest. Waters feels that it was the band's ability to change styles yet still remain essentially heavy that made them endure.

Jeff Waters: "What grabbed me about Priest was that they were able to do 50 different styles in one band, and that's what really turned me on to heavy metal music . . . K.K. and Tipton could do classical-influenced stuff and then they could do the blues-influenced things, and not only just rhythms and stuff but also guitar solos that were blues[y]. Then this Halford guy was screaming like some kind of banshee and yet he was an opera-style singer . . . [they were] just like the ultimate band for me

. . . you can see how they changed in a way, but they still have those roots."

Controversial in some respects, *Point Of Entry* was different from any-thing that Priest had recorded before or since. *Sounds* writer Geoff Barton was keener than others to praise it, giving the album four-and-a-half stars out of five. In his review he wrote enthusiastically: "Somehow Halford's heavies have managed to create mayhem in the Mediterranean and prove themselves the exception to the rule by coming up with an LP that sounds like it was recorded on a demolition site than under sleepy Spanish skies."

Barton was eager to hear more of the melodic vibe Priest had created. "I personally find this new JP music tremendously exciting. Less contrived and a good deal more spontaneous than albums old . . . *Entry* adds up to 40 minutes of champion churnola."

Of course, the band themselves were pleased with *Point Of Entry*. A gushing Downing described it to *Sounds* a few months after its release as "the best recording we've ever made."

After the success of *British Steel*, it was argued that Priest compromised their sound in order to make a more radio-friendly album with such songs as 'Heading Out To The Highway'. No doubt CBS thought a softening of the band's edges could be a potential money-spinner. Aside from a couple of duff moments, *Point Of Entry* stands alongside *Turbo* as one of Priest's most underrated albums, and it could be said that the AOR-cum-melodic-hard-rock approach served the band well in the long run.

Bewilderingly, the record company decided to release 'Don't Go' as the first single (on February 21), which didn't help the album's sales, nor did it sell particularly well in its own right, reaching only 51 in the UK charts. 'Hot Rockin'' – a much better song – was released on April 26 but fared even worse, struggling to 60. 'Heading Out To The Highway' (which was the correct choice for lead single in the US) and 'Desert Plains' would have been better representations of the album.

Promotional clips, directed by Julien Temple, were made for 'Don't Go', 'Heading Out To The Highway' and 'Hot Rockin''. Leather-clad Halford looked remarkably similar to Freddie Mercury in Queen's 'Crazy Little Thing Called Love' video, even sporting a camp moustache.

For ardent American Priest fans, perhaps the most frustrating and annoying aspect of the album was its hideous artwork, which depicted a vast highway stretching into the sunlight. As a consequence of the cover's ambiguity (no band pictures, small title, plain colours and basically nothing eye-catching) the label sensibly, but belatedly, ordered that future ship-ments had stickers with the Judas Priest name placed on them. In addition, a black and white band photo was also put on future copies to mark it as a Judas Priest album and not an unofficial bootleg.

Point Of Entry began with the riff-filled 'Heading Out To The Highway', a melodic slice of Eighties metal – loud, brawny and infectious, and a subsequent classic in Priest's extensive back catalogue. 'Don't Go', one of the weaker songs on the album with a slow, almost plodding pace, was almost entirely devoid of anything memorable, the short guitar solo salvaging an otherwise mundane song. Despite its hopeless lyrics, 'Hot Rockin'' was rollicking good fun, with an immediately likable anthemic chorus that was great for arena metal such as Priest's, while 'Turning Circles' had a wonderfully melodic texture.

As in many of the songs on *Point Of Entry*, Priest veered off into the AOR/melodic hard rock field, which at the time was mostly dominated by such acts as Foreigner, Journey, Toto, Styx, and Boston. 'Desert Plains' was a brave attempt on Priest's behalf at trying to capture the melodic and slick approach of the aforementioned bands. At the time, it didn't acquire Priest a new fan base but, years later, such songs would enjoy a significant amount of popularity among audiences who yearned for more melodic metal as opposed to the ferocity of something like 'Painkiller'.

'Solar Angels' became Priest's concert opener, with a distinctive solo and Halford's vocals at their most harmonic. The chorus to 'You Say Yes' was nothing short of irritating. The fun but disposable 'All The Way' opened like an AC/DC song with a short riff – simple and to the point. Compared to the power of tracks like 'Desert Plains' and 'Heading Out To The Highway', 'Troubleshooter' was a pretty lame effort while 'On The Run' finished the album on another melodic note.[*]

Despite the criticism the album received at the time, 'Desert Plains', 'Solar Angels', 'Heading Out To The Highway' and 'Hot Rockin'' have since become live favourites and cherished among Priest enthusiasts.

As promotion for the release of the new album, the band set out on a tour taking them through Europe from February 13 to March 6, playing Holland, France and Germany with Saxon in support. The show in Amsterdam on February 14 was recorded for future use as live B-sides and extra tracks on 12″ singles. Suffice to say the audience that night – as on pretty much every night on the tour – was ecstatic. From the start of May to the end of July, Priest trekked around the States, with two sold-out

---

[*] The bonus tracks on the 2001/02 reissue were 'Thunder Road', an unreleased demo from the *Ram It Down* sessions in Denmark during December 1987, and a too-fast live version of 'Desert Plains'.

nights at New York's Palladium and shows in San Antonio, Los Angeles, Houston, Chicago, Philadelphia and Minneapolis, among other cities. A different act – Iron Maiden, The Joe Perry Project, Max Webster, Savoy Brown, Ranger and Whitesnake – supported on alternate nights.

By this point, Iron Maiden and Judas Priest had cleared the air and become friendly. K.K. Downing told *Sounds* in August, 1981: "Earlier on in this tour, the singer [Paul Di'Anno] came up to me and said, 'Look, I'm sorry about what happened,' and explained that they'd all acted in a really big-headed way, then, one by one, the others apologised and that was fine. The silly thing is that I don't know why they said it in the first place because they all claim to be Priest fans!"

Yet all was not entirely amicable, as Downing told *Metal Hammer* writer Dave Ling in 1987, "I still don't like 'em, it's just a personal thing . . . They didn't treat us with respect . . . They've always been trying to dethrone us and they always will be trying to."

While most reviews of Priest's 1981 world tour were ecstatic, some writers observed how the band were being heavily influenced by the stage show of other acts. In a review of Priest's November gig at the Hammersmith Odeon, Geoff Barton wrote: "Sunday night . . . a brash, garish and glitzy combo. With their stage show ripped off from the Kiss tour before last (I kid you not) . . ." Barton was, however, in favour of the new set, concluding by calling the night "one of '81's finest, methinks."

In defence of Priest's overblown stage show, Downing told *Sounds*: "I think there's a place for bands like us and Kiss with elaborate stage ideas. Basically it's just playing songs and creating an image for each song."

Halford immediately took to America: the vastness, the differing land-scapes and cities, the (perceived) freedom of speech and the friendly inter-action. The others were not as enamoured of the continent, fed up with the constant trips back and forth across the Atlantic. "At first I hated America," Tipton told *Sounds* in 1981, "but now I've come to accept it, to accept that the food isn't very good and that people are sometimes going to say idiotic things to me."

Both Tipton and Downing accepted that America was a necessary evil if Priest's career was to have any lasting impact. "Judas Priest are very successful in the States at the moment," Downing said in the same *Sounds* chat. "Our album's sold half a million in three months, so it looks as if we're as important as any other band."

During September and October, Priest returned to Ibiza to record new material at Sound Studios. Halford told *Kerrang!* in their January, 1982 issue: "We've recorded seven new songs and as usual we'll be aiming for a total of 10. The material is varied: some of the songs are as intricate as *Sin After Sin* and *Stained Class*, others are as raw and as primitive as *British Steel* and there are those that are in the style of *Point Of Entry* . . . It'll probably be the heaviest thing we've put out . . . We go back to the studios at the beginning of the year . . ."

Exhausted after months on the road and in the studio, Priest toured Britain for the first time in 18 months. However, as Downing explained to *Sounds*, "[it was] too soon after the previous tour and because we hadn't a new show. Fortunately, we're no longer in the position in the UK where we need to promote new records by touring."

This attitude only served to stoke up British fans' ire at Priest's absence from the UK stage, and members of the band admitted that they were worried, as Halford told *Kerrang!* in 1982: "There was a little concern for the fact that we'd spent so much time away that people might come to the shows and put us on trial so to speak . . ."

Starting in Hull on November 6, Priest played Manchester, Leicester, Bristol, Cardiff, Birmingham, Glasgow, Newcastle, Sheffield, Crawley, London, Southampton and finally Poole on November 24. It would be their last extensive UK tour for some time.

Support act were German rockers Accept. Guitarist Wolfgang Hoffman has fond memories of the winter trek. "It put us right on the spot internationally. It was also the time when we got professional management, international record deals, etc." Judas Priest and their entourage treated the young German band well, even though Accept's management kept their charges on a tight leash.

Wolfgang Hoffman: "The policy of our management has been totally firm, we came to the venue, performed and left – which we kept doing all our professional life . . . We did not hang out with them . . . If musicians hear each other's records, it is very possible they will influence each other, and our singer Udo Dirkschneider was definitely looking up to Rob Halford."

Revered rock/metal producer Michael Wagener, who was the original guitar player in Accept, recalled the tour. "I remember the guys from Judas Priest as being extremely nice. The drummer for Accept had 40 inch-deep kick drums and, when we played in Glasgow, the stage was 15-feet high. When we all arrived for a soundcheck, the crew had set up the backline so we only had about a foot-and-a-half in front of the drums. The guys in Judas Priest made their crew move the whole backline back five feet, so we had more room. They always gave us all the PA and most of the non-special lights for the show. Great people . . ."

When asked how many times he saw Priest live during that 1981 tour, Wagener responded, "At least 32 times! I watched every single show from the side of the stage, fascinating, very professional . . . I have nothing but great memories from the time with Judas Priest and I wish there would be more to come, I would love to get a chance to work with them."

1981 ended with European dates with Def Leppard in Germany, Switzerland, France, Belgium and finally Holland on December 14. A date in Puerto Rico was also added. After deciding to reject the material from the autumn '81 Ibiza sessions, the band returned to Sound Studios in early 1982 to start afresh with Allom and Austin. The band found themselves short of songs and, during an impromptu studio jam, the hit single 'You've Got Another Thing Comin'' was devised. Like Bon Jovi's 'Living On A Prayer' or Van Halen's 'Jump'. the song became an arena rock staple, and received a burst of renewed popularity when the American fast-food chain Burger King used the song for one of its television commercials in 1999.

Screaming For Vengeance was mixed in Florida at Beejay Record Studios, Orlando and Bayshore Recording Studios, Coconut Grove, and mastered in New York. When released in the UK on July 17, it reached number 11 in the top 40, lasting a mere three weeks in the chart. In America, it was a different story, where the album clocked up over a million sales, giving Priest their very first double-platinum record. By January 1985 it had sold in excess of 1,300,000 copies.[*]

Screaming For Vengeance would quickly become one of the decade's most defining metal albums, influencing bands such as Slayer, Metallica, and Therapy?, whose bassist Michael McKeegan gives due credit: "On a personal level I first got into Priest in 1983 when I bought *Screaming For Vengeance* in a record shop in Newcastle-upon-Tyne . . . I'd seen pictures in *Kerrang!* and knew 'Breaking The Law' from before, so it seemed like a safe bet . . . Priest have always been one of those bands everyone in Therapy? agreed on . . . I think it was mainly because they sounded so distinctive and had a keen ear for songwriting, something we always tried to apply to Therapy?, no matter how noisy or eccentric the music became."

Screaming For Vengeance was the also first Judas Priest album Timothy Owens, a young teenager from Ohio, heard.

Tim Owens: "I think my first [Priest] memory was probably when I heard *Screaming For Vengeance*. I heard 'Electric Eye' and I wasn't a fan

---

[*] Bizarrely, when the album was released in South Korea, the first few shipments were missing the monstrous title track.

before that . . . I thought, 'Man even I'm like, 'I don't know about this!' But when I heard 'Electric Eye' I thought, 'Wow! This is cool stuff. This is unbelievable.'"

'The Hellion', a 42-second instrumental, opened proceedings immediately followed by 'Electric Eye', a song about an Orwellian society of surveillance cameras peering into every nook of society. Both songs became permanent fixtures in the band's live act. 'Riding On The Wind' was a pounding, drum-led piece that proved Holland was a more than competent drummer, contrary to the harsh criticism he was receiving from some quarters of the music press. 'Bloodstone' opened with an immediately distinguishable riff, leading into a familiar anthemic chorus. '(Take These) Chains' was melodic hard rock that would not have been out of place on *Point Of Entry*. Halford's vocals were filled with anguish on 'Pain And Pleasure', which featured another significant guitar solo.

'Screaming For Vengeance' was a fierce riff attack with Halford at his screeching best. 'You've Got Another Thing Comin'' was followed by 'Fever', which built up to a crescendo, demonstrating that Priest could ally melody with their twin-lead guitar attack. 'Devil's Child' was rather clichéd but worked a treat live thanks to its hand-waving, all-sing-together chorus.*

The album was generally well received, typified by *Sounds'* review: "*Screaming* marks the viperous vicar's return with all the vitriolic 'Vengeance' threatened in the title . . . so forget the Sinner. *Long live the Hellion!*"

The album sleeve, designed by Doug Johnson, based on initial artwork by John Berg, featured a silver metallic eagle known as 'The Hellion' in flight past the burning sun. Originally, Priest wanted to feature a character, or mascot, similar to Iron Maiden's Eddie. Released on August 21, 'You've Got Another Thing Comin'' only peaked at 66 in Britain, but it became Priest's biggest hit in the States and an instant crowd pleaser. The video, filmed at Kempton Park, was directed by Julien Temple. While no video accompanied '(Take These) Chains', the second single taken from the album, a live video of 'The Hellion/Electric Eye', directed by Mick Anger, aired in December.

After rehearsing at New York's SIR Studios, Priest hit the road on Halford's birthday, August 26, covering practically the length and breadth of North America (with some Canadian shows) in October and early

---

* The 2001/02 reissue included the previously unreleased 'Prisoner Of Your Eyes', also recorded by Halford solo, 'Heart Of A Lion' and a live version of 'Devil's Child'.

November. The tour, totalling over 100 gigs in America alone, included New York (where Priest played their first sold-out show at Madison Square Gardens on October 2), New Jersey, San Diego, San Francisco, Seattle, Chicago, and Philadelphia.

To mirror the album's opening triple-whammy, the set began with 'The Hellion', 'Electric Eye' and 'Riding On The Wind' before the band tore through a 'best of' set containing such Priest classics as 'Sinner', 'Breaking The Law', 'Metal Gods' and 'The Ripper'. Support on selected dates was Iron Maiden, who had a new singer with them, the formidable Bruce Dickinson – arguably the only heavy metal singer who could give Rob Halford a run for his money. Maiden were on the brink of metal stardom themselves with the album *The Number Of The Beast*, released in March, 1982. As well as being their second joint US tour, it was the third and final time Priest and Maiden would tour together.

While the critics raved, there were comments on the similarity and competition between both bands. A *Sounds* review of the Madison Square Gardens' gig said: "Iron Maiden are very nearly terrific . . . they riff hard and ferociously, with an anthemic edge that assures us that they're British." Of Judas Priest, the same reviewer wrote: "Priest gives us 90 minutes of sharp staging, symmetry and design that doesn't smother the band and their strengths, but rather highlights them . . . Priest put on a consistently great and totally engrossing show."

Krokus, Uriah Heep, Coney Hatch and Heaven were Priest's opening acts for the duration of the US tour, which finished on December 12 at the Mid-south Coliseum in Memphis. The show was filmed and released as a VHS home video, *Judas Priest Live*, and shown repeatedly on MTV in 1984.[*] The gig showed Judas Priest at their prime, with a stage show that wasn't as cheap and unimaginative as the early years yet not as over-the-top as the Turbo: Fuel For Life tour of 1986. An exhilarating set, which opened with 'The Hellion/Electric Eye' and climaxed with 'Hell Bent For Leather', remains an awe-inspiring example to other metal bands.

What was particularly pleasing to Priest about the 1982 US tour were the new developments in sound equipment. Halford told *Kerrang!* in 1982: "Using radio gear is another great advantage because it gives you a hell of a lot more freedom to move around. With all of us using leads it was getting a bit like spaghetti junction on stage! Nowadays, Kenny's gone cordless and I'm using a radio mike."

---

[*] It was reissued on DVD in 2006 as *Live Vengeance '82*.

The advancement of onstage radio equipment also meant that the band could synchronise their stage movements with greater ease. "It's nothing we work out," Tipton told *Sounds* in August 1982. "It's just things we fall into over a tour."

Despite the progression in their career, having risen to the top of the heavy metal circuit in America, Judas Priest were experiencing difficulties with their management team of Jim Dawson and Mike Dolan at Arnakata Management Inc. The partnership ended during the 1982 US tour. Halford confessed to *Kerrang!* in 1990 that their ex-manager (allegedly Dawson) "had a drug problem." Initially, Priest took care of business themselves with the Secret Management Associates Inc, while retaining the services of Mike Dolan until mid 1983, when Priest started a fruitful and long-lasting managerial relationship with Bill Curbishley's Trinifold Management.

Curbishley had made a name for himself in the business as a tough, no-bullshit type of character, hence such names as 'Wild' Bill Curbishley. In 1976 he was appointed (and remains) manager of The Who but – as they had (temporarily) split after a farewell US tour finished in December 1982, Curbishley was left with time on his hands. He had noticed Judas Priest's large attendances at US arenas and, after talks took place, a contract was signed during the second leg of Priest's US tour, which started on January 12, 1983. Jayne Andrews later joined the band's management team in the Eighties with a more 'hands on' role, under the job title 'Management Co-ordinator'.

Due to the mass appeal of *Screaming For Vengeance* in America, Priest had to postpone plans for a European tour until the following year to make room for more American dates. It further angered their UK fans, who craved to see the band in action. Halford told *Sounds* in August 1982: "People who are totally unaware just assume away, they think, 'Oh, they're going to America chasing money' . . . Bands just don't make money on the road any more, it's a fact of life."

After playing the last date on the second US leg in Honolulu, Hawaii on February 21, Priest took a break due to exhaustion before playing at the US Festival in San Bernardino, California, organised by Apple Computers. With a strong turnout of around 200,000 people, the band gained serious mainstream attention, even though they were sandwiched between Canadian soft rocker Bryan Adams and Crosby, Stills and Nash. The final US date for 1983 was in Texas on June 8.

At the behest of their new management team and record label, Priest flew to Ibiza the day after the US Festival to write and record the follow-up to *Screaming For Vengeance*. "I suppose it took a month to write," Halford told *Kerrang!*

Sounds had reported in mid 1982 that Priest's next album was tentatively scheduled for a November release in to coincide with a tour, but recording was prolonged and thus the initial plans for its release were scrapped.

"We've certainly spent longer than ever in the studio," Downing told *Sounds* in December 1983, "but we've also had quite a few technical problems with equipment breaking down. In a way though, I think that the time spent has enabled us to put together the best album we've ever done."

While in Ibiza, Downing was run over by a taxi during a drunken night out. Fortunately, he escaped with little injury and work resumed almost immediately. The productive relationship with Tom Allom continued. "He's a great all-rounder and the sounds we get he enhances and makes better," Tipton told *Sounds* in '83. "He knows exactly what's required from us and what our fans expect . . . Tom's an excellent engineer and he makes the most of what we give." Replacing Louis Austin as engineer was Mark Dodson.

After several months recording in Ibiza, which took them beyond the November date, the album was mixed in DB Recording Studios and Bayshore Studios in Miami and mastered at New York's Sterling Sound. It was the longest time they had spent making an album. CBS quite clearly wanted Priest to repeat the success of *Screaming For Vengeance*, possibly outselling that album. "It's got all the basic elements of *Screaming For Vengeance* and it runs along the same basic formula," Tipton told *Sounds*. "That wasn't intentional – we didn't set out to come up with an exact copy. That's just the way we write these days. We've tried to cover every angle on it and I think it'll fulfil everybody's demands."

Halford echoed his fellow band member's thoughts in a 1983 interview with *Kerrang!* prior to the album's release: "The success of that last album meant a great deal to us. It gave us the boost to go there and match the success of *Screaming For Vengeance* . . ." He was more than pleased with the finished product: "As far as production and everything else goes on this album, it probably has the most impact and is the most interesting HM LP I've heard in a very, very long time."

To drum up early support for *Defenders Of The Faith* and to appease dissatisfied UK fans who had not witnessed Priest on tour since November 1981, the band scheduled a UK winter tour with support from Quiet Riot. Priest did not hide their trepidation at playing Britain after almost two years away. Halford confessed to *Sounds*: "I still would like to believe, but I won't know until we get back, that they understand what we've been doing."

Tipton put it more bluntly: "We'll be the first to admit that we've let Britain and Europe slip . . . but everybody wants to make it in the States."

Rehearsals took place in Brixton, south London, with the tour beginning on December 12, taking them through Newcastle, Glasgow, Manchester, London, Leicester and Birmingham, until December 22.

"You don't review Judas Priest," Mick Wall wrote in *Kerrang!* "Don't be asking me to do that, you just get into it or do the other thing. Friday night's show was one you would have wanted to get into, I have never seen them perform better."

Quiet Riot front man Kevin DuBrow hasn't forgotten the impact the tour had on his band.

Kevin DuBrow: "*Metal Health* [Quiet Riot's latest album] was released worldwide . . . we wanted to try and break the European market and the tour was offered to us. Up to that point we had done tours with ZZ Top, Scorpions, Loverboy, Iron Maiden, Black Sabbath and for the most part we had no trouble getting with the audience and, in our minds, kinda blowing everybody away, because we were the young upstarts on the tours. We didn't blow Iron Maiden away but we gave them a run for their money with the audience. But with Judas Priest, of all the bands we'd toured with – and I've been saying this for 25 years – they were the best band we ever worked for. Without a doubt! They were like a machine . . . Before we had released *Metal Health*, *Screaming For Vengeance* was on everybody's CD player or cassette deck."

DuBrow admits that Priest was the only band each member of Quiet Riot collectively liked. "When they toured with the album that 'Exciter' is on [*Stained Class*] . . . they played Los Angeles; me and Randy Rhoads went to see them and from that point on we were big fans. So when we got the offer to support Judas Priest it was . . . more a matter of excitement that we got to see them play every night. You never think about it in terms of getting worried . . . we were fans more than anything. [Although we played with] the Scorpions, ZZ Top, Iron Maiden and Black Sabbath, Judas Priest was actually the only band we were big fans of. So, I mean, it was cool to see them play 'Metal Gods' every night, because they did it a bit differently from the record. The vocal melody was much cooler than on the album, and they were still doing 'Bloodstone', which is my favourite song by them. And the guitar sounds were just as good as they were on the record. When we toured with the Scorpions, the guitar sounds weren't as cool as they were on the records."

The American group were taken aback by Priest's generosity on the road. Kevin DuBrow: "The first night we played with them was in Edinburgh and Rob Halford came in . . . as soon as he got there and introduced himself, he was like the ultimate rock'n'roll gentleman. The next day I think we did Birmingham and we had breakfast with both K.K. and Glenn. You know, a lot of the time the headlining acts are pompous asses, but these guys were so nice. It's so funny because [recently] I saw both K.K. and Glenn in Los Angeles and it was like no time had passed at all; they were just as good as they always were and it was just pretty, pretty amazing."

Quiet Riot were not invited to jam with Priest on stage. "I think the funniest thing is when we played Leicester with them and they insisted that the audience needed to stop spitting on our bass player Rudy Sarzo, and I thought that was hilarious. But they were angry and it was obvious . . . they kept gobbing on him. It was really, really funny. The Priest guys went over amazingly well, as I said, they were a machine."

The British tour was interrupted by two shows at the Rock, Pop, Heavy Metal Festival in Dortmund, Westfalenhalle, Germany on the weekend of December 17 and 18. The festival had a stellar cast featuring such titans as Iron Maiden, Ozzy Osbourne, Def Leppard, the Scorpions, Quiet Riot, Krokus and the Michael Schenker Group.

Reviewing Priest's performance in *Sounds*, Garry Bushell wrote: "To me they're pantomime of the first order and Halford is the perfect panto dame, corpulent, convivial, coruscating and comical."

An unnamed *Kerrang!* writer was not as smitten: "I couldn't decide whether to laugh or grit my teeth but the music was excellent, if a touch relentless."

Defenders Of The Faith was unleashed in the UK on January 28, 1984. Like its predecessor, *Screaming For Vengeance*, the British chart returns (number 19 in the UK, five weeks on the charts) failed to match the US (top 20 in the *Billboard* Top 200 Albums charts, reaching platinum status by 1988). In the January, 1985 issue of *Kerrang!*, a disappointed Halford told Howard Johnson: "Everyone wants to top their last album and I'd be a liar if I said that I wasn't disappointed with the sales of *Defender* . . . We did about 800,000 copies and sales are virtually at a halt now, whereas *Screaming* . . . is still selling!"

Fans took to the album title as it suggested Priest were defending the rock'n'roll faith, their aim being to spread heavy metal around the globe. "Well, I suppose it's pretty obvious really," Halford told *Kerrang!* at the time of the 1983 British tour. "It's HM, isn't it?"

Another similarity to *Screaming For Vengeance* was the creation of a new fantastical creature, again designed by Doug Johnson, called 'The Metallion'. The album bore two singles in 1984 – the rip-roaring 'Freewheel Burning', which reached number 42, making it their biggest single in the UK since 'United' in 1980, and 'Some Heads Are Gonna Roll'.

The video for 'Freewheel Burning', directed by Wayne Isham, latched on to the video game craze of the Eighties. The furiousness of the song was represented by a car-racing game (played by a kid at an arcade). Halford can actually be seen *inside* the game, driving one of the cars. Shots of the band playing the song were also inserted into the clip. Surprisingly there was no video for 'Some Heads Are Gonna Roll'. However, a promo was made for 'Love Bites', directed by Keef (Keith MacMillan), which was a fabricated live video with no audience.

Whereas *British Steel* and *Screaming For Vengeance* had at least one metal anthem apiece, Halford admitted to *Kerrang!* that "we simply didn't have a strong single on *Defenders . . .*'" In his *Sounds* review, Geoff Barton declared the album to be "a dynamite selection, harking back to the glories of *Sad Wings Of Destiny* days by way of its electric energy and 'magnum opus' feel."

Defenders Of The Faith began with the highly energetic and ferocious 'Freewheel Burning' – easily one of Priest's most accomplished metal songs. In the age of Eighties thrash bands such as Metallica and Slayer, Priest had to prove to their fans that they could still deliver the goods. Reviewing the single, Howard Johnson of *Kerrang!* summed up: "'Freewheel Burning' is hammer-down, ball-breakin' hard rock . . ."

'Jawbreaker' was one of several songs that caused a stir in the Eighties with the Parents Music Resource Center (PMRC) thanks to its controversial gay lyrical content. 'Rock Hard, Ride Free' was another in a line of arena metal anthems that Priest had become adept at making. As the band were now playing 15,000–25,000 capacity arenas in the States, such songs succeeded in uniting their followers. 'The Sentinel' was another fast, ferocious riff-based song, with Halford hitting some ridiculously high notes. 'Love Bites', led by a highly charged melody with Halford's forceful lyrics, was picked as the tour's opening song.

'Eat Me Alive' – an homage to oral sex – would prove to be the album's most controversial song. 'Some Heads Are Gonna Roll' received strong rotation on American airwaves; an anomaly considering it wasn't the best song on the album. The pace slowed for the sultry power ballad, 'Night Comes Down'. 'Heavy Duty' plodded like a dinosaur – huge drum beats, repetitious riffs and strong bass. The sounds of a live crowd merged the latter with the album's chest-beating, anthemic title track.*

Defenders Of The Faith has retained its appeal among Priest and metal fans in general. Michael McKeegan (of Therapy?): "For me there's not a weak moment on *Defenders Of The Faith*. It was the second Priest album I bought and it was a big step on from *Screaming . . .* in terms of speed and aggression. The soloing is brilliant throughout and every song has a big chorus . . . 'Rock Hard, Ride Free' and 'Eat Me Alive' are two favourites, and 'The Sentinel' is in my top three all-time Priest faves."

The wrestler Chris Jericho, singer of the band Fozzy, is also a huge Priest fan, having laid down cover versions of 'Freewheel Burning' and 'Riding On The Wind'. "Priest is an influence on any metal band who came into existence post-1980. *Defenders Of The Faith* is my all-time favourite Priest record and 'The Sentinel' is a masterpiece . . . We used to do a lot of covers and Priest is one of Fozzy's collective favourite bands. We chose those songs because they rule but are not exactly 'hits'. We also did a version of 'Metal Gods' that rules but hasn't been released yet."

By 1984, thrash metal in the States – primarily based around bands from the San Francisco Bay area – had become a force to be reckoned with. Metallica's masterful 1983 album *Kill 'Em All* was the touchstone for a new type of metal with sonic riffs, fluid bursts of electric energy, harsh vocals and sporadic bouts of aggression.

From around the time of *Defenders Of The Faith* to the end of the decade, thrash reigned supreme on the metal circuit – both in terms of album sales and touring. Other important bands and early albums from the time, which spearheaded the way for this new sub-genre of heavy metal, included such titans as Anthrax with *Fistful Of Metal*, Slayer with *Show No Mercy*, Megadeth with *Killing Is My Business . . . And Business is Good!* and Exodus with *Bonded By Blood*. Metal Church, Testament, Watchtower and Voivod were also founding practitioners of the genre.

Like its parent category, the origins and influences of thrash are often debated. Judas Priest can lay a claim to being a forebear of the movement with the remarkable kick-drum speed of 'Exciter' from *Stained Class* and the sheer ferocity of 'Riding On The Wind' (*Screaming For Vengeance*).

"If you listen to some of the so-called thrash metal, you can hear a bit of

---

* The 2001/02 reissue featured the previously unreleased ballad, 'Turn On Your Light', and a live recording of 'Heavy Duty/Defenders Of The Faith'.

the old, frantic Priest guitars in there, the stuff we used to do more in our early days," Halford told *Kerrang! Mega Metal*. "It's good."

Other significant early examples include Black Sabbath's 'Symptom Of The Universe', Motörhead's 'Overkill' and, surprisingly, Queen with the ultra-fast 'Sheer Heart Attack' and 'Stone Cold Crazy' (Metallica covered the latter on *Garage Inc.*) Thrash also inherited traits from American punk rock, primarily from the fast aggression of Iggy and the Stooges, and the Ramones.

Priest got wind of this burgeoning scene on the west coast of America. With a faster, more forceful and aggressive brand of modern metal, they needed to prove that they could compete with the bands they had influenced without moving away from their own style and melody. "I wouldn't say that we ignore the state of the music scene," Halford told *Kerrang!* in the mid Eighties, "we always look at it from year to year . . . [but] we do seem to follow our own path!"

Having toured the UK at the end of 1983, Priest set their sights on the rest of the world for the following year. Supported by American right-wing gonzo Ted Nugent and NWOBHM band Raven, the tour began in Europe on January 20, passing through Denmark, Sweden, France, Holland, Spain, Germany and Switzerland, finishing at the end of February. The North American tour, supported by Saxon and Great White, began on March 16 and finished on August 10. Against a backdrop of the *Defenders Of The Faith* cover, the stage show was based around 'The Metallion', which, with its elongated claws and venomous illuminating eyes, could have sprung to life from the pages of an Isaac Asimov story.

In a review of the Priest/Great White gig at Toronto's Maple Leaf Gardens, a *Kerrang!* journalist acknowledged Priest's enthusiasm for their support bands. "Openers Great White did excellently . . . thanks to the headliners' generous allocation of sound and lights . . ." Priest "were utterly masterful from the moment Halford emerged from the jaws of the colossal Metallian, which dwarfed the inarguably vast stage . . . Musically, Priest are lethal but largely predictable . . ."

The tour did not go without its controversy. During a sold-out show at Madison Square Garden on June 18, fans rioted, causing half-a-million-dollars worth of damage, resulting in Judas Priest being banned from playing there again. It remains unclear as to whether the ban has been lifted.

After finishing a Japanese tour in September at Tokyo's renowned Budokan, Priest came off the road. Yet there was still work to be done for a follow-up to *Defenders Of The Faith*, so the band headed off again to Spain as Halford told *Kerrang!*: "We've been here for the whole of November; we'll be here for about half of December before taking a Christmas break and then coming back to work through January."

A quiet period followed but, as Halford told *Kerrang!*: "What I will say, though, is that our new stage show will be *very* spectacular! Priest will be back again – count on it!"

EIGHT

1985–1989

". . . We are very fortunate because as a band we've always been on the up, always getting more successful . . . Each album has got a new sound or direction . . ."

– Glenn Tipton speaking to *Metal Hammer* in May, 1987

IN the mid Eighties, the Parents Music Resource Center (PMRC), founded in May, 1985 and led by Tipper Gore, the wife of future Democratic Vice President Al Gore, was a powerful, firmly established organisation with important political connections.

Gore's team of four wives and mothers (whom the press dubbed the 'Washington Wives') consisted of Susan Baker (wife of Treasury Secretary James Baker), Pam Howar (wife of Washington estate agent Raymond Howar) and Sally Nevius (wife of Washington City Council Chairman John Nevius). Their aim was to censor popular music and in some cases actually place a ban on anything they believed incited violence, illicit sex, rape and other such controversial and morally repugnant themes.

Rob Halford was not overly concerned at the rise of the PMRC, telling *Metal Hammer* in 1989: ". . . There will always be a group of people who'll oppose this form of music, be it heavy metal, rock'n'roll, whatever we call it. There will always be someone bitching . . . There's always someone in any walk of life that doesn't like what you do."

After writing letters of protest and being generally persistent with their mission, the PMRC managed to persuade record companies to agree to put warning stickers on records, advising on the songs' lyrical content. This came into practice on November 1 and was comically dubbed 'the Tipper sticker' by the media. Some bands and artists challenged the PMRC's stance. Indeed, Dee Snider (of Twisted Sister) got a chance to say his piece when he testified in the US Senate against their policies.

The PMRC published a list of 15 songs that they believed to be morally corrupting. Judas Priest were high up on the hit list at number three with

'Eat Me Alive', from *Defenders Of The Faith*. Ranked alongside Priest in the 'Filthy 15' were Prince, Madonna, AC/DC, Twisted Sister, W.A.S.P, Def Leppard, Mercyful Fate, Black Sabbath, Mary Jane Girls, Vanity, Mötley Crüe, Venom and, bizarrely, Cyndi Lauper and Sheena Easton. The songs in question seem tame in comparison with contemporary rap and hip-hop tunes. The Prodigy's 'Smack My Bitch Up' (both song and video) would have sent Tipper Gore into seizures had it been released in 1985.

The PMRC was not the only political activist group in America during the Reagan years. The Moral Majority, formed in 1979 under the initial moniker 'Christian Voice' by conservative Christian fundamentalists, aimed to suppress abortion, homosexuality and any other sin the Bible preached against. Predictably, heavy metal was perceived as a danger to the typical God-fearing American suburban family, and such artists as Ozzy Osbourne, Mötley Crüe, Judas Priest and W.A.S.P were all in the Moral Majority's sights. The campaign disbanded in 1989, but Jerry Falwell, the televangelist who was one of the movement's original founders, formed a second political group called, unimaginatively, The Moral Majority Coalition, in 2004.

"Quite honestly . . . I feel we were tagged unfairly," Halford told *Metal Hammer* after the controversy had died down. "'Eat Me Alive' is a spoof caricature sexual song . . ."

However, regardless of either the Moral Majority or the PMRC's witch-hunting techniques, Priest were to be connected with a far more serious incident with far-reaching repercussions (see Chapter Nine).

In terms of press, live shows and TV appearances, 1985 was a quiet year for Judas Priest, unusually so considering the tight schedule they had lived by in over a decade of relentless recording and touring. Halford told *Kerrang!* in 1987: "We were expected every 18 months to have recorded an album and toured the world with it . . . The break we took has proven we can come up with something different and give the term heavy metal a new meaning . . ." It was the right moment for the band to take a well-earned respite. Having cracked America with *Screaming For Vengeance* in 1982 the band were financially secure, an important factor in any such move. However, both their record company and management felt that there was still some work to be accomplished in the studio and on the road.

On July 13, Priest performed at Live Aid – the mammoth charity concert extravaganza organised by ex-Boomtown Rats singer Bob Geldof. Priest arrived on the Philadelphia stage at 4.26, playing a 10-minute set featuring 'Living After Midnight', 'The Green Manalishi (With The Two-Pronged Crown)' and 'You've Got Another Thing Comin''.

Halford also took part in Hear 'n Aid, a heavy metal charity organised by ex-Black Sabbath and Rainbow singer Ronnie James Dio, bassist Jimmy Bain and current Def Leppard guitarist Vivian Campbell. The aim was to emulate the enormous success of the hugely popular Live Aid-related recordings, 'Do They Know It's Christmas?' by Band Aid and USA For Africa's 'We Are The World'. Dio, Campbell and Bain quite rightly felt that the industry ignored heavy metal acts when it came to raising money for charity, so they set up their own in May, 1985, recording an album, *Stars*, at a Hollywood studio. Among the 40 heavy metal/rock artists were Don Dokken, Kevin DuBrow, Geoff Tate and Blackie Lawless. Rumours that Dio will reunite the stars of Hear 'N' Aid continued to circulate for several years.

The thrash metal scene was harsher, more aggressive and significantly rawer than LA's 'hair metal' bands, as they were affectionately known. The latter bands were more extreme in a fashion sense even if their music was more pop-orientated, aimed at mass radio play and chart success. The likes of Mötley Crüe, Twisted Sister, Quiet Riot, Ratt and Poison had a glam-rock image that was in many ways more important (and entertaining) than their music, which in the case of Poison left a lot to be desired. Bizarrely, the images of some hair metal bands, with their outlandish hair and multi-coloured leather, made an impact on Priest. "We watch very carefully and with much interest bands like Mötley Crüe . . ." Tipton told *Sounds* in May, 1986.

The writing for the album that was to become *Turbo* (the title purportedly influenced by Tipton and Downing's love of Porsche Turbos) began back in November, 1984 in Marbella, Spain. Writing sessions and rehearsals lasted until the early summer of 1985, when they were interrupted by the Live Aid and Hear 'n Aid dates. For the recording, the band chose not to work in Ibiza; instead, they headed for Compass Point, Nassau, with Tom Allom, recording up until Christmas, with mixing being completed in January, 1986 at New York's Record Plant. Initially *Turbo* was intended as a double album, to be called 'Twin-Turbo', marking Priest's tenth studio release. A total of 18 songs were recorded at Compass Point but CBS felt production and shipping costs would be too high. As Tipton told *Sounds* in May, 1986, charging more money for a double album "defeated the object of the exercise."

Several excellent songs were not used including 'Heart Of A Lion' (handed over to LA metal band Racer X for their second album *Second Heat*), 'Red, White And Blue', 'All Fired Up', 'Fight For Your Love', 'Under The Gun' and 'Prisoner Of Your Eyes', although some were uncovered over a decade later and used as bonus tracks on the 2001/02 series of Judas Priest album reissues.

Despite many fans' and writers' misgivings at the time of its release, *Turbo* has a rightful stake in heavy metal history. Inevitably influenced by *Eliminator*-era ZZ Top, it was the first metal album to be completely digitally recorded, using only guitar synthesisers on the album to produce a more melodic, smooth sound. Rob Halford confessed to *Hard Rock* in 1986: "We went into the writing not really with the full intention of using them [guitar synthesisers] as extensively as we have done."

It was certainly a controversial move to use guitar synthesisers, and many listeners poked fun at their new sound. Priest were disappointed and taken aback by such negative responses. K.K. Downing told *Sounds* in July, 1987: "We thought . . . *Turbo* would be the next *Pyromania* or *Back In Black* . . . But it backfired on us a bit, it didn't take us forward." Released in the UK on April 19, *Turbo* reached a disastrous 33, the band's worst chart position in the UK since the pre-*Unleashed In The East* years, lasting just four weeks in the charts. It predictably fared much better in the States, going in at number 50 on the *Billboard* Top 200 in its first week, peaking at 17, eventually going gold and then platinum.

The artwork, which depicted a hand holding onto a joystick, was again designed by Doug Johnson. Latching on to the phenomenal success of MTV and the music video market, a pair of videos – for 'Turbo Lover' and 'Locked In' – were directed by Wayne Isham, whose previous work consisted of Mötley Crüe's 'Smokin' In The Boys Room' and 'Home Sweet Home'. Influenced by the success of the *Mad Max* films starring Mel Gibson, the videos showed the band driving through vast desert landscapes on Harley Davidsons. In 'Locked In', Halford was captured and subsequently tortured by science-fiction creatures called 'bio-mecca-droids', who, incidentally, happened to be men-eating women. Priest were never a serious band when it came to acting in front of the camera in the Eighties, as Tipton told *Sounds* in 1986 on the set of 'Locked In': "We've taken all sorts of ideas . . . the whole storyline is very tongue-in-cheek."

It was obvious that after seeing the success of bands like Def Leppard, Mötley Crüe and Poison, Priest intended broadening their appeal to attract a more extensive fan base with a smoother album production, as Tipton told *Sounds*: "You can always learn from others, especially the youngsters."

Turbo began with 'Turbo Lover', a slick song that remains heavily featured in Priest's live act. The pop-fuelled, soft-rock 'Locked In' was the obvious choice for a single, while 'Private Property' was yet another anthemic hands-in-the-air pop-metal song with a fun chorus. The jovial 'Parental Guidance' was Priest's riposte to the PMRC's attack. 'Rock You All Around The World' was heavier compared with its lighter pre-decessors, but like 'Private Property', it featured a commercial pop chorus. 'Out In The Cold' utilised an eerie synthesised intro, while 'Wild Nights, Hot And Crazy Days', showed Priest boldly attempting a Bon Jovi-style power ballad anthem. 'Hot For Love' was unremarkable, but 'Reckless' had a killer lick and another terrific crowd-cheering chorus. The song was in line as the lead theme to the hit movie *Top Gun*, but Priest turned the request down. Berlin's 'Take My Breath Away' was chosen instead and won an Academy Award and a Golden Globe for 'Best Original Song'. More than two decades later it is still a widely known song and a karaoke staple. If 'Reckless' had been the lead theme to a Hollywood movie it could have taken Priest to even greater stratospheric success.[*]

In the November, 2004 issue of *Classic Rock*, *Turbo* was voted one of 'The 20 Most Underrated Rock Albums Ever' alongside other under-estimated works like Motörhead's *Orgasmatron*, Queen's *Made In Heaven*, and AC/DC's *Fly On The Wall*.[†]

Priest had not toured since playing Japan in September, 1984, so they were eager to get back on the road. The promotional tour, dubbed Turbo: Fuel For Life, starting on May 2 in Albuquerque, New Mexico, was the band's biggest stage production thus far, with 'The Hellion' as the centrepiece, its giant claws lifting the guitarists from the stage floor giving them a full view of the ecstatic audience. The band had a new look to match their new sound; each member puffed their hair up and even Halford grew his hair longer. The new image appeared to be influenced by science-fiction themes, as each band member had his own specially designed uniform. They also sported coloured leathers designed by the LA-based designer Ray Brown. Halford told *Kerrang! Mega Metal*: "If anything we all really felt it was time for a bit of a change. Nothing too drastic, just more colour . . . we all feel good in new clothes . . ."

Support on the tour came from the underrated, melodic hard-rock band

---

[*] Bonus tracks on the 2001/02 reissue were a live version of 'Locked In' and *Turbo* sessions out-take, 'All Fired Up'.

[†] Perhaps Priest will go back to the *Turbo* album and re-release it the way it was intended as an 18-track double album. There is certainly a fan demand for it.

Dokken. Filmmakers Jeff Krulik and John Heyn documented the show at the Capital Center in Landover, Maryland on May 31 for their rockumentary *Heavy Metal Parking Lot*, which captured a metal audience waiting anxiously in the car park for the venue's doors to open. Most of the fans appeared drunk, stoned and over-excited. It became something of a cult classic, and even the controversial American filmmaker John Waters was said to have been disturbed by it. Since 1986, Krulik has made a number of documentaries about popular culture, parodying *Heavy Metal Parking Lot* in 2000 with the similarly titled *Harry Potter Parking Lot*.

Back in the UK, Derek Oliver, a journalist for *Kerrang!*, reported on Priest's show at the LA Sports Arena in May. ". . . I then tottered giggling into the depths of the Judas Priest stage set where I chanced upon a meeting with our old friend Jonathan Valen, drummer for Legs Diamond . . . Valen has taken to temporarily plying his trade within the colossal sanctuary of Priest's moveable scenery . . . he [Holland] is a drummer with nowhere to go and I wonder what it is that keeps him in the spotlight and Valen hidden in the rigging?"

Despite an otherwise positive review, Oliver continued to slyly hint at the Valen/Holland anomaly when concluding: "The only scar on this planet was the reminder during Dave Holland's 'perfect' solo that perhaps all is not truthful in the rhythm department . . . Jonathan Valen is indeed a very concise percussionist!"

Since the review's appearance in the July, 1986 issue of *Kerrang!* Priest have been none too kind regarding Valen; predictably, their own version of events differs greatly from what both he and Oliver had to say regarding the drumming matter.

Tipton told writer Bryan Reesman in his 1998 Judas Priest essay for *Goldmine* magazine that Valen was a pretend rock star: "I think he [Valen] used to get changed every night into his stage clothes. He was a bit of a would-be star, and I think he took it upon himself to do an interview one day. I forget his name now."

Jonathan Valen: "The band actually blamed me for the article, thinking that I purposely called up the magazine and gave an interview to help promote my career but that was not true. My feeling was that a reporter who just happened along saw what had been going on and let the cat out of the bag."

Tipton maintains that because the band were using triggers on a new drum kit, they "got this guy to come out on the road for the first three weeks to nursemaid us . . . And somebody spotted him under the stage . . . so they were saying, 'Dave Holland isn't playing drums.'"

112

Jonathan Valen: "I'm not sure the boys in the band want their big secret unveiled to the public . . . I did play electric drums backstage for them, but they have made up some convoluted story about me being some kind of drum tech, to protect their image – they never wanted anybody to find out about it. When the article came out about my participation, they threatened [me] . . . never talk to anyone or else! This is the reason my name does not show up on their live record and why they have never spoken very highly about me.

"First of all, let me go on record as saying that at no time did I ever take the place of David Holland, and the band, at least to my knowledge, did not have a problem with his playing. He was their drummer and my role was more like a percussionist playing in and out of David's beats – I played the double bass drum parts and filled in drum breaks to make the songs sound more thunderous. These parts would have required a drummer with four hands and would have been impossible for one drummer to do, so naturally David and I sat down and just worked the parts out together. My duties also included triggering a Prophet 5 VS via the Octapad on all the background vocal parts, along with sound effects and also some guitar effects that Kenny asked me to play. You see today acts just sequence the whole song and all play to a click track, but back in those days, 16 seconds of sample time was all you got, and unless you had a drummer or someone with great timing doing it, there would have been a definite train wreck.

"Priest were on the cutting edge of technology at the time in a big way, and you can't fault them for giving their fans one hundred per cent. The marching snare drum solo in 'The Sentinel' on the Judas Priest live record [*Priest . . . Live!*] is one very obvious place that you can hear me, and all of that was played by me every night hand to hand, it was not sequenced. I had many drum fills and what I call bombing runs until the article written in *Kerrang!* came out. At that time, the band went into denial mode about my presence and cut lots of my parts, still allowing me the solo in 'The Sentinel', but no more freedom to do anything that might be obvious to the audience.

"This whole business about keeping it secret doesn't make any sense to me. If the band would have just acknowledged me and my presence there would be no controversy, and people would have just accepted the fact that in the Eighties this kind of situation happened all the time in many bands. I really wish they would have given me credit on the record because I worked very hard for them, and I feel that I have every right to be proud of my accomplishments. By keeping my name off the record it helped to squelch the rumours that were flying around. But now there is more drama surrounding it.

"I have played on Patrick O' Hearn's *Rivers Gonna Rise* album, a record with Terry Bozzio – one of the greatest progressive drummers in the world, so why would I try to ruin my integrity and reputation by making up a story about playing with Judas Priest?!"

Valen made the valid point that if he did not play drums on the tour the band would have sued for slander as soon as the *Kerrang!* story was published. "Those guys are ruthless businessmen and would never have let this kind of public relations nightmare exist," he reasoned. "The last time I spoke to them was after the final show on August 31 at the CNE stadium in Toronto, Canada. I did receive a letter from Ian Hill some time after the tour, but I never heard from anyone else in the band.

"The *Kerrang!* piece actually helped me in some ways, documenting what had actually happened. And because of it, it allowed an opportunity to have the truth be known. I am convinced that without that article the chances are pretty good that the creative cast of the band may have succeeded in the cover-up. I'm thankful that that reporter saw what was going on and reported it."

How was Valen treated by the Priest road crew?

Jonathan Valen: "The road crew for the most part were awesome. There were, however, some characters that gave me a bit of grief, but I could deal with it; I don't wish to name names. I saw no tension with the band members because everyone pretty much kept to themselves. Rob would always arrive in a limo and we would arrive on a bus. Even when I had a bad night and would come to the dressing room with my tail between my legs, the boys would just say, 'Hey lad, tomorrow is a new day, don't worry about it . . .' I can recall Mick Brown and Jeff Pilson . . . trying to distract me when I was playing during shows and, because of the fact that very few people could see me, there were always some kind of antics going on behind the scenes."

Valen holds a positive opinion of Holland's drumming. "Dave Holland is, in my opinion, extremely talented, and I will always be grateful for his friendship and professionalism . . . The guitar players in the band said in an article that I came out on the road with them for a week as a consultant because of my knowledge of samplers – that is completely untrue. It had been explained to me that the reason they brought me into the project was because when a band member leaves a group, the fans might view this as a break-up, and two heads were better than one . . .

"I've been completely honest with you and have no reason to make up

114

such a story. I'm doing my best to prove what I did for Judas Priest but it was 20 years ago . . ."

Despite the recriminations the experience brought, Valen remains grateful for his time on the tour. "Let me say thank you to Rob Halford, Ian Hill, Glenn Tipton, Dave Holland and Kenny Downing for an amazing adventure, something I will remember forever . . . Hope the truth doesn't get me killed!"

To support Valen's contention, Michael Schenker Group singer David Van Landing stated: "I met Jonathan Valen out on tour with Judas Priest on the 'Turbo' tour. I was friends with Rob Halford and saw many of the shows from backstage. I saw Jon with drumsticks in his hands and he was on his way to start the show. When I asked him what he did for the band, he told me he was playing on some of the more difficult drum stuff, and I watched him do it. So it makes sense that they would eventually replace Dave Holland down the road with a more technically gifted player . . ."

Adding further credence to Valen's assertion, American DJ Howard Howes was a carpenter and mechanic on the tour, and fixed 'The Hellion' whenever it broke down. He told the author: "I don't really fancy getting involved in this in an official capacity, but [working] on that tour I did see [Valen] programming and playing some electronic drums and effects . . ."

Derek Oliver looked back on the controversy from a 20-year perspective: "It's not uncommon to find bands 'augmenting' their live sound with offstage keyboard/guitar/backing vocalists or even tapes, and I'd seen a fair bit of that sort of thing going on before so it didn't really surprise me when Jon Valen told me why he was there. It was weird, however, to climb inside the stage set and see a little area set aside for Jon's equipment so that he could play along [with] Priest, beefing up the sound. I'd seen Dave Holland play before and always thought it looked a bit odd that he was such a 'light' player, and yet the sound coming out of the PA was always big and bombastic. When I watched the gig it all fell into place – the syn drums, triggers, explosions, etc. Despite that, I thought they were great; consummate showmen and the crowd lapped it up . . .

"The trouble with being a journalist is that you're always looking for an angle, and Jon Valen handed me one on a sliver platter. I remember thinking that the guys back at the office are gonna love this, and wrote the review accordingly. Like an idiot, I was so wrapped up in the story that I failed to note the set list and reported that [Priest] played a couple of songs that hadn't been aired, thus undermining my integrity, but the fact remained they did have a secret drummer and Dave Holland wasn't entirely responsible for the sound.

"Geoff Barton, the *Kerrang!* editor at the time, told me that in the days following publication he received an angry telephone call from, I believe, K.K. Downing, who complained bitterly that they had been stitched up, etc. Geoff, bless him, stood by the review and proffered that K.K.'s reaction was, if understandable, somewhat flawed in light of the overriding evidence. I think Geoff had uncovered a similar story a few years prior to this incident, having noticed an offstage guitarist ghosting for Michael Schenker during an MSG concert, so he was supportive and, like a good newspaper man, always up for a bit of dirt.

"I guess my feelings on the matter have been erased by time and distance but I do remember thinking how weird it was to have seen this band very early in their career at a small gig promoting the *Sad Wings Of Destiny* LP, and then to be watching them playing a huge sports arena in Los Angeles with thousands of screaming fans punching the air . . . and a second percussionist under the stage!"

Priest journeyed around Canada for much of July with Bon Jovi as support, after the US tour with Dokken finished at the end of June. A second Stateside leg was arranged for July and August with support from Krokus. The Swiss rockers, whose 1983 album *Headhunter* was produced by Tom Allom, had previously supported Priest on the American Screaming For Vengeance tour and had appeared with them at the Dortmund Festival in 1983.

Marc Storace [Krokus lead singer]: "We lived on the same apartment complex in Los Angeles [Oakwood Gardens] for a few months and played tennis with K.K. and Glenn to keep fit a couple of times. They were both great guys to hang around with . . . I'm a terrible tennis player myself . . . so I really played for the fun of it and simply to share the good company. [They're a] very cool band – they treated us so well, and I'd love to tour with them any time again!"

With rave reviews following Judas Priest all over North America, British journalists flew to the States eager to witness the band in action. The top rock and metal music rags such as *Kerrang!*, *Metal Hammer* and *Sounds* were uniform in their praise for the new stage set and show. On September 28 the Turbo: Fuel For Life tour hit Europe, journeying through Holland, Germany, Spain, Belgium, France, Denmark, Sweden, Norway and Finland, with support from Warlock, a young German metal band fronted by Doro Pesch.

Doro Pesch: "It was our very first big tour – it was actually the day when I quit my day job as a graphics artist. My manager called and said,

'Oh, you wanna quit your job?' And I said, 'Why?' And he said, 'Well, I think we can go on tour with your favourite band in the world!' and I said, 'You must be kidding! No way!' and he said, 'Yes, Judas Priest!' I was blown away. I said, 'OK' . . . I went to my boss and I said, 'Well, I just want to let you know I'm going on tour and I want to quit the job.' He said, 'Are you crazy?' I said, 'Well, maybe, but I wanna try it.' And I think he said, 'OK girl, you're crazy but good luck.'"

Doro recalls the huge venues the tour played, quite a leap from the much smaller clubs Warlock were used to. "I remember '86 was the peak of heavy metal and with the big stadiums, it was unbelievable. Scandinavia had the big ice-sport venues and I guess every day it was between 20,000 and 30,000 people or even more. It was fantastic, and [Priest] were super-nice to us. We didn't expect anything. And actually we got treated good, and I learned from that and I thought if I ever had a support band then I wanna treat them as good as we were treated.

"On the last couple of days, we did [talk to them] but back then nobody could really speak English out of the whole band – what shall we talk about? Years and years later we met them again at a Judas Priest concert in Munich, and it was such a great experience that we could [have a] conversation, exchanging jokes. But in '86, I think our drummer was 15 or 16 years old, and we were really young and inexperienced so . . ."

The language barrier did not stop Priest from being polite and appreciative to their support acts.

Doro Pesch: "We had a tour bus but the budget was really low . . . the Priest guys were nice and said, 'You guys, you know, take what you want from the catering' and we could have it every day, dinner and stuff . . . We ate when they finished because I think as a support band you have to play [by] the rules and not get on the nerves of the headliner. We tried our best to put on a good show, to always be on time and to do everything good. And then to talk a little bit, just sometimes to say, 'Hi, how are you doing?' and 'Have a great show!' It was a very friendly tour . . . I didn't feel like I couldn't talk to them . . .

"We [were] always treated well, I think almost every day we did a sound check and it was perfect. I remember one of the concerts, I forget which country, but we were doing our thing and the audience was excited, and then suddenly I turned around and all the guys from Priest were watching us from the side of the stage and I almost got a heart attack . . . we tried, of course, to play even better, but it was like when your idol is watching you, the pressure is on. I remember the very last gig. We wanted to give them something as thanks. We picked up a card and I meditated about what I wanted to say . . . I couldn't catch any sleep and then I think I wrote one line, like 'Thank you, for the spirit.' After 10 hours of thinking about it, out came one line!"

Disappointingly, and to the frustration and anger of their British fans, Priest once again completely bypassed their native country. "It's a shame that we can't go in and play big enough places to put on the full show . . ." Downing told *Metal Hammer* in 1987. "We could do Hammersmith for two nights and have difficulty in selling the second night . . . When you have support bands supporting you and they go down pretty bad, and then two months later the support band's doing four Hammersmiths and you only did two, you think to yourself, 'What the fuck's going on here?' . . . We don't want to go back to Bristol Colston Hall and have difficulty getting a 4X12 light on stage."

After the European shows, Priest finished the year playing four Japanese gigs. In terms of venue sizes and audience attendances, Turbo: Fuel For Life was the biggest and most fantastically overblown tour yet for Judas Priest.

Asked by *Hard Rock* for Priest's plans for 1987, Halford replied: ". . . I would imagine the next logical step would be the long-awaited next live Priest album . . . In '87, I would imagine you'd see us doing a few isolated dates around America . . ." The band spent 1987 off the road, choosing to concentrate on writing and recording their next album in Spain. The first of the year's recording activities in January, much to the horror of heavy metal purists around the world, was the most unlikely of partnerships. Peculiarly, Judas Priest collaborated in a Paris studio with disposable pop wizards Mike Stock, Matt Aitken and Pete Waterman (SAW) on three tracks – 'I Will Return', 'You Keep Giving Me The Runaround' (both written by SAW) and a cover of The Stylistics' 'You Are Everything'.

The collaboration had come about through Bill Curbishley's associations with SAW. On the relationship in the studio, Waterman says there were no arguments and "they were great" to work with. By an uncanny coincidence, David Howells, the co-founder of Gull Records, managed the production team. Regarding the songs, Howells says, "I thought they sounded great at the time, particularly 'You Are Everything', but I have no idea what happened to the tracks."

Perhaps, after the poor sales of *Turbo*, Priest were eager to restore their commercial standing. Whatever the motivation, the band had a change of heart and the three tracks remain unreleased. "We actually did three tracks together, just as an experiment," Tipton told *Metal Hammer* in 1988, "but we can't afford at this stage in our career to do anything that isn't Judas Priest."

Rob Halford (*Metal Hammer*): "Another thing is that we realised that whatever we did with these guys would go slap bang on the radio. I think that answers the people who say that we are just doing it for the hit singles."*

At the time of pre-preparation for the album that would become *Ram It Down*, Downing told *Sounds'* Mary Anne Hobbs: "So the next album is going to be cram jam full of nasty, gritty, horrible metal songs." The band had already written and demoed several songs, as Downing informed *Metal Hammer*: "One's called 'Ram It Down' and there's another called 'Hard As Iron', 'Sharp As Steel', and there's another one called 'Love You To Death', which is a bit filthy."

It seemed the failure of *Turbo* to take off had proved a learning curve for Priest, who decided to return to the hard-edged metal they had helped to patent. In the meantime, to buy some time, the band toyed with a double package consisting of unreleased studio material on one disc and live material on the other to keep fans happy. This idea never materialised and gradually evolved into the straightforward double *Priest . . . Live!* released in Britain on June 13, reaching the 47 position but dropping from the charts after only two weeks.

Recorded at the Dallas and Atlanta shows on the Turbo: Fuel For Life US tour, the track listing was the right balance of older Priest material with a large selection of songs from *Turbo*, consisting of: 'Out In The Cold', 'Heading Out To The Highway', 'Metal Gods', 'Breaking The Law', 'Love Bites', 'Some Heads Are Gonna Roll', 'The Sentinel', 'Private Property', 'Rock You All Around The World', 'Electric Eye', 'Turbo Lover', 'Freewheel Burning', 'Parental Guidance', 'Living After Midnight' and 'You've Got Another Thing Comin' '†

If there were doubters after *Turbo*, *Priest . . . Live!* showed critics that the band could still deliver the goods on stage. *Sounds* concluded its four-star review with, "Priest may be unfashionable, but they are certainly not irrelevant."

Kerrang! gave the double album full marks, saying, "This album captures

---

* It's often been claimed that the SAW tracks are in the secure hands of Judas Priest, although Waterman says he still has copies of the songs, saying, "It's a shame the tracks were never put out."
† The 2001/02 reissue added: 'Screaming For Vengeance', 'Rock Hard Ride Free' and 'Hell Bent For Leather'.

the essential essence of a major rock band reaching an unprecedented peak in their career, a band in full flight . . ." In *Metal Hammer*, Dave Ling wrote, "The packaging's truly naff, but the vinyl inside it would stand up under the scrutiny of even the band's most stern critics. Buy it."*

As 1988 approached, Priest and Tom Allom switched recording locations from sunny Spain to Puk Recording Studios in a bitterly cold Denmark. "We came here to work harder," Tipton told *Metal Hammer*. "We've always been sidetracked on previous albums . . . So everyone agreed to go somewhere where there was nothing to do but work . . . This album has really gelled, it locked into place and found its own theme."

The album had a working title of *Monsters Of Rock*, but the band felt this was clichéd and unoriginal so it became *Ram It Down*. "We had a lot of problems with the record company trying to change that name!" Tipton revealed to *Metal Hammer* before the record's release. "They said it was a sexist title!"

Released on May 28, 1988, *Ram It Down* reached number 24 in the UK charts and lasted a fairly healthy (by their standards) five weeks in the charts while going gold in the US. The band were displeased at the way the album was handled; indeed, the only single released from *Ram It Down* was a frankly bizarre cover of Chuck Berry's 'Johnny B. Goode', which happened to be the title track to a forgettable American college caper called *Johnny Be Good*, starring Anthony Michael Hall, Robert Downey Jr, Uma Thurman and Jennifer Tilly. Halford told *Metal Hammer* in 1988 that the producers of the film "wanted a metal band to do a metal version of 'Johnny B. Goode' and we were on the list."†

The promotional video, directed by Wayne Isham, was shot at Amsterdam's Roxy Theatre, showing Priest in full flight in front of a small audience of just a few hundred fans. The film itself received a universal panning, flopping as a consequence. It seemed that Priest's first endeavour into the world of film soundtracks had been ill-advised.

Ram It Down began with the skull-crushing title track, one of only two stand-out tracks on the album. Unfortunately, after such a promising start, much of the album failed to approach the same ferocity. 'Heavy Metal', a lame attempt at creating another arena metal anthem, was cliché-ridden

---

* A live VHS, recorded at the Dallas show on June 27, 1986, accompanied the album's release. The set list for the video differed from the album so fans weren't buying the same show twice. (It was released on DVD in 2003 as *Electric Eye*.)
† Released in the UK on April 23, the single reached a disastrous number 63 in the charts, dropping out after only two weeks.

and poorly executed. 'Love Zone' and 'Come And Get It' were badly written and had no real focus. The angry, unmelodic 'Hard As Iron', originally recorded for *Turbo*, must have received drastic alterations, as it would not have slotted in comfortably among the hook-laden material on that album. 'Blood Red Skies' was the other highpoint, a long and sweeping epic similar to 'Victim Of Changes' and 'Beyond The Realms Of Death'. The visual imagery of 'Blood Red Skies' may have been influenced by the magnificent sunset above Halford's new home in Phoenix, located in the middle of the Arizona desert.

Despite the title, 'I'm A Rocker' was a heavy but plodding nonentity and was surprisingly resurrected on Priest's 2005 world tour. 'Johnny B. Goode' was not only a pointless cover version but the worst song on the album. 'Love You To Death', another leftover from the *Turbo* sessions, was almost entirely dispensable. The dull 'Monsters Of Rock' concluded Priest's weakest album since their debut, *Rocka Rolla,* in 1974.*

For their 1988 world tour, dubbed The Mercenaries Of Metal, Priest decided to trim down the huge production that they and many rock bands used throughout the Eighties, as Tipton told *Kerrang!*: "We've decided, for one reason or another, to go out with just a great live show and very few gimmicks – no 70-foot monsters or whatever."

Commencing on May 7, 1988 in Stockholm, Sweden, Priest's first tour after a 16-month break took in Norway, Denmark, Germany, Holland, Belgium, France, Spain, Italy and Switzerland, then returned to Germany before reaching the UK in June. Initially, the Philadelphia glam metal band Cinderella were scheduled to support on the entire European leg, but they had to pull out to resume production on their second album *Long Cold Winter*. Instead, Bonfire opened for Priest on each European date. Riding high with the release of their second album *Fireworks*, it was quite a coup for the German band as their singer Claus Lessmann confirms: "We had just finished our headline tour of Germany and then being on tour with Priest was a real big thing for us."

British fans breathed a sigh of relief when dates were announced for Priest's first UK jaunt since the end of 1983. "For me, it will be a big sentimental thrill to be back on a British stage," Halford told *Kerrang!* before the tour opened in Birmingham on June 12, playing London, Leicester, Edinburgh, Newcastle, Manchester, Newport and Sheffield.

Lessmann has fond memories of touring with the self-proclaimed Metal

---

* The 2001/02 reissue included live versions of 'Night Comes Down' and 'Bloodstone' as bonus tracks.

Gods: "They were real gentlemen . . . we were rockers and we had so much fun. They were real good colleagues and acted like gentlemen. I mean, it always happens, when you get technical problems you don't get a sound check one night, but that's no problem, we're all pros . . . It's a headliner's tour and it's your part just to support them and if they treat you good, it's no problem . . . those guys were real gentlemen."

Like previous support bands, Bonfire were not given the opportunity to perform with Priest on stage but Lessmann does remember one particular night.

Claus Lessmann: "[Bonfire] come from the south part of Germany and I think it was in Sheffield, the last show [on June 22], when we went into a costume shop and bought some Bavarian costumes that looked very, very stupid because they weren't original, they were more that carnival kind of thing . . . [Rob Halford] was singing 'Metal Gods' and we were going up stage, walking on the catwalk, and everybody in the band already saw us and [they] were laughing and the audience was laughing, but Rob didn't know what was going on. Then he turned around in all this leather stuff and looked at these Bavarian-dressed idiots onstage during the song 'Metal Gods'. Rob said something like this had never happened to him and he had so much fun . . ."

Beginning in July, a North American tour, supported by Cinderella, finished in Portland, Oregon on October 23. Despite the shows being successful and well-received, including the songs 'Sinner' and 'Beyond The Realms Of Death', which the band hadn't played in years, fans and critics were dissatisfied with the new material. In a 1989 *Kerrang! Mega Metal* feature, an unnamed journalist made some valid points: "[Judas Priest] need a major rethink, and I believe new blood is necessary in two positions: behind the mixing desk . . . and behind the drum kit." Whether or not the band took notice of this feature is not known, yet changing producers and drummers is exactly what happened . . .

In 1989, Dave Holland left Judas Priest. Al Atkins, who had gotten to know Holland well over the years, says, "I remember Dave telling me that he decided to leave them on two accounts; one being his aging mother and his sister [in Northampton] who was struggling to look after her mum with M.S. (multiple sclerosis.) The other was that after all the years he had played drums for Priest, they still wouldn't make him a member of the band and they just paid him a set wage, which really pissed him off. After a few vodkas, he would tell me some unbelievable stories, but I couldn't prove them to be true . . ."

It was also rumoured that certain band members forced him to leave because his standard drumming skills grew redundant. The band wanted to move back to the double-kick drum approach of the Les Binks-era for their next album, and Holland's style was not complex or rhythmic enough for what they had in mind.

Tipton had his own thoughts on Holland's departure, telling *Metal Hammer*: "He had a terrible year and we thought enough was enough. We parted amicably. In a way, it was good timing, because we knew we wanted to change direction slightly."

However, as Al Atkins says, "They distance themselves with all past members. It's as if they all never existed . . . Dave told me he was set up but we will never know."

Whatever the real version of events, the quest for a new drummer began while writing and rehearsing for the next album began at a Spanish studio in early 1989. K.K. Downing told *Metal Hammer*: "We are putting ideas together as individuals, at the moment . . . and then we'll go into the studio as soon as we feel they are good and ready."

Scott Travis – born September 6, 1961 in Norfolk, Virginia – got wind of Priest's need for a drummer through his former Racer X colleague, singer Jeff Martin, who was friends with Rob Halford. Travis mailed a selection of Racer X tapes to the Judas Priest management team. In the January, 1990 issue of *Metal Hammer*, Tipton said: "As you can imagine we were inundated with applicants for the job, even though we never advertised we were looking for a new drummer, word got around."

The band liked what they heard and flew Travis to southern Spain where he auditioned by playing three songs. The chemistry between Travis and the members of the band was evident from his tremendous drumming abilities alongside some demo work that was played during the audition. Halford admitted to *Metal Forces* magazine in 1990 that Travis gave the band a renewed sense of enthusiasm. Being now able to play songs such as 'Riding On the Wind' was ". . . down to Scott's ability, because Dave wasn't a double bass drummer so we couldn't do 'Exciter' . . . we are now able to play stuff that Les Binks was playing."

Travis' appointment as Priest's new drummer was officially confirmed at the start of 1990 when recording for what was to become *Painkiller* began.

"Just another 10 years and Scott can call himself a real member of Priest!" Downing jokingly told *Metal Hammer* in February, 2005. Only time would tell on the matter . . .

There was also a change in the production department. For the first time since *Unleashed In The East*, Priest dispensed with Tom Allom's services and hired Chris Tsangarides, who had been the engineer on *Sad Wings Of Destiny* back in 1976. The band were now looking to achieve a different, less lazy sound compared with the thrash bands dominating the metal scene in the States.

After rehearsing for several weeks at an old rented mill in Spain, the band decamped to Miraval Studios (surrounded by acres of vineyards) in southern France. Preparation, rehearsals and recording for the album overlapped into January before finishing up in March, 1990. A spot of recording was also completed at Wisseloord Studios in Holland, where the album was mixed. The tapes were then flown to London in the spring where they were mastered at Townhouse Studios.

The end of the decade found Judas Priest in an angry frame of mind. An absurd yet burdensome court case loomed, causing frustration and bitterness that was to make them vent their wrath in their music.

NINE

1990–1991

". . . if we'd lost the case I don't know if we'd have been able to find enough enthusiasm in our hearts to go on tour."
– Glenn Tipton speaking to *Metal Hammer* in December, 1990

DECEMBER 23, 1985. The scene: a dark church schoolyard that could have taken its eerie setting from a Hammer Horror film starring Peter Cushing. Instead of the misty Yorkshire Moors, the location was Reno, Nevada in the USA. James Vance, aged 20, and 18-year-old Raymond Belknap both had criminal records arising from behavioural and antisocial issues, with a family history of domestic violence and other seriously harmful concerns. They had dropped out of high school and drifted from job to job as a couple of loners with a disturbing fascination with guns.

After hours of getting stoned on marijuana and consuming a 12-pack of beer while continuously playing Judas Priest's 1978 album *Stained Class*, the two close friends made a suicide pact after trashing Vance's bedroom in a fit of rage; it is believed the only items that were not destroyed were the turntable and the heavy metal albums the pair regularly played. The highly intoxicated men then went to the schoolyard and shot themselves with a 12-gauge shotgun. Belknap was killed instantly but Vance lived for another three years with a severely disfigured face. Somehow the blast diverted off into another direction, ripping off part of his jaw and mouth. What was more painful? Instant death or three further years of mental and physical torture? It was a pathetic end to two wasted lives.[*]

Weeks later, at the beginning of 1986, their parents sought the advice of Reno-based attorneys Vivian Lynch and Kenneth McKenna in the belief that it was Judas Priest's music that had driven their sons to such drastic

---

[*] Vance became addicted to the medication he took and died at the Washoe Medical Center on Thanksgiving Day in 1988 after complications from the many operations he had to undergo. He fathered a child and ironically died a born-again Christian.

125

actions. They claimed that the pair were forced, or rather instructed, to kill themselves because of hidden messages in the song 'Better By You, Better Than Me'. Supposedly, phrases such as "Let's be dead" and "Do it, do it, do it" could be heard when the track was played backwards.*

In a similar case from 1984, a 19-year-old man identified only as John M. shot himself in the head and died instantly after listening to Ozzy Osbourne's 'Suicide Solution' from the *Blizzard Of Ozz* album. It was claimed that the song promoted suicide. However, the court ruled that Osbourne and his label (coincidentally CBS) were protected by the First Amendment of the Constitution, which declared freedom of speech, and the case was dismissed before going to court.†

Judas Priest received a subpoena in 1986 and, for the next three years, the families' legal wrangle against the band, CBS and Betagrance Ltd (the company that was associated with the making of *Stained Class*) simmered. In September, 1989, Reno-based Judge Jerry Carr Whitehead made a court order despite Priest and their record label's attempt to file for a motion of dismissal after the subpoena was heard in '86. Whitehead ruled that subliminal messages were an invasion of privacy. On July 17, 1990, *The New York Times* reported that Priest and CBS were being "charged in a [$6.2 million] civil suit with the liability arising from the manufacture and marketing of a faulty product, as well as negligence and intentional and reckless misconduct."

"If this had arisen in Great Britain, it would never even have got past the first few months," Halford pointed out to *Kerrang!*

During the five years prior to the trial, perhaps the most absurd rumours directed at Judas Priest from right-wing evangelical Christian politicians, American conservative groups, and the tabloid press, centred on claims that the members were Satanists and practised Satanism through their music. Of course, with a name like Judas Priest, songs such as 'Beyond The Realms Of Death, albums called *Sin After Sin* and a famous symbol nicknamed 'the devil's tuning fork', right-wing forces leapt at the chance to attack the band and their music. But as noted occult historian and writer Gavin Baddeley observed in his book *Lucifer Rising: Sin, Devil Worship & Rock 'N' Roll*, Judas Priest have no references to Satanism in their music,

---

* Hidden – or subliminal – messages referred to a type of mind control where a signal or series of words and images is unwittingly sent to the human mind below a conscious level, thus potentially affecting a person's actions without being traceable.

† Osbourne has vigorously defended his song, saying it was written as a personal tribute to AC/DC singer Bon Scott, who killed himself in 1980 after a night of heavy drinking and partying. A flow of similar lawsuits followed Osbourne throughout the Eighties.

nor did they wear crucifixes, relying almost entirely on the archetypal heavy metal image of denim and leather.

It could have been that the plaintiffs viewed the imagery on the *Sad Wings Of Destiny* sleeve and jumped to the conclusion that the band members were, indeed, devil worshippers. Thankfully, Judge Whitehead ruled against the prosecution introducing any such evidence.

The Vance and Belknap case was not the only instance of Judas Priest being associated with a grisly killing. Four months before the double suicide pact, on August 17, 1985, the bodies of an elderly Chinese couple were found drenched in blood at home in a quiet suburb near San Francisco. The man was shot dead and his wife was sexually assaulted and left to die. The gunshot wound left her paralysed for life. The attack was part of serial killer Richard Ramirez's bloodthirsty satanic rampages around California. Ramirez (dubbed 'The Night Stalker') had drawn a pentagram and other Satanic references in lipstick across the walls of the house. Next to the symbols were the words 'Jack The Knife' from Priest's song 'The Ripper' from *Sad Wings Of Destiny*.

Ramirez left an AC/DC cap at the scene of one of his crimes. Once the press got hold of the story they erroneously misquoted the AC/DC song 'Night Prowler' (from *Highway To Hell*) in subsequent articles. Ramirez was wearing an AC/DC T-shirt when he was arrested and hummed the song to his captors. By this point in the mid Eighties, AC/DC had also become heavily associated with Satanism, while ludicrous rumours circulated that AC/DC stood for 'Anti-Christ/ Devils Child' and 'Away Christ/Devil Comes'.

Dangerous outsiders such as Vance, Belknap and Ramirez interpreted Priest and AC/DC's lyrics far too literally, missing their comical attitude, irony and theatrical melodrama. In *Satanic Killings*, author Frank Moorhouse wrote, "To the ears of Ramirez, these fantasies were the heroic acts of men who lived outside the law, black-clad outlaws who scorned society and never had to face the penalties of living within. Men who were doing the Devil's work."

The Judas Priest trial began in August at Washoe County District Court. Attorney Suellen Fulstone represented the band and their record label while the complainants' team was headed by Lynch and McKenna. The fact that Judge Whitehead had agreed the case could be televised angered the band, as Tipton told Joel McIver in a 2005 *Metal Hammer* interview: "What people don't understand is that one of the boys survived, horribly disfigured . . . the boy knew that he would be on TV, facing a band that he'd always loved, in front of millions of people. And he died of a drug overdose. So I ask myself, who really killed that guy?"*

Attorney Lynch told the court that hidden messages in Judas Priest's music were the cause of Vance and Belknap's suicide pact and that the band were "meddling in the mysteries of the human mind." The pair's love of heavy metal and Judas Priest evidently "pushed them over the edge." Lynch offended and annoyed the band and everybody on their team when stating, "This was not a suicide. This was an adventure; a journey to a better place. What they planned was good, because Judas Priest said it was good." The judge ordered the band to surrender to the court the original master tapes for *Stained Class* but, because the album was recorded in 1978 for very little money, neither the band nor their management could find them.

Small protests of support were regularly held outside the court throughout the trial, and there were also autograph opportunities for fans. There was no jury during the court case but a total of 60 witnesses took the stand for the complainants, including members from Vance and Belknap's families, local police officers and computer and audio experts. Perhaps the most bizarre witness was Dr. Wilson Bryan Key, an author (*Subliminal Seduction*) and American campaigner who raised the highly controversial issue of subliminal messages back in the Seventies. Key claimed subliminal messages were hidden on Ritz crackers and in Abraham Lincoln's beard on five dollar bills, as well as in famous works of art and artefacts. He claimed that Judas Priest had taped the phrase "do it" and then reversed it into the master tape.

Priest admitted that they had previously used backward vocals but not on 'Better By You, Better Than Me'. Halford told *Kerrang!* the device was employed for 'Love Bites' off *Defenders Of The Faith* but "it's not a backward message . . . we reversed some words – to 'bites love' or something! – to get an effect." Another of Key's ludicrous assertions was that in the *Stained Class* artwork there was a hidden message containing 'sui', the first three letters of the word suicide.

Each band member attended court in smart suits and sat aloof behind their table of attorneys. In her opening statement, Fulstone said that Vance and Belknap had led "sad and miserable lives". Inevitably, with such emotionally cold upbringings and tumultuous personal histories, the tragic

* The entire court ordeal was documented by David Van Taylor in a TV film called *Dream Deceivers*.

ending to their lives occurred "long before any connection with heavy metal music."[*]

On August 24, Judge Whitehead delivered a verdict of not guilty. Both the band and their record label were cleared on all counts of causing the suicides of James Vance and Raymond Belknap. Whitehead concluded that Judas Priest's music did not carry subliminal messages. However, he understood that backward messages did exist in the songs, but that was merely down to common sound and not intentional. Neither Judas Priest nor CBS were ordered to pay any damages to either family but it cost band and label over $250,000 in legal fees. Halford told reporters after the trial's conclusion that it was important that Judas Priest stood for the American Constitution, heavy metal music and themselves, "which is rather ironic considering it was four Englishmen."

The outcome was a tremendous weight off their backs. However, the band were particularly annoyed with Suicidal Tendencies' singer Mike Muir's comments to *Metal Hammer* in 1990, claiming that the court case and everything associated with it was merely a publicity stunt that Priest had triggered after the poor sales of *Ram It Down*. Tipton wrote a lengthy letter to the magazine, which was printed in the November/December, 1990 issue. "What an idiot!" Tipton wrote. "Such illiterate comments could only come from someone desperate for attention . . ." A personal spat between both bands ensued.[†]

Painkiller was released on September 22, reaching 26 in both the UK and US. It fared less well than *Ram It Down*, staying in the charts for only a fortnight. Rather insensitively, CBS used the slogan 'Backward or forward – this album kills!' In response to the album's publicity, Halford told *Metal Hammer*: "Apart from this sad aspect, the rest of the affair was absolutely ridiculous and very stupid . . . CBS tried to make it clearer to everybody that the whole thing has to be seen with a sense of humour."

However, the critics were unanimous in their praise for what they called an earth-shattering return to form. In *Metal Hammer*, Chris Welch wrote: "This album more than makes up for the slight diversions detected in recent work and is all together better produced and more solid in its direction than *Ram It Down*." In a five-star review, *Kerrang!* declared that "*Painkiller* is a welcome return for these acknowledged masters of the genre . . ."

---

[*] In his book *Satanic Killings*, author Frank Moorhouse wrote that Americans were "all too willing to confuse 'Satanism' with parental neglect."
[†] The author endeavoured to speak to Mike Muir but he refused to be interviewed.

Painkiller began with the enormously powerful and highly charged title track. Straight away it was evident how much of a difference Scott Travis made as Priest's new drummer; the killer double-bass drum intro could not have been achieved by the lesser talents of Dave Holland. 'Hell Patrol' was a roaring slaughterhouse of riffs, which, during the Gulf War of 1990–1991, did not seem entirely irrelevant. 'All Guns Blazing' furiously screeched and wailed; Tipton and Downing's dual guitars were in fine shape, each riff and solo crystal clear. 'Leather Rebel' began with a tremendously sharp riff before all hell broke loose in a matter of seconds. 'Metal Meltdown' was Priest's noble attempt at playing thrash metal despite their age. 'Night Crawler' was lyrically superficial, but gripping nonetheless. 'Between The Hammer And The Anvil' was one of the less familiar songs on the album; no doubt the band were thinking of the looming court case when they wrote it. 'A Touch Of Evil' was a fantastically dark, gothic epic, by far one of the better songs in the Priest arsenal. 'Battle Hymn' was a short, fairly pointless instrumental piece that lead on to the powerful 'One Shot At Glory', which would not have felt out of place on either *Defenders Of The Faith* or *Screaming For Vengeance*. Rob Halford was not wide of the mark when he told *Kerrang!* in 1991: "... *Painkiller* really represents more of what I always feel Priest is about. It's very tough, very strong and powerful. There are no real weak spots on it ..."*

Priest used the album to vent their frustration at the ludicrous court case while showing off the prowess of their new drummer. While the power and sheer anger of *Painkiller* sounds unrelenting more than a decade after its release, the album has divided fans into those who feel it sacrifices Priest's traditional melodic approach, evident on albums like *Defenders Of The Faith* and *Turbo*, and those who admire its proximity to the thriving thrash metal scene. Others attacked the album for its simplistic and often daft lyrics. However, in terms of overall quality, fans were in agreement that *Painkiller* harked back to such earlier career highlights as *British Steel* and *Screaming For Vengeance*. In addition, the comic book-inspired fantasy artwork, showing the Priest symbol surrounded by a burning city, was a return to the *Sad Wings Of Destiny*-era.

Powerful promotional videos were made for 'Painkiller' and 'A Touch Of Evil'. The black and white video for 'Painkiller', directed by Wayne

---

* The 2001/02 reissue included a previously unreleased track, the brooding 'Living Bad Dreams', which slotted well into the dark and angry mood of *Painkiller*, and a live version of 'Leather Rebel'.

Isham, showed the band in true blistering form. The constant use of strobe lights reflected the song's anger. Director Julien Temple used a montage of circus characters and a factory to represent 'A Touch Of Evil'. It was mostly shot in black and white, although the splashes of colour were effective.

Such was the kudos attached to *Painkiller* that Judas Priest were nominated for their first Grammy award.

The band made their first live concert appearance with Travis on September 13 at the Concrete Foundations Forum Conference in Los Angeles. Held over a three-day period (from September 13–15), it was the third time the Forum had acted as a worldwide conference on the rock and metal scene. Other bands on the bill included Pantera, Alice In Chains and Exodus. While there, Halford gave a keynote 20-minute speech on the current heavy metal scene, his beliefs against censorship and Priest's recent court case. Halford told *Metal Hammer* shortly after the conference that he felt, "Everyone in a democratic society should have their own opinion and should be able to express themselves freely."

Despite a strong attendance of 3,000 people, only 700 fans were allowed into the ballroom at the Sheraton La Reina Hotel during each performance. Inevitably, Travis was riddled with nerves but for Priest it was an exciting moment, because it was the first time in many years that they got to play some older favourites. The 11-song set, which was broadcast on more than 200 radio stations around America, opened with 'Riding On The Wind' and included 'Grinder', 'Between The Hammer And The Anvil', 'The Green Manalishi (With The Two-Pronged Crown)' 'Bloodstone', 'Heading Out To The Highway', 'Leather Rebel', 'Painkiller', 'Living After Midnight' and the now controversial 'Better By You, Better Than Me'.

Rob Halford told *Metal Forces*: "That was just great, our first live performance with Scott. He had some sleepless nights before the first show, believe me!"

The immense Painkiller tour began in Canada on October 18 and shifted to the USA on November 1, with Testament and Megadeth as support. This time the centrepiece of the stage show (designed by Tom McPhillips) was the great futuristic creation known as the Metallion, which the band lovingly referred to as 'Metal Mickey'. The set list included older songs such as 'Beyond The Realms Of Death', 'The Ripper' and 'Victim Of Changes', which they had not played on the past few tours.

As with previous tours, Halford sported a new look (he had also successfully managed to stay teetotal for the past couple of years), shaving the whole of his head and with tattoos (of pterodactyls, the prehistoric flying reptiles) painted on both sides of his head. He told *Kerrang!*'s Mick Wall in 1991: "The head work was done after *Ram It Down*. I've always been fascinated by tattoos. From a psychological point of view it's a very deep thing to go through . . . It's very painful." Halford believed that by applying tattoos to his head and, over the next few years, the rest of his body, he was maturing and undergoing a change in his life, a spiritual transition. "There's something primordial about carrying something around on your skin for the rest of your life," he told *RAW* in 1991.

In a glowing review of the Sacramento gig on November 4, one *Kerrang!* journalist wrote: "Just be sure to buy your ticket and see it yourself. The Priest are back. For real."

The tour finished in Florida at the end of December and was a positive finale to a physically exhaustive and mentally draining year, which could have spelt the end of Judas Priest's career. Road work continued in 1991 throughout the US before a date at the massive Rock In Rio II Festival at the Maracana Stadium in Rio, Brazil on January 23, featuring Guns N' Roses, Faith No More, Billy Idol, Sepultura, Megadeth and Queensrÿche.

Tipton admitted to *Metal Hammer* shortly after the festival that they "had a lot of problems" with certain acts on the bill. "We just got on with it. We played the best we could . . . It was a shame we had a lot of restrictions imposed on us by other bands. But we'll say no more about that . . . It's nothing we had encountered before – just silliness and ego problems with other bands. We can't really understand that."

Reviewing the televised show, a *Metal Hammer* journalist wrote that Priest were "the absolute highlight of the whole festival . . . Metal Gods – without a doubt." The band then flew to Denmark to commence the European leg of the *Painkiller* tour on January 31, supported by the Canadian thrash metal band Annihilator and Pantera. The latter were on the road to promote *Cowboys From Hell*, their debut album for a major label, having released their first few albums independently. As was the case in the past, Priest scaled down their stage set for the European venues as Glenn Tipton told *Metal Hammer*: "It's got to be, because the venues in Europe will be five to six thousand seaters, whereas in America it could be up to 20,000."

An extensive European tour included some important shows in Yugoslavia and Slovenia, while a swing through Britain and Ireland included gigs in Aston Villa, Manchester, London, Newport, Sheffield, Newcastle, Edinburgh, Belfast and finally, Dublin. Reviewing the first night in Aston Villa, Birmingham, the long-standing *Kerrang!* journalist Jason Arnopp wrote: "As far as I'm concerned Metallic things don't come better than Judas Priest. They kill."

For Jeff Waters it was an honour for his "little band" Annihilator to tour with Judas Priest. Asked if the court case in Reno was still an issue during the *Painkiller* European tour, Waters says, "No, I think K.K. and I might have talked about it a bit . . . Personally, there was a lot of drinking and I don't remember half of the tour but . . . they did come out with a bit of *Screaming For Vengeance* [and] *Painkiller* anger in there, and I think a lot of that came from not just the writing and Halford's screaming but the combination of the drumming, with [Scott] Travis and an engineer mixer who did the drum sounds."

Waters couldn't help noticing the divisions between Halford and the rest of the band surfacing.

Jeff Waters: "It seemed to me that before the shows, K.K. and Tipton would always 'high five' me and be making jokes together. They were always chummy and happy with each other. Ian Hill always had a big smile on his face [drinking] his favourite red wine. Travis would be moping around like Scott Travis mopes around. But we noticed that Halford would always seem to arrive separately and leave with his bodyguard or assistant after the show, and I don't think I ever saw Halford and K.K. and Tipton together on the whole tour. It seemed like maybe he entered the stage from a different side or something, or they would always leave or come up to the venue in different cars . . . Maybe I'm reading something into that, maybe that was just part of how they'd always done it, but at that point it was something that we all wondered about. There seemed to be a separation there, but we did not see any arguments in the two or three months we did on the tour. I didn't see a single, negative thing going on with those guys and I guess that's because they were all professional enough to keep that out of the venue . . .

"K.K. was the only one I really hung out with much and we'd go party a bit . . . I can remember with Tipton, he was . . . looking after a lot of business on the *Painkiller* tour or having to deal with something [else]. I don't know what the issues were but I remember I was in the hallway in an arena somewhere and I interrupted him with a 'Hey Glenn', that kind of comment, and as he turned I realised, 'Oh shit! That was the wrong time to talk to the guy.' He shut off his stress and just smiled and said, 'Yes, Jeff, how can I help you?' I remember him being so willing to put off any of his own issues and to give a kid that loves his band the time of day. He was the busiest guy on that *Painkiller* tour. For some reason I guess it's his band in a way, his baby."

The Judas Priest/Annihilator/Pantera tour of 1991 has lived on in many people's memories. Jeff Waters: "If you can imagine what a great time that would be to see all those bands; Annihilator were on top of their game so to speak, Priest were writing *Painkiller*, and then you've got this new band [Pantera] who've just released an album in the States called *Cowboys From Hell*, and they were a force to take over the world. That was really a metal fan's dream over in Europe, and it was reflected in the fact that the tours were pulling anywhere from five [thousand] to 50,000 people. Fantastic."

Despite Priest's heavy touring schedule over the past year, Tipton still found time to play guitars on ex-topless model Sam Fox's song 'Spirit Of America', included on her 1991 album *Just One Night*. The pair became acquainted because both had homes in Spain. Fox admitted to Tipton that she was a keen rock fan and, while critics noticed that the album had a more rock-orientated approach than her previous pop output, it was commercially unsuccessful. If the Stock, Aitken and Waterman connection back in the late Eighties was too much for Priest fanatics to handle, then they were more than annoyed at this latest collaboration.

In April, Priest played three Japanese dates before a second US tour commenced in Salt Lake City on June 9. The American arena shows – not strictly part of the Painkiller world tour – were dubbed Operation Rock 'N' Roll with a bill, put together by Sony Music, consisting of co-headliner Alice Cooper and Motörhead, Metal Church and Dangerous Toys.

The tour was regarded as a disappointment in terms of ticket sales, with many empty seats. This was largely down to how the rock and metal scene had dramatically changed over the past few years. The Seattle-based grunge bands such as Mudhoney, Nirvana and Pearl Jam had all but eliminated the heavy metal and hard rock scene of the Eighties in favour of an aggressive, introspective type of alternative rock. No more make-up, leather clothes and puffy hair. Although dubbed grunge bands, Alice In Chains and Soundgarden used heavy metal influences in their approach.

However, it was not totally a rough ride for longhaired metal rockers during 1990–1992. Thrash bands like Metallica and Slayer had huge success with album sales and concert attendances; the former had the biggest album sales of their career in 1991 with the self-titled *Metallica* (often referred to as 'The Black Album'), which turned them into quite possibly the biggest band in America. Guns N' Roses and The Black Crowes also had albums high in the charts. There were also successes for what were commonly referred to as the 'old school' rock bands. Def Leppard's 1992 album *Adrenalize* was a huge hit, instigated by its lead single 'Let's Get Rocked', and after the death of Freddie Mercury in November 1991, Queen had an enormous resurgence of success. However, the Operation Rock 'N' Roll tour felt the strain.

Jason McMaster (Dangerous Toys vocalist): "The climate was not about heavy metal at all, summer 1991 was not about headbangers . . . The media and corporate music companies were all following the dollar bill and it was Pearl Jam, Nirvana and the Seattle wave that was taking it to the shopping malls. It was not very underground at all, so the fans and press were interested in asking us if the tour was failing, as the shows were not selling out and a few dates had dropped from lack of ticket sales. I would never let my guard down; I defended hard rock and metal the entire time. Music fans were being spoon-fed whatever was hot, and it may not have been 'Operation Rock 'N' Roll' that they were filling their bellies with, but that doesn't mean that it was a waste of time. A few press people thought this could be their angle on a story. That tour made thousands of rock fans very, very happy.

"I never saw anyone not having a good time or not getting along. It had to be tough for Metal Church to open at five o'clock every night – it usually started in daylight just after doors opened [at] about 5:30 pm, and that had to be hard work. Dangerous Toys [played] in between Metal Church and Motörhead. It was a lot of hard work at first – finding our legs and feeling what was happening between the audience and the drum kit was strange at first, and knowing that Motörhead fans may not enjoy what we were doing was tough to learn. Hard-core fans of certain bands are not always gonna welcome you into their home at first, if you know what I mean."

Being such a big Judas Priest fan, McMaster was grateful to have had the opportunity of hanging out with the band, yet disappointed that Priest never gave more than a passing glance to Dangerous Toys. "[Priest] were always considerate and not much more than that. It was almost like wondering if they were flying in from their homes to every show, or if they were golfing in the morning and having tea on the way to the airports . . . I never found out. They were seemingly mysterious, but more than likely just enjoying their time before they had to go to the gig."

Inevitably with two strong headliners, there was some question as to who would top the bill. "I seem to remember there being some meetings between the management of Alice and Priest," says McMaster, "but I never heard of any sort of misunderstandings. I believe that market research was done by the management, and whoever was selling the most in those markets would be the one to headline. I seem to recall Alice and Priest swapping headline slots quite a bit." As with Jeff Waters, McMaster observed that he "never saw Rob [Halford] near any other members of Priest . . . strange!"

The final show, at the CNE Grandstand, Toronto on August 19, was the last Rob Halford and Judas Priest would play together for over a decade. During the tour Halford seemed pretty content, as he told *Metal Edge* magazine: "Even on our time off we're always calling each other on the phone, making plans."

During the opening song 'Hell Bent For Leather', due to a communication breakdown between the band and their entourage, Halford miscued his Harley Davidson ride on stage at the same time that the drum riser (structured on top of steps centre stage) was in motion. Consequently, a knock to the head left him temporarily unconscious. The band continued playing while wondering what was happening. With all the dry ice and smoke, it was difficult for the band to see until Tipton almost tripped over the singer's body. Despite a painful injury, Halford continued with the show.

The seeds were being sown for Halford's resignation from one of the world's most successful heavy metal bands.

TEN

1992–1995

"I wish Painkiller *had been even harder now. I want to go real hard-core, get really, really intense from now on."*
— Rob Halford speaking to *RAW* magazine in 1991

"IT'S true we were seriously considering packing it in . . ." Rob Halford told *RAW* at the start of 1991. "I mean, I don't want to be in a band with dwindling album sales, which has to play in front of 'more select' audiences . . . So, in a way, *Painkiller* has saved Judas Priest. It seems as if we now have more than one album left in us . . ."

Painkiller was a harsh album but Halford wanted to go even harder and faster. Spending the past couple of years on the road with such thrash and hard-core metal titans as Megadeth, Annihilator, Metal Church, Testament and Pantera had convinced Halford that a change of musical direction into harsher territory was necessary — something he felt would be impossible within the secure confines of Judas Priest. He was also purportedly annoyed at the tense relationship between Tipton and Downing leading up to *Painkiller.*

Pantera invited Halford to join them on stage in California in March, 1992 as they tore through 'Grinder' and 'Metal Gods' from the *British Steel* album.* Halford and Pantera also had time to record a song called 'Light Comes Out Of Black' for the *Buffy The Vampire Slayer* movie soundtrack. "We went into the studio and eight to 12 hours later, we finished the song," Halford told *Kerrang!* in 1993. "The movie sucked, but the song was OK!"

As a further sideline, Halford found time in his schedule to work with Ugly Kid Joe on the song 'Goddamn Devil', as well as joining Skid Row onstage for a blistering version of 'Delivering The Goods' (which subsequently made their *B-Side Ourselves* collection). Such was the growing gulf

---

* It was a lifelong ambition for guitarist Dimebag Darrell, who was later killed in tragic circumstances onstage in December, 2004. Halford was among the many rock and metal artists who passed on their condolences.

between Halford and the rest of Judas Priest that the singer felt he had no other choice to make. "I did this stuff with Pantera, with Skid Row and even with Ugly Kid Joe, and it made me think," Halford confided to *Kerrang!* "It gave me a lot of confidence that I may have been lacking . . ."

Thus a total shock was delivered to fans and indeed the entire heavy metal community in September, 1992 when it was formally announced that Rob Halford, singer for Judas Priest since 1973, had left the band. It was rumoured that he had informed the other members of his decision in an unequivocal fax sent in May. However, this was contradicted in a press statement from Halford's manager John Baxter: "Regarding the split up: I confirm Rob did not send a 'fax' to his former band members. One has not been produced by either party to date – so it can be concluded that the whole thing was a mud-slinging P.R. move by Judas Priest's representatives. Prior to departing, Rob spoke with each of them often via telephone. The last conversation took place two days prior to the dissolution of the agreements. Who told whom? Well, Rob's UK attorney informed Judas Priest's UK attorney of Rob's departure over the telephone and documents were couriered the next day. Rob also spoke to Judas Priest's attorney via telephone. Given he was Judas Priest's attorney from '81 forward, Rob had a good relationship with the individual. Rob asked this attorney if he should speak with Ken, Glenn and Ian regarding the matter, but the attorney said he'd handle it. From my conversation with Ken shortly afterwards, he told me their attorney delivered the news in a very cold way. I'm saddened to this day that the communication of Rob's departure from his agreements with Judas Priest was not handled with greater care."

Whatever the true version of events, it was that Halford had left Judas Priest. Almost inevitably, a bitter feud arose between both parties that grew stronger over the next few years, with issued statements being batted back and forth between lawyers. The tense relationship and difficulties Halford and his new management team, EMAS (acquired to oversee his solo career) had with Trinifold (Priest's management) was well documented in the music press.

Halford was said to be annoyed that he was not invited to participate in Priest's 20th-anniversary video and CD, as well as the reissue operation for their entire back catalogue. On the other side of the divide the others were angry at Halford's accusations in the press following his resignation, and sought legal help regarding their publishing rights over Halford's early solo material. In a series of press statements, parts of which were printed in a 1993 issue of *RAW*, Halford declared that he needed to "protect himself from Mr. Tipton, Downing and Hill's tyrannical behaviour." While Priest railed against the "demented mumblings of our ex-vocalist Robert Halford."

Halford temporarily fronted Black Sabbath for two nights at the Pacific Amphitheatre in Costa Mesa, California, from September 12–15. He had initially asked their manager, Sharon Osbourne, for tickets to see a Sabbath show in Phoenix, his adopted home. Not much later, Osbourne rang Halford back to ask him would he like to be in the band. Ronnie James Dio, who was briefly back singing in the current Sabbath line-up, had protested against opening for Ozzy Osbourne on the latter's No More Tours tour, so Halford was approached.*

Being keen to get a young band together with an energy and vitality that could match Pantera, in November, Halford announced the formation of Fight with guitarists Brian Tilse and Russ Parish (who quit, citing musical differences after the band's first album and tour to be replaced by Mark Chaussee), bassist Jay Jay and erstwhile Priest colleague, drummer Scott Travis. "Whether we continue with Scott or not doesn't mean we'll lose contact with him," Glenn Tipton told *Kerrang!* the following year. "He's a friend, a good lad. It's really up to him. He's been caught in the middle of it . . ."

Towards the end of July, 1993, Fight made their first live appearances, playing three separate shows at The Mason Jar – a small club in Phoenix. For the first time in many years, Halford was crippled with nerves before going on stage. As if to underline his uneasiness, no cameras or recording equipment were allowed into the building and fans were thoroughly searched prior to entering the premises.

Fight's first UK mini-tour in 1993 was a disaster, with poor ticket sales that caused a gig at London's Astoria to be downscaled to the neighbouring Astoria 2 (commonly known as the Mean Fiddler.) They were also booked to play at Nottingham's modest Rock City, hardly the Birmingham NEC. Despite the poor turnouts, a *Kerrang!* writer reviewing the London gig wrote: "Halford was excellent, hitting the highs and lows with effective ease . . . just maybe, he's done the right thing after all."

Fight also played Germany, Italy, Spain, France and Holland throughout '93. Halford was obviously influenced by his brief tenure in Sabbath,

---

* Halford's professional relationship with Black Sabbath continued in the mid-Nineties when he teamed up with guitarist Tony Iommi for a series of unreleased recordings. When Ozzy Osbourne suffered bronchitis during the 2004 Ozzfest tour, Halford stepped into the breach at Camden, New Jersey, on August 26.

as the set list included 'Sweet Leaf' and 'Symptom Of The Universe'. He could not entirely turn his back on his past as roaring versions of 'Solar Angels', 'Bloodstone', 'Freewheel Burning' and 'The Green Manalishi' proved. "Priest is still very much a part of my life," Halford confessed to *Kerrang!* in 1994. "It's something I can't let go of . . ."

However, Halford was quick to point out how Fight were different. "This band plays Priest tunes in a very different way from Priest, so they take on a different flavour, anyway."

Halford came under severe criticism from some quarters of the press for his endeavours, although certain broad-minded writers admired his change of direction. In 1993 Fight released a gritty, underrated debut album, *War Of Words*, followed by a filler EP, *Mutations* (1994), and their second and final album, *A Small Deadly Space* (1995). Despite the scepticism towards Fight, Cronos (from Venom) and Fozzy's Chris Jericho count themselves as fans. "I was really excited when [*War Of Words*] was first released," says Jericho, "and I dug the Pantera-esque quality of it. 'Into The Pit' and 'Nailed To The Gun' are classics."

Jon Oliva (Savatage): "Rob's solo stuff was good and hyper-aggressive. I don't think you can really compare it to classic Priest, so I won't even try."

Michael McKeegan (Therapy?): "I thought *War Of Words* was a brilliant album. [I] even had a chance to see Fight live in America in, I think, 1994. We'd been supporting the Rollins Band across town, so when we were done we jumped a cab over to the Fight show and caught the last five or six songs – very cool, especially as the encore started with 'Freewheel Burning."

The follow-up album, *A Small Deadly Space*, was not nearly as hard-hitting or overpowering as its excellent predecessor, although it did contain the destructive opener 'I Am Alive', and the lengthy title track. The relative failure of *A Small Deadly Space* and Fight's inability to attract their own following did little to boost Halford's confidence. After a tour of the USA playing support to Metallica and Anthrax in the summer of 1995, Fight quietly disbanded, having played just 38 shows. Halford told *Classic Rock* in 2000: "I felt that we'd got as much as we could get out of Fight at that time and knocked it on the head."

Meanwhile, in 1992, the remaining Judas Priest members Glenn Tipton, K.K. Downing, Ian Hill and Scott Travis soldiered on, trying to keep the name alive despite missing a singer. During the enforced lull, a retrospective double CD was released in 1993 with an accompanying video. Neither Halford nor Travis made an appearance, although the in-depth interviews with Downing and Hill revealed interesting detail on the Al Atkins years.

The track inclusion for *Metal Works '73–'93* was debatable ("The list of songs we went through was endless . . ." Tipton informed *Kerrang!*), with some fans bemoaning the omission of 'Riding On The Wind', 'Take On The World', 'The Ripper', 'Grinder' and 'Evening Star' in favour of 'Devil's Child' and 'Solar Angels', which didn't quite pack the same punch. Tipton was adamant that certain songs deserved a second chance. "There really is such a great selection of songs that some, like 'The Rage', we feel are a bit overlooked," he told *Kerrang!* " 'Blood Red Skies' is another . . . I feel that we offer a really great combination . . ." Certainly, there was no desire to include any bonus tracks to boost sales. "There's none of that shit." Tipton curtly informed *Kerrang!* during the album's promotion, referring to the release as "the end of chapter one and the beginning of chapter two."

Metal Works '73–'93 was released in the UK on May 8, reaching number 27, staying in the charts for a sole week before disappearing into the Priest back catalogue. The album cover by Mark Wilkinson, showing the Hellion and the Painkiller matched against each other in a duel, was a brilliant montage of characters, including the dreaded Metallion, from previous albums.

To promote the album a series of rock nights was held at various clubs in the UK with competitions and giveaways, but these didn't really help the album's sales.

After Halford's departure, it seemed that Tipton was now the directional force within the band. However, the long period of inactivity proved frustrating for the guitarist, who hatched plans for a solo album. K.K. Downing was less than enthused at the prospect, as he told the author in an interview for *Fireworks Melodic Rock* in 2006: "I always thought that, 'Well, if I did a solo wouldn't it sound just like Judas Priest?' And if it did wouldn't that probably be wasting a lot of good material? People would much prefer good songs played by the original band. So many people tried it, didn't they? And it didn't work at all."

Tipton told the author that "back in 1994/5 there was no Judas Priest as such and it didn't look as though there was going to be. I just started to write a bunch of songs." Tipton initially laid down some tracks in Wales with drummer Cozy Powell and Who bassist John Entwistle for Atlantic Records. However, with the young rock audience still hungry for grunge bands, the label thought the songs were out of touch. "I was undoubtedly disappointed at that point in time that they felt the line-up was a bit old school," Tipton said. "It was pretty harsh out there at the time."

Consequently, on the orders of his label, Tipton was flown to LA to work with some of the best young rock musicians southern California had to offer, such as Billy Sheehan, Shannon Larkin, C.J. DeVillar, Brooks Wackerman and future Metallica bassist Robert Trujillo. "They kept me on my toes and there was a lot of mutual respect," Tipton recalled. "They were great sessions and a lot came out of it."

The end product was Tipton's debut solo album *Baptizm Of Fire*.* The original idea to blend songs from both sessions didn't work, as Tipton explained to the author: "*Baptizm Of Fire* was more of a solo album while the Tipton, Entwistle and Powell songs were more of a band album." The Tipton-Powell-Entwistle sessions eventually came out under the title *Edge Of The World*. Sadly, neither of Tipton's cohorts lived to see the release of the album. On April 5, 1998, Powell perished in a horrific car accident, while on June 27, 2002, Entwistle died of a heart attack (caused by an unspecified amount of cocaine) in a room at the Hard Rock Hotel and Casino in Las Vegas. Speaking about Powell in 2006, Tipton told the author (for *Fireworks Melodic Rock*): "I just find it so difficult to believe he's still not around. He was a great person and a great drummer." The guitarist also praised Entwistle's talents: "He just proved to be a master of the bass guitar in every way. He was so in touch with his equipment and his techniques. He could play any sort of bass playing; he just blew me away really. I wasn't ready for the amount of talent he had."

Both *Baptizm Of Fire* and *Edge Of The World* were unimaginative, average rock albums, and were far less interesting than any of Halford's solo albums. The idea of a Tipton solo tour or any other musical endeavour was put on hold. "While Priest is in operation I would never ever contemplate going out on a solo level," the guitarist explained. "Solo albums are funny things, you've gotta do them for the right reasons. I did mine at a time when there was no Judas Priest but, in the future, if there is a big lull in Priest activities or if we retire, I would love to go out with guys like Rob Trujillo and Shannon Larkin."

In January, 1995 it was officially announced that Judas Priest were looking for a new singer.

---

* The album was not released until 1997 because recording sessions were interrupted when Priest's activities recommenced.

PART 4

VICTIM OF CHANGES: THE RIPPER YEARS

A publicity shot of Judas Priest Mark VII circa 1975-76. They still hadn't created their classic leather and studs image; left to right: Ian Hill, K.K. Downing, Rob Halford, Glenn Tipton and Alan Moore. (GERED MANKOWITZ)

Judas Priest Mark VII in the mid-seventies. Alan Moore left the band in 1976 for the second and final time. Left to right: Rob Halford, Alan Moore, Ian Hill, Glenn Tipton and K.K. Downing. (GERED MANKOWITZ)

Rob Halford in his famous black silver-studded outfit complete with bull-whip and bikers cap, circa 1978.
(FIN COSTELLO/REDFERNS)

The Mark IX line-up in the late seventies; left to right: Rob Halford, K.K. Downing, Glenn Tipton, Les Binks and Ian Hill.
(JILL FURMANOVSKY)

A very camp Judas Priest in 1977-1979 with Les Binks, Glenn Tipton, Rob Halford, Ian Hill and K.K. Downing.
(ADRIAN BOOT/RETNA)

Judas Priest on *Top Of The Pops* performing 'Take On The World' on 25th January 1979.
Drummer Les Binks left the band mid-1979 prior to the second leg of their US tour. **(LFI)**

Rob Halford and Glenn Tipton on stage in 1978/9.
By then their leather and studs image was in full force.
(KEVIN CUMMINS)

K.K. Downing playing one of his lethal
riffs in the late 1970s. **(LFI)**

Rob Halford in his full heavy metal stage gear outside and inside his house in Walsall from around 1980. (ROSS HALFIN)

Cause for celebration, left to right: Ian Hill, Dave Holland, Glenn Tipton and Rob Halford. (ROSS HALFIN)

K.K. Downing and Ian Hill backstage in the early eighties. (ROSS HALFIN)

Judas Priest on roller skates in New York's Central Park in late 1979. This was Dave Holland's first tour with the band and Priest's second US tour of 1979; left to right: Glenn Tipton, K.K. Downing, Dave Holland, Rob Halford and Ian Hill. (MICHAEL PUTLAND/RETNA)

In the early eighties, Rob Halford's traded in his world-famous Harley Davidson for a low-cost bicycle. (ROSS HALFIN)

Judas Priest in their early eighties heyday, when they were dominating arenas all over America; left to right: Dave Holland, K.K. Downing, Ian Hill, Glenn Tipton and Rob Halford. (EBET ROBERTS/REDFERNS)

ELEVEN

1996–2000

"My preference is to continue with Priest. If that's not to be, then I'm not going to lie down and die . . . my life has been Judas Priest."

– Glenn Tipton speaking to *Kerrang!*, 1993

BY the start of 1996, Judas Priest had received over one thousand audition tapes from various vocalists, including former Accept singer David Reece. Another candidate was Gamma Ray singer Ralf Scheepers. Despite his ambitions to front a new version of Priest, Scheepers was reluctant about the band's decision to continue with a new singer.

Ralf Scheepers: "I had mixed feelings and, to be honest, I just wrote my application because I was curious as to what would happen . . . I wrote my application in a short letter to the personal management of Judas Priest when I was still in Gamma Ray back in 1992. I never expected to get any answer! I was surprised when the first letter came in saying that they liked my voice and they wanted to see a video of me . . .

"The thing is that the relationship with Gamma Ray was not that good any more, as other members had started to sing their own songs in the studio, so I thought they don't really want to have a vocalist any more . . . all in all it was just waiting, waiting and waiting, but at last I received a positive answer from the management . . . along the lines of, 'The band have heard your material and were impressed . . . I promise that you will be invited for an audition . . .' That really gave me a good feeling! After waiting more than two years due to other activities of the Priest members, such as Glenn's solo album, etc., somehow I had the feeling that nothing would happen in the end . . . Then totally out of the blue a letter came saying that they were very sorry to inform me that they had found their man, but still appreciated my vocal abilities as I was one of the final 10 singers on their short list."

Scheepers, who went on to form his current band Primal Fear, occasionally crossed paths with Judas Priest. "I met the band on the *Jugulator* tour when they played in Stuttgart several years ago, and they invited me for a meet and greet. Glenn and K.K. spoke about the audition thing with me and I was really happy and had a great feeling afterwards. We met again several times as we played the same festivals here and there, and we always had good talks when we found some time to see each other . . ."

Combing through the rest of the audition tapes, the band and their management spent hours trying to find a singer that could equal or better Halford's prowess while not necessarily looking the same. Scott Travis happened to be given a videotape by his then girlfriend of a Judas Priest tribute band called British Steel, fronted by a young, bulky mid-Westerner named Timothy Owens, filmed at a small club in 1995. The fans who shot the video purportedly told Owens after the gig that they would get the tape to Priest because they knew Travis. Owens shrugged it off as a nice but implausible gesture.

Having already seen British Steel play live in his home state, Travis was reluctant to watch the video at first, because Judas Priest were not looking for a Halford-type character but an original singer with a more modern approach. However, Travis gave in to the persistence of his girlfriend. The drummer was sufficiently knocked out by how good Owens was and immediately contacted the rest of the band. Travis took the tape with him to England in February, 1996 and showed it to Tipton, Downing and Hill, who were at Rockfield Studios poring over the hundreds of audition tapes they had received.

Tim Owens: "It was almost like a year later, they'd given the tape to Scott. He was going back to England to work on some stuff and, you know, they were gonna look at some singers and he happened to bring that tape with him, so it was pretty cool."

Like Travis, the other band members could not believe how good Owens was. "We were totally amazed," Downing told *Metal Edge* in '96. "This guy had every quality and more of a young, strong Rob Halford . . . He's as good as if not better than Rob Halford." Priest's management immediately contacted Owens to validate who he was and to ask him if he had an up-to-date passport. "First they called and said Judas Priest is wanting to get hold of you," Owens recollected. "So then Jayne Andrews called me from Priest management – their co-ordinator or whatever her title is. She said, 'We'd like to have a meeting with you.' I thought, 'Wow! This is pretty amazing, man.' "

Owens was flown to England in February, 1996 for a live audition, just

146

two days after the band saw the tape. A new phase in Judas Priest's career was about to begin . . .

Timothy Steven Owens was born at Barberton Hospital in Akron, Ohio on September 13, 1967. Until joining Judas Priest, he had never been a fully professional singer, moving in and out of such mundane jobs as a door-to-door salesman selling office supplies, and a purchasing agent for a local law firm. Owens' father Troy had a warehouse job and his mother Sherri ran her own, home-based babysitting service.

As well as the Priest tribute act British Steel, Owens had previously sung in a number of amateur bands like Brainicide (originally called Dammage Inc.), US Metal, Alternation, Trust Of Fate, Seattle (obviously influenced by the Seattle grunge bands of the early Nineties) and, most popularly, Winters Bane.

Despite the notoriety British Steel achieved after Owens' rise to metal fame, the band was not intended as a long-term project. "It might have lasted a year," says Owens. "I'm not that certain on it. You know, it was basically done because of the band, Winters Bane, I was in. We were trying to make it . . . to play shows, and a promoter said the only way we really could do it was to make the band British Steel.

"[British Steel] was fun at first but you know everything loses speed . . . We didn't sound very good at the end. I didn't really want to do it in the first place. It just so happened that when people heard the Winters Bane record, they thought, 'You sing like Judas Priest – you sound like Rob Halford.' That was my favourite band so we did it . . . and at the end, no one was any good in the band, even myself. So I think that was the big thing with doing that band, but then Winters Bane started going sour and so did British Steel, so I left to do other stuff."

Upon arriving in England for the first time, Owens was greeted by Priest's management co-ordinator, Jayne Andrews. "Jayne picked me up and we drove to Wales . . . to practise. The band were [at Rockfield] at the time and it was pretty amazing walking in and seeing those guys. I walked in and saw Ian [Hill] first and it was like, 'Wow! This is pretty amazing.'"

Inevitably, Owens was nervous at the prospect of singing in front of his heroes in an unfamiliar country, but he relished the challenge. "You know, the funny thing is that I didn't think I was going to have to do anything. I mean they were like, 'We want to meet with you . . . we don't know if you have to sing yet.' So I really wasn't knowing if I was gonna have to sing. One of the first things they said when I got off the plane was, 'We're gonna get you ready and we're gonna do this tomorrow.' And I just looked at them and said, 'So let's do it now' . . . that's how it was. That was very odd, you know. I probably hadn't sung a Judas Priest song for a year up to that point . . . talk about someone not being ready and prepared!"

After a good night's sleep to get over his jet lag, Owens was eager to begin. He was first asked to sing 'Victim Of Changes'.

Tim Owens: "It was just like the story goes – I sang the first line and Glenn said, 'OK, you've got the gig.' I was pretty amazed really, I couldn't believe it. And he's like, 'No, go ahead and sing the rest of the song, I was kidding.' I'm thinking I could quite possibly be the fastest person to make a band and the fastest person to get fired. So it was pretty funny, but I had to do it and sing the rest . . . I said, 'Can I sing another one?' So I sang 'The Ripper' and that's how I got the nickname 'The Ripper' . . . Glenn just started calling me 'The Ripper' as did Ken. I went into a room and they said, 'Listen, you made it, but you can't tell anybody. You can tell your parents and your family but you can't tell anybody else,' so it was kind of a long plane ride home. I waited to tell them till I got home . . . so it was a pretty exciting moment. It was life changing and the thing was that it came out of nowhere; it wasn't something I'd aspired to and I didn't even send them a demo."

For a young man from Ohio, who was one minute fronting a little-known tribute band and the next, actually becoming the real singer in the real Judas Priest, it must have seemed little short of surreal.

Coincidentally, Priest's old rivals Iron Maiden had a new singer after their popular frontman Bruce Dickinson had left to pursue a solo career. Blaze Bayley, formally of the Midlands band Wolfsbane, fronted Maiden from 1994 to 1999. Whereas Priest were not too concerned about the nationality of their new singer, Maiden bassist and main man Steve Harris was adamant that he wanted somebody British as Dickinson's replacement. Similarly to Halford, Dickinson had grown distanced from the rest of the band. Also, similarly to Halford, his solo albums were of varying quality. Fans and critics were displeased with the two albums Bayley and Maiden created together but they fared a lot better, commercially, than the two studio albums Priest made with Owens.

Tim Owens: "The thing was, I think the guys in Priest had picked a singer that could . . . match Halford's vocals . . . I think that's what they wanted to do. I don't have to be somebody else to sing Judas Priest, but I still have to explain to people that's why they picked me. I think the tribute band thing was a curse at times because you have to explain it, but I think the point of that was that I could sing it and that was the difference."

Owens' rise from school choirboy to an international heavy metal star was chronicled in Andrew C. Revkin's *New York Times* article ('Metalhead becomes Metal God: Judas Priest fan is elevated to lead vocalist'), published in 1997. This eventually formed the basis for a mediocre Hollywood movie, *Rock Star* (originally called *Metal God*) in 2001, starring Mark Wahlberg (ironically, Wahlberg was a former rap star) and *Friends* actress Jennifer Aniston. The film centred on a fictional band named Steel Dragon. The role of the lead singer was played by actor Jason Flemyng, but his voice was dubbed by Soto and Michael Matijevic. A number of real-life rock stars took part in bringing the music of Steel Dragon to life in the film, namely Jeff Scott Soto, Zakk Wylde, Jeff Pilson and Jason Bonham, among other less famous names.

Initially, Priest were involved in the making of the film, offering supervision on the story and soundtrack. However, after a series of arguments ensued, the band walked away from the project. "*Rock Star* was a good idea, but it turned out to be a fucking bunch of crap," Tim Owens told *Classic Rock* in 2004. "The songs were terrible and so was the singing. Ugh!"

Owens was aghast that Priest did not receive the same degree of attention that other metal bands enjoyed in certain circles.

Tim Owens: "I really don't know about the album sales. I would think in the States Priest have sold more than Iron Maiden, I don't know. I'm not real sure on that. I've always said that, to me, and I'm not talking about my era with Judas Priest, I'm talking about Judas Priest in the Eighties when they were at their best, they were always underrated."

The appointment of Judas Priest's new singer was announced to the music press in May, 1996. At the same time, Priest parted company with Sony Music, whom they had been with since 1976, and formed their own Priest Music Ltd, which allowed them full control over distribution.

"We negotiated our deal with Columbia/Sony, with whom we haven't had a good relationship for many years, to be honest," Downing informed *Metal Edge* at the time of negotiations in 1996. "We haven't been happy and we want a better relationship with a new label."

In Europe, Priest eventually signed with the revered German metal label SPV in 1996 and, in the US, with CMC International. Work began on a new album almost straight away. Recorded at Silvermere Studios in Wisley, Surrey and mastered at Whitfield Street Studios, *Jugulator* was conceived during 1996 and the first half of '97 with Tipton, Downing and Sean Lynch handling production.

Tim Owens: "I made it [into the band] February 6, I think [and] we rehearsed in May. I think it was somewhere there. I worked on 'Burn In Hell' and I think 'Bullet Train' and maybe some of 'Death Row' . . . I wanted to do good. I wanted to get it, so I was pretty hard on myself. I mean that was the thing – you wanted to prove to them that you could do it.

"I really didn't write much and, if I ever did, they wouldn't have listened. There were times when they wanted me to pronounce words a different way than I would have usually pronounced them, and I respected that. I respected Glenn and Ken and the guys. [They] knew that I'd just slowly move in on it."

Around this time, former Judas Priest lead singer and co-founder Al Atkins recorded his album *Victim Of Changes*. Needless to say, Trinifold, Priest's management company, were not pleased. "They just said I couldn't use the Judas Priest name on the sleeve," Atkins explained.

Some viewed the album as a cynical cash-in, especially as Judas Priest were gearing up for the release of a new album themselves. As a cheeky response to Trinifold's displeasure and the lukewarm reception to *Victim Of Changes*, Atkins toyed with the idea of touring as the 'Judicator'. "This was just one name flying around when Dave Holland and myself got together," says Atkins. "Another was Steel Force, but we went for just Atkins/Holland in the end . . ."

The metal scene had changed dramatically since the last Judas Priest album in 1991. After Kurt Cobain's suicide in 1994, the impact of grunge music had subsided, with post-grunge metal bands like Korn and System Of A Down beginning to make waves in the mid- to late-Nineties with their distinctive and imaginative fusion of alternative rock with old school metal influences derived from such titans as Maiden and Priest. Nu-metal (a fusion of rap and metal) became mainstream with Papa Roach, Linkin Park and Limp Bizkit at the forefront. Yet these bands and their ilk became over-exposed and struggled to find an enduring audience after the era came to a standstill after just a few years of mainstream popularity.

Released on October 16, 1997, *Jugulator* was hailed by some critics and fans as a robust comeback, although others claimed that it was as uncreative and unimaginative as 1988's *Ram It Down*. In terms of quality and units, *Jugulator* was eclipsed by Columbia's collection *Living After Midnight: The Best Of Judas Priest*, released around the same time, which chronicled the band's career from the late Seventies to *Painkiller* in 1990.

Jugulator did not reach the UK Top 40, although it just about entered the *Billboard* chart, making it to 82. At the time it was suggested that *Jugulator* sold a poor 40,000 units in the US; certainly the sales were weaker compared with previous efforts, despite a major promotional tour. "We have never done this much publicity before the release of an album," Downing told *Hard Roxx* magazine at the time of its release. *Jugulator* achieved some degree of commercial success in other territories, making the Top 20 chart in Germany and Japan.

The rather ludicrous sleeve illustrated a new breed of monster to join the ranks of the Metallion, the Hellion and the Painkiller. K.K. Downing told *Hard Roxx*: "Anybody who knows Priest and Priest history will know that over the years we have adhered ourselves to the archetypal heavy metal imagery that goes with the music . . . The Jugulator himself is a character who lives inside a volcano and comes out at night to prey on everything that moves, ripping their throats out . . ."

Jugulator began with the throat-ripping title track, featuring brutal guitars and powerful vocals so hard and heavy they could have been made at a Black Country steel factory. Yet it lacked a melody. 'Blood Stained' was an improvement, with an arena-chanting chorus and Downing and Tipton's infectious dual guitars, although Owens' vocals felt forced. 'Dead Meat' contained lyrics that could have been written better by a college student. 'Death Row' was an average metal song, which did not begin as eerily as intended thanks to Tipton's comical spoken intro. Like 'Blood Stained' it had a chest-beating chorus that went down well with the fans who saw the band on tour at the time. 'Decapitate' was led by firm guitars and steady, robust drums, but any initial feeling of excitement failed to ignite. 'Burn In Hell', one of the better songs, was wisely included in the band's live act. A steady build-up led to all hell breaking loose with fiery guitars, pounding drums and sinister vocals. Similar to its predecessors, 'Brain Dead' was cliché-ridden and, appropriately enough, brain dead; it was devoid of any melody, excitement and the usual Priest traits.

'Abductors' showed Owens' awesome vocal capability with some truly harsh tones and plenty of energy, but again the lyrics were absolute nonsense. 'Bullet Train' was a modern slice of power metal that would not have seemed out of place on *Painkiller*. The epic closer, 'Cathedral Spires', has often been compared with the equally underrated and ignored 'Blood Red Skies'. Chris Jericho of Fozzy rated the song very highly, saying " 'Cathedral Spires' is in my top 10 Priest songs of all time."

With *Jugulator*, Priest succeeded in making a darker, heavier album than *Painkiller*. However, upon listening, enthusiasm for a new version of Judas Priest quickly waned. The problem was they had lost their flair for melodic riffs, and Tipton and Downing's ridiculously lame B-grade lyrics only made staunch fans pine for Halford's introspective observations.

'Bullet Train' was released as an exclusive promotional-only single and was nominated for a prestigious Grammy award in the 'Best Metal Performance' category, which would prove to be Owens' proudest memory from his tenure in Judas Priest. "I've got so many [memories] really but I think that, probably, being nominated for a Grammy in America and going to the Grammys was the best," he says. "It was an amazing time . . ."

A promotional video for 'Burn In Hell' was also made, although the song was not released as a single. " 'Burn In Hell' was tough . . ." Owens recalls, "long and hot and my first video shoot . . . tough, over and over and over . . . flames in front of me . . . It was a lot harder than I thought it would be. The video was amazing though."

Jugulator failed to match Halford-era Priest at their best (*Defenders Of The Faith*, *Screaming For Vengeance*) or worst (*Rocka Rolla*, *Ram It Down*). Some saw it as a reaction to Halford's Pantera-influenced Fight albums. "Maybe [Halford] thought the Priest thing wasn't heavy enough – hence *Jugulator*!" Downing told *Record Collector* in May, 2005.

Although Owens and Halford could both hit high notes with consummate ease, Halford was much more credible, feeling as comfortable singing a ballad as any type of metal song. The question posed was: maybe the band had not picked the right singer after all? Owens is humble enough to state that if Halford had still been in Judas Priest, the album would have sounded entirely different.

If *Jugulator* did not please some fans, then the host of Judas Priest tribute albums from the mid-Nineties onwards certainly did. The band themselves were keen to hear these offerings, and it was claimed that Rob Halford recorded a contribution with Phoenix-based metal band Sacred Reich for one particular album but it was declined for inclusion, allegedly due to hostility between Halford and his ex-colleagues. The first tribute album – 1997's *A Tribute To Judas Priest: Legends Of Metal* – featured Testament, Helloween, Mercyful Fate, Fair Warning, Overkill and Iced Earth. Several similar albums have since followed, and even Fifties American crooner Pat Boone paid his own special tribute by recording a laid-back version of 'You've Got Another Thing Comin'' on his 1997 heavy metal covers album *In A Metal Mood: No More Mr. Nice Guy*.

The new-look Judas Priest started touring in the USA on January 30, 1998, finishing on March 2 with support from Motörhead. Unlike Blaze Bayley, who could not cope with Iron Maiden's strenuous touring schedule, which ultimately led to his departure, Owens proved he had the physical and vocal muscle to survive the rigours of life on the road.

Tim Owens: "It was great, man, it was unbelievable! We always had good tours and we always had fun, and I think that was the big thing about us, that we all got along and had fun. Even from the start they made me feel like I'd known them forever, even though their posters were on my wall. We became really good friends, the tour was great, and really the crowd was very accepting. I know people might not have wanted to accept me but, once I started singing and we started playing, we would win them over and there'd be chants of 'Ripper' out in the crowd. As a matter of fact the first place I got a good 'Ripper' chant was in London. So it was kind of a cool experience that the place I was worried of playing the most was the first one that gave me the biggest 'Ripper' chant."

After a couple of months on the road in the US, Priest flew to Europe with guests Gorefest, the death metal band from Holland. "They were much heavier but I enjoyed them a lot actually," Owens says.

Gorefest guitarist Frank Harthoorn: "I think we just made them an offer, and [we] were one of four or five acts they were considering. Being on the same label probably helped out, but Priest have always taken really heavy bands on tour with them, such as Slayer or Pantera. They're definitely not afraid of a challenge, though in their case, they don't need to be anyway. We did the whole European leg of the Jugulator tour with Priest. This was actually one of only two times we've ever played in the UK, and we were pretty nervous about the [London] Astoria gig especially. Turned out we had one of our best nights there. We always thought the UK hated us, and maybe they did, but if so the crowd certainly didn't show it."

By the end of the tour, Harthoorn was pleased with the way his band was treated by Judas Priest: "I think we were treated fine, yeah. As long as you know that, as a support act, you will be restricted in lights and sound, and you can live with that, then there's really no problem. We had the benefits of playing to their audience, which is much larger than we would ever pull ourselves. I'd say that's a fair trade."

Unlike previous support bands, the guys in Gorefest did not socialise with the headliners. Frank Harthoorn: "We always kept a respectful distance between ourselves and them – in fact, we were advised to do so by certain people in their entourage. Not that that mattered much, these are some of my all-time metal heroes, I don't want to bore them with my drunken behaviour . . . Ripper was the guy who always dropped by to say hello and have a drink. I think even he was a little intimidated by being in this band, so every other evening he snuck out and joined us for a slightly less glamorous beer. Top fella, really friendly, and loving his music."

It was certainly a great opportunity for Gorefest to catch Priest in action. "As much as I could," says Harthoorn. "Like every band, they had their on and off nights. When they're off, they're still pretty good, but when they're on, they really become this huge metal machine. It's a wonderful thing to watch, and with most of these songs, you just can't go wrong, can you?"

Beginning on March 18 in Germany, Priest played a few dates in Eastern Europe in Poland, Slovakia and the Czech Republic, before the European tour finished in Portugal on April 28. Only two dates were played in the UK, one at the London Astoria on April 11 and the second at Wolverhampton Civic Hall the following night. In a way, the weak ticket sales were a reflection of the apathy towards the *Jugulator* album in Britain. The band toured Japan in May and played a couple of dates in Mexico on September 17 and 19 before a second American tour in September and October with Megadeth as support. The tour resulted in a terrific live album, *'98 Live Meltdown*, which hardly made an impact in the charts not like *Unleashed In The East* and *Priest . . . Live!* However, the sheer power of Owens' vocals and the band themselves was incredible, and the set list was well-chosen, with old classics such as 'The Ripper', 'The Sentinel' and 'Grinder' rubbing shoulders with the newer songs. 'Rapid Fire' was particularly dynamic and proved that Owens could give Rob Halford a run for his money in terms of live performances.

Meanwhile, Halford's solo career had indefinitely stalled. At the end of 1997, he told Gerri Miller, the former editor at *Metal Edge*, that "metal is dead and I am done with it."

Obviously this came as a major shock to heavy metal fans. "I think I didn't express myself quite clearly then," he reflected to *Rock Hard* in April, 2000. "What I meant – and I pointed that out a little later – was that in the metal genre, big changes aren't possible. Classic metal had defined itself in the Seventies and Eighties and I didn't see any outstanding new bands. Look at the bands on the cover of your magazine: Metallica, Thin Lizzy, Running Wild, all bands that have existed for many years. Of course metal isn't really dead, I'm not so stupid that I would really claim something like that, but I don't expect in the near future some mega-bands will appear. And I can't imagine that a young musician will create something really new out of the old influences, which has the same musical meaning. Maybe I'm wrong and there is somewhere a 16-year-old new Randy Rhoads genius who proves me to be wrong. I hope so. I wish nothing more than to see the new Sabbath, Priest, Maiden or Metallica – a bunch of kids who blow everything away – very young bands who have the characteristics of classic metal in them."

The "metal is dead" quote continued to haunt Halford. "I tried to fudge my way out of that by saying, 'I didn't really mean that,'" he told *Launch* in August, 2000. "What I meant was the metal where I came from, bands like Priest and stuff, there's no more bands like that. When in reality, there are bands of that ilk from Europe. I think that just went to prove my emotional state of mind at that time. I remember I was sitting on the bus with Gerri Miller, I was just so frustrated and not settled, and I made that ridiculous statement that metal is dead, which is a fucking stupid thing to do.

"I've been confronted all over Europe by that statement, and I've just been making amends by saying that I was off my John Rocker. It was a stupid thing to say, and you've got to be able to admit your mistakes, and that was a big mistake on my part. Metal fans are extremely loyal, devoted people, and if you rub them up the wrong way, like I did, you've got to step up to the plate and put your hands up and go, 'I'm sorry.'"

Despite the anger of his feelings about contemporary metal, Halford had begun a series of writing sessions with producer Bob Marlette and Marilyn Manson guitarist John Lowery (a.k.a. John 5.) It was during the mid-Nineties and through a chance meeting with Trent Reznor of Nine Inch Nails at a bar in New Orleans that those songs changed direction, from their early rock-orientated demos to something entirely different. With Reznor credited as executive producer, the industrial metal album *Voyeurs* by Two – as the Reznor/Halford project was called – came out in the UK in March, 1998 on Reznor's Nothing Records label. "It was that one-off moment to work with a genius like Trent Reznor." Halford told *Classic Rock* in 2000. "I knew it was really going to set people off."

Voyeurs was greeted with apathy by the metal press and hard-core Halford fans. While it sounded interesting on first hearing, it quickly grew tiresome. Aside from the odd track such as the opening songs 'I Am A Pig' (for which gay porn filmmaker Chi Chi LaRue directed a promotional video) and 'Stutter Kiss', the rest of the album was difficult to enjoy, because the distinctive Halford vocal traits and twin-guitar attacks of Judas Priest were absent.

Yet other metal musicians were able to appreciate the album in a different light. Jeff Waters (Annihilator): "It's just not what you would expect.

155

Well, I can sort of see why somebody would want to like Two . . . There were some critics, if I remember, back then that said [Halford] left Priest to try and get his creativity out and to do something different, which makes sense, and anybody would want to do that after years in a band. Even to step out for a day or a week or a year to try something different would be fun or refreshing . . . But I remember a lot of critics saying he's jumping on the bandwagon of the music that's happening now with Nine Inch Nails and Marilyn Manson and all that stuff. And I thought, well, I have to step back and listen to it because if I myself had stepped out of this Annihilator thing and did something totally different, I'd want somebody to give it a chance, and I did and thought, 'Well, oh yeah, it's pretty good for what it is.' If you don't think about Judas Priest, it's pretty good."

Perhaps of more interest to fans than the album was an interview Halford gave in February, 1998 on the MTV show *Superrock*. Aside from talking about the Two project, he let slip that he was gay. "It was very unplanned and spontaneous," Halford told *Classic Rock* in 2000. "It wasn't calculated . . . It came out of my mouth on MTV in New York and was very unplanned."

The news was hardly a major shock to the metal world, who had a fair idea as to Halford's sexuality through his lyrics and image. It was just a matter of wondering if he would ever 'come out'. Halford also admitted in an interview with American gay and lesbian newspaper, *The Advocate*, in May '98, that the other Priest members knew about his homosexuality but it was always his decision to tell the public and not theirs.

"If I hadn't have left Judas Priest, I wouldn't have done it," he confessed to *Classic Rock*'s Geoff Barton in a 2004 interview. "I wouldn't have said I was gay. It would have been wrong."

In the interviews that followed the *Superrock* show, Halford never shied away from speaking about his sexuality. His spur-of-the-moment admission could have seriously damaged his career, although at that point his popularity could not have gotten any lower. Nevertheless, in the macho world of heavy metal, where virility and potency with the opposite sex were regarded as vital, it came as a surprise to some that a heavy metal star was gay. "You could lose a record deal, a fan base. It's really difficult for any musician to come out," Halford confirmed to *The Advocate*.

Tim Owens: "Well, there was always a bit of a rumour back then [about Halford]. To me, I was younger so I didn't look [at Priest] and think 'Umm, they're gay.' It just wasn't leather and spikes to me . . . In hindsight, I look back at all of Rob's outfits and think, 'Maybe he is gay' but I didn't think that then at all. It was the music that attracted me to them. When it came out that Rob was gay and they were really talking about it . . . the record sales weren't really that big anyway, in all honesty. If he had come out in 1982, I don't really know what would have happened."

Owens has a point – the most notable example being Queen. Freddie Mercury never publicly admitted he was gay but when Queen made a disco-orientated rock album in 1982 called *Hot Space*, fans in America quickly caught on. In the video to 'Body Language', Mercury's campness was on full display. Consequently, Queen lost popularity in the States. Halford was fortunate in choosing a more enlightened age to express his sexuality.

After a short break to rest from their world tour, in 1999, Judas Priest returned to Silvermere Studios in Surrey to write and record material for what became *Demolition*. Some recording also took place at Riverside Studios, with Glenn Tipton as the main producer and arranger of the entire album. As with *Jugulator*, Sean Lynch co-produced.

The making of *Demolition* took longer than usual and rumours persisted that Owens disagreed with the others over the songwriting. As it stood, Owens was not permitted to submit any material as the songwriting was exclusively tied up between Tipton and Downing, although, surprisingly, Chris Tsangarides received a songwriting credit with Tipton on 'Subterfuge', and Travis (his first songwriting credit on a Priest album) with Tipton on 'Cyberface'.

Jeff Waters: "I think when you're plucking out a new singer who doesn't have a lot of experience in writing songs, and all of a sudden you have to come up with a new Judas Priest album, Tipton was right to take over the reins and say, 'OK, I'm going to direct you through this.' He's like the director of the band, I'd say. At the same time, I can see it from a different angle because I'm in a band where I'm sort of the leader, and I can see why somebody needs to take a little bit more [control]."

Despite any differences, Owens is insistent that he much preferred the recording of *Demolition* to that of its predecessor. "I really didn't [contribute] much," he says, "I respected that and I respected Glenn and Ken."

Priest were announced on the Ozzfest bill for the summer of 1999, but at the time they were busy working on new material while having intense negotiations with Atlantic Records. A summer 2000 US arena tour (with Nazareth and the Scorpions in support) was also cancelled, with the band claiming they needed more time to work on the album.

Not only were there stories circulating that Owens was considering leaving Judas Priest over songwriting credits but rumours were rife that Travis had permanently returned to Racer X after being dissatisfied with the overlong delay in recording *Demolition*. It seemed that all was not well in the band . . .

TWELVE

2001–2002

"I wish we did more with videos and touring . . . well, just more of everything, actually . . . I knew Rob was gonna come back eventually anyway."

— Tim Owens speaking to the author in 2006

*D*EMOLITION was finally released in the UK on July 16, 2001 to unenthusiastic reviews and low sales, with only approximately 100,000 copies sold in the US, reaching a dismal 165 in the *Billboard* Top 200 Albums chart. Atlantic Records and Judas Priest ended their contractual agreement and in 2002, Priest signed a North American deal with SPV (who owned the band's UK rights). *Demolition* didn't even chart in the UK. Suffice to say, the album was a commercial and artistic disaster, as Chris Jericho says, "*Demolition* has grown on me over the years but when it was first released I thought it was bollocks." Didn't everybody?

Demolition began with the vicious 'Machine Man', which lacked the vital Priest characteristics (it was unleashed as the album's lead single). The unmelodious 'One On One' and 'Hell Is Home' had an incredible amount of anger but both sadly lacked Downing and Tipton's dual guitars; it seemed as if their trademark riffs and solos had been thrown into a void and forgotten about. 'Jekyll And Hyde', 'Devil Digger' and 'Bloodsuckers' were lame metal songs with yet more B-grade lyrics. 'In Between' had some surprisingly tender moments, while 'Feed On Me' was an improvement with solid riffs, pounding drums and the presence of a strong melody. It was, by far, the best track on the album. 'Subterfuge' was a heavy affair with an industrial vibe, but again it didn't sound like typical Priest at all. 'Lost And Found' was a surprisingly good ballad but it felt out of place, sandwiched between the dark metal dirges. 'Cyberface' lumbered along like an elephant's fearsome footsteps, while 'Metal Messiah' concluded proceedings with a terrible mixture of sound and distortions. The 'rapping' parts were uncomfortable, verging on ridiculous, and it was a bad choice to end an album that had already sunk under the weight of its ludicrousness.*

Judas Priest began a Demolition world tour in Switzerland on June 8, 2001, in support of their worst album. When it came to deciding which songs to play, the band wrote down the title of every song they'd ever recorded and placed the names into a hat. Each song picked was included in the set. Supported by Savatage, the European leg included a string of prestigious metal festivals such as the enormous Bang Your Head!!! Festival in Germany. In June, the tour played Glasgow, London, Manchester, Birmingham and Portsmouth.

Before arriving in the UK, Savatage guitarist Chris Caffery noted in his online diary on the Savatage website that "the ferry ride" to the UK "was kinda humorous," noting that there "were tons of drunken English people taking their clothes off and dancing. Unfortunately, they were all fat and old. Yuk!"

Singer Jon Oliva admits that both bands never really had a chance to socialise. "We had drinks a few times," he remembers, "but they were so friggin' busy on tour. No chance to sit down and have a normal meal . . . They were very cool to us [though] – class guys all the way really."

Oliva watched Priest perform almost every night and particularly admired Owens, who often wore a flamboyant silver jacket while on stage. "I've known Tim for a long time. He's a great guy and one bad-ass singer . . . I think Ripper did an awesome job. He had amazing shoes to fill!"

Caffery also had tremendous respect for Priest and Tim Owens, as he noted in his diary: "Of course when Priest hit the stage it was a whole new ball game. They are just too cool. Ripper rules. He is definitely one of the best [singers] out there. I watched their whole set and went to say hello to the band. K.K. sat me down to talk, we became good friends as the weeks went on. There was our daily discussion of tech talk . . . going over the show's disasters onstage! The guys were so cool. They said if I needed anything to ask. Even if it was their dressing room if ours sucked. They were so cool. You see, this tour was a very special thing for me. When I was 12 years old, I had won a contest to see and meet Judas Priest. This was the 'British Steel' tour. For the next four or five tours they always gave me and my brother tickets and passes. I remember K.K. asking me what I wanted to be when I grew up. I said that I wanted to be like him. He remembers

---

* Pointless re-recorded versions of 'Rapid Fire' and 'The Green Manalishi (With The Two-Pronged Crown)' were added as bonus tracks to the CD reissue. To the annoyance of some Priest fans, Japan received an extra track called 'What's My Name'.

all of this and it was special for me to be opening for him, but also special for him to see a direct product of himself opening for them. There was an instant bond. Tim Owens is a good friend, too. He was psyched to watch us every night. As were we to see him."

Birmingham, the birthplace of heavy metal, was Caffery's favourite city: "The [Birmingham] show was a good one. Great city for metal. Priest still have family here. They had a party afterwards and we all hung out and had a blast. K.K. gave me three of Rob Halford's old belts. This little boy was living one of his biggest dreams and loving every second. K.K. was very complimentary to my guitar playing. He would always make jokes about how I could fill in for him and no one would notice! We were very similar onstage!"

The European tour finished on July 10, followed by a quick South American tour in September, but a planned US tour (with Anthrax and Iced Earth) due to begin in LA on September 14 was cancelled after the terrorist attacks on New York's World Trade Center three days before. The tour was postponed until the following year.

Priest toured Europe, followed by Australia and Japan in December, finishing 2001 with a terrific one-off gig (supported by NWOBHM stalwarts Saxon) at London's Brixton Academy for a live DVD release. A promotional video for 'Lost And Found' was filmed during the sound-check. By now, Owens felt right at home in Judas Priest, and the rest of the band revelled in his enthusiasm. Reviewing the show in *Classic Rock*, Malcolm Dome wrote: "Tonight will soon be available on DVD. Beg, borrow or steal a copy, because if it comes even close to capturing the atmosphere and performance in the flesh, it'll be a classic. Gig of the year, I reckon."

The DVD *Live In London*, released in 2002, was succeeded the following year by a double live album, which contained the complete 26-song set list. As with *'98 Live Meltdown*, *Live In London* failed to set the charts alight (entering neither the UK Top 40 nor the US *Billboard* Top 200 Albums). What had delighted fans about the 'Demolition' tour was the reintroduction of long-discarded songs, such as 'Exciter' and 'Devil's Child', to the set. Unfortunately they were not included on the live album, although 'Running Wild', 'Desert Plains' and 'United' made the final cut.

In 2002, Priest began their rearranged tour of the USA and Canada with Anthrax on January 17 in Las Vegas, finishing on February 19. As a committed Judas Priest fan, Scott Ian was overjoyed that Anthrax was given an opportunity to tour with his metal heroes. Ian has nothing but praise for Halford replacement Tim Owens.

Scott Ian (Anthrax): "Among all that insanity of 9/11 one of our stresses was, 'Oh no, is the Priest tour gonna get cancelled? And how are we gonna get to tour with them now?' Of course, that was a very, very minor thing compared to everything else going on in the world, but in our little small world of Anthrax, we were like, 'Oh shit! We still wanna tour with Priest!' When they told us that it was gonna happen a couple of months later we were really excited. It was fucking awesome man! They treated us amazingly and it was great to get to see them every night, you know, with Ripper . . . It was like a dream come true . . . We never got to play with them back in the early Eighties . . . so it's just one of those bands where you always wish, 'God, I hope some day I get to tour with those guys.'"

After the North American dates, Priest returned to Europe for a tour that began in France at the beginning of March and finished in Spain on April 7. A second North American tour started in July and finished in Chicago in August, after which the band took a well-earned rest.

Controversy greeted the band at the end of the tour. In August, 2002, the People For The Ethical Treatment Of Animals (PETA) sent Trinifold Management a request that allegedly asked for Priest to stop wearing leather on stage and to change the song and album title from 'Hell Bent For Leather' to 'Hell Bent For Pleather', arguing that the titles convinced young fans to copy their idols by wearing real leather. The band's reply reportedly claimed they wore artificial leather and that the names of both song and album would remain as they were. The matter was quickly dropped.

Having spent most of the Nineties in a commercial and critical wilderness, by 2000, Halford had a new mentor, producer and guitarist Roy Z,[*] and manager John Baxter, and had rightfully reclaimed his title of Metal God.

Before hooking up with Halford, LA-born producer, guitarist and songwriter Roy Z was chiefly known for his work with Bruce Dickinson and his own band Tribe Of Gypsies, a cult hard-rock outfit that merged Z's metal and rock leanings with his Latin heritage. His primary influences were such virtuoso guitarists as Uli Jon Roth, Michael Schenker, Frank Zappa, Jeff Beck, Jimi Hendrix and Carlos Santana.

---

[*] Roy Z's real name is Roy Ramirez. He changed it during the Eighties because of its association with the Californian serial killer Richard Ramirez, and because he felt he would not gain any attention with an ethnic name. He became Roy Zerimar but it was shortened to 'Z'.

Going under the unimaginative band moniker Halford, the singer hooked up with guitarists Patrick Lachman and Mike Chlasciak, bassist Ray Riendeau and drummer Bobby Jarzombek. "After experimenting and doing so much in metal, it was a time to refocus and go to the places where I felt I could do the best work and feel most comfortable," Halford explained to *Classic Rock* in 2000.

His 'comeback' album, appropriately titled *Resurrection*, took 18 months to make and was released in 2000 on Sanctuary's Metal-Is label. In 2002, it was suggested on the internet that sales for *Resurrection* had totalled 60,000, not too far ahead of Priest's alleged figures for *Jugulator*, which only managed to shift a very poor 40,000 units in America. *Demolition* did slightly better but still not great with sales of just over 100,000 in the States. With such low returns it was no wonder Priest had difficulties with American record companies. It was a sobering reminder of how times had changed since the million-or-so sales Halford and Priest had achieved with albums such as *Screaming For Vengeance*.

Resurrection was a glorious return to form for Halford, with some critics hailing it as a metal masterpiece. In September 2000, Malcolm Dome wrote in *Classic Rock* that *Resurrection* "is a full-blown wallow in un-ashamed screaming British metal. It is perhaps the greatest album Judas Priest have never made."

Roy Z's production was impeccable, and songs such as 'Made In Hell', 'Cyberworld' and 'Locked And Loaded' remain quintessential heavy metal. *Resurrection* was a very personal album as Halford told *Classic Rock*: "*Resurrection* lays it out bare and tells you what I've gone through." Halford was given a rare opportunity to support the reunited Iron Maiden in 2000 on a massive tour, which included shows at Madison Square Garden in New York and Birmingham's NEC. The singer's relationship with Maiden was re-instigated by Halford's duet with Bruce Dickinson on 'The One You Love To Hate' on *Resurrection*.

Halford returned to his roots for the Maiden tour by playing older Priest numbers, which he also showcased on his own tour of small venues and major rock festivals from 2000–03. As well as songs from *Resurrection* and a few popular Fight songs, fans were more than delighted to hear 'Stained Class', 'Jawbreaker', 'Genocide', 'Running Wild', 'Tyrant' and 'Riding On The Wind'. It seemed that Halford was playing more of Judas Priest's older songs than Priest themselves though, to be fair, the band had recorded two new studio albums, which had to be promoted. At that point there appeared to be no reason why the singer should need to go back to his former band.

Halford hastily released the exhaustive 2-CD *Live Insurrection* in 2001. One journalist shrewdly noted in a *Classic Rock* review of the album that it was "as if Halford has lost so much time and credibility because of his mis-firing post-Priest projects that he now has to make it all up in the shortest available time span."

Several writing sessions took place during 2001 and, consequently, a second Halford studio album, *Crucible*, was released in 2002. Giving the album three stars out of five, Dave Ling wrote in his *Classic Rock* review that "*Crucible* is less obvious, less self-conscious than *Resurrection*." Most critics were not as struck by *Crucible* as they had been with its predecessor, but Halford and his band stuck to the same traditional metal formula although with much darker tones, as shown on songs like 'Golgotha'. 'One Will' and 'Betrayal' were particular highlights of the album.*

In between exhaustive touring, writing and recording, Halford found time to make a cameo in the independent American film *Spun*, directed by Swedish film maker Jonas Åkerlund. "Acting has been my big ambition all along," Halford had told *Hard Rock* in September, 1986. "I've always had an inclination to do something of that nature . . ." The film also starred Mickey Rourke, Brittany Murphy, John Leguizamo, Debbie Harry and Eric Roberts. "I did a couple of scenes with Mickey Rourke," Halford told the *Metro* newspaper in 2006. "He turned out to be a big fan of [Judas Priest]."

In 2002, while Judas Priest were off the road, Tim Owens toured small clubs and pubs with American band The Sickness, featuring former Winters Bane bassist Dennis Hayes and drummer Tim Semelsberger. As 2003 approached, rumours were rife that Owens and Judas Priest had fallen out and that Rob Halford was going to reunite with his old colleagues. There was even a highly publicised story that Owens was going to join a revamped Pantera, but both sides fiercely denied these rumours. Around this time Travis allegedly told Canadian magazine *Brave Words & Bloody Knuckles* that Halford was hopefully going to rejoin Judas Priest for a summer tour in 2003. However, Priest's management denied any suggestions of a reunion.

There was still a certain amount of bitterness and public bickering between both camps. Although in 2000 an olive branch of sorts was offered by Halford via a letter to the band expressing his thoughts and emotions about rebuilding their friendship. "I missed them, as friends and

---

* A third studio album by Halford is planned for 2008.

best mates," he confessed to *Classic Rock* at the time. "It was an incredibly private and personal letter and the result of that is we're getting along fine."

Yet Halford still felt that there was more to do as a solo artist. "I certainly don't feel as though I need to return to Priest," he told *Classic Rock* in July, 2002, "but there's still a great deal of affection . . . I'd love to play some shows with them again in the future."

The public spats persisted throughout the first few years of the new millennium. Perhaps what reignited the feud after Halford's letter was Owens' claims to the press in 2002 that Halford had lost his way, and had abandoned his metal roots with the last Fight album and the doomed Two project.

Halford replied via an interview in the August 2002 issue of *Classic Rock*: "So if Tim says I turned [my] back on metal because Fight and Two were commercial disasters, and that I just went back to metal because that's where I make my money . . . well, fuck you, Tim!" Owens has since claimed he is a fan of the Fight albums.

Even at the start of 2003, just months before Halford's highly publicised reunion with his former band, he was quoted in *Classic Rock*, "I am not a member of Judas Priest and I have no plans to reunite."

A decade on from Halford's departure in May, 1992, it seemed as if Halford and Judas Priest would never reunite, despite management efforts since 1999 to make it happen. "I can state categorically that Rob Halford will never sing with this band again, because he doesn't fucking deserve it," Downing told *Classic Rock* in May, 2001.

Yet collective work on a retrospective box-set brought back some previously forgotten memories, and the opportunity to mend an old friendship and go out on the road as a united band was simply too good to miss.

PART 5

UNITED:
RETURN OF THE METAL GOD

THIRTEEN

2003–2004

"I mean having been apart for 14 years we didn't really know what to expect. I anticipated that it would all go well and everything but you never know until you actually go out there . . ."
— Glenn Tipton in an interview with the author for *Fireworks*
Melodic Rock in 2006

WHILE Rob Halford chose to reside mostly in America, Glenn Tipton and K.K. Downing both had houses in England as well as holiday homes in Spain – a part of the world they had gotten to know over the years thanks to their previous recording sojourns there. Downing's English home, a grand manor called Astbury Hall in Shropshire, was estimated to be worth at least a couple of million pounds.

It had an indoor swimming pool, a state-of-the-art studio, a bar, a golf course, 300 acres of land and several garages to house Downing's collection of classic cars. Inevitably, with so much time spent on the road as well as recording and promoting, he did not spend all of his time there. In the early weeks of 2003, Downing was sued by his former girlfriend, Sarah Lissimore, who claimed she was owed money and a share of the estate from the sheer amount of work, money and expenses she poured into the home while Downing was on the road to promote the *Demolition* album. The case went to Birmingham County Court in February, 2003.

Lissimore purportedly met Downing in 1993 after he finished his relationship with another woman who claimed Downing told her he wanted to wear a wedding dress. On a rare occasion for any of the band members, UK tabloids noticed the story and published Downing's battle to keep his home. *The Sun* reported that Lissimore, who was in her mid-thirties at the time, told the court: "Ken told me he and Julie had stopped talking after he told her he would like to try a bride's dress on. He said they were in a restaurant together and she went dead silent."

Downing invited Lissimore to live with him but she claimed that she suffered years of mistreatment. Lissimore told the court: "I went to my solicitor because of the abuse I suffered year after year after year. [Downing] told me I could leave and he would give me a tank of petrol and that was it. I was shocked."

Lissimore sought £200,000 in damages to compensate for her time invested in the upkeep of the house and for ending her career in the pharmacy industry. She also claimed in court that Downing bought her an engagement ring from Argos despite his public admission that he did not want to get married, preferring to invest his time and money into his career and property. Downing retaliated by stating the piece of jewellery was not an engagement ring. He told the court: "She knew before she came to Astbury that I did not want to be married. Everything I do and every penny I have goes towards the estate . . . The idea that I would share Astbury is to my mind insulting. It's mine."

The judge delivered his verdict on April 4, 2003 and dismissed Lissimore's case, ordering her to pay up to £100,000 in legal costs. Things were to go from bad to worse for Lissimore when she was declared bankrupt on May 19, 2004 at Shrewsbury County Court.

Judas Priest had been in the rock and metal press a lot over 2001–03 and, while this was mostly due to their public bickering, some of the coverage was positive. 2001–02 saw the re-release of the band's entire Sony/Columbia/CBS back catalogue – from 1977's *Sin After Sin* to 1990's *Painkiller* – in remastered and expanded form with two bonus tracks per album. The CDs were released in three batches of four[*] and, as a complete set, the albums were met with glowing reviews. It was evident that a tremendous sense of renewed enthusiasm for the 'classic' line-up was in the air at the start of the new millennium.

While nothing was happening in the Judas Priest camp in terms of new material, the band began to compile a retrospective box-set to celebrate their 30th anniversary. After Halford's tour of Japan and the USA in February and March 2003, a series of meetings to discuss the box-set took place in England. It was at this juncture that Halford, Tipton, Downing and Hill began to properly rebuild their broken friendship. At one particular gathering at Halford's Walsall house (at the time he also had homes in Phoenix, San Diego and Amsterdam) the four seriously discussed getting back together. By the end of that meeting, the band were reunited.

Tipton told *Classic Rock* towards the end of 2004: "We had no intention

[*] For serious enthusiasts, a limited edition black and silver-studded collector's box-set was released to store the albums.

of talking about a reunion, but by the end of the afternoon we'd decided to get back together. It was that simple."

"We just looked at each other and said, 'I'll do it if you do it,'" Halford confessed to *Metro* in 2006. "Everybody left and I thought: 'Oh my God, the world has no idea what just happened.'"

Within a year of interviews and press statements claiming that Halford would never sing for Judas Priest again, the hatchets seemed to have been buried. "Priest has always been the combination of the incredibly unique-sounding vocals of Rob and the characteristics of K.K. and myself and the thunderous rhythm section of Scott Travis and Ian Hill," Tipton proclaimed to *Zero Tolerance* magazine in spring, 2005. "It's those five elements that make up one of the most unique bands in the world."

Owens knew his time was up when he looked at a blank schedule for 2002. "Two years between records? I was starting to realise I had no idea how I was gonna make a living," he told *Classic Rock* in early 2004. "And I'd just become a father. It was like, 'C'mon guys, just give me a clue what's happening.' I was still under contract, but I wasn't going home to a mansion and I didn't have a Batmobile. It was very frustrating."

"I felt comfortable about Tim departing this band," Downing told *Powerplay* in 2005, "because I felt that he would go out there and find the right band, make an album with the right songs . . . make a great album and have more success outside of Judas Priest."

Speaking to the author in 2006, Downing elaborated, "It's always difficult because Rob was not only tried and tested, he's a great talent and obviously, he is the voice of Judas Priest and you can't take that away. I mean at the time you think, 'Oh yeah, we can replace him' [but] as great as Ripper was – and he was great – it takes a long time in the fans' eyes to develop that, well, I can't really put it into words . . . but as we know Freddie's the voice of Queen, Jagger's the voice of the Stones, Daltrey's the voice of The Who . . . and who's the voice of Van Halen? – that one confuses me a bit. But I'm still a David Lee Roth fan myself."

When asked by the author if he could remember the last gig he played as the front man for Judas Priest and whether he knew at the time that it was going to be his last, Owens replied, "I'm not sure where it was but after we were off the road for a few months, I knew the end was near."

In fact, the last gig Owens performed as singer for Judas Priest was at Chicago's House of Blues on August 25, 2002. He was contacted by Priest's management in early 2003 informing him about the band's decision. "I got an email first," he says, "then we talked about it. No, I was fine with it. It was something that had to happen and we all knew it . . . so it wasn't that bad. Yeah, everything has been great and that's the whole thing I've said to people; it just worked out better for everybody."

"We all phoned him individually," Tipton told *Classic Rock*. "And he was great about it."

It was reported at the time that the decision for Halford to reunite with his former colleagues was made only a few weeks prior to the 'official' public announcement that Halford made in a phone interview with CNN on July 11, 2003. Speaking from Walsall, Halford told the American news station: "Priest is reunited after many years of rumours, the big thing being the fans." At the time there was a strong rumour that Halford was enticed by a 50 per cent cut of all profits. However, the band and their management denied this.

The official story that Halford, Tipton, Downing and Hill were reunited at long last (with Scott Travis) quickly spread around the world's music press and fan sites. At the time, it was suggested that an album was planned for 2004, with writing and recording sessions due to begin in October 2003. A world tour to promote the album and to celebrate 30 years of Judas Priest was also in the works. Speaking about the new album Halford told CNN: "We'll just do it like we always did. I'll sit down with Ken and Glenn and we'll start jamming, and we'll slowly put the jigsaw of metal together. I know we will make another terrific metal masterpiece."

In an article about the reunion on the CNN website (dated July 13, 2003) Tipton said, "We're going to maintain our friendship with Ripper. He's a great guy, in fact, he sent us an email yesterday, saying he agrees with the decision, you know, because he is a big Priest fan as well, like we all are in a way. He is such an incredible vocalist he is bound to go on to greater success in his own right. Once people know he's free I'm sure he'll be in demand."

Tim Owens: "I felt comfortable with all of them. I felt really comfortable with them so I mean, I don't think there was anything [bad] . . . we just had a good time . . . I don't speak to them as much as I did, but I still speak to them every now and then."

Owens made a point of seeing Priest on their world tour. "I thought it was fun, it was a good time. I'm not one to run and hide, you know . . . talk nice for the press and then behind backs . . . I'm a friend and I'll always be a friend. My wife and I went out and caught [the show] . . . it was a good time, and it was nice to see the guys and sit down with Rob and talk quite a bit, you know. They're just great guys, every one of them good friends. No one can ever take that away."

Scott Ian: "[Tim's] got the most uncanny metal voice I've ever heard.

He's incredible . . . really, they couldn't have gotten anybody better to follow Rob Halford. There's no one out there that could have done the job that he did . . . just from a personal and professional level I don't think [anyone] could have done a better job than Tim. He was just so professional about the whole situation, knowing who's shoes he was filling and just going in and doing the best job he could as a fan of Judas Priest and not wanting to disappoint anyone . . . and just being the utmost professional and a gentleman when Rob came back – I think Tim is amazing."

With such an incredible voice, Owens was not out of a job for long. Prior to his friendly 'dismissal', he had been approached by Iced Earth's Jon Schaffer to sing on their upcoming album *The Glorious Burden*, after the band's previous singer Matt Barlow quit for a career in law enforcement. Initially, Owens was hired merely as a session vocalist, but a rapport between Owens and Schaffer was quickly established. Schaffer told *Classic Rock* in February, 2004: "I saw Judas Priest in 1979 and 20 times since then, and I know Tim is a better singer than Rob Halford ever was. That's a bold statement, but it's true."

Owens settled comfortably into Iced Earth and committed himself to touring duties in support of *The Glorious Burden*, which was highly praised by critics upon its release and was better than anything Owens had created with Priest. Tim Owens: "Iced Earth's last album sold 200,000 copies. It might not be a lot to some people, but 200,000 nowadays for a metal band is good. I can see us headlining the festivals in a few years, which is great."

It seemed that things had worked out for the best for all concerned. "Ripper got a lot out of it," Downing told *Powerplay*. "He's got his name and his face in the world domain. I swear to God he has had more success instantly since he sang for Iced Earth than he did with Judas Priest. He's more accepted."

By 2006, Owens had formed a new band, Beyond Fear, with guitarists Jon Comprix and Dwane Bihary, drummer Eric Elkins and bassist Dennis Hayes.

Their debut album was released to strong reviews although some critics, including the author, noticed the similarity between tracks such as 'And . . . You Will Die' and 'Scream Machine' and songs on *Jugulator*. In an interview for *Fireworks Melodic Rock* at the time of the album's release, Owens told the author: "It's kind of nice that I've heard people say that this is the album Judas Priest should have made as their last album, or even when I was in the band. So . . . it's flattering. I mean, I don't agree with it, but that's a pretty cool thing to hear.

"I think 'Scream Machine' was intentionally made as a nod to really old-school, tongue-in-cheek, cheesy-type lyrics about metal and monsters. It was my purpose to make it that way and the funny thing is it's probably one of the best songs on the record. It could have been on a Priest record . . . It's awesome, it's a cool song. I'm such a big fan of *Painkiller* and some of the faster Maiden tunes, and 'We Rock' from Dio and Priest's *Screaming For Vengeance*."

Because Owens was not given the chance to offer songs to Judas Priest, what made the album interesting was his songwriting skills.

Tim Owens: "It's the same really, it's fun and satisfying that I'm singing my own songs, and I get to see these people sing my songs that I've written. And prove to people that I can write, and it's nice to do that. But I've enjoyed touring with all the bands that I've done. So it's really a good thing."

The idea that Owens was a 'hired hand' in Priest, as Dave Holland claimed, was certainly plausible. "Years ago I wanted to start writing," Owens told the author while on a European tour supporting the reformed Anthrax in early 2006. "I actually started when I was in Priest. I wrote a song called 'Save Me', which I submitted to them around *Demolition* time. They really didn't think it was Priest-like, so I started thinking then that I'd like to make music and put my own record out."

The author asked Owens about the chances of Beyond Fear opening for the reformed Judas Priest.

Tim Owens: "Well I think it would be an awesome idea! But I've already been told by Priest's management that it'll never happen . . . they didn't give me a reason. Actually they did. They said, 'Tim, you should just let go of the Judas Priest thing.' It's kind of a strange thing. You know we're all still friends and the guys are just awesome. What would be better than having Beyond Fear tour with Judas Priest? Somebody's saying no and that's the way it happens . . . I definitely think Beyond Fear touring with Priest would be a great idea, not only for the fans but also as a marketing idea. But let's just say it won't happen."*

As writing and recording progressed into 2004, the reunited Judas Priest limbered up with a series of festival appearances in the summer of 2004 to promote the 30-year (1974–2004) retrospective box-set and DVD *Electric Eye*. "It's a way to rekindle all of Priest's achievements and all that we'll be giving to the fans again in 2004," Halford told *Classic Rock*:

* At the time of writing (late 2006), Owens is back working with Iced Earth.

The 65-track, four-disc *Metalogy* CD and single-disc DVD box-set was issued on May 17, 2004 to ecstatic reviews from fans and critics. Reviewing the box-set in the May, 2004 issue of *Classic Rock*, Malcolm Dome gave it a full five-star review: "*Metalogy* is a lovingly crafted, beautifully observed celebration not just of Judas Priest but of heavy metal as a whole, because without this lot where would the genre be today? Nowhere near as colourful or creative."

Metalogy spanned Judas Priest's entire recording career, from the mid-Seventies Gull Records days to the SPV years with Tim Owens. The set included a number of unreleased tracks, but not the obscure 'Mother Sun' or anything from the SAW sessions of 1987. The December, 2006 issue of *Classic Rock* hailed the box-set as, "Arguably the greatest heavy metal box-set of them all," when it was named as the number one purchase in the '34 Best Box-Sets For Christmas'.

There was an incredible amount of excitement in the heavy metal world when Judas Priest announced their 'Reunited' tour of 2004. Commencing in Germany on June 2 and proceeding through Italy, Switzerland, Sweden, Holland, Czech Republic, Hungary, Bulgaria, Greece and Spain before finishing in Belgium on June 27, the band performed a total of 49 shows, including headlining spots at various festivals. Reviewing the Barcelona gig (June 24), *Classic Rock*'s Geoff Barton wrote: "And what a set list! . . . Now admit it: you wish you'd been there instead of me, don't you? Be patient."

Not everybody was completely bowled over by the reunion. Reviewing the band's June 10 gig at the Sweden Rock Festival in *Fireworks Melodic Rock*, Phil Ashcroft wrote: "It was time for the eagerly awaited reunion of Judas Priest with Rob Halford – although the muddy sound and unwillingness of Mr. Halford to attempt any of the higher notes put a damper on things . . . To be honest, Rob wasn't in the best form, and moved about like a malfunctioning automaton."

Support act on part of the tour were Annihilator, who had previously supported Judas Priest in 1991 on the European 'Painkiller' tour.

Jeff Waters: "The Priest guys got hold of me in 2004 when they were going to do the reunion and [Annihilator] got to go and open up for the first few shows . . . As a kid growing up I was such a massive fan of Priest. I mean I knew every single word, guitar riff, drum patterns and everything of every song of every album. And to be asked to tour with them once was huge, personally, and then to be asked when Halford finally comes back to the band again to come over and do the shows. It was . . . you can imagine."

175

Waters saw the differences between the Judas Priest of 1991 and the Judas Priest of the 21st century.

Jeff Waters: "When you get older, you'd sometimes love to go back and relive where you were a long time ago, and going on that tour was the same thing except you're standing there going, 'My God, these guys haven't aged', and you listen to the tunes and you realise these tunes are going to sound great 50 years from now . . . I got to see them from a pretty cool perspective when I toured with them on the Painkiller tour in 1990. You were seeing Priest at their prime [then], at their best . . . Going back and playing with them it was really cool, because I got to see them from the first gig . . . I think Halford had a little extra weight on him than he does now . . . But in 2004 Travis was just getting used to it, and Halford and Tipton and K.K. were all getting used to playing the stuff again in a group.

"As a musician, it was priceless to be able to stand there and watch the rehearsals and just to see that they were human, they make mistakes too, they have to practise to get as good as they are and they have to work at it. But then you watch them show after show and these guys are like, they want it, they still have the fire. A lot of guys at that age probably say, 'We don't care, we're making money', but [Priest] want to get real here, to do it again, to get back to where [they] were.

"[Rob's] the best in almost any [genre] . . . and [any] other singer in any other kind of music that takes a good listen to Halford would have to agree. When you ask a guy that's in his fifties to go out on the road and do what he does, there's not many other guys in the world that could do it other than Dickinson and maybe a couple of others but it's a unique freak of nature, there's no other Halford out there."

In early 2004, Priest were announced as second headliners under the reformed Black Sabbath for the annual summer Ozzfest tour of America, which began in Connecticut on July 10 and finished in Florida on September 2. The last scheduled date of the Ozzfest tour was arranged for September 4 in West Palm Beach, but was cancelled due to the fast-approaching Hurricane Frances. Joining Sabbath and Priest on the road were, among others, Slayer, Dimmu Borgir, Superjoint Ritual, Black Label Society, Slipknot, Lamb Of God, Hatebreed, Lacuna Coil and Atreyu. A selection of non-Ozzfest shows (with Slayer and Hatebreed supporting) were slotted in, including a date in Toronto on August 18.

The entire tour brought back memories for Downing and Hill supporting Sabbath at the Masonic Hall in Walsall back before Halford and Tipton joined the band. "I remember the show well," Downing told *Classic Rock* in 2004. "It was the first and only time that we shared a stage with Sabbath and we said never, ever again." Many journalists among the North American music press thought Priest stole the show on the Ozzfest tour, mainly due to the overfamiliarity of the set list from yet another reunion of the original Black Sabbath.

Judas Priest continued recording their "comeback" album, eventually titled *Angel Of Retribution* (the title was only decided at the last minute), at the Old Smithy in Worcestershire and Sound City in California with Roy Z until the end of 2004. From the outset, the band were looking for a live, vintage heavy metal sound akin to their earlier albums, so many of the songs were recorded in one take, to give a rawer edge. Tipton informed *Metal Hammer* in 2005 that they had difficulty at first "because we thought after 14 years apart, what do people expect from Priest? So in the end we just wrote what comes naturally to us . . . It's got some light and shade and it's got some powerful stuff."

Naturally, it was Halford who introduced Roy Z to the rest of the band after his excellent production on the two Halford studio albums. "He's absolutely the bollocks is Roy," Downing told the author in 2006. "He's an excellent guitar player as well. He's a real big guitar fan but, technically, he's great and the thing is, he like myself, is the reason why I think we make a great team. Really it's because of our roots and what we're like. When Roy was here last all we did was sit down, drink beer, and laying out CD's and rare footage of Thin Lizzy, Uli Jon Roth and Dio and Hendrix and all that stuff."

With Roy Z's masterful approach to production and new techniques, Priest had come a long way from their earlier recordings. Downing told *Powerplay* prior to the release of *Angel Of Retribution* that the album "is very switched-on technically. It was all done with Pro Tools, which is now becoming the industry standard. The main thing though, the nice thing about it as far as I'm concerned, is that we've finally got the sounds coming out of the speakers in the control room that we've got out there when we're playing the guitar. Technology has moved on a bit these days. It used to be really hard work to capture that sound and energy, but it's a lot easier now."

"I think that you can have the best of both worlds," Downing told the author for *Fireworks Melodic Rock*. "I mean I'm sitting here now surrounded by computers and stuff . . . all these programs. And you can do so much in a small room . . . fortunately, a lot of bands are actually able to make music at a low cost, so it's very beneficial in a way, but the downside is . . . maybe there are too many people doing it? I don't know, is that possible? The record companies in the old days might get a couple of new albums thrown at them a week, now maybe it's 300 or 3,000. So it's very difficult for these guys to plough through them really – 40 [to] 50 minutes at a time is quite time-consuming for these guys."

While euphoria surrounded Halford's return, ex-Priest drummer Dave Holland made less welcome headlines in 2004.

After leaving Priest in 1989, a brief Trapeze reunion occurred in the mid-Nineties featuring the original trio of Holland, Galley and Hughes. However, the reformation met with little success and they called it a day in 1994. Apart from drumming for Australian rock band The Screaming Jets on a European tour, Holland led a solitary existence at home in Stoke Bruerne, Northampton. He owned a drum shop and, for income, he gave private drum lessons while continuing with session work.

In 1996, Holland teamed up with Glenn Hughes, Tony Iommi and Don Airey for a series of sessions that were not released until 2004 on the Sanctuary label as *The 1996 DEP Sessions*, although bootlegs had been in circulation for years under the moniker *Eighth Star*.* Straight after the demo sessions, Holland played on Al Atkins' collection of new recordings of early Priest songs, *Victim Of Changes*.

Al Atkins: "We were approached by several big labels to record an Atkins/Holland album, featuring many star names, and we had been to London to meet up with them. Dave was also approached to record a solo album, which would feature all the artists he had played with over the years like Glenn on bass, Rob Halford on vocals, Don Airey on keyboards and even myself."

The fate of Holland's long-promised solo album, which was expected to feature Al Atkins, Glenn Hughes, Tony Iommi, Don Airey and The Moody Blues' Justin Hayward, will never be known.

On December 29, 2002, police searched Holland's Northampton cottage for evidence relating to claims of sexual assault and rape. The raid netted sex aids, pornographic magazines and videos. In August, 2003, the *Northampton Chronicle & Echo* reported that 55-year-old Dave Holland and his co-defendant, an unemployed 22-year-old, Spiros Laouitaris, from

---

* For the official release, the original drum tracks were replaced by Jimmy Copley, who also played drums on Iommi's self-titled debut solo album, released in 2000. Iommi told *Record Collector* in 2005: "The drum sound at the time, because they were just demos, wasn't particularly a very good drum sound. And also because of [Holland's] 'problem', I don't want to get involved in that."

Bourne Crescent, Kings Heath, Northampton, had been arrested and charged with a series of sexual assaults on a 17-year-old special needs boy. Laouitaris, who had a number of learning difficulties himself, had been charged with four counts of indecent assault. Holland had been charged with five counts of indecent assault and one count of attempted rape against the boy who (along with his family), for obvious legal reasons, remained unnamed throughout the case.

Over the coming months it was reported that the assaults took place on five separate occasions between June and December, 2002, when the boy stayed overnight at Holland's cottage. It was alleged that the boy was instructed to give oral sex and perform humiliating acts with a sex toy. Laouitaris allegedly took part in threesomes with Holland and the boy as well as other sex acts. Holland and Laouitaris both pleaded not guilty as they stood alongside each other in the dock for the initial hearing at Leicester Crown Court. The overweight drummer with greying hair looked remarkably different from the skinny, moustached man of the Eighties that Judas Priest fans were more familiar with. Wearing glasses and casually dressed, Holland did not utter a word, except to confirm his name and his pleas of not guilty. The pair were released on unconditional bail by Judge Charles Wide.

The trial began on January 15, 2004 at Northampton Crown Court. The Crown was represented by prosecuting counsel Maria Savvides while defence counsels Michael Joyce represented Holland and Nicola Cafferkey acted for Laouitaris. The victim was 18 when he gave evidence against Holland and his co-defendant, telling his horrific story to the judge and jury and others in attendance through a series of video statements taken by police, lasting two hours. Holland had started giving drum lessons to the boy at his cottage in late 2001. After seven months, in which a trusted friendship grew between the pair, the boy's parents, who had adopted him at the age of 10, allowed their son to stay overnight at Holland's home from June, 2002 until the boy admitted what had been happening. As reported in the *Northampton Chronicle & Echo*, Savvides said that the boy's parents "decided to give him drum lessons because it was something he was happy doing."

The paper also published the boy's statement: "[Holland] practically gave me a beer. He told me to go and have a shower and come down naked. Then he went upstairs to have a shower and then he put porn on the TV." After allegedly suffering a series of assaults on five separate occasions, the boy finally told his parents by letter in December, 2002 what had happened during the past few months. Via the video statements, he told the court: "I just said I didn't like it, please stop."

The paper also reported that Holland admitted to being bisexual, as well as admitting ownership of a large selection of pornographic tapes and magazines, sex toys and devices. He told the court: "The subject of sex came up. I told him I am bisexual. I don't know why. I'm the kind of person that if I feel someone should know something then I'll tell them. I believe he was of the same persuasion as myself."

Holland stood in front of the judge and jury on January 19 and told them: "He [the boy] certainly has made all this up . . . Maybe he has done something like this before, maybe I'm getting blamed for something because I have said something to inadvertently upset him."

The boy's father gave evidence to the court. He spoke about the façade Holland had allegedly created to lure the boy back to his home for the night ("He appeared to be a true gentleman. He seemed to get right down to his level and show a caring and understanding attitude to his needs"), and about the deep psychological damage that had been inflicted on his son. The boy's father grew curious and worried about his son's increasingly bizarre and erratic behaviour. The teenager would return home after visiting Holland's home and take several baths, which he didn't usually enjoy, and grew angry, depressed and frustrated for no apparent reason. "He started to come back very tired, with a sore throat, and he was very aggressive . . . During the time he was going to Dave's, we noticed he started scratching, bleeding and had blotches." At the time of the trial it was stated that the boy had to be taken out of school, a place for boys with learning difficulties, and taught at home because of his emotional trauma.

When police interviewed Laouitaris straight after his arrest, he strenuously denied taking part in any form of sexual contact with Holland and the boy. He said that he was not "really good friends" with Holland, contrary to popular belief, and during the trial, he said that he was not Holland's gay lover but they met up for "a bit of fun" on some occasions. However, when in the witness box, Laouitaris changed his story. He told the jury that Holland lied to the police and had forced him to lie to the police before the interview, saying that nothing had happened. Laouitaris admitted that he knew about the sexual assaults Holland made on the boy: "[Holland] wanted me to go there and he would let me off some of the money [I owed], if I went to the house to have a threesome."

The prosecution did not believe either story. Savvides claimed that Laouitaris had been to Holland's house on two of the five nights when the threesomes allegedly took place, and had done nothing to stop Holland from committing the assaults. She looked at the co-defendant and said firmly: "You were equally to blame. You knew that the boy was not consenting, that his head was being held down. You forced him and you indecently assaulted him."

After all the evidence and testimonies were presented it was understood that Holland had seduced both the boy and Laouitaris because of their learning difficulties. Holland abused his role as a paternal figure for his own sexual needs and satisfaction. A few days before the verdict was read, Judge Wide instructed the jury to disregard one count of indecent assault by Laouitaris because of a lack of evidence. He also told the jury to disregard Holland's sex life and concentrate on the specific charges of sexual assault and offences against the individual boy.

On Friday, January 23, the jury, which consisted of seven women and five men, deliberated for seven hours. In a stunning turn of events, Laouitaris was cleared of three counts of indecent assault. It was reported the jury unanimously agreed that he had been manipulated by Holland's deceit. The drummer had used his strong personality to exploit younger, more vulnerable people, and Laouitaris and the boy were attracted by Holland's former career as a rock star. Holland cried as the jury declared him guilty of attempted rape and five counts of indecent assault. As the police led him away, he continued sobbing, holding his head firmly in his hands. Holland was kept in custody until sentencing the following month.

Two decades before, Holland was enjoying enormous success along with his former colleagues on the *Defenders Of The Faith* world tour. Now he was on his way to prison.

If he had known his fate, would Holland have still done what he did?

Did his former colleagues know about his sexuality?

Had Holland ever admitted to anyone about his perverted sexual desires back in the Eighties?

Had Holland committed any other sex crimes on minors in the past?

Halford had recently come out, and a former close friend of Downing's alleges that he is bisexual too. If true, one can only imagine what that knowledge would have done to Judas Priest's career in America during the mid-Eighties.

On January 24, the *Northampton Chronicle & Echo* ran the headline: "ROCK STAR IS GUILTY OF SEX ABUSE." On February 14, the same newspaper's headline screamed: "JUDAS BEAST" as Holland began an eight-year prison sentence and was ordered to pay a fine of £10,000 towards the cost of the eight-day trial, paid for by the sale of the cottage he had owned for over 20 years. When Holland stood in Northampton

Crown Court the previous day, Judge Wide was particularly concerned that the drummer could pose a future threat, as it was alleged that other young men had visited his home. The judge told Holland: "You deliberately and calculatedly planned a strategy to abuse a boy who you know was exceptionally vulnerable . . . [You] deliberately, carefully and calculatedly planned to abuse him . . . You groomed his parents. You presented yourself as a potentially caring and beneficial influence on the boy's life . . . Once you gained their trust in that way, you were in a position to invite him to your home to abuse him." Holland was told that he would never work with children again and was consequently put on the Sex Offenders Register.

In a press statement, Judas Priest said: "We are as shocked as everyone by this news. However, we would like to point out that Scott Travis is Judas Priest's drummer and has been since 1989. We haven't had any contact with Dave Holland at all since we parted company with him over 15 years ago."

When the author began preparation for this book, he felt it only fair that Holland should get his own say on the matter. However, in late 2005, it wasn't possible to locate Holland's whereabouts.* Letters were posted to local papers in every quarter of the Midlands, and most of them were published. After several useless phone calls from readers who had nothing new to offer, the task was put on hold for a few weeks. The readers who did answer had already mentioned their stories in the press, leading one to suspect they liked having their name published. However, the author did receive one interesting unmarked, anonymous letter. Typed in black, bold letters, it read:

AFTER YOU HAVE READ THIS YOU WILL UNDERSTAND WHY IT IS ANONYMOUS

DAVE HOLLAND WAS ARRESTED AND CONVICTED FOR SEXUALLY PROCURING/ATTEMPTED CHILD RAPE/CHILD ABUSE

I KNOW BECAUSE THE BOY WAS A FRIEND

---

* His location was not made available due to the Data Protection Act 1998, which dictates how organisations hold information about British citizens and prevents such information being made public because it is seen as a violation of privacy.

The author's attention was diverted by other matters until he received an email during the autumn of 2006, giving details of a close friend of Holland's who was still in touch with the drummer despite his imprisonment. Yet hopes were quickly dashed as he refused to cooperate. I persisted, contacting the Prisoner Location Service; however, they too quashed any hopes of contacting Holland, invoking the Data Protection Act by stating that if Holland's location was made public, it could be a threat to his life.

The author even managed to obtain the correct address of Holland's cottage in the town of Stoke Bruerne. However, the Royal Mail quickly returned the letter with a sticker reading "addressee has gone away." A handwritten note on the envelope also read: "Return to sender. No longer at this address." The author persisted with the search, which had already been deemed a waste of time. Emails were sent to journalists who reported on the case back in 2003/4, some of whom had their own ideas regarding Holland's location, offering the names of local prisons in the Northamptonshire area. The author posted yet more appeals, hoping that Holland would get hold of one and, in turn, post a reply. Weeks went by before the author finally admitted defeat and gave up.

One morning during the winter of 2006, I received a shock. A small but thick brown envelope with a Northampton postmark arrived in the post. Inside was a letter, three single sides long and handwritten on A4-lined paper, signed by Dave Holland.

I had no reason to question the validity of the letter. The drummer had faded into obscurity, so it would seem futile for anybody to pass themselves off as him. What follows is a verbatim transcript of that letter:

Monday 6th Nov, 2006.

Dear Neil,

Thank you for contacting me & I apologise for the amount of time that it's taken to get back to you. I'm sorry that I cannot reveal my whereabouts to you, but suffice to say that there are several reasons for this & I can assure you that if you were in my shoes, you would do exactly the same. So, this letter comes to you via my family & I do hope that you receive it o.k.!

Firstly, I want to wish you well with your book & I hope you have real success with it when it eventually comes out. Secondly, I'm not at all surprised by the response that you've received from the band & their management & thirdly, I also & unfortunately, have to tell you that I'm not going to be able to help you either, but, for totally different reasons, I'm sure!

I was convicted & imprisoned for an offence that I didn't commit & like so many others in similar situations to the one in which I find myself, an offence that never even existed in the first place. I don't wish to dwell on this, but I would like you to, at least, partly understand my reasons for not being able to help you at the present time.

Like myself, before all of this happened to me, I'm sure you will be unaware of how the law works when it comes to accusations against someone that are of a sexual nature. The criteria that came to be applied could never be used to gain a conviction in any other type of offence whatsoever. In brief, it can, & often is, achieved by the simple act of "pointing a finger" at someone without any evidence whatsoever. I know that it probably seems impossible to believe, but I can assure you that it is a fact. With the absence of the ducking stool & the subsequent burning at the stake of the "guilty", there is absolutely no difference whatsoever between the criteria that is permitted to be applied in sex offence cases now & that which was applied in cases of witchcraft in the 17th century. This has to be changed, but it will be a long job, & the stigma that goes hand in hand with a sex offence, or just simply an accusation of one, will surely take even longer to rectify thanks to our "illustrious" red top press!

I am now, & after much work & effort that would be impossible to describe in any detail, more or less prepared for an appeal against my conviction, & during the course of my part of the preparation, the basis of a book, on what can only be described as the disgraceful & appalling institution that is this country's criminal justice system, began to take shape. So, like yourself, I am also writing what I hope will turn out to be a "best seller", although any financial gain that may come from it, however helpful towards putting back together some "semblance" of a life for myself when I get out of prison, will only ever be a secondary matter, or a "spin off", compared to how far I hope the book will go towards putting "right" a dreadful "wrong" that exists within our existing justice system.

After this book is finished (& finally getting to the point after I've probably bored you to tears!!) I will be writing a book about my life & career in the music business & about people that I've met & events & incidents that have taken place during the course of it, which of course, will include the final 10 years of it, those having been spent with "you

---

know who!!" *Although I really would like to help you with your book, Neil, I'm sure that you will appreciate that anything I let you have for yours (especially some of the more "juicy" bits!) I won't be able to use for mine!*

Anyway, I'll hang on to your address & drop you a line once I'm out & settled. In the meantime, I wish you all the luck in the world!

Sincerely,
Dave Holland

FOURTEEN

2005

"God knows what albums we would have made with Rob between Painkiller *and this album. It would have been interesting but it will never be seen . . ."*

– K.K. Downing speaking to *Powerplay* in 2005

*A*NGEL OF RETRIBUTION, Rob Halford's first album with Judas Priest since 1990's *Painkiller*, initially planned for release before Christmas 2004, was put back until early 2005 when it was hoped the re-scheduled date would boost sales. Another promotional marketing tool was an exclusive five-track "taster" – featuring 'Judas Rising', 'Deal With The Devil', 'Revolution', 'Worth Fighting For' and 'Hellrider' – that Priest and their management gave to journalists at special preview hearings in London and New York in late 2004 and at the start of the following year. A downloadable promotional video was made for 'Revolution'.

Released in the UK on March 12, *Angel Of Retribution* was a considerable commercial success, just making it into the Top 40 at 39. Although Halford told *Zero Tolerance* during the promotional run, "We've always been proud to say that we are a British heavy metal band," some fans noticed the irony that it took an American producer in California to make a British heavy metal record. The album gave Priest their first-ever number one anywhere in the world, in Greece, and entered the top 10 in Austria, Finland, Germany, Japan, Norway, Spain and Sweden. In America, *Angel Of Retribution* reached number 13, Priest's highest-charting position there, selling over 58,000 copies during its first week of release and shifting even more during the following weeks. It was estimated that sales of the album in the US were close to 200,000 after just a couple of months.*

---

* Hard-core fans were treated to a special limited-edition cardboard sleeve version with a bonus DVD that included a documentary and live performances filmed in Spain (Barcelona and Valencia) during the 2004 *Reunited* tour of: 'Breaking The Law', 'Metal Gods', 'A Touch Of Evil', 'Hell Bent For Leather', 'The Hellion/Electric Eye' 'Diamonds And Rust' and 'Living After Midnight'.

It was a grand achievement for a band that had successfully managed to extricate itself from a decade of commercial disasters and creative redundancy. However, some critics attacked the album's final song, 'Lochness', as being an overblown piece of nonsense. Prior to the album's release, *Classic Rock* editor Geoff Barton heard the preview disc and had raved; however, his (March 2005) review of the complete album dropped from a potential five to three stars, all because of this one track that sends "the entire record crashing down in flames . . . 'Lochness' is so ill-conceived, so long-drawn out, droning and dismal, that it single-handedly destroys what would otherwise have been a triumphant Halford-led return."

In an interview with *Metro* in March, 2006, Halford said the song was inspired by memories of a Scottish tour the band did during the early Seventies. After gigging in Inverness, and with little petrol left, they were consequently forced to sleep in their van by Loch Ness. In the singer's opinion, 'Lochness' "became this monumental metal epic we're really proud of."

Other critics were prepared to overlook this ill-advised anomaly. *Powerplay* wrote: "Just a few bars of opening track 'Judas Rising' are enough to tell you that Priest are back to doing what they do best. The solos and guitar flourishes are back, the soaring melodies and memorable choruses are back, and Rob Halford is back – sounding better than ever. Most importantly of all though, the band have written a set of first-class songs."

The sleeve harked back to the *Sad Wings Of Destiny*-era as Downing confirmed to *Classic Rock*, "The cover to the new one is a modern update of that." The former showed a sad, fallen angel – whereas *Angel Of Retribution* (as the title suggests) showed an angel rising, powerful and intimidating.

It wasn't just the sleeve that looked back to the past. Halford, Tipton and Downing were (mostly) in fine form lyrically, albeit in an introspective and nostalgic mood. Songs such as 'Deal With The Devil' namechecked places like Holy Joe's in West Bromwich, which the band had previously used for rehearsals in the late Sixties and early Seventies.

'Judas Rising' was an entirely appropriate opening track – raw, exciting, harsh and brimming with screeching menace. The *British Steel*-influenced 'Deal With The Devil' exemplified 21st century Priest. 'Revolution' had a more radio-orientated edge (hence its release as lead single) that showed Hill hadn't lost his musical chops – bringing back memories of the funk-filled 'The Rage'. 'Worth Fighting For' proved Halford had not lost his vocal delicacy on a strong power ballad, while on the opposite side of the coin, the grinding 'Demonizer' showcased his powerful metal screams.

'Wheels Of Fire' featured a sharp, distinct riff. For those who mistook Priest for only making heavy metal, a short, tender song like 'Angel' proved they were not totally one-dimensional. Like 'Last Rose Of Summer' (from *Sin After Sin*), 'Angel' fit remarkably well into an album of heavy (sometimes very heavy) songs.

The beastly 'Hellrider' was straight from the *Painkiller*-era; clichéd but fantastically good fun. The ballad 'Eulogy' was not nearly as effective as 'Angel', although the short bursts of piano added a tinkling ambience. As already discussed, 'Lochness' was dull, pretentious and at 13 minutes in length, overlong.

Overall, *Angel Of Retribution* was an excellent effort and a remarkable return to form after the dire *Demolition*. While lacking the ferocious intensity of *Painkiller*, it harked back to the melodic nature of *Screaming For Vengeance* and, as an appetising hint of what might follow, the album promised much.

Judas Priest began the European leg of their 'Angel Of Retribution' world tour in Denmark on February 23, with In Flames and Paradise Lost supporting, finishing in Spain on April 17 with Baron Rojo as the exclusive opening act. More dedicated Priest fans wondered if the set list would include anything off the *Jugulator* and *Demolition* albums. However, Downing told *Powerplay*: "No. I wouldn't expect Rob to ask me to perform stuff that I didn't play on, and I'm not going to ask him to perform stuff that he didn't play on."

While in Finland, Halford received an unexpected invitation to attend a special reception at Buckingham Palace, along with 500 other entertainment figures, to recognise the global success of British music. Halford flew to London for the special event held on March 1. A month later, a sold-out show, scheduled for April 6 in Katowice, Poland was among all scheduled entertainment cancelled as a mark of respect following the death of Pope John Paul II. The President of Poland declared five days of official mourning throughout the country.*

Fans in the UK were treated to a surprisingly lengthy tour, supported by Priest's old friends, the legendary German hard rockers Scorpions. "When I heard Rob Halford had gone back [to Priest,] that became my dream touring package," guitarist Rudolf Schenker told *Classic Rock* prior to the tour. "And it's a great way for us to come back to the UK."

---

* The gig was not re-arranged. It would have been the first show the Halford line-up of Judas Priest played in Poland. Previously, Priest played shows in Katowice in March, 1998 and March, 2002 with Tim Owens as vocalist.

The tour began on March 16 with a sold-out gig at London's Hammersmith Apollo, followed by Birmingham, Manchester, Belfast, Glasgow, Newcastle, Sheffield and Cardiff, finishing in Plymouth on March 31. Most of the shows were a total sellout, with second dates added in London and Manchester. The triumphant homecoming gig at Birmingham's NEC on March 19 was the biggest Judas Priest had headlined in their career and was filmed for a future DVD, but plans to release the footage have still not been confirmed; it's likely to be saved for another commemorative collection.

"We did record several shows during [the] tour," Tipton informed the author. "There's been a lot of live stuff released from Priest recently and we don't want there to be a glut or overdo it. So we have no actual plans at the moment; whether the footage will emerge eventually is another argument."

The UK set list featured 'The Hellion', 'Electric Eye', 'Metal Gods', 'Riding On The Wind', 'The Ripper', 'A Touch Of Evil', 'Judas Rising', 'Revolution', 'Hot Rockin'', 'Breaking The Law', 'I'm A Rocker', 'Diamonds And Rust', 'Deal With The Devil', 'Beyond The Realms Of Death', 'Turbo Lover', 'Hellrider', 'Victim Of Changes', 'The Green Manalishi (With The Two-Pronged Crown)' and 'Painkiller'. The encore consisted of 'Hell Bent For Leather', 'Living After Midnight' and 'You've Got Another Thing Comin''.

In a review of one of the Hammersmith shows, Malcolm Dome wrote: "Priest's performance is the epitome of what the genre is all about." *Record Collector* described the same gig as "an incredible, thoroughly enjoyable evening." Even some of the broadsheets were enthusiastic. *The Times* gave the concert four stars out of five: "Only a churl could fail to be thrilled to bits."

There were some churlish writers who were more impressed with the Scorpions' highly energetic show. Most of their criticisms were aimed at Halford, who was attacked for being overweight, overdressed and inflexible. Reviewing one of the Manchester gigs, Bruce Mee wrote in *Fireworks Melodic Rock*: "The Scorpions and Judas Priest are both from the same era, but live on stage they are light years apart. While Rob Halford was content to shuffle around like an old man, the Scorpions leap around with boundless enthusiasm and energy . . ."

Powerplay were more conciliatory in their review of the second Manchester gig: "With no effects to speak of, apart from some silly fuss with flags, this was all about the band nailing the songs we love. A friend of mine who saw them the night before said that Halford was a disgrace, out of condition, just a fat man in a long coat. Well, he may show his age, but he's certainly still got it . . . Great metal, just a slight sign of fatigue."

Priest toured Japan in May and the two sold-out shows at Tokyo's Budokan Hall on May 18/19 were also filmed for a DVD release. The US tour, including dates in Canada, began on May 30 in Ohio and finished on July 10 in Phoenix, with Queensrÿche as special guests. After a few weeks rest the tour resumed in September, taking in Mexico, Brazil, Argentina, Chile and Puerto Rico, with special guests Whitesnake.

The second leg of the North American tour began on September 23, finishing in Texas on November 1 with special guests Anthrax and Hatebreed. A special one-off gig, dubbed 'Priest Feast', was held in San Diego on October 30, with Rob Zombie and Anthrax supporting. Another band that took part in the show was Hoax UK – a band (made up of high school children) that was formed by Kiss' Gene Simmons via his TV show *Rock School*.

Scott Ian (Anthrax): "We went out for dinner a few times and we would hang out quite a bit after the shows . . . but more so on the *Demolition* tour than the last one we did with them. Glenn even told me that it was like the end of the cycle for them. They were all just pretty tired and really looking . . . to be done; they weren't really hanging out too much after the shows. It was right at the end, the last week or so, when we started hanging out, and that's when Glenn told us, 'I apologise, please don't think anything bad . . . we're all just tired and we all just wanna get home. We've been out for a year . . . ' So that was really sincere."

While on tour, Priest won the 'Metal Guru' award on October 4 at *Classic Rock*'s 'Roll Of Honour' ceremony held at the posh Café De Paris in London. Obviously the band could not attend, but Jayne Andrews collected the award on their behalf after a speech by journalist Geoff Barton, who recalled memories from first interviewing the band in 1976 as they were promoting *Sad Wings Of Destiny*. Other winners included Lemmy, Deep Purple, Queen with Paul Rodgers, Billy Idol and AC/DC.

Judas Priest's world tour finally came to a successful finish in Eastern Europe. From late November through to December, they played gigs in the Ukraine, Russia, Estonia, Latvia and Lithuania for the first time in their career. With 116 live dates completed, Priest played more shows in 2005 than any other year in their career. They were ecstatic with audience reactions from around the globe, as Tipton told the author: "You know, the kids are not stupid, they know when you are doing something genuinely or when you're just out there for the wrong reason. When we go on stage it's not just Priest on stage, it's us and the audience, and everybody sings along to the choruses and lead breaks now. It's just a wonderful occasion every night."

At the end of the two-year cycle of tour, album, tour, plus the exhaustive amount of interviews and obligatory promotional tasks that are necessary for a new album, there was still one big question left to answer: would this be just a one-off?

"We intend to do two, three, maybe four of five more albums," Tipton told *Zero Tolerance* in early 2005. "*Angel of Retribution* is a great Priest album, but it may not be our best-ever work . . . We've got to view this as a new beginning."

FIFTEEN

2006

"We've come a long way from London's old Marquee and all those other little clubs we used to play in the 1970s."

– Rob Halford speaking to *Metal Hammer* in 2006

THE year 2006 was a quiet one for Judas Priest, with only sporadic releases, reissues and live events. The band performed just two live shows, the first at a special charity event held at the Royal Albert Hall on March 31. Organised by The Who's Roger Daltrey for the Teenage Cancer Trust charity, the concert was in honour of the late British rock broadcaster Tommy Vance, who had a profound impact on hard rock and metal bands through his *Friday Rock Show*. The concert featured Boned (a favourite of Vance's), Ian Gillan, Scorpions and, thanks to Bill Curbishley's associations with Daltrey, Priest landed the headlining spot.

"Tommy was always a really good friend," Tipton told the author weeks before the concert, "and really supportive of Judas Priest and so many other bands in his career. He didn't want anything for it; some disc jockeys latch onto a band, but in Tommy's case he used to get a lot of bands under his wing, he used to help them, launch them and he was responsible for a lot of bands' success. He was just a great character."

Priest were nervous, as it was their first-ever gig at the revered venue. "It's my understanding that we're the first heavy metal band to play there." Halford told Geoff Barton hours before the event. "It'll also be the first time a Harley Davidson has entered the building." Reviewing Priest's performance, Sue Ashcroft wrote in *Fireworks Melodic Rock*: "It was a sing-a-long selection with 'Breaking The Law', 'Electric Eye', 'Metal Gods', and other gems, but finishing the night with 'Take On All The World'. This saw the entire cast coming on to join in. What a sight."

On May 25, at the Mandalay Bay Events Center in Las Vegas, Priest were honoured at the very first VH1 Rock Honours event alongside fellow Brits Queen and Def Leppard and token Americans Kiss. Godsmack performed a special Priest medley, while the band themselves played 'Breaking The Law' and 'You've Got Another Thing Comin'', bringing out the Harley Davidson for the latter song.

One of the biggest tributes paid to Judas Priest was the sheer amount of awards – 'Best Group Of The Year', 'Best Album Of The Year', 'Best Live Performance In Japan', 'Best Album Cover', and 'Best Vocalist Of The Year' – they won at the 2006 *Burrn!* magazine awards ceremony in Japan.

A live DVD was issued in the UK on January 23 entitled *Rising In The East*. The set list was pretty much the same as the UK tour with the exception of 'The Green Manalishi (With The Two-Pronged Crown)' being replaced by 'Exciter'. Needless to say, the latter's inclusion excited hardcore fans. In a sly reference to *Unleashed In The East*, Halford informed *Classic Rock*: "I'd like to stress that it's not been remixed or overdubbed in any way." *Live Vengeance '82* (originally released as *Judas Priest Live* on VHS) was released for the first time on DVD in February. Initially, it had been included in the *Metalogy* box-set, but fans craved for a stand-alone release. A 2-CD retrospective, *The Essential Judas Priest*, was released on September 25 including tracks off *Angel Of Retribution*, namely 'Judas Rising' and 'Revolution'.

Coming as a surprise to fans, K.K. Downing teamed up with Roy Z to produce *Storm Warning*, the debut album of bassist Mick Cervino's band, Violent Storm, featuring singer Matt Reardon and drummer Mike Sorrentino. The author asked Downing how he got involved.

K.K. Downing: "I have absolutely no idea than, you know, a few beers later . . . I saw those guys in Miami; they came to one of our shows when Ripper was in the band and we had a bit of a chinwag then . . . I was down in the old Costa Del Sol with a buddy of mine and we thought, 'Bugger me it's boring, let's fly to Barcelona . . . and have a few beers up there,' and that's what we did. Obviously, then I was talking to Mick and he said that he'd got something in the pipeline. He was thinking of asking a couple of guys to play and then it was real early days. He'd just got some material and it was never known what would ever happen, you know? And of course, I'm there going, 'Yeah! Yeah! Send me a couple of songs and I'll see what I think.' Of course, when I got the stuff I thought, Well it's kind of like in the rough stages . . . it's got some pretty good potential. I thought, 'Yeah, I could blow a couple of solos over this,' so I did and really didn't think too much of it. I'd done my part if you know what I mean . . .

"I said, 'What you really need is to get somebody to do a really good job on this.' So I thought I'll offload this on to Roy . . . He said, 'Well, yeah I could make it sound really, really good . . .' and one thing led to another, so then I got more and more involved with the arranging and the mixing, the artwork and the name and everything . . . just trying to basically give the guys the benefit of all of the years of, well, a lot of years of inexperience but more lately the experience that I've got first-hand really . . . it would be good to see a band with good potential doing this sort of material now in the 2000s. I think it's always a good thing. To be honest, I wish I could have had even more input earlier on but, then again, like Roy Z says, 'An album's never finished. You just have to hand it over at some point.'"

Downing admitted that because of the distance between each musician on the album, they rarely got together.

"I mean we met up in Las Vegas, in Los Angeles . . . Mick and all those guys were spread out all over the place, mainly in Miami. At one point, me and Roy were sending files backwards and forwards over the Internet and I'm going, 'No, no – the bass is far too low in that song . . .' So that was when we couldn't actually physically be together. So it was pulled together on a bit of a wing and a prayer to be honest . . . It's just basically going back quite a while now, I think we were doing the *Demolition* stuff at the time . . . but the main thing is that the band's really looking forward to getting out on tour and they always have been. They know that they've gotta have a record out otherwise they can forget it . . ."

Released in Britain on October 23, *Storm Warning* was a decent if somewhat clichéd melodic hard rock album. Guitar wizard Yngwie Malmsteen cropped up on 'Fire In The Unknown' and 'Pain', while Roy Z played guitars on the former and 'Screaming In Your Face'. Downing contributed guitars to 'War No More' and 'Deceiver'.

Rob Halford was also busy in 2006 with his own flurry of solo activity. On June 1, his management emailed a press release to journalists, which was also posted on Halford's official website, informing that he had acquired his entire back catalogue from Sanctuary Records UK and that *Resurrection* (2000), *Live Insurrection* (2001) and *Crucible* (2002) would be the first releases from Halford's new company Metal God Entertainment (MGE). In November, the albums were re-released in remastered form and made available exclusively on Apple iTunes Music Store.*

A promising new Halford song, 'Forgotten Generation', was made

---

* Plans to release them commercially had not been confirmed at the time of writing in winter 2006.

available to download on Apple iTunes Music Store. A 15-song compilation, *Halford: Metal God Essentials −Volume 1*, was also released, which included 'Forgotten Generation' as well as another new song, 'Drop Out'. *Silent Screams Singles EP* joined the latter in collecting Halford's career outside of Priest, while *K5 The War Of Words Demos*, also released in November, consisted of early, previously unreleased Fight material. Again, these were only made available via Apple iTunes.

A DVD documentary, *Fight: War Of Words − The Film* is expected in 2007 chronicling Fight's first year in 1992 when Halford decided to leave Priest and tour/record with his new band. A second forthcoming DVD release, *Live At Rock In Rio 2001*, sees Halford and his band finish their aptly titled Resurrection world tour at the annual rock festival in Brazil after completing almost a hundred shows, including dates with Iron Maiden and Queensrÿche. Downloadable trailers were made available on Halford's official website.

A new solo album, *Halford IV*, has been tentatively pencilled in for release in 2008, but with a new Judas Priest album and subsequent world tour expected in 2007–08, that could very easily change. As Halford, Tipton, Downing and Hill each approach 60, they certainly don't show any sign of slowing down.

SIXTEEN

2007

The Future

"Nostradamus, even in this new millennium, is still a very intriguing, mysterious character."

— Rob Halford speaking to *Classic Rock*, 2006

ON April 7, 2006, Judas Priest announced that their next project would be an entirely conceptual piece — their first — on the 16th-century French prophet Nostradamus. The idea is said to have come from Bill Curbishley, who thought it would be a wise move despite the lavishishness and boldness of the band's plans both in the studio and on stage.[*]

Priest won't be the first popular heavy metal band to tackle the life of the infamous prophet; he was the inspiration for Iron Maiden's song 'Die With Your Boots On' from their 1983 album *Piece Of Mind*. After the pretentious nonsense of 'Lochness', opinions are inevitably divided on the matter, with all sorts of questions being raised: will the album be over-blown rubbish? Why have they decided on this idea rather than a straight-forward rock record? Are they deluded enough to think they can achieve anything? Will Priest become a heavy metal version of Yes?

Judging by some of the comments the band have made, it seems Priest have been more influenced by Finnish symphonic metal band Nightwish than the progressive rock bands of the Seventies such as Yes, ELP and Jethro Tull. Halford spoke to *Classic Rock* about their new project: "The opportunities are there to bring in other dimensions, whether it's classical/symphonic, using orchestras, massive choirs." He joked that there would be more costume changes than during the past two tours.

---

[*] Coincidentally, Ozzy Osbourne had announced the previous year that he was writing a stage musical based on the life of the 19th century Russian mystic Grigory Rasputin, sometimes referred to as the "mad monk".

In his interview with Glenn Tipton for *Fireworks Melodic Rock*, the author tried to prise some clues out of him as to the new album: "We start next Monday actually. We've got a band meeting tomorrow. Rob's over in England now. We shall start writing Monday."

Could Priest fans expect another 'Lochness?': "Not at the moment," he said, "my lips are sealed. I'll get into serious trouble if I say anything."

In October 2006, the author briefly spoke to Downing: "We're working day and night. All the material is done; we're just recording it at the moment. We're a couple of weeks into it but it's a long project . . . we're definitely gonna release it when record companies like to release records, which is like end of January/early February. That type of period, whether it drags on a little bit remains to be seen. But it's a lot of work . . . we've made a good start and it's going to be very interesting."

At the time of writing (late 2006), some sources claim that the band have written 90 minutes of music, and there are tentative plans to perform the album in its entirety on stage during their own tour, but the usual 'best of' set list would be used for festival dates, which have yet to be announced.

K.K. Downing: "We don't know exactly how this project's gonna go yet. But we can certainly go out and play the festivals and do our own show."

It seems likely that the album will be released sometime before Christmas 2007, possibly to coincide with a series of festival appearances and a headlining tour, possibly from the end of 2007 into '08, before Halford reignites his solo band.

A concept album seems such a drastic and highly unusual move for a band that has pretty much followed the same path throughout their career, although there have been diversions, such as *Turbo*, which often failed. Perhaps they are looking to establish themselves outside of the heavy metal community, as Iron Maiden sought to do with their ambitious but successful album *A Matter Of Life And Death*.

"I don't think Priest have achieved true success," K.K. Downing declared to *Record Collector* in 2005. "Before I go six feet under I'd like to see the band where it deserves to be. So this is it. It's the only chance."

POSTSCRIPT

Heroes End

As Judas Priest show no signs of retiring after 30 years together, their standing in the rock and heavy metal world remains assured – as both pioneers and as an inspiration to those that have followed. So what better way to conclude proceedings than for Priest associates – past and present – to pay their respects to the Metal Gods.

David Howells (Gull Records): "Judas Priest worked hard to convince the media that they were worthy of attention. I'm still not convinced they get the respect they deserve even today. The public usually get it, once they get a chance to hear and see an act, but sometimes it's difficult to get past the media's prejudices."

John Hinch (Ex-Judas Priest drummer): "All I get is people coming up to me, 'Oh, you used to be in Judas Priest, didn't you?' . . . I've just given up noticing because you can't go, 'That was 30 years ago, I am now a man.' And it happens at the most peculiar times, I mean, you're talking pretty up- and up-business people, 'You used to be in Judas Priest. That's fantastic.' So that's it, you know – had a great time, wonderful, loved every bit of it and then packed it in. And no, I don't really regret it at all . . . when people go, 'Oh, you used to be in Judas Priest,' my attitude almost is, 'Well, that was another person.'"

Scott Ian (Anthrax): "Judas Priest are just a great metal band. They play great and make great songs. They created the template for mostly everything that came after them. All that music that they created still holds up well today . . . they're just awesome songs. The stuff that they were creating in the Seventies and early Eighties . . . It always sounds like Priest. Nobody else sounds like them . . . few metal bands are as good as they are. I mean 20 years later, even 30 years later, and nobody at all sounds like them. They're the original metal band!"

Conrad 'Cronos' Lant (Venom): "In my opinion, Judas Priest have been a major influence on the metal scene. There aren't any metal bands around today who could say they don't have at least a little Judas Priest in them somewhere. Any young metalheads out there who want to know where it all started should go and check out the first half dozen Judas Priest albums and give themselves a real metal education."

Kevin DuBrow (Quiet Riot): "I'd tour with Judas Priest again just to see them play every night. I saw them play for the first time in many, many years a few weeks ago [at the VH1 Rock Honours] and they were every bit as good as they were the last time I saw them. It was just great to see them together. They have such a great guitar sound . . . it's insane."

Brian Ross (Blitzkrieg): "Priest have influenced me greatly as a musician. They are the ultimate British metal band. They are everything that Blitzkrieg and every other British metal band should strive to be!"

Jason McMaster (Dangerous Toys): "Judas Priest took a lot of style and churned it out as their own manifestation of rock played with such power; maybe they were the first heavy metal band, as most of us know it – depending on who you talk to, of course. But the leather and metal spikes and the riffs from hell have taken bands to other heights with their music. Black Sabbath and Judas Priest seriously changed the landscape. There is Metallica and Slayer for a reason.

"The first band I was ever in played Judas Priest songs, and every other band I have ever been in played Priest songs, too. And even though I have always written and recorded my own material, Priest is always there influencing me, in my current band. During one of our songs in the live set, we always throw in a snippet of 'Heading Out To The Highway' and 'Devil's Child' – the fans go crazy every time."

Ralf Scheepers (Gamma Ray): "In the end everything that counts is respect, and I respect Judas Priest. Their success is more than evidence that they deserved everything they have achieved . . . I was a fan of the original line-up, now I am glad to see them together again, and I have a great time hearing their music again. Sometimes I forget that I am doing this profession on my own and jump around with the air guitar and sing along to their tunes."

Joe Lynn Turner (Ex-Rainbow/Deep Purple singer): "I am a fan. I saw them in New Jersey here last year with Queensrÿche and they were great . . . They were the consummate metal band and still are . . . They are still kicking it. They are the real deal . . . they are authentic . . . When I think of heavy metal I think of them . . . They helped define the genre."

Tim Owens (Beyond Fear): "I like both the records that I did with Judas Priest. I think they're both different and that's why I fell in love with Judas Priest, because they changed with every record."

Jeff Waters (Annihilator): "With a band like Judas Priest, I know that some people have said, 'Oh they didn't reach the levels of this or that', but you have to remember that for people like me and other bands out there, they would dream to be at Priest's level of not just sales but of live attendances, about having the respect of other people and musicians, about getting a number one and creating incredibly amazing songs. So anyway, Priest should be very happy where they are right now."

APPENDICES

CAST OF CHARACTERS

Al Atkins – still lives in West Bromwich with his family and is a solo artist with five albums under his belt, including his latest, *Demon Deceiver*. For details, visit http://www.alatkins.com/

Pete Boot – now retired, he organises concerts around the world under the banner *Fill Your Head With Rock* to help raise awareness of Parkinson's disease. He runs the website http://www.fillyourheadwithrockinternational.com/

Ernie Chataway – still based in the Midlands after a long time spent living in London, he plays the guitar and jams with the odd pub band.

John Ellis – has been a successful sales representative in the print industry for over 20 years.

Roger Glover – is the bassist in Deep Purple. He is also a respected songwriter and producer in his own right.

John Hinch – currently assists his wife with her company, which is engaged in event co-ordination. His drum kit, which he uses only occasionally, sits in the loft.

Dave Holland – has been in prison since 2004 on an eight-year sentence.

David Howells – owns the London-based music company Darah Music, which manages the producer/writer Steve Mac and songwriters such as Nicky Chinn.

Geraint Hughes – runs his own recording studio in Brighton.

Derek Oliver – works at the label Roadrunner Records and heads the reissue label Rock Candy Records with Dante Bonutto. Go to http://www.rockcandyrecords.co.uk/

Tim 'Ripper' Owens – has a successful working relationship with Iced Earth and is the front man and founder of the metal band Beyond Fear. For details visit, http://profile.myspace.com/index.cfm?fuseaction= user.viewprofile&friendid= 80714926 and http://www.timripperowens.com/

John Pasche – is presently working as a freelance designer. He has worked on a mixture of projects ranging from individual performance artists and the Philharmonic Orchestra to corporate identities for a new telecommunications company and a new café franchise. He also works on various projects for the BBC World Service Trust. For details visit, http://www.johnpasche.com/

Simon Phillips – is a successful session drummer and currently the drummer in Toto. For details visit, http://www.simon-phillips.com/

Jim Simpson – still runs his Birmingham-based label Big Bear Music. For details visit, http://www.bigbearmusic.com/

Bruno Stapenhill – plays in a covers band called The Cadence and gigs mostly in the south west of England. For details visit, http://www.thecadence.co.uk/

Jonathan Valen – works in post-production on shows for the Discovery Channel, and TV shows for a company called HD Studios in Marina Del Rey, California. He is currently working on a golf show, *Club House Golf*, and is also at work with Pat Regan, a well-known sound mixer. For details visit, http://www.jonathanvalen.com/index.html

CHRONOLOGY

The following is a summation of Judas Priest's career. There are some missing dates, which are due, mainly, to a lack of information. However, the author has endeavoured to be as accurate as possible with facts and dates that are currently available.

1947

19 July: Frederick (John) Hinch was born in Lichfield, Staffordshire
14 October: Allan John Atkins was born in West Bromwich, Midlands

1948

05 April: James Leslie Binks was born in Northamptonshire
05 April: David Holland was born in Northamptonshire
25 October: Glenn Raymond Tipton was born in Blackheath, Midlands

1951

20 January: Ian Frank Hill was born in West Bromwich, Midlands

25 August: Robert John Arthur Halford was born in Sutton Coldfield but raised on Lichfield Street in Walsall, Midlands

19 September: John Ellis was born in his grandmother's house in West Bromwich, Midlands

27 October: Kenneth Downing Jr. was born in West Bromwich, Midlands

1957

06 February: Simon Phillips was born in London

1961

06 September: Scott Travis was born in Norfolk, Virginia, USA

1967

13 September: Timothy Steven Owens was born in (Barberton Hospital) Akron, Ohio, USA (and has lived in the state all his life).

1969

(Exact date unknown) September: K.K. Downing auditioned as guitarist for Judas Priest but was turned down – Ernie Chataway got the job instead

25 November: Played showcase gig at The George pub. Audience included Robert Plant

1970

(Exact date unknown) March: Played a gig at Masonic Hall in Walsall

1971

16 March: First gig with K.K. Downing, Ian Hill and John Ellis at St. John's Hall, Essington

16 March *(Exact date unknown)* December: UK tour. Played over 40 British dates during that year

30 June: Played a gig at the Lafayette, Wolverhampton as support to the Chicago Blues Band

(Exact date unknown) July: Recorded 'Holy Is The Man' and 'Mind Conception' at Zella Records

26 July: Played a gig at Quaintways, Chester as support to Status Quo

02 September: Played a gig at the Kinetic Circus, Birmingham as support to Graphite

04 October: Played a gig at the Borough Hall, Stafford as support to Thin Lizzy

06 October: Played a gig at The Yeoman, Derby as support to Slade – John Ellis' last gig in Priest

1972

01 January–*(Exact date unknown)* December: UK tour. Played over 70 British dates during that year

17 February: Played a gig at Henry's Blues House, Birmingham as support to Trapeze

24 March: Played a gig at the Glen Ballroom, Llanelli in Wales as support to The Wild Angels

29 April: Played a gig at the Wellington Hall, Shropshire as support to Spirit

14 June: Played a gig at the Cedar Club, Birmingham as support to Dr. Ross

30 September: Played a gig at the County Cricket Club, Northampton as support to Curved Air

27 November: Played a gig at The Plaza, Old Hill with Glenn Tipton's ex-band The Flying Hat Band

16 December: Played a gig at the Boat Club, Nottingham as support to The Sensational Alex Harvey Band

1973

(Exact date unknown) January–06 September: British tour that started in Haywood and finished at Birmingham Town Hall. Played more than 25 gigs that year

(Exact date unknown) March: Played a gig at St. George's Hall, Liverpool as support to Budgie

(Exact date unknown) April: Played a gig at Birmingham College of Art and Food as support to Budgie. Audience included John Hinch and one Robert Halford

15 April: Played a gig at the Hippodrome, Birmingham as support to Family

29 April: Al Atkins' last gig with Priest at the Wellington Arms in Shropshire

(Exact date unknown) May: Atkins and Chris 'Congo' Campbell left Judas Priest

17 July: Records state that Rob Halford played his first gig with Priest at Bolton Town Hall on this date

1974

11 February–28 December: UK tour started at the Marquee Club in London (interrupted by foreign dates) and finished at the Royal Links Pavilion, Norfolk

19 February: Gig in Germany

04 March: Gig in Holland

25 March: Gig in Norway

07 April: Gig in Norway

23 August: *Rocka Rolla* was released in the UK

1975

21 February–6 September: UK tour started at the Main Hall in Latfield and finished at the Links Pavilion in Cromer

25 April: Recorded a performance on BBC TV's *The Old Grey Whistle Test* presented by Bob Harris

22 August: Performed at the 15th Annual Jazz and Blues Reading Festival at the Thameside Arena in Reading

11 October–28 December: UK autumn tour started at Slough College in London and finished at the Roundhouse in London

1976

26 March: *Sad Wings Of Destiny* was released in the UK

06 April–20 June: UK Sad Wings Of Destiny tour started at The Plaza, Truro and finished at the Roundhouse, London

1977

(Exact date unknown) March: Played at the Kuusrock Festival in Oulu, Finland

22 April–22 May: UK 'Sin After Sin' tour began at the Corn Exchange, Cambridge and finished at the Victoria Theatre, London

14 May: *Sin After Sin* was released in the UK – produced by Deep Purple bassist Roger Glover

(Exact date unknown) May: Drummer Les Binks joined the band

17 June–25 July: First US tour started at Civic Center, Amarillo, Texas and finished at the Coliseum, Oakland, California. Played support to REO Speedwagon on first date

08 July: Supported REO Speedwagon at the Haymaker's Club in Wheeling, Illinois

09 July: Performed at the Superjam '77 in St. Louis Missouri with REO Speedwagon, Ted Nugent and Gypsy

16 July: Supported REO Speedwagon at the Palladium Theatre in New York

23–24 July: Supported Led Zeppelin at the Day on the Green Festival – Oakland Coliseum, California

29 August: Played at the Blue Lagoon Ballroom, Cornwall

06–07 October: Supported AC/DC at the Volkshaus in Zurich, Switzerland

1978

19 January–*(Exact date unknown)* February: UK 'Stained Class' tour began at Cramer Links Park, West Runton and finished at the Civic Hall, Guildford

25 February: *Stained Class* was released in the UK

10 March–07 July: US tour as support to Angel, Foghat and B.T.O. started at the Palladium Theatre, NYC and finished at the Civic Center, San Antonio, Texas

25 July–05 August: Toured Japan.

Rob Halford backstage at Castle Donington in 1980. **(LFI)**

The band in action at the Monsters Of Rock festival at Castle Donington on 16th August 1980. **(LFI)**

Judas Priest at the US Festival at San Bernardino, California in May 1983, an event organized by Apple Computers. Bizarrely, Priest was sandwiched in-between Bryan Adams and Crosby, Stills & Nash. **(NEAL PRESTON/CORBIS)**

Ian Hill at Glen Helen Park, California in 1983 during Priest's US tour. **(NEAL PRESTON/CORBIS)**

Vintage Judas Priest: the Mark X line-up in complete head banging heavy metal attire in the mid-eighties; left to right: Glenn Tipton, K.K. Downing, Rob Halford, Dave Holland and Ian Hill. **(ROSS MARINO/RETNA)**

Rob Halford, acclaimed California drummer Jonathan Valen and Glenn Tipton backstage during the 1986 North American 'Turbo: Fuel For Life' tour. This photograph was taken on the night of the final gig of the tour at the CNE Grandstand in Toronto, Canada, which was also Valen's last ever gig with the band. It proved a bitter ending for their short-lived onstage collaboration. (COURTESY OF JONATHAN VALEN)

Drummer Jonathan Valen's controversial contribution to the 1986 North American 'Turbo: Fuel For Life' tour. Valen hasn't spoken to any of the band members since. (COURTESY OF JONATHAN VALEN)

Hell Bent For Leather: Halford on his famous Harley
Davidson in the eighties. (BOB LEAFE/FRANKWHITEPHOTOAGENCY)

Rob Halford and Glenn Tipton on stage circa 1986.
(EBET ROBERTS/REDFERNS)

Judas Priest underwent an image makeover during the time of the controversial *Turbo* album in 1986;
left to right: Dave Holland, K.K. Downing, Rob Halford, Glenn Tipton and Ian Hill. (GAB ARCHIVES/REDFERNS)

An infamous period in heavy metal: Judas Priest (left to right: Rob Halford, Ian Hill, K.K. Downing and Glenn Tipton) on trial at Washoe County District Court in Reno, Nevada in August 1990. A verdict of not-guilty was given by Judge Jerry Carr Whitehead on 24th August, 1990. (DAVID PARKER)

Rob Halford during the time of his short-lived post-Judas Priest project Fight in 1993. (DANA FRANK/RETNA)

Tim 'Ripper' Owens, Rob Halford's American replacement for the period 1996-2003. (ROSS HALFIN)

Former Judas Priest singer and co-founder Al Atkins and Judas Priest Mark I guitarist Ernie Chataway in 2006 at JB's in Dudley, West Midlands where Al played a gig that night to promote his acclaimed comeback album *Demon Deceiver*. (COURTESY OF AL ATKINS)

Back together: Glenn Tipton, Rob Halford and K.K. Downing reunited in New York in 2005. (DARAGH MCDONAGH/RETNA)

The complete stage set-up: Judas Priest performing vintage British heavy metal at the Tommy Vance memorial concert at the Royal Albert Hall in London on 31st March 2006. It was the band's first gig at the famous London venue. (SUE ASHCROFT)

All for one and one for all: Glenn Tipton, Rob Halford and K.K. Downing post-reunion. (ROSS HALFIN)

23 October: Performed a session at the BBC Studios

24 October – *(Exact date unknown)* November: UK X–Certificate tour supported by Lea Heart.

11 November: *Killing Machine* was released in the UK

15–16 December: Played two nights in New York – Stage One, Buffalo and at the Palladium Theatre, NYC

1979

20 January: First single 'Take On The World' was released and reached number 14 in the UK charts

25 January: Performed 'Take On The World' on BBC TV's *Top Of The Pops* programme

10 February–15 February: Toured Japan

27 February–6 May: Toured US

12 May–31 May: UK Killing Machine tour supported by Marseilles. Finished with two nights at the Hammersmith Odeon, London and one gig at the Birmingham Odeon

12 May: The single 'Evening Star' was released in the UK

17 May: Performed 'Evening Star' on BBC's *Top Of The Pops*

01 July: Played at the Dalymont Park Festival in Ireland

(Exact date unknown) July: Drummer Les Binks was asked to leave the band. He was replaced by ex–Trapeze drummer Dave Holland

01 September–09 November: Toured USA

06 October: *Unleashed In The East* was released in the UK – first Judas Priest album to be produced by Tom Allom

11 November–15 December: Toured Europe

1980

07–27 March: UK British Steel tour supported by Iron Maiden. Finished with two nights at the Odeon Theatre, Birmingham

27 March: Performed 'Living After Midnight' on BBC's *Top Of The Pops*

29 March: The single 'Living After Midnight' was released in the UK

01 April: Played the Rainbow Theatre as apart of Levi' Jeans 50th Anniversary

05 April: Played at the Kortrijk Festival, Belgium

12 April–26 April: Toured Europe

19 April: *British Steel* was released in the UK

09 May–05 August: Toured USA

07 June: The single 'Breaking The Law' was released in the UK

29 June: Played at the Grand Slam Super Jam in St. Louis, Missouri

16 August: Performed at the first Monsters of Rock Festival at Donington Park, headlined by Rainbow

23 August: The single 'United' was released in the UK. Played at the Neunkirchen Festival, Germany

28 August: Performed 'United' on BBC's *Top Of The Pops*

1981

21 February: The single 'Don't Go' was released

26 February: *Point Of Entry* was released in the UK

26 April: The single 'Hot Rockin'' was released

07–24 November: UK Point Of Entry tour started at the Manchester Apollo and finished at Wessex Hall, Poole. Support was from Accept

1982

17 July: *Screaming For Vengeance* was released in the UK

21 August: The single 'You've Got Another Thing Comin'' was released

26 August–12 December: Toured North America

1983

12 January–8 June: Toured US

06 November: Played a gig at Northlands Coliseum, Canada

12–22 December: UK tour started at City Hall Newcastle and finished with two nights at the Odeon Theatre, Birmingham. Support was from Quiet Riot

1984

06 January: Performed on the TV programme *The Tube*

20 January–21 February: Toured Europe

21 January: The single 'Freewheel Burning' was released in the UK

28 January: *Defenders Of The Faith* was released in the UK

16 March–10 August: Toured US

06 September–13 September: Toured Japan

1985

13 July: Performed at Live Aid in Philadelphia

1986

19 April: *Turbo* was released in the UK

02 May–31 August: Toured North America

31 May: Judas Priest perform at the Capitol Centre, Maryland, which was filmed for the documentary *Heavy Metal Parking Lot*

28 September–29 October: Toured Europe

4 December–13 December: Toured Japan

1987

12 June–22 June: Toured UK

13 June: *Priest . . . Live!* was released in the UK

22 July–23 October: Toured North America

1988

23 April: The single 'Johnny B. Goode' was released in the UK

28 May: *Ram It Down* was released in the UK – final Priest album produced by Tom Allom

12–22 June: UK *Ram It Down* tour began at the Powerhouse, Birmingham and finished at Sheffield's City Hall. Support was from Bonfire

1990

23 March: The single 'A Touch Of Evil' was released in the UK

13 September–23 December: Toured North America

22 September: *Painkiller* was released in the UK – last album with Rob Halford before he left to go solo

1991

09 January–15 January: Toured US

23 January: Played Rock In Rio II Festival at the Maracana Stadium, Brazil

31 January–17 March: Toured Europe (inc. Eastern Europe)

19–28 March: UK and Ireland Painkiller tour began at the Leisure Centre in Aston Villa and finished at Edinburgh Playhouse. Support was from Annihilator

12 April–15 April: Toured Japan

09 July–19 August: Toured North America

1992

(Exact date unknown) May: Rob Halford decides to leave – he tells the band of his decision via fax

07 September: It was publicly announced that Rob Halford had left Judas Priest

14–15 November: Rob Halford fronted Black Sabbath on stage at Pacific Amphitheatre, Costa Mesa, California

1993

24 April: The single 'Night Crawler' was released in the UK

08 May: *Metal Works '73–'93* was released in the UK

(Exact date unknown)–July: Fight world tour

01 September: Fight's debut album *War Of Words* was released in the UK

19 October–30 November: Fight world tour

1994

12 July: Fight's *Mutations* EP was released in the UK

21 August: Fight played one-off gig in Miami

1995

01 April: Fight's *A Small Deadly Space* was released in the UK

21 April–13 July: Fight toured North America

1996

(Exact date unknown): American singer Tim Owens joined Judas Priest – later became known as 'Ripper' Owens

1997

17 March: Glenn Tipton's debut solo album *Baptizm Of Fire* was released in the UK

16 October: *Jugulator* was released

1998

30 January–2 March: Toured USA

(Exact date unknown) February: Halford announced he was gay, live on MTV's *Superrock*

18 March–28 April: Toured Europe

30 March: Two's *Voyeurs* was released in the UK

11–12 April: Played two nights in the UK to promote the *Jugulator* album – London Astoria and Wolverhampton Civic Hall. Support was from Gorefest

13 May–20 May: Toured Japan

17 September: *'98 Live Meltdown* was released in the UK

17 September–19 September: Played two gigs in Mexico

22 September–31 October: Toured US

2000

19 July–21 December: Halford world tour

08 August: Halford released debut album *Resurrection* in the UK

2001

09 January–19 January: Halford toured South America

29 January: An announcement was made that Judas Priest's Sony/Columbia albums would be remastered and reissued with bonus tracks.

02 April: Halford's *Live Insurrection* was released in the UK

28 May: Single 'Machine Man' was released in the UK

08 June–10 June: Played festivals in Europe

13–18 June: UK *Demolition* tour started at the Barrowlands, Glasgow and finished at the Guildhall, Portsmouth. Support was from Savatage

18 June: *Classic Albums: British Steel* DVD was released in the UK

21 June–10 July: Toured Europe

16 July: *Demolition* was released in the UK

01 August–10 August: Toured South America

31 October–18 November: Toured Europe

30 November–07 December: Toured Australia

10 December–15 December: Toured Japan

19 December: One-off gig at Brixton Academy, London was recorded for a DVD release

2002

17 January–19 February: Toured US

14 March–7 April: Toured Europe (inc. Eastern Europe)

07 June–06 July: Halford played various rock/metal festivals around the world

25 June: Halford's second album *Crucible* was released in the UK

05 July–25 August: Toured US

01 July: *Live In London* was released on DVD in the UK

15 August: People For The Ethical Treatment Of Animals (PETA) asked in a formal letter that the band stop wearing leather and change the title of *Hell Bent For Leather* to 'Hell Bent For Pleather' (plastic leather)

12 October: Halford played at the Soyo Rock Festival in Seoul, South Korea

2003

13 January: *Live In London* (CD) was released in the UK

01 February–29 March: Halford world tour

(Exact date unknown): Tim Owens was asked to leave Judas Priest by e-mail

11 July: Rob Halford officially announced by phone live on CNN that he had re-joined Judas Priest

17 November: Iced Earth released *The Reckoning EP* in the UK with Tim Owens on vocals

24 November: Live DVD *Electric Eye* was released in the UK

2004

12 January: Iced Earth released *The Glorious Burden* in the UK – it was Tim Owens' first album since leaving Judas Priest

23 January: Dave Holland was found guilty of sexual abuse and attempted rape of a 17-year-old-boy

13 February: Dave Holland was sentenced to eight years and fined £10,000 for sexual abuse and attempted rape of a minor

17 May: Retrospective Judas Priest box set *Metalogy* was released in the UK

02 June–27 June: Played European festivals

10 July–2 September: Co-headlined the US Ozzfest with the original Black Sabbath (non-Ozzfest shows were added)

26 August: Halford fronted Black Sabbath live on stage at Tweeter Waterfront, Camden, New Jersey

2005

23 February–14 March: Toured Europe

12 March: *Angel Of Retribution* was released in the UK

16 March–31 March: Toured UK and Ireland

02 April–17 April: Toured Europe

08 May–19 May: Toured Japan

16 May: 'Worth Fighting For' single was released in the UK

30 May–10 July: Toured North America with Queensrÿche as special guests

01–16 September: Toured South America with Whitesnake as special guests

23 September–1 November: Second leg of US tour with Anthrax and Hatebreed as special guests

24 November–03 December: Toured Eastern Europe, which included dates in Russia

2006

23 January: Live DVD *Rising In The East* was released in the UK

09 February: Jayne Andrews announced that Priest had won in several categories at the *Burrn!* magazine awards in Japan

13 February: Live DVD *Live Vengeance '82* was released

07 March: Glenn Tipton's two solo albums were released simultaneously in the UK – *Edge Of The World* (first release) and *Baptizm Of Fire* (re-released with bonus tracks)

08 May: Ex-Priest vocalist Tim Owens and his band Beyond Fear released their self-titled debut album in the UK

24 May: Appeared as special guests on the US radio programme *Rockline*

28 May: Honoured at the first VH1 Rock Honours ceremony in Las Vegas

25 September: *The Essential Judas Priest* was released in the UK

23 October: Violent Storm's debut album *Storm Warning* was released in the UK – K.K. Downing's first non-Priest production credit

JUDAS PRIEST: A LINE-UP HISTORY

For a complete Judas Priest family tree, pay a visit to Al Atkins' excellent website at http://www.alatkins.com. I'd also like to personally thank Al Atkins, Ernie Chataway, John Ellis, John Hinch, Tim 'Ripper' Owens, Simon Phillips and Brian 'Bruno' Stapenhill for their assistance. The French fan site 'The French Metallian' was also very useful for this section. For details, go to http://judaspriest.free.fr

MARK I
1969–1970
Al Atkins – Vocals
Bruno Stapenhill – Bass
Ernie Chataway – Guitar
John Partridge – Drums

MARK II
1970–1971
Al Atkins – Vocals
K.K. Downing – Guitars
Ian Hill – Bass
John Ellis – Drums

MARK III
1971–1972
Al Atkins – Vocals
K.K. Downing – Guitars
Ian Hill – Bass
Alan Moore – Drums

MARK IV
1972–1973
Al Atkins – Vocals
K.K. Downing – Guitars
Ian Hill – Bass
Chris 'Congo' Campbell – Drums

MARK V
1973–1974
Rob Halford – Vocals
K.K. Downing – Guitars
Ian Hill – Bass
John Hinch – Drums

MARK VI
1974–1975
Rob Halford – Vocals

K.K. Downing – Guitars
Glenn Tipton – Guitars
Ian Hill – Bass
John Hinch – Drums

MARK VII
1975–1976
Rob Halford – Vocals
K.K. Downing – Guitars
Glenn Tipton – Guitars
Ian Hill – Bass
Alan Moore – Drums

MARK VIII
1977
Rob Halford – Vocals
K.K. Downing – Guitars
Glenn Tipton – Guitars
Ian Hill – Bass
Simon Phillips – (Session) Drummer

MARK IX
1977–1979
Rob Halford – Vocals
K.K. Downing – Guitars
Glenn Tipton – Guitars
Ian Hill – Bass
Les Binks – Drummer

MARK X
1979–1988
Rob Halford – Vocals
K.K. Downing – Guitars
Glenn Tipton – Guitars
Ian Hill – Bass
Dave Holland – Drums

MARK XI
1989–1992
Rob Halford – Vocals
K.K. Downing – Guitars
Glenn Tipton – Guitars
Ian Hill – Bass
Scott Travis – Drums

MARK XII
1996–2003
Tim 'Ripper' Owens – Vocals
K.K. Downing – Guitars
Glenn Tipton – Guitars
Ian Hill – Bass
Scott Travis – Drums

MARK XI REUNION
2003–Present
Rob Halford – Vocals
K.K. Downing – Guitars
Glenn Tipton – Guitars
Ian Hill – Bass
Scott Travis – Drums

SELECTIVE LIST OF NON-JUDAS PRIEST BANDS

Some fans ask the question: what other bands have Judas Priest members (both past and present) played in? Here is an alphabetical overview:

AL ATKINS
Al Atkins A.N.D.
The Bitta Sweet
Blue Condition
Jug Blues Band
Lion
The Reaction
Sugar Stack

LES BINKS
Eric Burdon
The Faintin' Goats
Fancy
Roger Glover
Lionheart
The Shakers
Tytan

ERNIE CHATAWAY
Bullion

ROB HALFORD
Athens Wood
Fight
Halford
Hiroshima
Lord Lucifer
Surgical Steel
Thark
Two

JOHN HINCH
The Bakerloo Blues Line
Hiroshima

DAVE HOLLAND
Al Atkins A.N.D.
Tony Iommi
Trapeze

ALAN 'SKIP' MOORE
Glad Stallion
Pendulum
Sundance
Tendency Jones

TIM 'RIPPER' OWENS
Alternation
Beyond Fear
British Steel
Damage Inc. (previously known as Brainicide)
Iced Earth
Seattle
Twist Of Fate
US Metal
Winters Bane

SIMON PHILLIPS
Asia
Jeff Beck
Jack Bruce
Stanley Clarke
Brian Eno
Mick Jagger
Phil Manzanera
Gary Moore
Mike Oldfield
PHD
Mike Rutherford
Michael Schenker
Derek Sherinian
Toto
Toyah
John Wetton
The Who (also played drums on solo albums by Roger Daltrey and Pete
    Townshend)

BRUNO STAPENHILL
The Bitta Sweet
Blue Condition
Bullion
The Cadence
Jug Blues Band
Lion
RAM
The Reaction

The Ryegee Explosion
Suicide
Sugar Stack

GLENN TIPTON
The Flying Hat Band
Merlin
Shave And Dry

SCOTT TRAVIS
Fight
Hawk
The Scream
Racer X

JUDAS PRIEST: TOUR DATES

*Like any band or artist aspiring to make an impact in their chosen musical genre,
Judas Priest took their music to the world. Having travelled far from Birmingham's
dingy backstreet clubs and pubs to that city's NEC, one of the biggest arenas
Britain has to offer, the band have played approximately 489 gigs in the UK
during their career to date and about 677 in the USA, an incredible achievement by
any standards.*

The author is greatly indebted to Kerrang!, Metal Hammer *and* Sounds *as
references when compiling UK dates from the Eighties to the present year. The
incredible archive site known as 'The French Metallian'
(http://judaspriest.free.fr/index.php?idm=m0) and Al Atkins' website
(http://www.alatkins.com/) were both valuable when listing international and pre-
Eighties dates. I would also like to thank Al personally for his assistance with the
earlier (1969–1973) tour dates. It has not been possible to note every single detail
but the listing is the most accurate possible on a basic level. To make reading easier,
I have listed the names of each album to whichever tour is relevant. If there was no
album released, I have simply referred to the continent in which the band were
touring at the time. Occasionally I have mentioned the support artist(s) too.*

*Looking at the following list is clearly enough evidence to show sceptics that Judas
Priest have spent most of their career working their arses off. So that hard work
should be immortalised!*

1969
BRITISH TOUR

25 November – The George Hotel, Walsall (England)

1970
BRITISH TOUR

(Exact date unknown) February – Masonic Hall, Walsall (England)
(Exact date unknown) February – Community Centre, Wednesbury (England)
(Exact date unknown) February – The George Hotel, Walsall (England)

8 March – Club Westbourne, Edgbaston (England)
9 March – Rugby Club, Shrewsbury (England)
11 March – Old Swinford Hospital School, Stourbridge (England)
13 March – Moor Farm Inn, Nottingham (England)
15 March – Hereford Town Hall, Hereford (England)

20 April – Youth Centre, Cannock (England)

1971
BRITISH TOUR

16 March – St. John's Hall, Essington (England)

7 April – Burntwood, Bath (England)
16 April – Three Mile Oak, West Bromwich (England)

1 May – Dudley Tech, Dudley (England)
8 May – Technical College, Walsall (England)
21 May – The Plaza, Old Hill (England)

01 June – Henry's Blues House, Birmingham (England)
18 June – Coppertops, Worchester (England)
19 June – Three Mile Oak, West Bromwich (England)
25 June – The Plaza, Old Hill (England)
30 June – Lafayette Club, Wolverhampton (England) *(Support to the Chicago Blues Band)*

02 July – Three Mile Oak, West Bromwich (England)
5 July – Central Hall, Birmingham (England)
10 July – Dudley Tech, Dudley (England)
12 July – The Gunn Inn, London (England)
26 July – Quaintways, Chester (England) *(Support to Status Quo)*
30 July – The Plaza, Old Hill (England)

08 August – Clouds, Derby (England)
14 August – The Village, Coventry (England)
21 August – Cavern Club, Liverpool (England)

02 September – Kinetic Circus, Birmingham (England) *(Support to Graphite)*
17 September – Coppertops, Worcester (England)
24 September – Cleopatra's, Derby (England)

04 October – Borough Hall, Stafford (England) *(Support to Thin Lizzy)*
06 October – The Yeoman, Derby (England) *(Support to Slade)*
09 October – Kinetic Circus, Birmingham (England) *(Support to Rory Gallagher)*
13 October – Yew Tree Centre, Walsall (England)
15 October – Community Centre, Newport (Wales)
16 October – Community Centre, Newport (Wales)
21 October – Café des Artistes, London (England)
22 October – Rose and Crown, London (England)
29 October – Zeppelin Club, Merton (England)

05 November – The Temple Club, London (England)
07 November – The Pheasantry, London (England)
12 November – Three Mile Oak, West Bromwich (England)
24 November – The Belfry, Birmingham (England)

03 December – Bromsgrove College, Broomsgrove (England)
05 December – Catacombs, Wolverhampton (England)
17 December – Distractions at the Bear, Burntwood (England)
24 December – Henry's Blues House, Birmingham (England)
28 December – Stoneground, Manchester (England)

1972
BRITISH TOUR

01 January – Hucknall MWC (Miners Club), Nottingham (England)
02 January – Gold Diamond, Nottingham (England)
03 January – Youth Wing, Penarth (Wales)
04 January – Bristol Legion, Cwmbach (Wales)
06 January – Youth Centre, Kincardine (Scotland)
13 January – Pavilion, Cheltenham (Scotland)

05 February – Underground Club, Worcester (England)
06 February – Magnet Club, West Bromwich (England)
09 February – Yew Tree Centre, West Bromwich (England)
17 February – Henry's Blues House, Birmingham (England) *(Support to Trapeze)*
18 February – Two J's Club, Essex (England)
20 February – Club Horn Hotel, Braintree (England)
26 February – The Greyhound Club, London (England)
28 February – Quarthouse, Chester (England)

04 March – Dudley Tech, Dudley (England)
09 March – Samantha's Blues Club, Leeds (England)
11 March – Manchester Centre, Manchester (England)
12 March – Bangor University (Arts Festival), Bangor (Wales)
13 March – City University, Northampton (England)
24 March – Glen Ballroom, Llanelli (Wales) *(Support to The Wild Angels)*
28 March – Rock City, Northampton (England)

05 April – Top Rank Suite, Doncaster (England)
12 April – Dix Club, Wolverhampton (England)
20 April – Youth Club *(Exact location unknown)* (Wales)
24 April – Dix Club, Wolverhampton (England)
28 April – Fag Club, Wigan (England)
29 April – Wellington Hall, Shropshire (England) *(Support to Spirit)*

09 June – College of Education, Swansea (Wales)
13 June – Ceda Club, Birmingham (England)
14 June – Ceda Club, Birmingham (England*) (Support to Dr. Ross)*
17 June – Laney Ballroom *(Exact location unknown)* (Wales)
20 June – Cleopatra's, Derby (England)
21 June – The Red Lion, Northampton (England)

11 July – Dudley Tech, Dudley (England)
12 July – Yew Tree Centre, West Bromwich (England)
13 July – Farafe Hotel *(Exact location unknown)* (Wales)
15 July – Walsgrove Hotel, Coventry (England)
21 July – Lafayette, Wolverhampton (England)

01 August – Henry's Blues House, Birmingham (England)
04 August – Dudley Tech, Dudley (England)
20 August – Moor Farm Inn, Nottingham (England)
27 August – *(Exact venue unknown)* Nottingham (England)
31 August – Mandy's, Coventry (England)

07 September – Town Hall, West Bromwich (England)
08 September – Plough and Harrow, Nottingham (England)
15 September – British Legion Club, Nottingham (England)
17 September – Moor Farm Inn, Nottingham (England)
24 September – Kinetic Circus, Birmingham (England)
28 September – The Babalou Club, Liverpool (England)
29 September – The Fighting Cocks, Mosely (England)
30 September – County Cricket Club, Northampton (England) *(Support to Curved Air)*

01 October – Angel Underground, Stafford (England)
02 October – King's Head, Stafford (England)
04 October – Borough Hall, Stafford (England)
05 October – Marquee, London (England)
06 October – The County, Northampton (England)
06 October – The Speakeasy, London (England)
07 October – Plough and Apron, Nottingham (England)
08 October – The Spectrum, Stockport (England)
09 October – Hotel *(Exact venue unknown)* Workington (England)
10 October – Angel Underground, West Bromwich (England)
10 October – *(Exact venue unknown)* Birmingham (England)
13 October – Pyramid Club, Liverpool (England)
13 October – Cavern Club, Liverpool (England)
14 October – Uniforum, Bradworth (England)
21 October – Cavern Club, Liverpool (England)
23 October – Quarthouse, Chester (England)
27 October – Fag Club, Wigan (England)
29 October – Brumling Budgie Club, London (England)

03 November – The Penthouse, Bridlington (England)
05 November – The Temple, West Bromwich (England)
13 November – The Top Rank, Doncaster (England)
20 November – Seven Stars, Haywood (England)
27 November – The Plaza, Old Hill (England) *(with The Flying Hat Band)*

14 December – Fantasia, Northampton (England)
16 December – Boat Club, Nottingham (England) *(Support to the Alex Harvey Band)*
21 December – Wellington Arms *(Exact location unknown)* (England)
26 December – Henry's Blues House, Birmingham (England)
(Exact date unknown) – Catacombs, Wolverhampton (England)
(Exact date unknown) – Spectrum, Stockport (England)
(Exact date unknown) – Fantasia, Northampton (England)
(Exact date unknown) –The Speakeasy, London (England)
(Exact date unknown) – Café Des Artistes, London (England)
(Exact date unknown) – Pedugh, Harrow (England)
(Exact date unknown) – The Pheasantry, Chelsea (England)
(Exact date unknown) – Zeppelin King *(Exact location unknown)* (England)

1973
BRITISH TOUR

(Exact date unknown) January – Seven Stars Club, Haywood (England)
(Exact date unknown) January – New Windmill Hall, Essex (England)

February – Tour of Scotland (No dates available – three weeks in total)

(Exact date unknown) March – St. George's Hall, Liverpool (England)
   (Support to Budgie)
(Exact date unknown) March – Nightclub *(Exact location unknown)* Southport
   (England)

(Exact date unknown) April – College of Art and Food, Birmingham
   (Support to Budgie)
12 April – Dix Club, Wolverhampton (England)
15 April – Hippodrome, Birmingham (England) *(Support to Family)*
29 April – Wellington Hall, Shropshire (England)

17 July – Town Hall, Bolton (England)
18 July – Town Hall, Castleford (England)
19 July – Houldsworth Hall, Manchester (England)
20 July – St. George's Hall, Liverpool (England)
21 July – Arts Centre, Huddersfield (England)
22 July – Memorial Hall *(Exact location unknown)* (England)
23 July – Memorial Hall, Northwich (England)
24 July – Borough Hall, Stafford (England)
26 July – Drill Hall, Lincoln (England)
27 July – City Hall, Hull (England)
28 July – Alexandra Palace, London (England)
29 July – Albany Hotel, Nottingham (England)
30 July – Boobs of Tiffany's, Merthyr (Wales)
31 July – Locarno, Coventry (England)

01 August – Pavilion, Hemel Hempstead (England)
02 August – Memorial Hall, Barry (Wales)
03 August – Guildhall, Plymouth (England)
04 August – City Hall, Truro (England)
11 August – Town Park, Harlow (England)
17 August – Global Village, London (England)
26 August – Kendal Festival, Westmorland (England)

(Exact date unknown) – Top Hat, Spennymoor (England)
(Exact date unknown) – Top Deck, Redcar (England)
(Exact date unknown) – Town Hall, Gainsborough (England)
(Exact date unknown) – Outlook, Doncaster (England)

06 September – Town Hall, Birmingham (England)

1974
EUROPEAN TOUR

11 February – Marquee, London (England)
19 February – *(Exact venue and location unknown)* (Germany)

04 March – *(Exact venue and location unknown)* (Holland)
15 March – Civic Hall, St. Albans (England)
25 March – *(Exact venue and city unknown)* (Norway)

07 April – *(Exact venue and location unknown)* (Norway)
13 April – Civic Hall, St. Albans (England)
22 April – Top Rank Suite, Doncaster (England)

09 May – Town Hall, Doncaster (England)
10 May – Town Hall, Leeds (England)
11 May – Floral Hall, Scarborough (England)
12 May – City Hall, Newcastle (England)
15 May – Heavy Steam Machine, Stoke-On-Trent (England)
16 May – Tiffany's Club, Derby (England)
17 May – City Hall, Sheffield (England)
18 May – Stoneground, Manchester (England)
19 May – King George's Hall, Blackburn (England)
21 May – Memorial Hall, Barry (Wales)
22 May – County Hall, Taunton (England)
22 May – Pavilion, Bath (England)
23 May – Norfolk Art College, King's Lynn (England)
24 May – Victoria Hall, Tonbridge (England)
25 May – City Hall, St. Albans (England)
26 May – Woodsville Hall, Gravesend (England)
27 May – Guildhall, Plymouth (England)
28 May – Town Hall, Torquay (England)
29 May – Town Hall, High Wycombe (England)
30 May – Top of the World, Guildford (England)
31 May – Community Centre, Slough (England)

01 June – Eversham Hall, Eversham (England)
01 June – Brighton Polytechnic, Brighton (England)
03 June – Sherwood Rooms, Nottingham (England)
04 June – Tiffany's Club, Hull (England)
05 June – Town Hall, Sittingbourne (England)
06 June – Westgate Hall, Canterbury (England)
07 June – King Alfred College, Winchester (England)
08 June – Liverpool Stadium, Liverpool (England)
09 June – Marquee, London (England)
14 June – Locarno Ballroom, Sunderland (England)
21 June – Mayfair Ballroom, Newcastle (England)

ROCKA ROLLA BRITISH TOUR

10 September – Arts Theatre, Huddersfield (England)
12 September – Windsor Hall, Blackburn (England)
13 September – St. George's Hall, Liverpool (England)
14 September – Lowther Pavilion, Blackpool (England)
15 September – Chesford Grange Hotel, Kenilworth (England)
16 September – Memorial Hall, Barry (Wales)
18 September – Drill Hall, Lincoln (England)
19 September – Marquee, London (England)
20 September – Pier, Hastings (England)
22 September – Woodville Hall, Gravesend (England)
23 September – Top Hat, Spennymoor (England)
24 September – Winter Gardens, Cleethorpes (England)
25 September – Civic Hall, Dunstable (England)
27 September – Penthouse, Scarborough (England)
28 September – Leas Cliff Hall, Folkestone (England)
30 September – Quaintways, Chester (England)

01 October – Civic Theatre, Halifax (England)
02 October – St. Andrew's Hall, Norwich (England)
05 October – Priory Ballroom, Scunthorpe (England)
06 October – Barbarellas, Birmingham (England)
07 October – Cooks Ferry Inn, London (England)
09 October – Lafayette, Wolverhampton (England)
10 October – Civic Theatre, Bedford (England)
11 October – Corn Exchange, Devizes (England)
12 October – Civic Hall, St. Albans (England)
14 October – Queens Hall, Narberth (Wales)
15 October – Glen Ballroom, Llanelli (Wales)
16 October – Town Hall, Swindon (England)
17 October – Queens Hall, Barnstable (England)
18 October – Flamingo, Redruth (England)
19 October – Country Ballroom, Taunton (England)
23 October – Pavilion, Cheltenham (England)
24 October – Manchester Polytechnic, Manchester (England)
25 October – City Hall, Newcastle (England)
27 October – Arts Theatre, Hull (England)
28 October – Town Hall, Walsall (England)
30 October – Plaza Ballroom, Guildford (England)

08 November – 76 Club, Burton-On-Trent (England)

28 December – Royal Links Pavilion, Norfolk (England)

1975

21 February – Main Hall, Latfield (England)

04 March – The Steam Machine, Hanley (England)
06 March – Top of the World, Stafford (England)
20 March – Cornwall Tech, Cornwall (England)
22 March – Liverpool Stadium, Liverpool (England)

05 April – Johnson Hall, Yeovil (England)
12 April – Town Hall, Birmingham (England)
13 April – Barbarellas, Birmingham (England)
30 April – Marquee Club, London (England)

03 May – 76 Club, Burton-On-Trent (England)
16 May – Marquee Club, London (England)
23 May – Poynton Civic Hall, Poynton (England)

05 June – The Highwayman, Threapwood (England)
14 June – Cloud Nine, Redditch (England)
20 June – Mayfair Ballroom, Newcastle (England)
27 June – Locarno, Sunderland (England)
28 June – City Hall, St. Albans (England)

05 July – Priority Hotel, Scunthorpe (England)
22 July – Cardiff Top Rank, Cardiff (Wales)
24 July – Cleopatra's, Derby (England)
25 July – Regency Ballroom, Derby (England)
27 July – Winning Post, Twickenham (England)
29 July – Ivanhoe's, Yorkshire (England)

02 August – Leas Cliff Hall, Folkestone (England)
03 August – Roundhouse, London (England)
07 August – Civic Hall, Dunstable (England)
09 August – Roundhouse Lodge, Dagenham (England)
14 August – Nagshead, High Wycombe (England)

15 August – Palace, Newark-On-Trent (England)
16 August – Casino Club, Wigan (England)
21 August – Hardrock, Manchester (England)
22 August – Reading Festival (Thameside Arena), Reading (England)
28 August – Winter Gardens, Penzance (England)
29 August – Blue Lagoon Ballroom, Cornwall (England)

05 September – Town Hall, Watford
06 September – Links Pavilion, Cromer

11 October – Slough College, Slough (England)
12 October – Roundhouse, London (England)
18 October – City Hall, St. Albans (England)
30 October – Dundee University, Dundee (Scotland)
31 October – Edinburgh University, Edinburgh (Scotland)

01 November – Glasgow University, Glasgow (Scotland)
05 November – Marquee, London (England)
14 November – Harrow College, Harrow (England)
15 November – Hitchin College, Hitchin (England)

05 December – North Cumberland College, North Cumberland
    (England)
07 December – Winning Post, Twickenham (England)
09 December – Ivanhoe's, Yorkshire (England)
12 December – Coventry Tech, Coventry (England)
28 December – Roundhouse, London (England)

1976
SAD WINGS OF DESTINY BRITISH TOUR

06 April – The Plaza, Truro (England)
09 April – Corn Exchange, Cambridge (England)
12 April – Town Hall, Birmingham (England)
14 April – Winter Gardens, Malvern (England)
17 April – City Hall, St. Albans (England)
18 April – Greyhound, Croydon (England)
25 April – Wyvern Theatre, Swindon (England)
30 April – Mayfair Ballroom, Newcastle (England)

04 May – King George's Hall, Blackburn (England)
06 May – Leeds Polytechnic, Leeds (England)
08 May – Technical College, Harlow (England)
09 May – Civic Hall, Guildford (England)
11 May – Queensway Hall, Dunstable (England)
12 May – Kursaal Ballroom, Southend (England)
13 May – Skindles, Maidenhead (England)
14 May – University, Slough (England)
15 May – Thames University, Kent (England)
27 May – New Victoria Theatre, London (England)
(Exact date unknown) May – Drill Hall, Lincoln (England)
(Exact date unknown) May – Civic Hall, Guildford (England)

20 June – Roundhouse Theatre, London (England)

1977
SIN AFTER SIN WORLD TOUR

(Exact date unknown) April – Kuusrock Festival, Oulu (Finland)
22 April – Corn Exchange, Cambridge (England)
23 April – Kursaal Ballroom, Southend (England)
24 April – Skindles, Maidenhead (England)
26 April – Top Rank, Cardiff (Wales)
27 April – Danebank Theatre, Crewe (England)
29 April – Pavilion, West Runton (England)
30 April – Cricket Club, Northampton (England)

01 May – Greyhound, Croydon (England)
02 May – Top Rank, Plymouth (England)
03 May – Pavilion, Hemel Hempstead (England)
05 May – Winter Gardens, Cleethorpes (England)
07 May – Empire Theatre, Liverpool (England)
08 May – Top Rank, Sheffield (England)
09 May – Town Hall, Birmingham (England)
12 May – ABC Ardwick Apollo, Manchester (England)
13 May – Mayfair Ballroom, Newcastle (England)
14 May – Coatham Bowl, Redcar (England)
15 May – Imperial, Blackpool (England)
16 May – Leeds Polytechnic, Leeds (England)

17 May – Drill Hall, Lincoln (England)
18 May – Civic Hall, Guildford (England)
19 May – Mayfair Ballroom, Newcastle (England)
20 May – Brunel Rooms, Swindon (England)
21 May – Pier Pavilion, Hastings (England)
22 May – New Victoria Theatre, London (England)

17 June – Civic Center, Amarillo, TX (USA) *(Support to REO Speedwagon)*
19 June – Texas Hall, Dallas, TX (USA)
20 June – Music Hall, Houston, TX (USA)
21 June – Municipal Auditorium, TX (USA)
22 June – Memorial Coliseum, Corpus Christi, TX (USA)
28 June – Music Hall, Oklahoma City, OK (USA)
30 June – Coliseum, Jackson, MS (USA)

01 July – Civic Center, Dothan, AL (USA)
02 July – Fox Theatre, Atlanta, GA (USA)
05 July – Municipal Auditorium, Charleston, SC (USA)
06 July – Freedom Hall, Johnson City, TN (USA)
07 July – Rupp Arena, Lexington, KY (USA)
08 July – Haymaker's Club, Wheeling, IL (USA) *(Support to REO Speedwagon)*
09 July – Busch Stadium (Superjam 1977,) St Louis, MO (USA)
16 July – Palladium Theater, New York, NY (USA) *(Support to REO Speedwagon and Starz)*
23 July – Oakland Coliseum, California (USA) *(Support to Led Zeppelin)*
24 July – Oakland Coliseum, California (USA) *(Support to Led Zeppelin)*

29 August – Blue Lagoon Ballroom, Cornwall (England)

06 October – Volkshaus, Zurich (Switzerland) *(Support to AC/DC)*
10 October – Volkshaus, Zurich (Switzerland) *(Support to AC/DC)*

1978
STAINED CLASS WORLD TOUR

19 January – Cramer Links Park, West Runton (England)
20 January – Corn Exchange, Cambridge (England)

21 January – Leeds University, Leeds (England)
22 January – Coventry Theatre, Coventry (England)
23 January – City Hall, Sheffield (England)
24 January – Top Rank, Cardiff (Wales)
26 January – Victoria Hall, Hanley (England)
27 January – Lancaster University, Lancaster (England)
30 January – Guildhall, Portsmouth (England)
31 January – Colston Hall, Bristol (England)

01 February – Civic Hall, Wolverhampton (England)
02 February – City Hall, Newcastle (England)
03 February – Music Hall, Aberdeen (Scotland)
04 February – Odeon Theatre, Edinburgh (Scotland)
05 February – Apollo Theatre, Glasgow (Scotland)
06 February – Free Trade Hall (Apollo Theatre), Manchester (England)
07 February – De Montfort Hall, Leicester (England)
09 February – Queensway Hall, Dunstable (England)
10 February – Hammersmith Odeon, London (England)
11 February – Odeon Theatre, Birmingham (England)
12 February – Town Hall, Middlesbrough (England)
(Exact date unknown) February – Civic Hall, Guildford (England)
25 February – St. George's Hall, Bradford (England)
(Exact date unknown) February – Pavilion, Hemel Hempstead (England)

10 March – Palladium Theater, New York, NY (USA) *(Support to Angel)*
11 March – Palladium Theater, New York, NY (USA)
17 March – Tarrant County Convention Center, Fort Worth, TX (USA)
18 March – Tarrant County Convention Center, Fort Worth, TX (USA)
23 March – *(Exact venue unknown,)* San Antonio, TX (USA)
25 March – Crazy Horse Saloon, Killeen, TX (USA)
28 March – Civic Arena, Killeen, TX (USA)

24 April – Civic Theater, San Diego, CA (USA)

7 May – Agora Theater & Ballroom, Cleveland, OH (USA)
12 May – Riverfront Coliseum, Cincinnati, OH (USA)
13 May – Rockne Hall, Allentown, PA (USA)

07 July – *(Exact venue unknown)* San Antonio, TX (USA)
25 July – Nakano Sun Plaza Hall, Tokyo (Japan)
29 July – Shiba Yubinchokin, Tokyo (Japan)

31 July – Koseinenkin Hall, Tokyo (Japan)

03 August – Koseinenkin Hall, Nagoya (Japan)
05 August – Festival Hall, Osaka (Japan)

X CERTIFICATE **BRITISH TOUR**

23 October – BBC Studios, London (England)
24 October – King George's, Blackburn (England)
25 October – City Hall, Newcastle (England)
26 October – Civic Hall, Wolverhampton (England)
27 October – Hammersmith Odeon, London (England)
28 October – BBC Radio, London (England)
29 October – Victoria Hall, Hanley (England)
30 October – Queensway Hall, Dunstable (England)
31 October – The Dome, Brighton (England)

01 November – Guildhall, Portsmouth (England)
02 November – City Hall, Sheffield (England)
03 November – De Montfort Hall, Leicester (England)
04 November – Lancaster University, Lancaster (England)
06 November – Empire, Liverpool (England)
07 November – Odeon, Edinburgh (Scotland)
08 November – Apollo, Glasgow (Scotland)
09 November – St. George's Hall, Bradford (England)
11 November – Assembly Rooms, Derby (England)
12 November – Hippodrome, Bristol (England)
13 November – Odeon, Birmingham (England)
14 November – Apollo, Manchester (England)
17 November – Hammersmith Odeon, London (England)
19 November – City Hall, Newcastle (England)
(Exact date unknown) November – *(Exact venue unknown)* Bournemouth
    (England)
(Exact date unknown) November – Sophia Gardens, Cardiff (Wales)
(Exact date unknown) November – City Hall, Sheffield (England)
24 November – Wirrina Stadium, Peterborough (England)

15 December – Stage One, Buffalo, NY (USA)
16 December – Palladium Theater, New York, NY (USA)

1979
KILLING MACHINE WORLD TOUR

10 February – Koseinenkin Hall, Tokyo (Japan)
13 February – Festival Hall, Osaka (Japan)
14 February – Festival Hall, Osaka (Japan)
15 February – Nakano Sun Plaza Hall, Tokyo (Japan)
27 February – Agriculture Hall, Allentown, PA (USA)
29 February – Louie's Rock City, Falls Church, VA (USA)

11 March – Mudd Club, New York, NY (USA)
15 March – Music Hall, Houston, TX (USA)
22 March – Civic Center, San Antonio, TX (USA)
29 March – Starwood Club, Los Angeles, CA (USA)
30 March – Starwood Club, Los Angeles, CA (USA)
31 March – Starwood Club, Los Angeles, CA (USA)

(Exact date unknown) April – El Mocambo, Ontario, Toronto (Canada)
(Exact date unknown) April – Crossroads, Bailey's, VA (USA)
10 April – Yakima Valley College, Washington, DC (USA)
11 April – Medford Armory, Medford, OR (USA)
13 April – Paramount Theater, Seattle, WA (USA)
21 April – *(Exact venue unknown)* San Diego, CA (USA)

04 May – International Amphitheater, Chicago, IL (USA)
06 May – Sports Arena, Milwaukee, WI (USA)
12 May – Apollo, Glasgow (Scotland)
13 May – Empire, Liverpool (England)
14 May – Assembly Rooms, Derby (England)
15 May – Apollo, Manchester (England)
16 May – Odeon Theatre, Birmingham (England)
17 May – Odeon Theatre, Birmingham (England)
18 May – Victoria Hall, Hanley (England)
19 May – New Theatre, Oxford (England)
20 May – Colston Hall, Bristol (England)
21 May – De Montfort Hall, Leicester (England)
22 May – Guildhall, Preston (England)
23 May – City Hall, Newcastle (England)
24 May – City Hall, Newcastle (England)
25 May – City Hall, Sheffield (England)
26 May – City Hall, Sheffield (England)

27 May – Gaumont Theatre, Southampton (England)
28 May – Hammersmith Odeon, London (England)
29 May – Hammersmith Odeon, London (England)

01 July – Dalymount Park Festival, Dublin (Ireland)

01 September – Nassau Coliseum, Uniondale, NY (USA)
03 September – *(Exact venue unknown)* New Haven, CT (USA)
08 September – Paramount Theater, Asbury Park, NJ (USA)
11 September – Forum Arena, Los Angeles, CA (USA)
14 September – Riverfront Coliseum, Cincinnati, OH (USA)
16 September – Freedom Hall (Kentucky State Fair,) Louisville, KY (USA)
20 September – Civic Center, Evansville, IN (USA)
21 September – Universal Amphitheater, Chicago, IL (USA)
22 September – Universal Amphitheater, Chicago, IL (USA)
24 September – Mecca Arena, Milwaukee, WI (USA)
30 September – Memorial Hall, Kansas City, MO (USA)

03 October – Music Hall, Houston, TX (USA)
05 October – Texas Hall University, Arlington, TX (USA)
11 October – Civic Center, Laredo, TX (USA)
14 October – El Paso Civic Center, El Paso, TX (USA)
17 October – Coliseum Arena, Seattle, WA (USA)
23 October – Civic Center, Santa Monica, CA (USA)
26 October – Hammond Civic Center, Hammond, IN (USA)
30 October – Ontario Theater, Washington, DC (USA)

03 November – Capitol Theater, Passaic, NJ (USA)
04 November – Palladium Theater, New York, NY (USA)
09 November – *(Exact venue unknown)* San Antonio, TX (USA)
11 November – Forest National, Brussels (Belgium)
12 November – Jaap Edenhal, Amsterdam (Holland)
13 November – Sartory Hall, *(Exact location unknown)* (Germany)
14 November – Ellenriederhalle, Hanover (Germany)
16 November – Grugahalle, Essen (Germany)
17 November – Kurnachtal-Halle *(Exact location unknown)* (Germany)
19 November – Niderbeiernhalle, Passau (Germany)
20 November – Stadthalle, Offenbach (Germany)
21 November – Westfalenhalle 3, Dortmund (Germany)
23 November – Messehalle 8, Hamburg (Germany)
24 November – Circus Krone, Munich (Germany)

25 November – Festhalle, Bern (Switzerland)
27 November – RT Halle, Regensburg (Germany)
28 November – Oberschwabenhalle, Ravensburg (Germany)
29 November – Freiheitshalle, Hof (Germany)

01 December – Friedrich-Ebert-Halle, Ludwigshafen (Germany)
02 December – Hemmerleinhalle *(Exact location unknown)* (Germany)
03 December – Eissporthalle, Berlin (Germany)
04 December – Stadthalle, Offenbach (Germany)
06 December – Parc des Expositions, Metz (France)
07 December – Palais des Sports, Reims (France)
08 December – Palais des Sports, Lille (France)
09 December – Pavillon de Pantin, Paris (France)
10 December – Palais des Sports, Lyon (France)
12 December – Maison des Sports, Clermond-Ferrand (France)
13 December – Palais des Sports, Montpellier (France)
14 December – Théâtre de Verdure, Nice (France)
15 December – Théâtre de Verdure, Nice (France)

1980
BRITISH STEEL WORLD TOUR

07 March – Cardiff University, Cardiff (Wales)
08 March – Leeds University, Leeds (England)
09 March – Colston Hall, Bristol (England)
10 March – Apollo Theatre, Manchester (England)
11 March – City Hall, Sheffield (England)
12 March – City Hall, Sheffield (England)
13 March – De Montfort Hall, Leicester (England)
14 March – Hammersmith Odeon, London (England)
15 March – Hammersmith Odeon, London (England)
16 March – Gaumont Theatre, Southampton (England)
18 March – Capitol Theatre, Aberdeen (Scotland)
19 March – Odeon Theatre, Edinburgh (Scotland)
20 March – Mayfair Theatre, Newcastle (England)
21 March – Mayfair Theatre, Newcastle (England)
22 March – Apollo Theatre, Glasgow (Scotland)
23 March – Deeside Leisure Centre, Queensferry (Scotland)
24 March – Empire Theatre, Liverpool (England)

25 March – Trentham Gardens Grand Hall Theatre, Stoke-On-Trent
   (England)
26 March – Odeon Theatre, Birmingham (England)
27 March – Odeon Theatre, Birmingham (England)

01 April – Rainbow Theatre, London (England)
03 April – *(Exact venue unknown)* London (England)
05 April – Kotrijk Festival, *(Exact location unknown)* (Belgium)
07 April – *(Exact venue unknown)* Plymouth (England)
08 April – *(Exact venue unknown)* London (England)
10 April – *(Exact venue unknown)* Grimsby (England)
12 April – Markthalle, Hamburg (Germany)
13 April – Neue Welt, Berlin (Germany)
14 April – Niedersachsenhalle, Hanover (Germany)
15 April – *(Exact venue and location unknown)* (Germany)
16 April – Hugenottenhalle, Neu-Isenburg (Germany)
18 April – Stadthalle, Erlangen (Germany)
20 April – Schwabinger Br, Munich (Germany)
21 April – Rosengarten, Mannheim (Germany)
22 April – Stadthalle, Karlsruhe (Germany)
25 April – Bataclan, Paris (France)
26 April – Forest National, Brussels (Belgium)

09 May – International Amphitheater, Chicago, IL (USA)
25 May – Will Rogers Auditorium, Fort Worth, TX (USA)
31 May – The Summit, Houston, TX (USA)

01 June – Civic Center, San Antonio, TX (USA)
02 June – Corpus Christi Coliseum, Corpus Christi, TX (USA)
06 June – Chaparral Center Arena, Midland, TX (USA)
07 June – County Coliseum, El Paso, TX (USA)
12 June – Veterans Memorial Coliseum, Phoenix, AZ (USA)
13 June – Long Beach Arena, Los Angeles, CA (USA)
15 June – SDSU Amphitheater, San Diego, CA (USA)
17 June – Coliseum Arena, Seattle, WA (USA)
19 June – Fox Warfield Theater, San Francisco, CA (USA)
21 June – Coliseum Complex, Portland, OR (USA)
25 June – Rainbow Music Hall, Denver, CO (USA)
29 June – Busch Stadium, St. Louis, MO (USA)

07 July – Rochester Auditorium, New York, NY (USA)

03 July – Convention Center, Asbury Park, NJ (USA)
04 July – Stage West, Hartford, CT (USA)
05 July – Nassau Coliseum, Hempstead, CT (USA)
07 July – Calderone Hall, Hempstead, NY (USA)
08 July – Towson Center, Towson, MD (USA)
12 July – Palladium Theater, New York, NY (USA)
22 July – Busch Stadium, St. Louis, MO (USA)
23 July – Wings Stadium, Kalamazoo, MI (USA)
25 July – Pekin Memorial Arena, Pekin, IL (USA)
26 July – Pekin Memorial Arena, Pekin, IL (USA)
27 July – Rockford Motor Speedway, Rockford, IL (USA)
28 July – Five Flags Center, Dubuque, IA (USA)
29 July – Wings Stadium, Kalamazoo, MI (USA)
30 July – Agora Theater & Ballroom, Cleveland, OH (USA)
31 July – Civic Arena, Pittsburgh, PA (USA)

02 August- The Garden, Boston, MA (USA)
03 August – Onondaga War Memorial, Syracuse, MY (USA)
05 August – O'Hara Arena, Dayton, OH (USA)
16 August – Donington Park (Monsters of Rock Festival) (England)
23 August – Neunkirchen Festival, Nuremberg (Germany)

1981
POINT OF ENTRY WORLD TOUR

13 February – Rodahal, Kerkrade (Holland)
14 February – Japp Edenhal, Amsterdam (Holland)
16 February – Hippodrome, Paris (France)
17 February – Hippodrome, Paris (France)
19 February – Hemmerleinhalle, Neunkirchen (Germany)
20 February – Messehalle, Stuttgart (Germany)
26 February – *(Exact venue unknown)* Kassel (Germany)
26 February – Rhein-Main-Halle, Wiesbaden (Germany)
28 February – *(Exact venue unknown)* Strasbourg (France)

01 March – *(Exact venue unknown)* Cambrai (France)
06 March – Ostseehalle, Kiel (Germany)
06 May – Indiana Convention Center, Indianapolis, IN (USA)
08 May – International Amphitheater, Chicago, IL (USA)
09 May – Metro Center, Rockford, IL (USA)

14 May – Metro Center, Minneapolis, MN (USA)
15 May – Civic Auditorium Music Hall, Omaha, NE (USA)
22 May – Oakland Auditorium, Oakland, CA (USA)
23 May – Long Beach Arena, Los Angeles, CA (USA)
25 May – SDSU Amphitheater, San Diego, CA (USA)
27 May – Selland Arena, Fresno, CA (USA)
30 May – Seattle Center, Seattle, WA (USA)

04 June – Veterans Memorial Coliseum, Phoenix, AZ (USA)
09 June – *(Exact venue unknown)* McAllen, TX (USA)
10 June – *(Exact venue unknown)* Laredo, TX (USA)
11 June – Convention Center Arena, San Antonio, TX (USA)
13 June – Moody Coliseum, Dallas, TX (USA)
14 June – Sam Houston Coliseum, Houston, TX (USA)
21 June – Universal Amphitheater, Chicago, IL (USA)

01 July – Capital Center, Largo, MD (USA)
02 July – Convention Hall, Asbury Park, NJ (USA)
15 July – O'Hara Arena, Dayton, Ohio
18 July – Auditorium Theater, Rochester, NY (USA)
22 July – Palladium Theater, New York, NY (USA)
26 July – Fairgrounds, Allentown, PA (USA)
29 July – Civic Center, Baltimore, MD (USA)
30 July – Tower Theater, Philadelphia, PA (USA)
31 July – Dr Pepper Festival Pier 9, New York, NY (USA)

07 November – Apollo, Manchester (England)
08 November – Apollo, Manchester (England)
09 November – De Montfort Hall, Leicester (England)
10 November – Colston Hall, Bristol (England)
11 November – Sophia Gardens, Cardiff (Wales)
12 November – Odeon Theatre, Birmingham (England)
13 November – Odeon Theatre, Birmingham (England)
15 November – Apollo Theatre, Glasgow (Scotland)
16 November – City Hall, Newcastle (England)
17 November – City Hall, Newcastle (England)
18 November – City Hall, Sheffield (England)
19 November – City Hall, Sheffield (England)
20 November – Leisure Centre, Crawley (England)
21 November – Hammersmith Odeon, London (England)
22 November – Hammersmith Odeon, London (England)

23 November – Gaumont Theatre, Southampton (England)
24 November – Wessex Hall, Poole (England)
27 November – Rhein-Main-Halle, Wiesbaden (Germany)
28 November – Grugahalle, Essen (Germany)
29 November – Stadthalle, Esslington (Germany)
31 November – Saarlandhalle, Saarbrücken (Germany)

01 December – Stadthalle, Offenbach (Germany)
02 December – Schwarzwaldhalle, Karlsruhe (Germany)
03 December – Friedrich-Ebert-Halle, Ludwigshafen (Germany)
04 December – Rudi Sedlmayer Halle, Munich (Germany)
05 December – Palais de Beaulieu, Lausanne (Switzerland)
06 December – Maison des Sports, Clemond-Ferrand (France)
07 December – Pavilion Espace Ballard, Paris (France)
08 December – Hall Rhemus, Strasbourg (France)
09 December – Palais des Sports, Lille (France
11 December – Forest National, Brussels (Belgium)
12 December – Jaap Edenhal, Amsterdam (Holland)
13 December – Grugahalle, Essen (Germany)
14 December – Markthalle, Hamburg (Germany)
(Exact date unknown) December – Roberto Clemento Coliseum, San Juan
    (Puerto-Rico)

1982
SCREAMING FOR VENGEANCE WORLD TOUR

26 August – Stabler Arena, Bethlehem, PA (USA)
28 August – East Troy, Alpine Valley, WI (USA)
29 August – Prairie Capital Convention Center, Springfield, IL (USA)

03 September – County Coliseum, El Paso, IL (USA)
07 September – Coliseum Arena, Houston, TX (USA)
10 September – Convention Center, San Antonio, TX (USA)
11 September – Reunion Arena, Dallas, TX (USA)
14 September – Kiel Auditorium, St. Louis, MA (USA)
15 September – Municipal Auditorium, Kansas City, MO (USA)
16 September – *(Exact venue unknown)* Lincoln, NE (USA)
17 September – Metro Center, Minneapolis, MN (USA)
19 September – Metro Center, Minneapolis, MN (USA)

21 September – Rosemont Horizon, Chicago, IL (USA)
22 September – Richfield Coliseum, Cleveland, OH (USA)
23 September – O'Hara Arena, Dayton, OH (USA)
25 September – Cobo Hall, Detroit, MI (USA)
26 September – Wings Stadium, Kalamazoo, MI (USA)
28 September – *(Exact venue unknown)* Hunnington, IN (USA)
29 September – Ohio Center, Columbus, OH (USA)

01 October – Centrum, Worchester, MA (USA)
02 October – Madison Square Garden, New York, NY (USA)
03 October – City Island, Harrisburg, PA (USA)
06 October – Civic Center, Portland, ME (USA)
07 October – Civic Center, Providence, RI (USA)
08 October – Civic Center, Glens Falls, NY (USA)
09 October – Coliseum, New Haven, CT (USA)
11 October – Broome County Arena, Binghamton, NY (USA)
12 October – The Spectrum, Philadelphia, PA (USA)
13 October – Civic Arena, Pittsburgh, PA (USA)
15 October – Memorial Auditorium, Buffalo, NY (USA)
16 October – Onondaga War Memorial, Syracuse, NY (USA)
17 October – Capital Center, Landover Hills, MD (USA)
19 October – Civic Center, Baltimore, MD (USA)
20 October – *(Exact venue unknown)* Salisbury, MD (USA)
21 October – *(Exact venue unknown)* Norfolk, VA (USA)
22 October – Meadowlands Arena, Rutherford, NJ (USA)
23 October – War Memorial, Rutherford, NJ (USA)
24 October – The Arena, Winnipeg (Canada)
26 October – Verdun Auditorium, Quebec, Montreal (Canada)
28 October – Maple Leaf Gardens, Ontario, Toronto (Canada)
31 October – Expo Center, Arlington (Canada)

04 November – The Arena, Winnipeg (Canada)
15 November – Coliseum, Seattle, WA (USA)
17 November – Lawlor Events Center, Reno, NY (USA)
23 November – Veterans Memorial Coliseum, Phoenix, AZ (USA)
27 November – Sports Arena, San Diego, CA (USA)

01 December – Tingley Coliseum, Albuquerque, NM (USA)
05 December – Cincinnati Gardens, Cincinnati, OH (USA)
09 December – Sunrise Theater, Columbia, TN (USA)
12 December – Mid-South Coliseum, Memphis TN (USA)

1983

12 January – Tingley Coliseum, Albuquerque, NM (USA)
16 January – Greensboro, Greensboro, NC (USA)
21 January – MECCA Auditorium, Milwaukee, WI (USA)
24 January – Lansing Civic Center, Lansing, MI (USA)
30 January – *(Exact venue unknown)* Duluth, MN (USA)
31 January – Hammonds Student Center, Springfield, MO (USA)

14 February – Frank Erwin Center, Austin, TX (USA)
21 February – NBC Arena, Honolulu, HI (USA)
29 February – Glen Helen Regional Park, San Bernardino, CA (USA)

08 July – Convention Center, Houston, TX (USA)

06 November – Northlands Coliseum, Edmonton (Canada)

12 December – City Hall, Newcastle (England)
13 December – Apollo Theatre, Glasgow (Scotland)
15 December – Apollo, Manchester (England)
16 December – Hammersmith Odeon, London (England)
20 December – De Montfort Hall, Leicester (England)
21 December – Odeon Theatre, Birmingham (England)
22 December – Odeon Theatre, Birmingham (England)

1984
DEFENDERS OF THE FAITH WORLD TOUR

20 January – Falkoner Theatre, Copenhagen (Denmark)
21 January – Isstadion, Stockholm (Sweden)
23 January – Scandinavium, Gothenburg (Sweden)
25 January – Parc des Expositions, Nancy (France)
26 January – Parc Expo Center, Rouen (France)
27 January – Jaap Edenhal, Amsterdam (Holland)
30 January – Maison des Sports, Clermond-Ferrand (France)

01 February – Sport Palace, Barcelona (Spain)
02 February – Estadio Koman Vacerio, Madrid (Spain)
03 February – Velódromo Anoeta, San Sebastian (Spain)
05 February – Marseille Stadium, Marseille (France)

07 February – Théâtre de Verdure, Nice (France)
09 February – Palais d'Hiver, Lyon (France)
10 February – Hall Tivoli, Strasbourg (France)
11 February – Espace Ballard, Paris (France)
13 February – Stadthalle, Offenbach
14 February – Hemmerleinhalle, Nuremburg (Germany)
17 February – Böblingen Sporthalle, Stuttgart (Germany)
18 February – Eulachalle, Winterthur (Switzerland)
19 February – Rudi Sedlmayerhalle, Munich (Germany)
20 February – Rhein-Neckarhalle, Heidelberg (Germany)
21 February – Philipshalle, Düsseldorf (Germany)

16 March – *(Exact venue unknown)* Niagara Falls, NY (USA)
21 March – Nassau Coliseum, Uniondale, NY (USA)
23 March – Meadowlands Arena, East Rutherford, NJ (USA)
25 March – Civic Center, Providence, RI (USA)
28 March – The Forum, Montreal (Canada)
30 March – Quebec Coliseum, Quebec (Canada)

02 April – Maple Leaf Gardens, Ontario (Canada)
06 April – Richfield Coliseum, Richfield (USA)
07 April – Wings Stadium, Kalamazoo, MI (USA)
11 April – Civic Center, Baltimore, MD (USA)
14 April – Freedom Hall, Louisville, KY (USA)
30 April – Reunion Arena, Dallas, TX (USA)

02 May – Tingley Coliseum, Albuquerque, NM (USA)
04 May – Sports Arena, Long Beach, CA (USA)
05 May – Sports Arena, Long Beach, CA (USA)
09 May – Sports Arena, San Diego, CA (USA)
24 May – Coliseum, Portland, OR (USA)
25 May – *(Exact venue unknown)* Spokane, WA (USA)
26 May – Tacoma Dome, Tacoma, WA (USA)
28 May – Pacific Coliseum, Vancouver (Canada)
30 May – Northlands Coliseum, Edmonton (Canada)
31 May – Veterans Memorial Coliseum, Phoenix, AZ (USA)

02 June – The Agridome, Regina (Canada)
04 June – The Arena, Winnipeg (Canada)
13 June – Joe Louis Arena, Detroit, MI (USA)
14 June – Rosemont Horizon, Rosemont, IL (USA)

16 June – Capitol Center, Landover, MD (USA)
17 June – Capitol Center, Landover, MD (USA)
18 June – Madison Square Garden, New York, NY (USA)
22 June – Spectrum, Philadelphia, PA (USA)
30 June – Hollywood Sportatorium, Hollywood, FL (USA)

17 July – Kansas Coliseum, Wichita, KS (USA)
25 July – Lawlor Events Center, Reno, NV (USA)
27 July – Cow Palace, San Francisco, CA (USA)
28 July – Cow Palace, San Francisco, CA (USA)
29 July – Irvine Meadows, Laguna Hills, CA (USA)
31 July – Salt Palace, Salt Lake City, UT (USA)

07 August – City Island, Harrisburg, PA (USA)
08 August – Ohio Center, Columbus, OH (USA)
09 August – Saginaw Civic Center, Saginaw, MI (USA)
10 August – Alpine Valley Music Theater, East Troy, WI (USA)

06 September – Miyagi Ken Sports Center, Sendai (Japan)
07 September – NHK Hall, Shibuya, Tokyo (Japan)
08 September – Kokaido Hall, Nagoya (Japan)
10 September – Festival Hall, Osaka (Japan)
11 September – Festival Hall, Osaka (Japan)
13 September – Nihon Budokan Hall, Tokyo (Japan)

1985
LIVE DATES

13 July – J.F.K. Stadium (Live Aid), Philadelphia, PA (USA)

1986
TURBO WORLD TOUR

02 May – Tingley Coliseum, Albuquerque, NM (USA)
09 May – Irvine Meadows, Laguna Hills, CA (USA)
10 May – Sports Arena, San Diego, CA (USA)
11 May – Forum Arena, Los Angeles, CA (USA)
12 May – Forum Arena, Los Angeles, CA (USA)
14 May – Selland Arena, Fresno, CA (USA)

15 May – Oakland Coliseum, Oakland, CA (USA)
16 May – Cal Expo Center, Sacramento, CA (USA)
18 May – Tacoma Dome, Tacoma, WA (USA)
22 May – Metrocenter, Minneapolis, MN (USA)
23 May – Kiel Auditorium, St. Louis, MO (USA)
25 May – Civic Center, St. Paul, MN (USA)
26 May – Veterans Memorial Auditorium, Des Moines, IA (USA)
28 May – Joe Louis Arena, Detroit, MI (USA)
29 May – O'Hara Arena, Dayton, OH (USA)
31 May – Capitol Center, Landover, MD (USA)

01 June – The Spectrum, Philadelphia, PA (USA)
04 June – Civic Center, Providence, RI (USA)
05 June – Centrum, Worchester, MA (USA)
06 June – Meadowlands Arena, East Rutherford, NJ (USA)
08 June – Nassau Coliseum, Uniondale, NY (USA)
17 June – Civic Center, Lakeland, FL (USA)
18 June – Hollywood Sportatorium, Miami, FL (USA)
21 June – The Summit, Houston, TX (USA)
22 June – Frank Erwin Center, Austin, TX (USA)
23 June – Convention Center, San Antonio, TX (USA)
25 June – Country Coliseum, El Paso, TX (USA)
26 June – Coliseum Odessa, Acton, TX (USA)
27 June – Reunion Arena, Dallas, TX (USA)
28 June – Lloyd Noble Arena, Norman, OK (USA)

14 July – PNE Coliseum, Vancouver (Canada)
17 July – Northlands Coliseum, Edmonton (Canada)
19 July – The Arena, Winnipeg (Canada)
22 July – Maple Leaf Gardens, Toronto (Canada)
23 July – The Forum, Montreal (Canada)
24 July – Quebec Coliseum, Quebec (Canada)
27 July – Ontario Civic Center, Ottawa (Canada)
29 July – RPI Fieldhouse, Troy, NY (USA)
31 July – Civic Center, Portland, ME (USA)

03 August – Sports Arena, Toledo, OH (USA)
05 August – Civic Arena, Pittsburgh, PA (USA)
06 August – Cincinnati Gardens, Cincinnati, OH (USA)
08 August – Saginaw Civic Center, Saginaw, MI (USA)
09 August – Joe Louis Arena, Detroit, MI (USA)

10 August – Hoffman Estates, Poplar Creek, IL (USA)
12 August – Market Square Arena, Indianapolis, IN (USA)
14 August – *(Exact venue unknown)* Green Bay, WI (USA)
15 August – Alpine Valley, East Troy, WI (USA)
16 August – Five Seasons Center, Cedar Rapids, IA (USA)
19 August – Kansas Coliseum, Wichita, KS (USA)
22 August – Starwood Amphitheater, Nashville, TN (USA)
27 August – Civic Center, Baltimore, MD (USA)
29 August – Meadowlands Arena, East Rutherford, NJ (USA)
31 August – CNE Grandstand, Toronto (Canada)

28 September – Ijsselhallen, Zwolle (Holland)
30 September – Stadthalle, Offenbach (Germany)

01 October – Stadthalle, Offenbach (Germany)
02 October – Böblingen Sporthalle, Stuttgart (Germany)
03 October – Carl Diem Halle, Würzburg (Germany)
04 October – Eulachalle, Winterhalle (Switzerland)
05 October – Olympiahalle, Munich (Germany)
08 October – Pabellón Real Madrid, Madrid (Spain)
09 October – Pabellón Real Madrid, Madrid (Spain)
11 October – Velódromo Anoeta, San Sebastian (Spain)
13 October – Palacio Municipal de Deportes, Barcelona (Spain)
15 October – Friedrich-Ebert-Halle, Ludwigshafen (Germany)
16 October – Saarlandhalle, Saarbrücken (Germany)
17 October – Grugahalle, Essen (Germany)
18 October – Forest National, Brussels (Belgium)
19 October – *(Exact venue unknown)* Paris (France)
22 October – Eilenriedhalle, Hanover (Germany)
23 October – Falkoner Theatre, Copenhagen (Denmark)
24 October – Isstadion, Stockholm (Sweden)
25 October – *(Exact venue unknown)* Gothenburg (Sweden)
27 October – Drammenshallen, Oslo (Norway)
29 October – Ishallen, Helsinki (Finland)

04 December – Nihon Budokan Hall, Tokyo (Japan)
06 December – Kokaido Hall, Nagoya (Japan)
10 December – Festival Hall, Osaka (Japan)
13 December – *(Exact venue unknown)* Yokohama (Japan)

1988
RAM IT DOWN WORLD TOUR

07 May – Isstadion, Stockholm (Sweden)
08 May – *(Exact venue unknown)* Gothenburg (Sweden)
09 May – Skedsmohallen, Oslo (Norway)
10 May – KB Hallen, Copenhagen (Denmark)
12 May – Deutschlandhalle, Berlin (Germany)
14 May – Ijsselhallen, Zwolle (Holland)
15 May – Forest National, Brussels (Belgium)
16 May – *(Exact venue unknown)* Paris (France)
18 May – Palais des Sports, Toulouse (France)
20 May – Sports Palace, Barcelona (Spain)
21 May – Velódromo Anoeta, San Sebastian (Spain)
22 May – Palacio des Deportes, Madrid (Spain)
23 May – Palacio des Deportes, Madrid (Spain)
26 May – Palatrussardi, Milan (Italy)
27 May – Palasport, Florence (Italy)
29 May – Patinoire de Malley, Lausanne (Switzerland)
31 May – Carl Diem Halle, Wurzburg (Germany)

01 June – Friedrich-Ebert-Halle, Ludwigshafen (Germany)
02 June – Olympiahalle, Munich (Germany)
04 June – Open Air Festival, Lübeck (Germany)
05 June – Weser Ems Halle, Oldenberg (Germany)
07 June – Stadthalle, Offenbach (Germany)
08 June – Halle 10, Ulm (Germany)
09 June – Böblingen Sporthalle, Stuttgart (Germany)
10 June – Sporthalle, Cologne (Germany)
12 June – Powerhouse, Birmingham (England)
13 June – Hammersmith Odeon, London (England)
14 June – Hammersmith Odeon, London (England)
16 June – De Montfort Hall, Leicester (England)
17 June – Playhouse, Edinburgh (Scotland)
18 June – City Hall, Newcastle (England)
19 June – Apollo, Manchester (England)
21 June – Centre, Newport (Wales)
22 June – City Hall, Sheffield (England)

22 July – CNE Grandstands, Toronto (Canada)
23 July – Maple Leaf Gardens, Toronto (Canada)

24 July – Civic Center, Ottawa (Canada)
27 July – Centrum, Worchester, MA (USA)
27 July – Orange County Fairgrounds, New York, NY (USA)
28 July – Nassau Coliseum, Uniondale, NY (USA)
29 July – Meadowlands Arena, East Rutherford, NJ (USA)
30 July – Nassau Coliseum, Uniondale, NY (USA)
31 July – Civic Center, Providence, RI (USA)

02 August – The Spectrum, Philadelphia, PA (USA)
05 August – *(Exact venue unknown)* Saratoga, NY (USA)
06 August – War Memorial, Rochester, NY (USA)
07 August – Coliseum, New Haven, CT (USA)
08 August – Broome County Arena, Binghamton, NY (USA)
09 August – Memorial Coliseum, Buffalo, NY (USA)
10 August – *(Exact venue unknown)* Hershey, PA (USA)
12 August – Capital Center, Largo, MD (USA)
13 August – Capital Center, Largo, MD (USA)
14 August – Coliseum, Hampton, VA (USA)
15 August – Ohio Center, Columbus, OH (USA)
16 August – O'Hara Arena, Dayton, OH (USA)
17 August – Richfield Coliseum, Cleveland, OH (USA)
19 August – *(Exact venue unknown)* Toledo, OH (USA)
20 August – The Palace, Auburn Hills, IN (USA)
21 August – Castle Farms Music Center, Charlevoix, MI (USA)
23 August – Market Square Arena, Indianapolis, IN (USA)
24 August – Rosemont Horizon, Chicago, IL (USA)
26 August – Alpine Valley, East Troy, WI (USA)
27 August – Metrocenter, Minneapolis, MN (USA)
29 August – Bonner Springs, Kansas City, KS (USA)
30 August – Kiel Auditorium, St. Louis, MO (USA)

08 September – Coliseum, Greensboro, NC (USA)
09 September – Coliseum, Charlotte, NC (USA)
10 September – Starwood Amphitheater, TN (USA)
11 September – Boutwell Auditorium, Birmingham, AL (USA)
13 September – Mid-South Coliseum, Memphis, TN (USA)
14 September – The Omni, Atlanta, GA (USA)
16 September – Memorial Coliseum, Jacksonville, FL (USA)
17 September – Civic Center, Lakeland, FL (USA)
18 September – Hollywood Sportatorium, Miami, FL (USA)
20 September – The Coliseum, Shreveport, LA (USA)

21 September – Lakefront Arena, New Orleans, LA (USA)
23 September – Starplex Amphitheater, Dallas, TX (USA)
25 September – Convention Center, San Antonio, TX (USA)
27 September – Frank Irwin Center, Austin, TX (USA)
28 September – Coliseum, Lubbock, TX (USA)
29 September – County Coliseum, El Paso, TX (USA)

01 October – Salt Palace, Salt Lake City, UT (USA)
02 October – McNichols Arena, Denver, CO (USA)
04 October – Tingley Coliseum, Albuquerque, NM (USA)
06 October – Veterans Memorial Coliseum, Phoenix, AZ (USA)
07 October – Cow Palace, San Francisco, CA (USA)
08 October – Cow Palace, San Francisco, CA (USA)
09 October – Storeline Amphitheater, Mountain View, CA (USA)
11 October – Selland Arena, Fresno, CA (USA)
12 October – Sports Arena, San Diego, CA (USA)
13 October – Forum Arena, Los Angeles, CA (USA)
14 October – Forum Arena, Los Angeles, CA (USA)
15 October – Irvine Meadows, Laguna Hills, CA (USA)
16 October – Irvine Meadows, Laguna Hills, CA (USA)
19 October – Center Coliseum, Seattle, WA (USA)
(Exact date unknown) October – Coliseum, Spokane, WA (USA)
22 October – PNE Coliseum, Vancouver (Canada)
23 October – Coliseum Portland, OR (USA)

1990
PAINKILLER WORLD TOUR

13 September – Concrete Foundations, Los Angeles, CA (USA)

18 October – The Forum, Montreal (Canada)
19 October – Quebec Coliseum, Quebec (Canada)
23 October – Maple Leaf Gardens, Ontario (Canada)
25 October – The Arena, Winnipeg (Canada)
28 October – Olympic Saddledome, Calgary (Canada)
31 October – PNE Coliseum, Vancouver (Canada)

01 November – Coliseum, Portland, OR (USA)
02 November – Coliseum, Spokane, WA (USA)
03 November – Lawlor Events Center, Reno, NV (USA)

04 November – ARCO Arena, Sacramento, CA (USA)
05 November – Oakland Coliseum, Oakland, CA (USA)
07 November – Activity Center, Tempe, AZ (USA)
08 November – Forum Arena, Los Angeles, CA (USA)
09 November – Irvine Meadows, Laguna Hills, CA (USA)
10 November – Sports Arena, San Diego, CA (USA)
11 November – Sports Arena, San Diego, CA (USA)
12 November – Salt Palace, Salt Lake City, UT (USA)
14 November – UTEP Special Events Center, El Paso, TX (USA)
17 November – Reunion Arena, Dallas, TX (USA)
19 November – The Summit, Houston, TX (USA)
20 November – McNichols Arena, Denver, CO (USA)
21 November – Tingley Coliseum, Albuquerque, NM (USA)
23 November – Expo Center, Tulsa, OK (USA)
24 November – Municipal Auditorium, Kansas City, MO (USA)
25 November – Civic Center, Omaha, NE (USA)
27 November – Ohio Center, Columbus, OH (USA)
28 November – Rosemont Horizon, Chicago, IL (USA)
29 November – Civic Center, St. Paul, MN (USA)

01 December – Market Square Arena, Indianapolis, IN (USA)
02 December – Richfield Coliseum, Cleveland, OH (USA)
03 December – O'Hara Arena, Dayton, OH (USA)
05 December – The Palace, Detroit, MI (USA)
07 December – Centrum, Worchester, MA (USA)
08 December – Coliseum, New Haven, CT (USA)
09 December – Capitol Center, Largo, MD (USA)
11 December – The Omni, Atlanta, GA (USA)
13 December – Coliseum, Hampton, VA (USA)
14 December – Meadowlands Arena, East Rutherford, NJ (USA)
15 December – Nassau Coliseum, Uniondale, NY (USA)
16 December – The Spectrum, Philadelphia, PA (USA)
17 December – Civic Arena, Pittsburgh, PA (USA)
19 December – Coliseum, Charlotte, NC (USA)
20 December – The Arena, Miami, FL (USA)
23 December – *(Exact venue unknown)* Orlando, FL (USA)

1991

09 January – Cumberland County Civic Center, Portland, ME (USA)

10 January – Broom County Arena, Binghamton, NY (USA)
12 January – Civic Center, Providence, RI (USA)
14 January – Knickerbocker Arena, Albany, NY (USA)
15 January – Kingston Armory, Kingston, PA (USA)
23 January – Maracana Stadium (Rock In Rio II Festival), Rio de Janeiro (Brazil)
31 January – KB Hallen, Copenhagen (Denmark)

01 February – Scandinavium, Gothenburg (Sweden)
02 February – Isstadion, Stockholm (Sweden)
04 February – Ishallen, Helsinki (Finland)
06 February – Rockefeller, Oslo (Norway)
08 February – Grugahalle, Essen (Germany)
09 February – Sporthalle, Hamburg (Germany)
11 February – Eissporthalle, Berlin (Germany)
12 February – Eilenriedhalle, Hanover (Germany)
14 February – Saarlandhalle, Saarbrücken (Germany)
15 February – Oberschwabenhalle, Ravensburg (Germany)
16 February – Carl Diem Halle, Wurzburg (Germany)
18 February – Stadthalle, Offenbach (Germany)
19 February – Olympiahalle, Munich (Germany)
20 February – B.A. Zelt, Vienna (Austria)
21 February – Icestadium, Graz (Austria)
23 February – Festhalle *(Exact city unknown)* (Switzerland)
24 February – Stadthalle, Bolzano (Italy)
25 February – Tivoli, Ljubljana (Slovenia)
26 February – Dom Sportova, Zagreb (Yugoslavia)

01 March – Tendastrice, Rome (Italy)
02 March – Palasport, Brescia (Italy)
04 March – Hanns-Martin-Schleyer-Halle, Stuttgart (Germany)
05 March – Friedrich-Ebert-Halle, Ludwigshafen (Germany)
06 March – Rhein Moselhalle, Koblenz (Germany)
08 March – The Bullring, Zaragoza (Spain)
09 March – Velódromo Anoeta, San Sebastian (Spain)
10 March – Palacio des Deportes, Madrid (Spain)
12 March – Le Transbordeur, Lyon (France)
13 March – *(Exact venue unknown)* Lisbon (Portugal)
15 March – Rijnhal, Arnhem (Holland)
16 March – Forest National, Brussels (Belgium)
17 March – *(Exact venue unknown)* Paris (France)

19 March – Leisure Centre, Aston Villa (England)
20 March – Apollo, Manchester (England)
22 March – Hammersmith Odeon, London (England)
23 March – Hammersmith Odeon, London (England)
24 March – Centre, Newport (Wales)
26 March – City Hall, Sheffield (England)
27 March – City Hall, Newcastle (England)
28 March – Playhouse, Edinburgh (Scotland)
30 March – Ulster Hall, Belfast (Northern Ireland)
31 March – S.F.X., Dublin (Ireland)

12 April – Festival Hall, Osaka (Japan)
13 April – Japan Arena, Yokohama (Japan)
15 April – Olympic Pool, Yoyogi (Japan)

OPERATION ROCK & ROLL NORTH AMERICAN TOUR

09 July – Salt Palace, Salt Lake City, UT (USA)
12 July – Irvine Meadows, Laguna Hills (USA)
13 July – Cal-Expo Amphitheater, Sacramento (USA)
14 July – Shoreline Amphitheater, Mountain View (USA)
16 July – Red Rocks, Denver, CO (USA)
18 July – 5 Seasons Arena, Cedar Rapids, IA (USA)
19 July – Target Center, Minneapolis, MN (USA)
20 July – The World, Chicago, IL (USA)
21 July – Starwood Amphitheater, Nashville, TN (USA)
23 July – The Sundome, Tampa, FL (USA)
24 July – The Arena, Orlando, FL (USA)
25 July – Lakewood Amphitheater, GA (USA)
27 July – The Summit, Houston, TX (USA)
28 July – Starplex, Dallas, TX (USA)
30 July – Palladium Carowinds, Charlotte, NC (USA)
31 July – Walnut Creek, Raleigh, NC (USA)

02 August – Starlake Amphitheater, Pittsburgh, PA (USA)
03 August – Pine Knob Music Theater, Detroit, MI (USA)
04 August – Hollyday Star Theater, Merryville, IN (USA)
06 August – Deer Creek Music, Indianapolis, IN (USA)
07 August – Richfield Coliseum, Richfield, OH (USA)
08 August – Cayuga County Fairgrounds, Weedsport, NY (USA)
09 August – Meadowlands Arena, East Rutherford, NJ (USA)

10 August – The Spectrum, Philadelphia, PA (USA)
11 August – Lake Compuce, Bristol, CT (USA)
13 August – Seapac, Portland, ME (USA)
14 August – Great Woods, Boston, MA (USA)
15 August – Capitol Center, Largo, MD (USA)
16 August – Middletown Speedway, Middletown, NY (USA)
17 August – The Forum, Montreal (Canada)
19 August – CNE Grandstand, Toronto (Canada)

1998
JUGULATOR WORLD TOUR

30 January – Boathouse, Norfolk, VA (USA)
31 January – Grady Cole, Charlotte, NC (USA)

02 February – 9:30 Club, Washington, DC (USA)
03 February – Avalon Ballroom, Boston, MA (USA)
04 February – The Chance, Poughkeepsie, NY (USA)
06 February – Roseland, New York, NY (USA)
07 February – Electric Factory Ballroom, Philadelphia, PA (USA)
08 February – Metropol, Pittsburgh, PA (USA)
10 February – State Theater, Kalamazoo, MI (USA)
11 February – RPM Warehouse, Toronto (Canada)
13 February – State Theater, Detroit, MI (USA)
14 February – Newport Music Hall, Columbus, OH (USA)
15 February – Agora Theater & Ballroom, Cleveland, OH (USA)
17 February – Brewery, Louisville, KY (USA)
18 February – Egyptian, Indianapolis, IN (USA)
19 February – House of Blues, Chicago, IL (USA)
20 February – Modjeska, Milwaukee, WI (USA)
23 February – The Rage, Vancouver (Canada)
24 February – Roseland Theater, Portland, OR (USA)
26 February – Stockton Civic Center, Stockton, CA (USA)
28 February – Warfield Theatre, San Francisco, CA (USA)

01 March – Universal Amphitheater, Los Angeles, CA (USA)
02 March – 4th & B, San Diego, CA (USA)
18 March – E-Werk, Cologne (Germany)
19 March – E-Werk, Cologne (Germany)
20 March – Stadthalle, Gross-Umstadt (Germany)

22 March – Congree B, Stuttgart (Germany)
23 March – *(Exact venue unknown)* Augsburg (Germany)
24 March – Stadthalle, Memmingen (Germany)
26 March – Kurhalle, Vienna (Austria)
27 March – Sports Hall, Zilina (Slovakia)
28 March – Spodek, Katowice (Poland)
29 March – Small Sports Hall, Prague (Czech-Republic)
31 March – Eissporthalle, Halle (Germany)

01 April – Arena, Berlin (Germany)
02 April – Docks Club, Hamburg (Germany)
03 April – Vega, Copenhagen (Denmark)
05 April – Grugahalle, Essen (Germany)
06 April – Music Hall, Hanover (Germany)
08 April – Ancienne Belgique, Brussels (Belgium)
09 April – Ijsselhallen, Zwolle (Holland)
11 April – Astoria, London (England)
12 April – Civic Hall Wolverhampton (England)
14 April – *(Exact venue unknown)* Paris (France)
15 April – Friedrich-Ebert-Halle, Ludwigshafen (Germany)
16 April – Stadhalle, Furth (Germany)
17 April – Colosseum, Munich (Germany)
19 April – Palacquatica, Milan (Italy)
20 April – Hafen, Innsbruck (Austria)
21 April – Volkshaus, Zürich (Switzerland)
23 April – Vall D'Hebron, Barcelona (Spain)
24 April – Sports Palace, Madrid (Spain)
25 April – Velódromo Anoeta, San Sebastian (Spain)
26 April – The Bullring, Zaragoza (Spain)
28 April – Cascais Pavilion, Lisbon (Portugal)

13 May – Shibuya Public Hall, Tokyo (Japan)
14 May – Shibuya Public Hall, Tokyo (Japan)
16 May – Diamond Hall, Nagoya (Japan)
17 May – Skala Espacio, Fukuoka (Japan)
18 May – Koseinenkin Hall, Nagoya (Japan)
20 May – U-Port, Tokyo (Japan)

17 September – Palacio De Los Deportes, Mexico City (Mexico)
19 September – Auditorio Coca-Cola, Monterrey (Mexico)
22 September – Rockin' Rodeo, Bakersfield, CA (USA)

23 September – 4th & B, San Diego, CA (USA)
24 September – Galaxy Theatre, Santa Ana, CA (USA)
26 September – Celebrity Theatre, Phoenix Theater, AZ (USA)
27 September – House of Blues, Los Angeles, CA (USA)
28 September – House of Blues, Los Angeles, CA (USA)
29 September – Hard Rock Hotel, Las Vegas, NV (USA)
30 September – Midnight Rodeo, Albuquerque, NM (USA)

06 October – Ariel Theater, Houston, TX (USA)
07 October – Far West Rodeo, San Antonio (USA)
08 October – Buckets Sports Bar, Corpus Christi, TX (USA)
10 October – The New Roadhouse, San Benito, TX (USA)
11 October – Midnight Rodeo, Waco, TX (USA)
13 October – Midnight Rodeo, Amarillo, TX (USA)
14 October – Ruby's Roadhouse, Lubbock, TX (USA)
15 October – The Caravan of Dreams, Fort Worth, TX (USA)
16 October – Malibu Alley, Shreveport, LA (USA)
17 October – Joe's Big Bamboo, Little Rock, AK (USA)
19 October – House of Blues, New Orleans, LA (USA)
20 October – House of Blues, Orlando, FL (USA)
21 October – The Button South, Fort Lauderdale, FL (USA)
23 October – The Masquerade, Atlanta, GA (USA)
24 October – House of Blues, Myrtle Beach, SC (USA)
26 October – Agora Theater & Ballroom, Cleveland, OH (USA)
27 October – Newport Music Hall, Columbus, OH (USA)
28 October – House of Blues, Chicago, IL (USA)
30 October – Calvin Theater, Northampton, MA (USA)
31 October – Hammerstein Ballroom, New York, NY (USA)

2001
DEMOLITION WORLD TOUR

08 June – Konzertfabrik Z7, Pratteln (Switzerland)
09 June – Gods of Metal Festival, Milano (Italy)
10 June – Mind Over Matter Festival, Wiesen (Austria)
13 June – Barrowlands, Glasgow (Scotland)
14 June – Apollo, Manchester (England)
15 June – Astoria, London (England)
17 June – Academy, Birmingham (England)
18 June – Guildhall, Portsmouth (England)

21 June – Colosseum, Munich (Germany)
23 June – Graspop Metal Festival, Dessel (Belgium)
24 June – With Full Force Festival, Leipzig (Germany)
25 June – E-Werk, Koln (Germany)
26 June – The Docks, Hamburg (Germany)
28 June – Amphitheater, Gelsenkirchen (Germany)
29 June – Bang Your Head Festival, Balingen (Germany)

01 July – Rockwave Festival, Athens (Greece)
04 July – Pabellón de Mendizorroza, Victoria (Spain)
05 July – La Cubierta, Madrid (Spain)
06 July – Alcazares, Murcia (Spain)
07 July – San Felipe Neri, Cadiz (Spain)
09 July – Feria De Muestras, Valladolid (Spain)
10 July – Vall D'Hebron, Barcelona (Spain)

01 September – Obras Sanitarias, Buenos Aires (Argentina)
04 September – Bar Opiniao, Porto Alegre (Brazil)
05 September – ATL Music Hall, Rio de Janeiro (Brazil)
06 September – Credicard Hall, Sao Paulo (Brazil)
07 September – Credicard Hall, Sao Paulo (Brazil)
09 September – Teatro Metropolitan, Mexico City (Mexico)
10 September – Teatro Metropolitan, Mexico City (Mexico)

01 November – Hofter Lo, Antwerp (Belgium)
03 November – Kulturbolaget, Malmö (Sweden)
04 November – Amager Bio, Copenhagen (Denmark)
05 November – Rockfeller, Oslo (Norway)
06 November – Train, Aarhus (Denmark)
08 November – Kaaren, Gothenburg (Sweden)
09 November – Varmekyrkan, Norrköping (Sweden)
10 November – Brewery, Stockholm (Sweden)
11 November – Club Rainbow, Ronneby (Sweden)
13 November – House Of Culture, Helsinki (Finland)
15 November – Estraden, Gävle (Sweden)
16 November – Culturhouse, Jonkoeping (Sweden)
18 November – Zeche, Bochum (Germany)
30 November – Metropolis, Perth (Australia)

02 December – Thebarton Theatre, Adelaide (Australia)
03 December – The Palace, Melbourne (Australia)

05 December – Enmore Theatre, Sydney (Australia)
07 December – The Arena, Brisbane (Australia)
10 December – Nakano Sun Plaza, Tokyo (Japan)
11 December – Nakano Sun Plaza, Tokyo (Japan)
12 December – Koseinenkin Hall, Osaka (Japan)
14 December – Diamond Hall, Nagoya (Japan)
15 December – Zepp, Fukuoka (Japan)
19 December – Brixton Academy, London (England)

2002

17 January – House of Blues, Las Vegas, NV (USA)
18 January – Universal Amphitheater, Los Angeles, CA (USA)
19 January – Warfield Theatre, San Francisco, CA (USA)
20 January – House of Blues, CA (USA)
23 January – Paramount Theater, Denver, CA (USA)
25 January – Deep Ellum Live, Dallas, TX (USA)
26 January – Villa Real, McAllen, TX (USA)
27 January – Aerial Theater, Houston, TX (USA)
29 January – House of Blues, New Orleans, LA (USA)
30 January – Edge 2000, Jacksonville, FL (USA)

01 February – House of Blues, Orlando, FL (USA)
02 February – Jannus Landing, Tampa, FL (USA)
03 February – Orbit, Boynton Beach, FL (USA)
04 February – Dekalb Atlanta Center, Atlanta, GA (USA)
06 February – Pierres Fort Wayne, Indianapolis, IN (USA)
07 February – Riviera Theater, Chicago, IL (USA)
08 February – Eagles Auditorium, Milwaukee, WI (USA)
09 February – Agora Theater & Ballroom, Cleveland, OH (USA)
10 February – Newport Music Hall, Columbus, OH (USA)
12 February – The Docks, Toronto (Canada)
14 February – Orpheum, Boston, MA (USA)
15 February – Roseland Ballroom, New York, NY (USA)
16 February – Electric Factory, Philadelphia, PA (USA)
17 February – Nation, Washington, DC (USA)
17 February – Nation, Washington, DC (USA)
19 February – Palace of Auburn Hills, Auburn Hills, IN (USA)

13 March – *(Exact venue unknown)* Paris (France)

14 March – Turbinenhalle, Oberhausen (Germany)
15 March – Columbiahalle, Berlin (Germany)
16 March – Hype Park, Osnabruck (Germany)
17 March – Spodek, Katowice (Poland)
18 March – Aladin, Bremen (Germany)
19 March – Paegas Arena, Prague (Czech-Republic)
20 March – Capitol, Hanover (Germany)
22 March – Schlachthof, Dresden (Germany)
23 March – Filharmonie, Stuttgart (Germany)
25 March – Hugenottenhalle, Frankfurt (Germany)
26 March – Stadthalle Furth, Nuremberg (Germany)
27 March – The Volkshaus, Zurich (Switzerland)
29 March – Pepsi Music Club, Vienna (Austria)
30 March – SAP Hall, Budapest (Hungary)

01 April – Orpheum, Graz (Austria)
02 April – *(Exact venue unknown)* Ljubljana (Slovenia)
04 April – Razzmatazz 1, Barcelona (Spain)
05 April – Republicca, Valencia (Spain)
06 April – Aqualung, Madrid (Spain)
07 April – Polideportivo, Pamplona (Spain)

05 July – Hard Hat Concert Hall, Toledo, OH (USA)
06 July – RIB & Music Festival, Akron, OH (USA)
07 July – Summerfest, Milwaukee, WI (USA)
09 July – The Pageant, St. Louis, MO (USA)
11 July – The Surf Ballroom, Clear Lake, IA (USA)
12 July – Playmaker's Pavilion, Fargo, ND (USA)
13 July – Kinsmen Rock the Valley, Saskatchewan, Craven (Canada)
14 July – Quest Club, Minneapolis, MN (USA)
16 July – Metropol, Pittsburgh, PA (USA)
17 July – The Palladium, Worchester, MA (USA)
19 July – Convention Hall, Asbury Park, NJ (USA)
20 July – Hampton Beach Casino, Hampton Beach, NH (USA)
21 July – Bald Hill Amphitheater, Farmingville, NY (USA)
22 July – The Chance, Poughkeepsie, NY (USA)
24 July – Innsbrook Pavilion, Glen Allen, VA (USA)
25 July – The Recher Theater, Baltimore, MD (USA)
26 July – Electric Factory, Philadelphia, PA (USA)
27 July – Northern Lights, Clifton Park (USA)
29 July – Webster Theater, Hartford, CT (USA)

31 July – The Asylum, Slidell, LA (USA)

01 August – Aerial Theater, Houston, TX (USA)
02 August – Sunken Gardens Amphitheater, San Antonio, TX (USA)
03 August – Canyon Club, Dallas, TX (USA)
04 August – The Pavilion, Lubbock, TX (USA)
06 August – Far West Entertainment, El Paso, TX (USA)
08 August – House of Blues, Las Vegas, NV (USA)
09 August – House of Blues, Los Angeles, CA (USA)
10 August – House of Blues, Anaheim, CA (USA)
11 August – Cajun House, Scotsdale, AZ (USA)
13 August – Camel Rock Casino, Santa Fe, NM (USA)
14 August – Ogden Theater, Denver, CO (USA)
16 August – Shrine Auditorium, Billings, MT (USA)
17 August – Party in the Pasture, Beulah, ND (USA)
19 August – Big Easy Concert House, Boise, ID (USA)
20 August – Roseland Ballroom, Portland, OR (USA)
21 August – Fillmore, San Francisco, CA (USA)
24 August – Royal Oak Music Theater, Detroit, MI (USA)
25 August – House of Blues, Chicago, IL (USA)

2004
REUNITED WORLD TOUR

02 June – Stadion Sporthalle, Hanover (Germany)
04 June – Rock In The Park, Nuremburg (Germany)
05 June – Arena Parco Nord, Bologna (Italy)
06 June – Festhalle, Frauenfeld (Switzerland)
08 June – Trepow Arena, Berlin (Germany)
10 June – Sweden Rock Festival, Sölvesborg (Sweden)
12 June – Arrow Rock Festival, Lichtenvoorde (Holland)
13 June – *(Exact venue unknown,)* Oberhausen (Germany)
14 June – T Mobile Arena, Prague (Czech-Republic)
16 June – Kisstadion, Budapest (Hungary)
18 June – Akademic Stadium, Sofia (Bulgaria)
20 June – Rock Wave Festival, Athens (Greece)
24 June – Olympic Arena, Barcelona (Spain)
25 June – Metal Mania Festival, Valencia (Spain)
27 June – Graspop Metal Festival, Dessel (Belgium)

10 July – Meadows Music Theater, Hartford, CT (USA)
12 July – Tweeter Center, Boston, MA (USA)
14 July – Tommy Hilfiger @ Jones Beach, Wantagh, NY (USA)
16 July – PNC Bank Arts Center, Holmdel, NJ (USA)
17 July – Chippewa Valley Festival Grounds, Cadott, WI (USA)
20 July – Germain Amphitheater, Columbus, OH (USA)
22 July – Starwood Amphitheater, Nashville, TN (USA)
24 July – Fiddler's Green, Denver, CO (USA)
26 July – Idaho Center Amphitheater, Nampa, ID (USA)
27 July – White River Amphitheater, Seattle, WA (USA)
29 July – Shoreline Amphitheater, San Francisco, CA (USA)
30 July – Sleep Train Amphitheater, Marysville, CA (USA)
31 July – Hyundai Pavilion, San Bernardino, CA (USA)

03 August – Journal Pavilion, Albuquerque, NM (USA)
04 August – Don Haskins Center, El Paso, TX (USA)
05 August – Smirnoff Music Center, Dallas, TX (USA)
07 August – Verizon Wireless Amphitheater, San Antonio, TX (USA)
08 August – Cynthia Woods Mitchell Pavilion, Woodlands, TX (USA)
10 August – Verizon Amphitheater, Kansas City, KS (USA)
12 August – UMB Pavilion, St. Louis, MO (USA)
14 August – Alpine Valley Music Theater, East Troy, WI (USA)
17 August – MI/DTE Energy Center, Detroit, MI (USA)
18 August – Molson Amphitheater, Toronto (Canada)
19 August – Blossom, Cleveland, OH (USA)
21 August – Tweeter Center, Chicago, IL (USA)
24 August – Verizon Wireless Music Center, Indianapolis, IN (USA)
26 August – Tweeter Waterfront, Camden, NJ (USA)
28 August – Post Gazette Pavilion, Pittsburgh, PA (USA)

29 August – Mohegan Sun Casino, Uncasville, CO (USA)
31 August – Alltel Pavilion, Raleigh, NC (USA)

02 September – Tampa Bay Amphitheater, Tampa Bay, FL (USA)

2005
ANGEL OF RETRIBUTION **WORLD TOUR**

23 February – Valbyhallen, Copenhagen (Denmark)
25 February – Lofbergs Lila Arena, Karstad (Sweden)

26 February – Globe, Stockholm (Sweden)
28 February – Ice Hall, Oulu (Finland)

02 March – Ice Hall, Tampere (Finland)
03 March – Hartwell Arena, Helsinki (Finland)
05 March – Scandinavium, Gothenburg (Sweden)
08 March – Spektrum, Oslo (Norway)
10 March – Grugahalle, Essen (Germany)
11 March – Stadthalle, Offenbach (Germany)
13 March – Zenith, Munich (Germany)
14 March – Böblingen Sporthalle, Stuttgart (Germany)
16 March – Hammersmith Apollo, London (England)
17 March – Hammersmith, Apollo, London (England)
19 March – NEC, Birmingham (England)
21 March – Apollo, Manchester (England)
22 March – Apollo, Manchester (England)
24 March – Odyssey, Belfast (Northern Ireland)
26 March – SECC, Glasgow (Scotland)
27 March – Arena, Newcastle (England)
28 March – Arena, Sheffield (England)
30 March – Arena, Cardiff (Wales)
31 March – Pavilions, Plymouth (England)

02 April – Brabanthal Den Bosch Arena, Den Bosch (Holland)
04 April – Zwickau, Zwickau (Germany)
07 April – Sports Arena, Brno (Czech-Republic)
08 April – Bank Austria Hall, Vienna (Austria)
10 April – Mazda Palace, Milan (Italy)
12 April – Vistalegre, Madrid (Spain)
13 April – Atlantico Pavilion, Lisbon (Portugal)
14 April – Coliseo, La Coruna (Spain)
16 April – Bullring, Zaragoza (Spain)
17 April – Badalona, Barcelona (Spain)

08 May – Pacifico, Yokohama (Japan)
10 May – Citizen's Auditorium, Nagoya (Japan)
11 May – Kosei Nenkin Kaikan (Japan)
13 May – Yubin Chokin Hall, Hiroshima (Japan)
14 May – Zepp, Fukuoka (Japan)
16 May – Castle Hall, Osaka (Japan)
18 May – Nippon Budokan, Tokyo (Japan)

19 May – Nippon Budokan, Tokyo (Japan)
30 May – Blossom Music Center Stadium, Cuyahoga Falls, OH (USA)

01 June – Xcel Energy Center, St. Paul, MN (USA)
03 June – Tweeter Center, Chicago, IL (USA)
04 June – DTE Energy Center, Detroit, MI (USA)
05 June – Molson Amphitheater, Toronto (Canada)
07 June – Darien Lake Performing Arts Center, Darien, Buffalo, NY (USA)
08 June – Verizon Wireless Arena, Manchester, NH (USA)
10 June – PNC Bank Arts Center, Holmdel, NJ (USA)
11 June – Mohegan Sun, Uncasville, CT (USA)
12 June – Tweeter Center, Mansfield, MA (USA)
14 June – Montage Mountain, Scranton, PA (USA)
15 June – Giant Center, Hershey, PA (USA)
17 June – Tommy Hilfiger @ Jones Beach Theater, Wantagh, NY (USA)
18 June – Tweeter Waterfront Center, Camden, NJ (USA)
19 June – Nissan Pavilion, Washington, DC (USA)
21 June – Hi Fi Buys Amphitheater, Atlanta, GA (USA)
22 June – Ford Amphitheater, Tampa, FL (USA)
23 June – Sound Beach Amphitheater, West Palm Beach, FL (USA)
25 June – Verizon Wireless, San Antonio, TX (USA)
26 June – Smirnoff Amphitheater, Dallas, TX (USA)
28 June – Journal Pavilion, Albuquerque, NM (USA)
29 June – Coors Amphitheater, Denver, CO (USA)

01 July – Hilton Amphitheater, Reno, NV (USA)
02 July – Shoreline Amphitheater, San Francisco, CA (USA)
04 July – Clark County Amphitheater, Ridgefield, WA (USA)
06 July – White River Amphitheater, Seattle, WA (USA)
08 July – Verizon Wireless Amphitheater, Irvine, CA (USA)
09 July – Mandalay Bay, Las Vegas, NV (USA)
10 July – Cricket Pavilion, Phoenix, AZ (USA)

01 September – Auditorio Coca-Cola, Monterrey (Mexico)
03 September – Palacio des los Deportes, Mexico City (Mexico)
06 September – Estadio Gigantinho, Porto Alegre (Brazil)
08 September – Claro Hall, Rio de Janeiro (Brazil)
09 September – Arena Skol, Sao Paulo (Brazil)
11 September – Ferrocarril Oeste, Buenos Aires (Argentina)
13 September – Pista Atletica, Santiago (Chile)
16 September – Roberto Clemente Coliseum, Puerto Rico (Puerto-Rico)

23 September – Soaring Eagle Casino, Mt. Pleasant, MI (USA)
25 September – Riverbend Music Center, Cincinnati, OH (USA)
27 September – Assembly Hall, Champaign, IL (USA)
28 September – Rockford Metrocentre, Rockford, IL (USA)
29 September – Wings Stadium, Kalamazoo, MI (USA)

01 October – Cellular Center, Milwaukee, WI (USA)
02 October – The Mark of the Quad Cities, Moline, IL (USA)
04 October – State Theater, Portland, OR (USA)
05 October – Arena At Harbor Yard, Bridgeport, CT (USA)
07 October – Paul E Tsongas Arena, Lowell, MA (USA)
08 October – Landmark Theater, Syracuse, NY (USA)
09 October – Borgato Casino & SPA, Atlantic City (USA)
11 October – Mid Hudson Civic Center, Poughkeepsie, NY (USA)
12 October – Bell Center, Montreal (Canada)
14 October – Corell Center, Ottawa (Canada)
15 October – John Labatt Center, Ontario (Canada)
18 October – MTS Center, Winnipeg (Canada)
20 October – Rexall Place, Edmonton (Canada)
21 October – Pengrowth Saddledome, Calgary (Canada)
23 October – Pacific Coliseum, Calgary (Canada)
24 October – Vernon Multiplex, Vernon (Canada)
26 October – The E Center of West Valley, Salt Lake City, UT (USA)
28 October – Konocti Harbor Resort & SPA, Kelseyville, CA (USA)
29 October – Sports Arena, San Diego, CA (USA)
30 October – Long Beach Arena, Long Beach, CA (USA)

01 November – Anselmo Valencia Amphitheater, Tucson, TX (USA)
24 November – Palace of Sports, Kiev (Ukraine)
27 November – Luzhniki Arena, Moscow (Russia)
29 November – New Ice Arena, St. Petersburg (Russia)

01 December – Saku Arena, Tallin (Estonia)
02 December – Kipsala Hall, Riga (Latvia)
03 December – Ice Hall, Vilnius (Lithuania)

2006
LIVE DATES

31 March – Royal Albert Hall, London (England)

ROB HALFORD: TOUR DATES

In between leaving Judas Priest in 1992 and returning to the line-up in 2003, Halford worked just as hard as Priest on the global live circuit. Particularly on the Halford (the band) tours, he played a large selection of Judas Priest tracks, some of which had not been played live in front of an audience for many years. Again, trying to gain complete details has not been entirely possible.

BLACK SABBATH

1992

14 November – Pacific Amphitheater, Los Angeles, CA (USA)
15 November – Pacific Amphitheater, Los Angeles, CA (USA)

2004

26 August – Tweeter Waterfront, Camden, NJ (USA)

FIGHT

1993
WAR OF WORDS WORLD TOUR

(Exact date unknown) July – The Mason Jar, Phoenix, AZ (USA)
(Exact date unknown) July – The Mason Jar, Phoenix, AZ (USA)
(Exact date unknown) July – The Mason Jar, Phoenix, AZ (USA)
19 October – *(Exact venue unknown)* Frankfurt (Germany)
20 October – *(Exact venue unknown)* Hamburg (Germany)
21 October – *(Exact venue unknown)* Bonn (Germany)
23 October – *(Exact venue unknown)* Munich (Germany)
24 October – *(Exact venue unknown)* Stuttgart (Germany)
25 October – *(Exact venue unknown)* Milan (Italy)
27 October – *(Exact venue unknown)* Barcelona (Spain)
28 October – *(Exact venue unknown)* Madrid (Spain)
30 October – Elysée Montmartre, Paris (France)

01 November – *(Exact venue and location unknown)* (Holland)
03 November – Rock City, Nottingham (England)
04 November – Astoria 2, London (England)
30 November – *(Exact venue unknown)* Denver, CO (USA)

1994
MUTATIONS NORTH AMERICAN TOUR

21 August – *(Exact venue unknown)* Miami, FL (USA)

1995
A SMALL DEADLY SPACE NORTH AMERICAN TOUR

21 April – La Semana Alegre, TX (USA)

14 June – Blind Melon's, Buffalo, NY (USA)
15 June – Metropol, Pittsburgh, PA (USA)
16 June – Phantasy Theater, Cleveland, OH (USA)
17 June – The Ritz, Detroit, MI (USA)
18 June – Vic Theater, Chicago, IL (USA)
20 June – The Rave, Milwaukee, WI (USA)
21 June – First Avenue, Minneapolis, MN (USA)
23 June – Mississippi Nights, St. Louis, MO (USA)
24 June – Lone Star *(Exact location unknown)* MO (USA)
26 June – Rack-n-Roll, Colorado Springs, CO (USA)
27 June – After The Gold Rush, Denver, CO (USA)
28 June – Upper Country, Salt Lake City, UT (USA)
30 June – Town Pump, Vancouver (Canada)

01 July – Under The Rail, Seattle, WA (USA)
02 July – Roseland, Portland, OR (USA)
05 July – Easy Street, Reno, NV (USA)
06 July – Fillmore, San Francisco, CA (USA)
07 July – Ventura Theater, Ventura, CA (USA)
08 July – The Palace, Los Angeles, CA (USA)
09 July – Bachannal, San Diego, CA (USA)
11 July – Huntridge Theater, Las Vegas, NV (USA)
12 July – The Rock, Tucson, AZ (USA)
13 July – Electric Ballroom, Phoenix, AZ (USA)

HALFORD

2000
RESURRECTION WORLD TOUR

19 July – The Mason Jar, Phoenix, AZ (USA)
20 July – Launchpad, Albuquerque, NM (USA)
22 July – Diamond Ballroom, Oklahoma City, OK (USA)
23 July – Royal Groove, Lincoln, NE (USA)
25 July – Ranch Bowl, Omaha, NE (USA)
28 July – The Canopy, Urbana, IL (USA)

01 August – Air Canada Center, Toronto (Canada)
02 August – Molson Center, Montreal (Canada)
03 August – Colisee Arena, Quebec (Canada)
05 August – Madison Square Garden, New York, NY (USA)
06 August – Tweeter Center, Boston, MA (USA)
08 August – Meadows Music Center, Hartford, CT (USA)
09 August – Cumberland County Civic Center, Portland, ME (USA)
11 August – Starlake Amphitheater, Pittsburgh, PA (USA)
12 August – E-Center, Philadelphia, PA (USA)
13 August – Coors Light Amphitheater, Scranton, PA (USA)
15 August – Pine Knob Amphitheater, Detroit, MI (USA)
16 August – Darien Lake Amphitheater, Buffalo, NY (USA)
17 August – PNC Arts Center, Holmdel, New Jersey, NJ (USA)
19 August – Riverport Amphitheater, St. Louis, MO (USA)
20 August – Sandstone Amphitheater, Kansas City, MO (USA)
23 August – Blossom Music Center, Cleveland, OH (USA)
25 August – UIC Pavilion, Chicago, IL (USA)
26 August – Marcus Amphitheater, Milwaukee, WI (USA)
27 August – Roy Wilkins Auditorium, Minneapolis, MN (USA)
29 August – World Arena, Colorado Springs, CO (USA)
30 August – Red Rocks Amphitheater, Denver, CO (USA)

01 September – Starplex Amphitheater, Dallas, TX (USA)
02 September – Woodlands Pavilion, Houston, TX (USA)
03 September – Sunken Garden, San Antonio, TX (USA)
04 September – Sunken Garden, San Antonio, TX (USA)
06 September – University of Texas, El Paso, TX (USA)
08 September – Mesa Del Sol, Albuquerque, NM (USA)

09 September – Desert Sky Pavilion, Phoenix, AZ (USA)
10 September – Irvine Meadows, Irvine, CA (USA)
12 September – Sports Arena, San Diego, CA (USA)
13 September – Universal Amphitheater, Los Angeles, CA (USA)
15 September – Centennial Garden, Bakersfield, CA (USA)
16 September – Shoreline Amphitheater, San Jose, CA (USA)
17 September – Aladdin Theater, Las Vegas, NV (USA)
20 September – Tacoma Dome, Tacoma, WA (USA)
21 September – Pacific Coliseum, Vancouver (Canada)

10 October – Medina Entertainment Center, Hamel, MN (USA)
11 October – House of Blues, Chicago, IL (USA)
12 October – The Rave Bar, Milwaukee, WI (USA)
14 October – Harpo's Concert Theater, Detroit, MI (USA)
15 October – Orbit Room, Grand Rapids, MI (USA)
17 October – Palladium, Worcester, MA (USA)
18 October – Roseland Ballroom, New York, NY (USA)
19 October – Webster Theater, Hartford, CT (USA)
21 October – Birch Hill Night Café, Old Bridge, NJ (USA)
22 October – 9:30 Club, Washington, DC (USA)
24 October – The Trocadero, Philadelphia, PA (USA)
25 October – Northern Lights, Clifton Park, NY (USA)
29 October – Elysée Montmartre, Paris (France)
30 October – O13, Tilburg (Holland)
31 October – Axionhal, Geel (Belgium)

02 November – SECC, Glasgow (Scotland)
03 November – MEN, Manchester (England)
04 November – NEC Arena, Birmingham (England)
06 November – Grugahalle, Essen (Germany)
08 November – Pumpehuset, Copenhagen (Denmark)
09 November – Kulturbolaget, Malmö (Sweden)
10 November – Solnahallen, Stockholm (Sweden)
12 November – Rockfeller, Oslo (Norway)
14 November – Docks, Hamburg (Germany)
15 November – Columbiahalle, Berlin (Germany)
17 November – Sübahnhof, Chemnitz (Germany)
18 November – Babylon, Munich (Germany)
19 November – Longhorn, Stuttgart (Germany)
21 November – Konzertfabrik Z7, Pratteln (Switzerland)
22 November – Tenax, Firenze (Italy)

23 November – Rolling Stone, Milan (Italy)
25 November – Aqualung, Madrid (Spain)
26 November – Jam Club, Bergara (Spain)
28 November – *(Exact venue unknown)* Hardenberg (Holland)
29 November – Pier, Bremen (Germany)
30 November – Capitol, Hanover (Germany)

03 December – JB's Club, Dudley (England)
04 December – Rock City, Nottingham (England)
06 December – Astoria 2, London (England)
08 December – Rodon Club, Athens (Greece)
09 December – Rodon Club, Athens (Greece)
14 December – Diamond Hall, Nagoya (Japan)
15 December – Zepp, Fukuoka (Japan)
16 December – Koseinenkin Hall, Osaka (Japan)
19 December – Zepp, Sendai (Japan)
20 December – Shibuya Kokaido, Tokyo (Japan)
21 December – Shibuya Kokaido, Tokyo (Japan)

2001

09 January – Sports Palace, Mexico City (Mexico)
13 January – Velez Sarsfield Stadium, Buenos Aires (Argentina)
15 January – Velodromo, Santiago (Chile)
19 January – Barra Da Tijuca, Rio de Janerio (Brazil)

2002
CRUCIBLE WORLD TOUR

07 June – Sweden Rock Festival, Sölvesborg (Sweden)
08 June – Gods of Metal Festival, Milan (Italy)
29 June – Bang Your Head Festival, Balingen (Germany)
01 July – RockWave Festival, Athens (Greece)
03 July – Akademic Stadium, Sofia (Bulgaria)
05 July – With Full Force Festival, Leipzig (Germany)
06 July – Graspop Metal Festival, Dessel (Belgium)

12 October – Soyo Rock Festival, Seoul (South Korea)

2003

01 February – House of Blues, Las Vegas, NV (USA)
02 February – House of Blues, Los Angeles, CA (USA)
07 February – House of Blues, Anaheim, CA (USA)
11 February – Shibuya Kokaido, Tokyo (Japan)
13 February – Zepp, Fukuoka (Japan)
14 February – Nenkin Hall, Osaka (Japan)
15 February – Shibuya Kokaido, Tokyo (Japan)
19 February – Zepp, Sapporo (USA)
28 February – L'Amour, Brooklyn, NY (USA)

01 March – L'Amour, Brooklyn, NY (USA)
29 March – The Avalon, San Francisco, CA (USA)

JUDAS PRIEST: SELECTIVE LIST OF SUPPORT BANDS

Another deciding factor when discussing Judas Priest's concerts is their knack for picking young, aspiring bands and helping them achieve their own success by giving them support slots. Priest have also helped older bands reconnect with their audience while collecting new and younger fans along the way viz: the Scorpions in 2005. Since their difficulties supporting Foghat in 1978, Priest made an unofficial promise to treat their support bands with respect. This is a selective list of bands who have supported Judas Priest over the years. In alphabetical order they are:

Accept (1981)
Annihilator (1991 & 2004)
Anthrax (2002 & 2005)
Baron Rojo (2005)
Bon Jovi (1986)
Bonfire (1988)
Cinderella (1988)
Coney Hatch (1982)
Dangerous Toys (1991)
Def Leppard (1980)
Dokken (1986)
Gorefest (1991)
Great White (1983)

Hatebreed (2004 & 2005)
Heaven (1982)
In Flames (2005)
Jailbait (1974)
Joe Perry Project (1981)
Krokus (1982 & 1986)
Lea Heart (1978)
Iron Maiden (1980, 1981 & 1982)
Magnum (1977)
Marseille (1979)
Max Webster (1981)
Megadeth (1990 & 1998)
Metal Church (1991)
Motorhead (1991 & 1998)
Ted Nugent (1983)
Pantera (1991)
Paradise Lost (2005)
Queensrÿche (2005)
Quiet Riot (1983)
Ranger (1981)
Raven (1983)
Savatage (1998)
Savoy Brown (1981)
Saxon (1981, 1983 & 2001)
Scorpions (1980 & 2005)
Slayer (2004)
Testament (1990)
Uriah Heep (1982)
Warlock (1986)
Whitesnake (1981 & 2005)
Rob Zombie (2005)

AND THE LEAD BREAK BELONGS TO . . . ?

SELECTIVE LIST OF JUDAS PRIEST LEAD BREAKS

Judas Priest fans have often wondered which lead guitar solo belongs to either Glenn Tipton or K.K. Downing. Here is a partial list of their lead guitar work from the CBS/Sony albums from 1977 to 1990. The Sounds *spin-off* Guitar Heroes *offered a great deal of help with the author's research for this section for the years 1977 to 1983, while the rest are credited in the liner notes for the 2001/02 Sony reissues.*

SIN AFTER SIN
'Sinner' – First lead: Glenn. Middle: K.K. Final lead: Glenn
'Diamonds And Rust' – Licks Glenn
'Starbreaker' – Both split between Glenn/K.K.
'Last Rose Of Summer' – Glenn
'Let Us Prey/Call For The Priest' – Split lead breaks:
    K.K./Glenn/K.K./Glenn
'Call For The Priest' – Split lead breaks: K.K./Glenn/K.K./Glenn
'Raw Deal' – Glenn
'Here Come The Tears' – Glenn
'Dissident Aggressor' – K.K.

STAINED CLASS
'Exciter' – First lead: Glenn/second lead harmony
'White Heat, Red Hot' – Glenn
'Better By You, Better Than Me' – Licks Glenn
'Stained Class' – Glenn
'Invader' – Glenn
'Savage' – K.K.
'Beyond The Realms Of Death' – Slow lead Glenn/fast lead K.K.
'Heroes End' – Glenn

KILLING MACHINE
'Delivering The Goods' – Glenn
'Rock Forever' – Both harmonising
'Evening Star' – Split lead: Glenn/K.K. – slow echo Glenn
'Hell Bent For Leather' – Glenn
'Killing Machine' – Glenn
'Running Wild' – Middle: Glenn. End: K.K.
'Before The Dawn' – K.K.
'Evil Fantasies' – Licks: K.K. Slide: Glenn. End: K.K.
'Burnin' Up' – K.K.

UNLEASHED IN THE EAST
'Exciter' – First lead: Glenn/second lead harmony
'Running Wild' – Middle: Glenn. End: K.K.
'Sinner' – First lead: Glenn. Middle: K.K. Final lead: Glenn

'The Ripper' – Glenn
'The Green Manalishi (With The Two-Pronged Crown)' – Split lead:
    K.K./Glenn/K.K./Glenn
'Diamonds And Rust' – Licks Glenn
'Victim Of Changes' – First lead: K.K. Second: lead Glenn
'Genocide' – Licks: Glenn/K.K./both – lead Glenn
'Tyrant' – First lead: Glenn/second lead harmony

BRITISH STEEL
'Rapid Fire' – Lead: K.K./Glenn/K.K./Glenn
'Metal Gods' – Glenn
'Grinder' – Glenn
'Living After Midnight' – Glenn
'You Don't Have To Be Old To Be Wise' – Lead: Glenn/K.K.
'The Rage' – K.K.
'Steeler' – Middle: K.K. Lead licks: K.K./Glenn/K.K./Glenn

POINT OF ENTRY
'Heading Out To The Highway' – Harmony lead
'Don't Go' – K.K.
'Hot Rockin'' – Lead: K.K./Glenn
'Turning Circles' – Glenn
'Desert Plains' – Lead: K.K./Glenn/K.K./Glenn
'Solar Angels' – Glenn
'All The Way' – Glenn
'Troubleshooter' – Lead: Glenn/K.K.
'On The Run' – Glenn

SCREAMING FOR VENGEANCE
'Electric Eye' – Glenn
'Riding On The Wind' – Lead: K.K./Glenn/K.K./Glenn
'Bloodstone' – Lead: Glenn/K.K. (interlinked through drum fill)
'(Take These) Chains' – Lead: K.K./Glenn
'Pain & Pleasure' – Lead: Glenn/K.K./Glenn/both
'Screaming For Vengeance' – Lead: K.K./Glenn/both
'You've Got Another Thing Comin' – Glenn
'Fever' – First lead: Glenn. Second lead: Glenn/K.K./together
'Devil's Child' – K.K.

DEFENDERS OF THE FAITH
'Freewheel Burning' – Glenn

'Jawbreaker' – K.K.
'Eat Me Alive' – Divided into four equally shared quarters:
    K.K./Glenn/K.K./Glenn
'Rock Hard Ride Free' – Intro: Glenn. Harmony sections: K.K./Glenn.
    Lead break: K.K./Glenn and end harmony sections: K.K./Glenn
'Some Heads Are Gonna Roll' – Split into two parts: K.K./Glenn
'Night Comes Down' – Both
'The Sentinel' – Split into seven parts:
    Glenn/K.K./Glenn/K.K./Glenn/K.K./Both

TURBO
'Turbo Lover' – Glenn
'Locked In' – Split into five parts: K.K./Glenn/K.K./Glenn. Melody: K.K.
    and arpeggios and run: Glenn
'Private Property' – Glenn
'Parental Guidance' – First half: Glenn. Second half, K.K.
'Rock You All Around The World' – Glenn (solos and licks)
'Out In The Cold' – Song intro: Glenn. First half of solo: K.K. Second half
    of solo: Glenn
'Wild Nights, Hot And Crazy Days' – K.K.
'Hot For Love' – K.K. (harmony section: both)
'Reckless' – Song intro: both. Solo: Glenn. Licks: K.K.
K.K. and Glenn played all synthesised guitars

PRIEST . . . LIVE!
'Out In The Cold' – First half: Glenn. Second half: K.K.
'Heading Out To The Highway' – K.K. then Glenn
'Metal Gods' – Glenn
'Breaking The Law' – K.K.
'Some Heads Are Gonna Roll' – First half: Glenn. Second half: K.K.
'The Sentinel' – Split into seven parts:
    Glenn/K.K./Glenn/K.K./Glenn/K.K./both
'Private Property' – Glenn
'Rock You All Around The World' – Glenn
'Electric Eye' – Glenn
'Turbo Lover' – Glenn
'Freewheel Burning' – Glenn
'Parental Guidance' – First part: Glenn. Second part: K.K.
'Living After Midnight' – Glenn
'You've Got Another Thing Comin'' – Glenn

RAM IT DOWN

'Ram It Down' – Split into seven sections:
K.K./Glenn/K.K./Glenn/K.K./Glenn/Glenn and K.K. Fourth
section up to harmonies is by Glenn. Fifth section with harmonies is
by K.K. Sixth section after harmonies, up top and through stop is
Glenn and the seventh section up to the vocal entry is K.K. and
Glenn

'Heavy Metal' – Intros and solos: Glenn

'Love Zone' – Split into five sections: Glenn/K.K./Glenn/K.K./Glenn
and K.K.

'Come And Get It' – First half: K.K. Second half: Glenn

'Hard As Iron' – First sections: K.K. Harmony section: Glenn and K.K.
Third section: Glenn. Final harmony section: Glenn and K.K.

'Blood Red Skies' – Main solo: K.K. End parts: Glenn

'I'm A Rocker' – All licks and solos: Glenn

'Johnny B. Goode' – Split into four parts: K.K./Glenn/K.K. (harmony
section) K.K. and Glenn

'Love You To Death' – Solo: K.K.

'Monsters Of Rock' – Intro and solos: K.K.

PAINKILLER

'Painkiller' – Middle of song: Glenn. End of song: K.K.

'Hell Patrol' – First half of lead break: K.K. Second half of lead break:
Glenn

'All Guns Blazing' – Full lead: Glenn

'Leather Rebel' – Glenn and K.K. with K.K. at the end of the lead break

'Metal Meltdown' – First half of intro: K.K. Second half of intro: Glenn.
First section of lead break: K.K. Second section of lead break: Glenn.
Third section of lead break: K.K. Fourth section of lead break: Glenn

'Night Crawler' – Glenn and K.K.

'Between The Hammer And The Anvil' – First half of lead break: K.K.
Second half of lead break: Glenn

'A Touch Of Evil' – All: Glenn

'One Shot At Glory' – Opening lick: Glenn. Second verse entry lick: K.K.
First section of lead break: K.K. Second section of lead break: Glenn.
Third section of lead break: K.K. and Glenn. Outro: Glenn

JUDAS PRIEST: UK CHART POSITIONS

What follows is a list of Judas Priest singles and albums that have made it into the British charts, according to the 19th edition (2005) of the British Hit Singles & Albums (Guinness World Records, Ltd).

Judas Priest have spent a total of 80 weeks in the UK album charts with 14 albums, and a reported 13 singles that spent 51 weeks in the UK charts. Those albums and singles that did not make the charts have also been listed here. The number in brackets indicates how long each release lasted in the charts.

ALBUMS

Rocka Rolla – released August 23, 1974 (-)
Sad Wings Of Destiny – released March 26, 1976 (-)
Sin After Sin – released May 14, 1977; number 23 (6)
Stained Class – released February 25, 1978; number 27 (5)
Killing Machine – released November 11, 1978; number 32 (9)
Unleashed In The East – released October 6, 1979; number 10 (8)
British Steel – released April 19, 1980; number 4 (17)
Point Of Entry – released February 26, 1981; number 14 (5)
Screaming For Vengeance – released July 17, 1983; number 11 (3)
Defenders Of The Faith – released January 28, 1984; number 19 (5)
Turbo – released April 19, 1986; number 33 (4)
Priest . . . Live! – released June 13, 1987; number 47 (2)
Ram It Down – released May 28, 1988; number 24 (5)
Painkiller – released September 22, 1990; number 26 (2)
Metal Works '73–'93 – released May 8, 1993; number 27 (1)
Jugulator – released October 16, 1997; number 47
'98 Live Meltdown – released September 17, 1998; number 74
Demolition – released July 16, 2001 (-)
Live In London – released July 1, 2002 (-)
Angel Of Retribution – released March 12, 2005; number 39 (2)

SINGLES

Take On The World – released January 20, 1979; number 14 (10)
Evening Star – released on May 12, 1979; number 53 (4)
Living After Midnight – released May 29, 1980; number 12 (7)

Breaking The Law – released June 7, 1980; reached number 12 (6)
United – released August 23, 1980; number 26 (8)
Don't Go – released February 21, 1981; number 51 (3)
Hot Rockin' – released April 25, 1981; number 60 (3)
You've Got Another Thing Comin' – released August 21, 1982; number
    66 (2)
Freewheel Burning – released January 21, 1984; number 42 (3)
Johnny B. Goode – released April 23, 1988; number 64 (2)
Painkiller – released September 15, 1990; number 74 (1)
A Touch Of Evil – released March 23, 1991; number 58 (1)
Night Crawler – released April 24, 1993; number 63 (1)
Machine Man – released May 28, 2001 (-)
Worth Fighting For – released May 16, 2005 (-)

SELECTIVE DISCOGRAPHY/ FILMOGRAPHY (UK)

JUDAS PRIEST

STUDIO ALBUMS, CDs

The 12 Judas Priest albums from 1977's Sin After Sin *to 1990's* Painkiller *are listed as per the Sony/Columbia reissues, which were released in three batches of four CDs during 2001–2002. A rather nifty black and silver-studded collector's box was released to store them but is now deleted. Each CD includes bonus tracks, which in total adds up to 26 songs. The nine bonus studio tracks had never been released before and neither had the 17 live tracks.*

The Gull Records albums are also listed as reissues. All albums state the original release date. Catalogue numbers on the Gull CDs vary depending on which version. The Gull albums listed below are the two most recent (and available) versions.

With all the reissues and unofficial releases, the Judas Priest discography gets confusing, but the entire back catalogue is listed here. Wherever possible, catalogue numbers have been included for each release, although it has not been possible to acquire all details.

Rocka Rolla

Year of Release: 1974
Label: Gull Records/Snapper
Catalogue Number (UK): SDPCD124
Track Listing: One For The Road/Rocka Rolla/Winter/Deep Freeze/Winter Retreat/Cheater/Never Satisfied/Run Of The Mill/Dying To Meet You/Caviar And Meths/Diamonds And Rust★
★*Bonus track included on the 2003 Snapper reissue*

Sad Wings Of Destiny

Year of Release: 1976
Label: Gull Records/Snapper

Catalogue Number (UK): SMMCD562
Track Listing: Victim Of Changes/The Ripper/Dreamer
Deceiver/Deceiver/Prelude/Tyrant/Genocide/Epitaph/Island Of
Domination

Sin After Sin

Year of Release: 1977
Label: Columbia/Sony Music Entertainment
Catalogue Number (UK): 5021272
Track Listing: Sinner/Diamonds And Rust/Starbreaker/Last Rose Of
Summer/Let Us Prey/Call For The Priest/Raw Deal/Here Come The
Tears/Dissident Aggressor/Race With The Devil★/Jawbreaker (Live)★
★*Bonus tracks included on the 2001/02 Sony/Columbia reissue*

Stained Class

Year of Release: 1978
Label: Columbia/Sony Music Entertainment
Catalogue Number (UK): 5021282
Track Listing: Exciter/White Heat, Red Hot/Better By You, Better Than
Me/Stained Class/Invader/Saints In Hell/Savage/Beyond The Realms Of
Death/Heroes End/Fire Burns Below★/Better By You, Better Than Me
(Live)
★*Bonus tracks included on the 2001/02 Sony/Columbia reissue*

Killing Machine (released as Hell Bent For Leather in the US)

Year of Release: 1979
Label: Columbia/Sony Music Entertainment
Catalogue Number (UK): 5021292
Track Listing: Delivering The Goods/Rock Forever/Evening Star/Hell
Bent For Leather/Take On The World/Burnin' Up/The Green Manalishi
(With The Two-Pronged Crown)+/Killing Machine/Running
Wild/Before The Dawn/Evil Fantasies/Fight For Your Life★/Riding On
The Wind★
+*On the initial 1979 release, this song only appeared on the US version*
★*Bonus tracks included on the 2001/02 Sony/Columbia reissue*

British Steel

Year of Release: 1980

Label: Columbia/Sony Music Entertainment
Catalogue Number (UK): 5021312
Track Listing: Rapid Fire/Metal Gods/Breaking The
Law/Grinder/United/You Don't Have To Be Old To Be Wise/Living
After Midnight/The Rage/Steeler/Red, White & Blue★/Grinder (Live)★
★Bonus tracks included on the 2001/02 Sony/Columbia reissue

Point Of Entry

Year of Release: 1981
Label: Columbia/Sony Music Entertainment
Catalogue (UK): 5021322
Track Listing: Heading Out To The Highway/Don't Go/Hot
Rockin'/Turning Circles/Desert Plains/Solar Angels/You Say Yes/All
The Way/Troubleshooter/On The Run/Thunder Road★/Desert Plains
(Live)★
★Bonus tracks included on the 2001/02 Sony/Columbia reissue

Screaming For Vengeance

Year of Release: 1982
Label: Columbia/Sony Music Entertainment
Catalogue Number (UK): 5021332
Track Listing: The Hellion/Electric Eye/Riding On The
Wind/Bloodstone/(Take These) Chains/Pain And Pleasure/Screaming
For Vengeance/You've Got Another Thing Comin'/Fever/Devil's
Child/Prisoner Of Your Eyes★/Devil's Child (Live)★
★Bonus tracks included on the 2001/02 Sony/Columbia reissue

Defenders Of The Faith

Year of Release: 1984
Label: Columbia/Sony Music Entertainment
Catalogue Number (UK): 5021342
Track Listing: Freewheel Burning/Jawbreaker/Rock Hard, Ride
Free/The Sentinel/Love Bites/Eat Me Alive/Some Heads Are Gonna
Roll/Night Comes Down/Heavy Duty/Defenders Of The Faith/Turn
On Your Light★/Heavy Duty/Defenders Of The Faith (Live)★
★Bonus tracks included on the 2001/02 Sony/Columbia reissue

Turbo

Year of Release: 1986
Label: Columbia/Sony Music Entertainment
Catalogue Number (UK): 5021352
Track Listing: Turbo Lover/Locked In/Private Property/Parental
Guidance/Rock You All Around The World/Out In The Cold/Wild
Nights, Hot & Crazy Days/Hot For Love/Reckless/All Fired Up★/
Locked In (Live)
★Bonus tracks included on the 2001/02 Sony/Columbia reissue

Ram It Down

Year of Release: 1988
Label: Columbia/Sony Music Entertainment
Catalogue Number (UK): 5021372
Track Listing: Ram It Down/Heavy Metal/Love Zone/Come And Get
It/Hard As Iron/Blood Red Skies/I'm A Rocker/Johnny B. Goode/Love
You To Death/Monsters Of Rock/Night Comes Down
(Live)★/Bloodstone (Live)★
★Bonus tracks included on the 2001/02 Sony/Columbia reissue

Painkiller

Year of Release: 1990
Label: Columbia/Sony Music Entertainment
Catalogue Number (UK): 5021392
Track Listing: Painkiller/Hell Patrol/All Guns Blazing/Leather
Rebel/Metal Meltdown/Night Crawler/Between The Hammer And The
Anvil/A Touch Of Evil/Battle Hymn/One Shot At Glory/Living Bad
Dreams★/Leather Rebel (Live)★
★Bonus tracks included on the 2001/02 Sony/Columbia reissue

Jugulator

Year of Release: 1997
Label: SPV Records
Catalogue Number (UK): SPV085–18782
Track Listing: Jugulator/Blood Stained/Dead Meat/Death
Row/Decapitate/Burn In Hell/Brain Dead/Abductors/Bullet
Train/Cathedral Spies

Demolition

Year of Release: 2001
Label: SPV Records
Catalogue Number (UK): SPV088–72420CD
Track Listing: Machine Man/One On One/Hell Is Home/Jekyll And
Hyde/Close To You/Devil Digger/Bloodsuckers/In Between/Feed On
Me/Subterfuge/Lost And Found/Cyberface/Metal Messiah/Rapid
Fire★/The Green Manalishi (With The Two-Pronged Crown)★

★Bonus tracks included on the 2001 SPV limited-edition cardboard sleeve package that also comes with a colour sticker and guitar pick. The catalogue number for the standard edition is SPV07672422.

Angel Of Retribution (Dualdisc)

Year of Release: 2005
Label: Sony BMG Records
Catalogue Number (UK): 5193003
Track Listing: Judas Rising/Deal With The Devil/Revolution/Worth
Fighting For/Demonizer/Wheels Of Fire/Angel/Hellrider/Eulogy/
Lochness
★Live DVD – Breaking The Law/Metal Gods/A Touch Of Evil/Hell
Bent For Leather/The Hellion/Electric Eye/Diamonds And Rust/Living
After Midnight

★Bonus DVD included on the 2005 limited-edition cardboard sleeve package that also features a 40-minute documentary from the 2004 'Reunited' tour. The catalogue number for the standard edition is 5193002.

LIVE ALBUMS, CDs

Unleashed In The East: Live In Japan

Year of Release: 1979
Label: Columbia/Sony Music Entertainment
Catalogue Number (UK): 5021302
Recorded at the Koseinenkin Hall and Nakano Sun Plaza Hall in Tokyo,
Japan in 1979 as part of the 'Killing Machine'/'Hell Bent For Leather'
Japanese tour.
Track Listing: Exciter/Running Wild/Sinner/The Ripper/The Green
Manalishi (With The Two-Pronged Crown)/Diamonds And Rust/Victim
Of Changes/Genocide/Tyrant/Rock Forever★/Delivering The Goods★/
Hell Bent For Leather★/Starbreaker★

★Bonus tracks included on the 2001/02 Sony/Columbia reissue

(The early copies of this album contained a free 7" EP with live tracks that featured Rock Forever/Hell Bent For Leather/Beyond The Realms Of Death. The catalogue number is SJP1. It was actually released as a regular 12" in Holland with the catalogue number CDS12–1864.)

Priest . . . Live!

Year of Release: 1987
Label: Columbia/Sony Music Entertainment
Catalogue Number (UK): 5021362
Recorded in Dallas, Texas and Atlanta, Georgia in 1986 as part of the 'Turbo: Fuel For Life' world tour.
Track Listing: **Disc 1** – Out In The Cold/Heading Out To The Highway/Metal Gods/Breaking The Law/Love Bites/Some Heads Are Gonna Roll/The Sentinel/Private Property
Disc 2 – Rock You All Around The World/The Hellion/Electric Eye/Turbo Lover/Freewheel Burning/Parental Guidance/Living After Midnight/You've Got Another Thing Comin'/Screaming For Vengeance★/Rock Hard, Ride Free★/Hell Bent For Leather★
★Bonus tracks included on the 2001/02 Sony/Columbia reissue

'98 Live Meltdown

Year of Release: 1998
Label: SPV Records
Catalogue Number (UK): SPV08918542
Recorded at various world venues as part of the 1998 'Jugulator' world tour.
Track Listing: **Disc 1** – The Hellion/Electric Eye/Metal Gods/Death Row/Grinder/Rapid Fire/Blood Stained/The Sentinel/A Touch Of Evil/Burn In Hell/The Ripper/Bullet Train/Beyond The Realms Of Death/Death Row
Disc 2 – Metal Meltdown/Night Crawler/Abductors/Victim Of Changes/Diamonds And Rust/Breaking The Law/The Green Manalishi (With The Two-Pronged Crown)/Painkiller/You've Got Another Thing Comin'/Hell Bent For Leather/Living After Midnight

Live In London

Year of Release: 2003
Label: SPV Records
Catalogue Number (UK): SPV09274262

Recorded at Brixton Academy, London on December 19, 2001 as part of the 'Demolition' world tour.
Track Listing: **Disc 1** – Metal Gods/Heading Out To The Highway/Grinder/Touch Of Evil/Blood Stained/Victim Of Changes/The Sentinel/One On One/Running Wild/The Ripper/Diamonds And Rust/Feed On Me/The Green Manalishi (With The Two-Pronged Crown)
Disc 2 – Beyond The Realms Of Death/Burn In Hell/Hell Is Home/Breaking The Law/Desert Plains/You've Got Another Thing Comin'/Turbo Lover/Painkiller/The Hellion/Electric Eye/United/Living After Midnight/Hell Bent For Leather

COMPILATIONS/COLLECTIONS, CDs

Best Of Judas Priest
Year of Release: 1978
Label: Gull Records
Catalogue Number (UK): GULP1026
Track Listing: Dying To Meet You/Never Satisfied/Rocka Rolla/Diamonds And Rust/Victim Of Changes/Island Of Domination/Ripper/Deceiver
(This CD version was released in 1987 and is now deleted)

Metal Works '73–'93
Year of Release: 1993
Label: Columbia/Sony Music Entertainment
Catalogue Number (UK): 5021382
Track Listing: **Disc 1** – The Hellion/Electric Eye/Victim Of Changes/Painkiller/Eat Me Alive/Devil's Child/Dissident Aggressor/Delivering The Goods/Exciter/Breaking The Law/Hell Bent For Leather/Blood Red Skies/Metal Gods/Before The Dawn/Turbo Lover/Ram It Down/Metal Meltdown
Disc 2 – Screaming For Vengeance/You've Got Another Thing Comin'/Beyond The Realms Of Death/Solar Angels/Bloodstone/Desert Plains/Wild Nights, Hot And Crazy Days/Heading Out To The Highway/Living After Midnight/A Touch Of Evil/The Rage/Night Comes Down/Sinner/Freewheel Burning/Night Crawler

Living After Midnight: The Best Of Judas Priest
Year of Release: 1997

Label: Columbia/Sony Music Entertainment
Catalogue Number (UK): 4872429
Track Listing: Better By You, Better Than Me/Take On The World/The Green Manalishi (With The Two-Pronged Crown)/Living After Midnight/Breaking The Law/United/Hot Rockin'/You've Got Another Thing Comin'/The Hellion/Electric Eye/Freewheel Burning/Some Heads Are Gonna Roll/Turbo Lover/Locked In/Johnny B. Goode/Ram It Down/Painkiller/A Touch Of Evil/Night Crawler
★Reissued in 2001/02 as part of the Sony remastered series

Genocide

Year of Release: 2000
Label: Snapper
Catalogue Number (UK): SMDCD273
Track Listing: **Disc 1** – One For The Road/Rocka Rolla/Winter/Deep Freeze/Winter Retreat/Cheater/Never Satisfied/Run Of The Mill/Dying To Meet You/Caviar And Meths/Diamonds And Rust★
Disc 2 – Victim Of Changes/The Ripper/Dreamer Deceiver/Deceiver/Prelude/Tyrant/Genocide/Epitaph/Island Of Domination

Metalogy

Year of Release: 2004
Label: Columbia/Legacy (*This box set includes material from various labels: Gull, Sony/Columbia, CMC International, SPV, Atlantic and JVC.*)
Catalogue Number (UK): 5128933
Track Listing: **Disc 1** – Never Satisfied/Deceiver/Tyrant/Victim Of Changes (Live)/Diamonds And Rust (Live)/Starbreaker (Live)/Sinner/Let Us Prey/Call For The Priest/Dissident Aggressor/Exciter/Beyond The Realms Of Death/Better By You, Better Than Me/Invader/Stained Class/The Green Manalishi (With The Two-Pronged Crown (Live)★
Disc 2 – Killing Machine/Evening Star/Take On The World/Delivering The Goods/Evil Fantasies/Hell Bent For Leather/Breaking The Law (Live)/Living After Midnight/Rapid Fire/Metal Gods/Grinder (Live)★/The Rage/Heading Out To The Highway/Hot Rockin' (Live)/Troubleshooter/Solar Angels/Desert Plains/The Hellion/Electric Eye (Live)/Screaming For Vengeance
Disc 3 – Riding On The Wind/Bloodstone/You've Got Another Thing Comin'/Devil's Child/Freewheel Burning/Jawbreaker/The Sentinel/

Love Bites (Live)★/Eat Me Alive/Some Heads Are Gonna Roll/Rock Hard, Ride Free/Night Comes Down/Turbo Lover/Private Property/Parental Guidance/Out In The Cold/Heart Of A Lion (Demo)★
Disc 4 – Ram It Down/Heavy Metal/Come And Get It/Blood Red Skies/Painkiller/Between The Hammer & The Anvil/A Touch Of Evil/Metal Meltdown/Night Crawler/All Guns Blazing/Jugulator/Blood Stained/Machine Man/Feed On Me
DVD – The Hellion/Electric Eye/Riding On The Wind/Heading Out To The Highway/Metal Gods/Bloodstone/Breaking The Law/Sinner/Desert Plains/The Ripper/Diamonds And Rust/Devil's Child/Screaming For Vengeance/You've Got Another Thing Comin'/Victim Of Changes/Living After Midnight/The Green Manalishi (With The Two-Pronged Crown)/Hell Bent For Leather
(NOTE: *This DVD was originally released as* Judas Priest Live *on VHS and then* Live Vengeance '82 *on DVD in 2006. It appeared on DVD for the first time in this box-set.*)
★*Previously unreleased tracks*

The Essential Judas Priest

Year of Release: 2006
Label: Sony
Catalogue Number (UK): SNY92554.2
Track Listing: **Disc 1** – Judas Rising/Breaking The Law/Hell Bent For Leather/Diamonds And Rust/Victim Of Changes/Love Bites/Heading Out To The Highway/Ram It Down/Beyond The Realms Of Death/You've Got Another Thing Comin'/Jawbreaker/A Touch Of Evil/Delivering The Goods/United/Turbo Lover/Painkiller/Metal Gods
Disc 2 – The Hellion/Electric Eye/Living After Midnight/Freewheel Burning/Exciter/The Green Manalishi (With The Two-Pronged Crown)/Blood Red Skies/Night Crawler/Sinner/Hot Rockin'/The Sentinel/Before The Dawn/Hell Patrol/The Ripper/Screaming For Vengeance/Out In The Cold/Revolution

OTHER

Judas Priest: Interview Picture Disc
Year of Release: 1987
Label: Baktabak
Catalogue Number (UK): BAK2054

SINGLES

Rocka Rolla/Never Satisfied (7")

Year of Release: 1974
Label: Gull Records
Catalogue Number (UK): GULS6
Extra Tracks:

The Ripper/Island Of Domination (7")

Year of Release: 1976
Label: Gull Records
Catalogue Number (UK): GULS31

Diamonds And Rust/Dissident Aggressor (7")

Year of Release: 1977
Label: CBS Records
Catalogue Number (UK): 5222

Better By You, Better Than Me/Invader (7")

Year of Release: 1978
Label: CBS Records
Catalogue Number (UK): 6077

Before The Dawn/Rock Forever (7")

Year of Release: 1978
Label: CBS Records
Catalogue Number (UK): 6794

The Ripper/Victim Of Changes (7")

Year of Release: 1979
Label: Gull Records
Catalogue Number (UK): GUL71

Take On The World/Starbreaker (Live) (7")

Year of Release: 1979
Label: CBS Records
Catalogue Number (UK): 6915

A 12" version was also released with the extra live track 'White Heat, Red Hot'. The catalogue number is CBS126915.

Evening Star/Beyond The Realms Of Death (7")

Year of Release: 1979
Label: CBS Records
Catalogue Number (UK): 7312

A limited edition 12" version was also released, which was pressed in clear vinyl and contained the extra track 'The Green Manalishi (With The Two-Pronged Crown'). The catalogue number is CBS 127312.

Living After Midnight/Delivering The Goods (Live) (7")

Year of Release: 1980
Label: CBS Records
Catalogue Number (UK): 8379

A 12" version was also released with the extra live track 'Evil Fantasies'. The catalogue number is 128379.

Breaking The Law/Metal Gods (7")

Year of Release: 1980
Label: CBS Records
Catalogue Number (UK): 8644
A cassette single with Breaking The Law/Metal Gods/Living After Midnight/United was also released.

United/Grinder (7")

Year of Release: 1980
Label: CBS Records
Catalogue Number (UK): 8897

Don't Go/Solar Angels (7")

Year of Release: 1981
Label: CBS Records
Catalogue Number (UK): 9520

Evening Star/Starbreaker (7" – reissue)

Year of Release: 1981
Label: CBS Records
Catalogue Number (UK): Unknown

Hot Rockin'/Trouble Shooter/Breaking The Law (Live) (7″)

Year of Release: 1981
Label: CBS Records
Catalogue Number (UK): A1153

A 12″ version was also released with the extra tracks 'Breaking The Law' and a live version 'Living After Midnight'. The catalogue number is CBS A12–1153.

You've Got Another Thing Comin'/Exciter (Live) (7″ picture disc)

Year of Release: 1982
Label: CBS Records
Catalogue Number (UK): A2611

(Take These) Chains/The Judas Priest Audiofile (7″)

Year of Release: 1982
Label: CBS Records
Catalogue Number (UK): A2822

Tyrant/Rocka Rolla/Genocide (12″)

Year of Release: 1983
Label: Gull Records
Catalogue Number (UK): GULS 76–12

6 Track Hits (Cassette)

Tracks: Sinner/Exciter/Hell Bent For Leather/Ripper/Hot Rockin'/
The Green Manalishi (With The Two-Pronged Crown)
Year of Release: 1983
Label: Pickwick
Catalogue Number (UK): 7SC 5018

Freewheel Burning/Breaking The Law (7″)

Year of Release: 1984
Label: CBS Records
Catalogue Number (UK): A4054

Some Heads Are Gonna Roll/The Green Manalishi (With The Two-Pronged Crown) (7″)

Year of Release: 1984
Label: CBS Records
Catalogue Number (UK): A4298

A 12″ version was also released with the extra track 'Jawbreaker'. The catalogue number is TA4298.

Turbo Lover/Hot For Love (7″)

Year of Release: 1986
Label: CBS Records
Catalogue Number (UK): Unknown

Locked In/Reckless (7″)

Year of Release: 1986
Label: CBS Records
Catalogue Number (UK): A7144

A 12″ version in a poster sleeve was also released with an extended version of 'Locked In', 'Reckless' and live versions of 'Desert Plains' and 'Freewheel Burning'. The catalogue number is QTA7144.

Johnny B. Goode/Rock You All Around The World (7″)

Year of Release: 1988
Label: Atlantic Records
Catalogue Number (UK): A9114

★This version is the special limited-edition collector's gatefold package.

(A 12″ version was also released with the extra live track 'Turbo Lover'. The catalogue number for the 12″ is AT9114. A 3″ CD single (A9114 CD) was also released, which carried both tracks and a live version of 'Living After Midnight' as well. No other singles were released from the Ram It Down *album.)*

Living After Midnight/Breaking The Law (7″)

Year of Release: 1989
Label: Old Gold
Catalogue Number (UK): OG9864

Painkiller/United/Better By You, Better Than Me (CD)

Year of Release: 1990
Label: CBS Records
Catalogue Number (UK): CBS467290

Bullet Train (exclusive promo CD)

Year of Release: 1997
Label: SPV Records
Catalogue Number (UK): *N/A*

Machine Man/Subterfuge/Burn In Hell★ (CD)

Year of Release: 2001
Label: SPV Records
Catalogue Number (UK): SPV056–72453CDS-E
★A CD extra video clip

Revolution (download only)

Year of Release: 2005
Label: Sony BMG
Catalogue Number: *N/A*

Worth Fighting For (CD)

Year of Release: 2005
Label: Sony BMG
Catalogue Number (UK): JPCDPROI

VHS

Judas Priest Live

Year of Release: 1993
Label: CMV
Catalogue Number (UK): 49820–2
Track Listing: The Hellion/Electric Eye/Riding On The Wind/Heading
Out To The Highway/Metal Gods/Bloodstone/Breaking The Law/
Sinner/Desert Plains/The Ripper/Diamonds And Rust/Devil's
Child/Screaming For Vengeance/You've Got Another Thing Comin'/
Victim Of Changes/Living After Midnight/The Green Manalishi (With
The Two-Pronged Crown)/Hell Bent For Leather

Fuel For Life

Year of Release: 1986
Label: CBS Fox
Catalogue Number (UK): 7104–50
Track Listing: Living After Midnight/Breaking The Law/Don't Go/
Heading Out To The Highway/Hot Rockin'/You've Got Another Thing
Comin'/Freewheel Burning/Love Bites/Locked In/Turbo Lover

Priest . . . Live!

Year of Release: 1987
Label: Vision Video Ltd
Catalogue Number (UK): WD233
Track Listing: Out In The Cold/Locked In/Heading Out To The
Highway/Breaking The Law/Love Bites/Some Heads Are Gonna Roll/
The Sentinel/Private Property/Desert Plains/Rock You All Around The
World/The Hellion/Electric Eye/Turbo Lover/Freewheel Burning/
The Green Manalishi (With The Two-Pronged Crown)/
Parental Guidance/Living After Midnight/You've Got Another Thing
Comin'/Hell Bent For Leather/Metal Gods

Painkiller

Year of Release: 1991
Label: Sony BMG
Catalogue Number (UK): 499042
Track Listing: Painkiller/Locked In/Love Bites/Hot Rockin'/You've Got
Another Thing Comin'/Breaking The Law/Living After Midnight/
Freewheel Burning/A Touch Of Evil

Metal Works '73–'93 (Documentary with live footage)

Year of Release: 1993
Label: SMV Enterprises
Catalogue Number (UK): 2004962

DVDs

Classic Albums: British Steel

Year of Release: 2001
Catalogue Number (UK): EREDV163
Label: Eagle Vision

The following live DVDs have been listed in the order of their recording rather than release date:

Live Vengeance '82

Year of Release: 2006
Label: Columbia/Sony BMG
Catalogue Number (UK): 82876749109
Recorded at Mid South Coliseum, Memphis on December 12, 1982 as part of the 'Screaming For Vengeance' world tour.
Set List: The Hellion/Electric Eye/Riding On The Wind/Heading Out To The Highway/Metal Gods/Bloodstone/Breaking The Law/Sinner/Desert Plains/The Ripper/Diamonds And Rust/Devil's Child/Screaming For Vengeance/You've Got Another Thing Comin'/Victim Of Changes/Living After Midnight/The Green Manalishi (With The Two-Pronged Crown)/Hell Bent For Leather
(A limited-edition digipack was also released at the same time. The catalogue number is 82876786779.)

Electric Eye

Year of Release: 2003
Label: Sony/SMV Enterprises
Catalogue Number (UK): 2021939
Recorded in Dallas, Texas and Atlanta, Georgia in 1986 as part of the 'Turbo: Fuel For Life' world tour
Set List: Out In The Cold/Locked In/Heading Out To The Highway/Breaking The Law/Love Bites/Some Heads Are Gonna Roll/The Sentinel/Private Property/Desert Plains/Rock You All Around The World/The Hellion/Electric Eye/Turbo Lover/Freewheel Burning/The Green Manalishi (With The Two-Pronged Crown)/Parental Guidance/Living After Midnight/You've Got Another Thing Comin'/Hell Bent For Leather/Metal Gods

Live In London

Year of Release: 2002
Label: SPV Records
Catalogue Number (UK): SPV55474267
Recorded at Brixton Academy, London on December 19, 2001 as part of the 'Demolition' world tour
Set List: Metal Gods/A Touch Of Evil/Blood Stained/Victim Of

Changes/One On One/Running Wild/The Ripper/Diamonds And
Rust/Feed On Me/Burn In Hell/Hell Is Home/Breaking The Law/
Desert Plains/Turbo Lover/Painkiller/The Hellion/Electric Eye/
United/Living After Midnight/Hell Bent For Leather

Rising In The East
Year of Release: 2005
Label: Warner Music Vision
Catalogue Number (UK): 0349705042
Recorded at the Budokan Hall, Tokyo, Japan on May 18–19, 2005 as part
of the 'Angel Of Retribution' world tour.
Set List: The Hellion/Electric Eye/Metal Gods/Riding On The Wind/
The Ripper/A Touch Of Evil/Judas Rising/Revolution/Hot Rockin'/
Breaking The Law/I'm A Rocker/Diamonds And Rust/Worth Fighting
For/Deal With The Devil/Beyond The Realms Of Death/Turbo Lover/
Hellrider/Victim Of Changes/Exciter/Painkiller/Hell Bent For Leather/
Living After Midnight/You've Got Another Thing Comin'

PROMO VIDEOS

Living After Midnight
Year of Release: 1980 (March)
Director: Julien Temple

Breaking The Law
Year of Release: 1980 (June)
Director: Julien Temple

Don't Go
Year of Release: 1981 (February)
Director: Julien Temple

Heading Out To The Highway
Year of Release: 1981
Director: Julien Temple

Hot Rockin'

Year of Release: 1981 (April)
Director: Julien Temple

You've Got Another Thing Comin'

Year of Release: 1982 (August)
Director: Julien Temple

The Hellion/Electric (Live)

Year of Release: 1982 (December)
Director: Mick Anger

Freewheel Burning

Year of Release: 1984 (January)
Director: Wayne Isham

Love Bites

Year of Release: 1984
Director: Keith MacMillan

Locked In

Year of Release: 1986
Director: Wayne Isham

Turbo Lover

Year of Release: 1986
Director: Wayne Isham

Parental Guidance

Year of Release: 1987
Director: Wayne Isham

Johnny B Goode

Year of Release: 1988 (April)
Director: Wayne Isham

Painkiller
Year of Release: 1990 (September)
Director: Wayne Isham

A Touch of Evil
Year of Release: 1991 (March)
Director: Julien Temple

Burn In Hell
Year of Release: 1997
Director: *Unknown*

Lost And Found
Year of Release: 2001 (December)
Director: Aubrey Powell

Revolution (download only)
Year of Release: 2005 (March)
Director: *Unknown*

FILMOGRAPHY

(Judas Priest have not officially endorsed the following films but they are worth seeing.)

Heavy Metal Parking Lot
Year of Release: 1986
Director: Jeff Krulik

Rock Star
Year of Release: 2001
Director: Stephen Herek

NOTABLE TV PERFORMANCES (UK)

Rocka Rolla

Programme: *The Old Grey Whistle Test* (BBC)
Broadcast: 25/4/75

Dreamer Deceiver/Deceiver

Programme: *The Old Grey Whistle Test* (BBC)
Aired: 25/4/75

Take On The World

Programme: *Top Of The Pops* (BBC)
Aired: 25/1/79

Evening Star

Programme: *Top Of The Pops* (BBC)
Aired: 17/5/79

Living After Midnight

Programme: *Top Of The Pops* (BBC)
Aired: 27/3/80

United

Programme: *Top Of The Pops* (BBC)
Aired: 28/8/80

Behind The Music: Judas Priest

Programme: *Behind The Music* (VH1)
Aired: 23/9/01

Diamonds And Rust/Worth Fighting For (Acoustic)

Programme: VH1 Special
Aired: 2005

VH1 Rock Honours

Performed on May 25, 2006 in Las Vegas
Aired: 02/6/06

JUDAS PRIEST TRIBUTE ALBUMS

A Tribute To Judas Priest: Legends Of Metal
Year of Release: 1997
Label: Century Media
Catalogue Number (UK): 7 277017 711523
Track Listing: The Hellion/Electric Eye (Helloween)/Rapid Fire
(Testament)/Saints In Hell (Fate Warning)/The Ripper (Mercyful Fate)/
Exciter (Strapping Young Lad)/Burnin' Up (Doom Squad)/Love Bites
(Nevermore)/Tyrant (Overkill)/Grinder (Kreator)/The Ripper (Iced
Earth)

A Tribute To Judas Priest Vol. 2: Delivering The Goods
Year of Release: 2000
Label: Century Media
Catalogue Number (UK): 7 277017 712520
Track Listing: Exciter (Gamma Ray)/Beyond The Realms Of Death
(Blind Guardian)/Sinner (Devin Townsend)/Bloodstone
(Stratovarius)/Painkiller (Angra)/Metal Gods (U.D.O.)/Dissident
Aggressor (Forbidden)/Desert Plains (Iron Savior)/Jawbreaker (Rage)/
Screaming For Vengeance (Virgin Steele)/Victim Of Changes (Gamma
Ray)/Night Crawler (Radakka)/You've Got Another Thing Comin'
(Saxon)

Hell Bent For Metal: A Tribute To Judas Priest
Year of Release: 1999
Label: Dwell
Catalogue Number (UK): 1017
Track Listing: Eat Me Alive (Angel Corpse)/Hell Patrol (Sanctorum)/
Steeler (Winters Bane)/ Beyond The Realms Of Death (Agent Steel)/
Electric Eye (Scary German Guy)/Hell Bent For Leather (Soulless)/The
Ripper (Equinox)/Metal Meltdown (Aurora Borealis)/ Dreamer Deceiver
(Steel Prophet)/Breaking The Law (Crematorium)/The Sentinel
(Prototype)/Desert Plains (Division)/You've Got Another Thing Comin'
(Vital Remains)

Hell Bent For Metal Vol. 2: A Tribute To Judas Priest
Year of Release: 2000
Label: Dwell

Catalogue Number (UK): B00004TFFA
Track Listing: Freewheel Burning (Cage)/The Green Manalishi (With The Two-Pronged Crown) (Burning Inside)/Grinder (Speed)/Rapid Fire (Defekt)/Tyrant (Tyrant)/Devil's Child (Acheron)/Diamonds And Rust (Seven Witches)/Screaming For Vengeance (Blood Coven) Exciter (Killswitch)/Riding On The Road (Debauchery)/Delivering The Goods (Dissaray)/Sinner (Engrave)

Breakin' the Law: An Industrial Rock Tribute To Judas Priest

Year of Release: 2001
Label: Zebra
Catalogue Number (UK): CDMZEB17
Track Listing: The Hellion/Electric Eye (Jani Lane)/You've Got Another Thing Comin' (Joe LeSte)/Hell Bent For Leather (Taime Downe)/Heading Out To The Highway (Chaz)/Turbo Lover (Jizzy Pearl)/Rock Forever (Spike)/The Green Manalishi (With The Two-Pronged Crown) (Electric Hellfire Club)/Steeler (Alex Mitchell)/Living After Midnight (Marq Torien)/Hot Rockin' (Phil Lewis)/Breaking The Law (Kory Clarke)/Delivering The Goods (John Corabi)

A Tribute To The Priest

Year of Release: 2002
Label: *Unknown*
Catalogue Number (UK): *Unknown*
Track Listing: Hell Bent For Leather (Annihilator)/Metal Gods (Primal Fear)/Delivering The Goods – Live (Skid Row)/Riding On The Wind (Witchery)/Screaming For Vengeance (Iced Earth)/Jawbreaker (Siebenburgen)/Breaking The Law (Hammerfall)/Electric Eye (Benediction)/Painkiller (Death)/All Guns Blazing (Silent Force)/Dreamer Deceiver (Steel Prophet)/Never Satisfied (Armored Saint)/The Green Manalishi (With The Two-Pronged Crown) (Therion)/Diamonds And Rust (Thunderstone)

Tribute To Judas Priest: Acero Argentino

Year of Release: 2006
Label: *Unknown*
Catalogue Number (UK): GLD GK 48171
Track Listing: You've Got Another Thing Comin' (Kefren)/Turbo Lover (Horcas)/Painkiller (Patan)/Metal Meltdown (Maley)/Metal Gods

(Renacer)/Screaming For Vengeance (Razones Concientes)/A Touch Of Evil (Lorihen)/The Hellion/Electric Eye (Tren Loco)/All Guns Blazing (Serpentor)/Hell Patrol (Mistica Power)/Breaking The Law (Metal Proyect)/Freewheel Burning (Jason)/Bloodstone (Atenas)/Ram It Down (Atavica)/Deal With The Devil (Lord Kraven)/Living After Midnight (Saul Blanch)

ROB HALFORD

STUDIO ALBUMS, CDs

In between leaving and rejoining Judas Priest, Rob Halford formed three bands – Fight, Two and Halford. All of his non-Priest music endeavours are listed under this solo heading as well as some new collections. A series of albums were reissued and remastered in November, 2006 but were only made available on i-Tunes Music Store, so these have not been included here.

FIGHT
War Of Words
Year of Release: 1993
Label: Epic
Catalogue Number (UK): SNY57372.2
Track Listing: Into The Pit/Nailed To The Gun/Life In Black/Immortal Sin/War Of Words/Laid To Rest/For All Eternity/Little Crazy/Contortion/Kill It/Vicious/Reality, A New Beginning

FIGHT
Mutations (EP: Collectors Edition)
Year of Release: 1994
Label: Epic
Catalogue Number (UK): SNY66127.2
Track Listing: Into The Pit (Live)/Nailed To The Gun (Live)/Freewheel Burning (Live)/Little Crazy (Live)/War Of Words (Bloody Tongue Mix)/Kill It (Dutch Death Mix)/Vicious (Middle Finger Mix)/Immortal Sin (Tolerance Mix)/Little Crazy (Straight Jacket Mix)

FIGHT
A Small Deadly Space
Year of Release: 1995
Label: Epic
Catalogue Number (UK): EK66649
Track Listing: I Am Alive/Mouthpiece/Legacy Of Hate/Blowout In The Radio Room/Never Again/Small Deadly Space/Gretna Greene/Beneath The Violence/Human Crate/In A World Of My Own Making

TWO
Voyeurs
Year of Release: 1998
Label: Eastwest/Warner Music
Catalogue Number (UK): 3984–22089–2
Track Listing: I Am A Pig/Stutter Kiss/Water's Leaking/My Ceiling's Low/Leave Me Alone/If/Deep In The Ground/Hey, Sha La La/Wake Up/Gimp/Bed Of Rust

HALFORD
Resurrection
Year of Release: 2000
Label: Metal–Is/Sanctuary
Catalogue Number (UK): MTAL85200.2
Track Listing: Resurrection/Made In Hell/Locked And Loaded/Night Fall/Silent Screams/The One You Love To Hate/Cyberworld/Slow Down/Twist/Temptation/Drive/Saviour

(A limited-edition CD box-set with a poster and postcard was also released. The catalogue number is MISBX001.)

HALFORD
Crucible
Year of Release: 2002
Label: Metal–Is/Sanctuary
Catalogue Number (UK): MISCD020
Track Listing: Park Manor/Crucible/One Will/Betrayal/Handing Out Bullets/Hearts Of Darkness/Crystal/Heretic/Golgotha/Wrath Of God/ Weaving Sorrow/Sun/Trail Of Tears/She*/Fugitive*

*Listed as bonus tracks on the limited-edition collectors set. The catalogue number is MISBX020.

LIVE ALBUMS, CDs

HALFORD
Live Insurrection
Year of Release: 2001
Label: Metal-Is/Sanctuary
Catalogue Number (UK): MISDD007
Track Listing: **Disc 1** – Resurrection/Made In Hell/Into The Pit/Nailed To The Gun/Light Comes Out Of Black/Stained Class/Jawbreaker/Running Wild/Slow Down/The One You Love To Hate (featuring Bruce Dickinson)/Life In Black/Hell's Last Saviour/Sad Wings/Saviour/Silent Screams
Disc 2 – Intro/Cyberworld/The Hellion/Electric Eye/Riding On The Wind/Genocide/Beyond The Realms Of Death/Metal Gods/Breaking The Law/Tyrant/Screaming In The Dark★/Heart Of A Lion★/Prisoner Of Your Eyes★

★*These are studio tracks, the latter two being re-recordings of shelved Priest songs from the* Turbo *album.*

HALFORD

Disney House Of Blues Concert (DEP)
Year of Release: 2004
Label: RHML UK/ EMAS Inc/DEP Music TM
Track Listing: Painkiller/Jawbreaker/Resurrection/Made In Hell/One Will/Hearts Of Darkness/Into The Pit/Golgotha/Cyberworld/The Hellion/Electric Eye/Riding On The Wind

PROMO VIDEOS

TWO

I Am A Pig
Year of Release:
Director: Chi Chi LaRue

HALFORD

Betrayal
Year of Release: 2002 (June)
Director: Salzy

GUEST APPEARENCES

KROKUS
Album: Headhunter
Track: Ready To Burn
Year of Release: 1983
Label: Arista
Catalogue Number (UK): *Unknown*

HEAR 'N AID (VARIOUS ARTISTS)
Track: Stars
Year of Release: 1986
Label: *Unknown*
Catalogue Number (UK): *Unknown*

SKID ROW
Album: B-Side Ourselves
Track: Delivering The Goods
Year of Release: 1992
Label: Warner
Catalogue Number (UK): *Unknown*

PANTERA
Album: Buffy The Vampire Slayer (Movie Soundtrack)
Track: Light Comes Out Of Black
Year of Release: 1992
Label: Columbia
Catalogue Number (UK): CK52854

UGLY KID JOE
Album: America's Least Wanted
Track: Goddamn Devil
Year of Release: 1992
Label: Mercury
Catalogue Number (UK): 512571–2

VARIOUS ARTISTS
Album: Nativity In Black
Track: The Wizard (Performed by the Bullring Brummies feat. Rob

Halford, Geezer Butler, Bill Ward, Brian Tilse & Wino)
Year of Release: 1994
Label: Columbia
Catalogue Number (UK): 4776712

QUEENS OF THE STONE AGE
Album: Rated R
Track: Feel Good Hit Of The Summer
Year of Release: 2000
Label: Interscope Records
Catalogue Number: 490863–2

FURIOUS IV
Album: Is That You?
Track: *Unknown*
Year of Release: 2003
Label: Naked Jain
Catalogue Number (Import): *Unknown*

GLENN TIPTON

STUDIO ALBUMS, CDs

The following solo albums are the 2006 Rhino Records reissues. Baptizm Of Fire (first released on Atlantic Records) was remastered and expanded in 2006 alongside Edge Of The World, which saw the light of day for the first time that year. The latter was released under the heading of 'Tipton, Entwistle & Powell'.

Baptizm Of Fire
Year of Release: 1997
Label: Rhino
Catalogue Number (UK): 8122733332
Track Listing: Hard Core/Paint It Black/Enter The Storm/Fuel Me Up/ Extinct/Baptizm Of Fire/The Healer/Cruise Control/Kill Or Be Killed/ Voodoo Brother/Left For Dead/Himalaya★/New Breed★

★*Previously unreleased bonus tracks*

TIPTON, ENTWISTLE & POWELL
Edge Of The World
Year of Release: 2006
Label: Rhino
Catalogue Number (UK): 8122733522
Track Listing: Unknown Soldier/Friendly Fire/The Holy Man/Never Say Die/Resolution/Searching/Give Blood/Crime Of Passion/Walls Cave In/Edge Of The World/Stronger Than The Drug

TIM 'RIPPER' OWENS

STUDIO ALBUMS, CDs

Like Rob Halford, Tim Owens has never recorded a solo album per se, preferring the security of a band environment. Here is a selective list of the official albums from the bands he has been in outside of Judas Priest.

WINTERS BANE
Heart Of A Killer
Year of Release: 1993
Label: Century Media
Catalogue Number (UK): *Unknown*
Track Listing: **Disc 1** – Wages Of Sin/Blink Of An Eye/Heart Of A Killer/Horror Glances/The Silhouette/Reflections Within/Haunted House/Night Shade/Winters Bane/Cleansing Mother
Disc 2 – Wages Of Sin (Live)★/Blink Of An Eye (Live)★/Heart Of A Killer (Live)★/Horror Glances (Live)★/Silhouette (Live)★/Reflections Within (Live)★/Haunted House (Live)★/Fear Of Death (Live)★/Cleansing Mother (Live)★/My Dagger's Revenge (Demo Version)★/Eyes Of The Deceiver (Demo)/Seven Nations (Instrumental Demo Version)
★Bonus tracks included on the 2000 Century Media reissue

WINTERS BANE
Redivivus
Year of Release: 2006
Label: Metal Heaven
Catalogue Number (UK): METAL00022
Track Listing: Seal The Light/Spark To Flame/The World/Dead Faith/

Catching The Sun/Remember To Forget/Burning Bridges/Waves Of
Fury/Despise The Lie/Catching The Sun/Remember To Forget/Seal
The Light/Furies

ICED EARTH
The Reckoning (EP)
Year of Release: 2003
Label: SPV Records
Catalogue Number (UK): SPV05674983
Track Listing: The Reckoning (Don't Tread On Me)/When The Eagle
Cries (Unplugged)/Valley Forge/Hollow Man

ICED EARTH
The Glorious Burden
Year of Release: 2004
Label: SPV Records
Catalogue Number (UK): SPV08574972
Track Listing: **Disc 1** – The Star-Spangled Banner
(Instrumental)/Declaration Day/When The Eagle Cries/The Reckoning
(Don't Tread On Me)/Greenface/Attila/Red Baron/Blue Max/Hollow
Man/Valley Forge/Waterloo/When The Eagle Cries (Unplugged)
Disc 2 – The Devil To Pay/Hold At All Costs/High Water Mark

BEYOND FEAR
Beyond Fear
Year of Release: 2006
Label: SPV Records
Catalogue Number (UK): SPV99862
Track Listing: Scream Machine/And You Will Die/Save Me/The Human
Race/Coming At You/Dreams Come True/Telling Lies/I Don't Need
This/Words Of Wisdom/My Last Words/Your Time Has Come/
The Faith

PROMO VIDEOS
ICED EARTH
The Reckoning
Year of Release: 2004 (March)
Director: Brian Smith

SCOTT TRAVIS

STUDIO ALBUMS, CDs

Before joining Judas Priest, Scott Travis had a good stint (which continues to this day) in the LA metal band Racer X. He was also the drummer in Fight with Rob Halford.

RACER X
Street Lethal
Year of Release: 1986
Label: Shrapnel
Catalogue Number (UK): SHR1023.3
Track Listing: Frenzy/Street Lethal/Into The Night/Blowin' Up The Radio/ Hotter Than Fire/On The Loose/Loud And Clear/Y.R.O./ Dangerous Love/ Getaway/Rock It

RACER X
Second Heat
Year of Release: 1988
Label: Shrapnel
Catalogue Number (UK): RR349601
Track Listing: Sacrifice/Gone Too Far/Scarified/Sunlit Nights/Hammer Away/Heart Of A Lion/Motorman/Moonage Daydream/Living The Hard Way/Lady Killer

RACER X
Technical Difficulties
Year of Release: 1999
Label: Mascot
Catalogue Number (UK): M7046CD
Track Listing: Phallic Tractor/Fire Of Rock/Snakebite/Technical Difficulties/Miss Mistreater/Bolt In My Heart/17th Moon/Waiting/ Poison Eyes/B.R.O./God Of The Sun/Give It To Me/The Executioner's Song/Children Of The Grave

RACER X
Superheroes
Year of Release: 2000
Label: Mascot
Catalogue Number (UK): M7056CD
Track Listing: Superheroes/Let The Spirit Fly/Godzilla/Dead Man's Shoes/King Of The Monsters/Mad At The World/Evil Joe/That Hormone Thing/Viking Kong/Time Before The Sun/O.H.B.(One Hot Bitch)

RACER X
Getting Heavier
Year of Release: 2002
Label: Mascot
Catalogue Number (UK): M7077CD
Track Listing: Dr. X/Lucifer's Hammer/Golden God/Bucket Of Rocks/Go-GG-Go/Heaven In '74/Everything's Everything/Empty Man/The Siren's Eye/Ghost Dance/Endless/Catapult To Extinction

FIGHT
War Of Words
Year of Release: 1993
Label: Epic
Catalogue Number (UK): SNY57372.2
Track Listing: Into The Pit/Nailed To The Gun/Life In Black/Immortal Sin/War Of Words/Laid To Rest/For All Eternity/Little Crazy/Contortion/Kill It/Vicious/Reality, A New Beginning

FIGHT
Mutations (EP: Collectors Edition)
Year of Release: 1994
Label: Epic
Catalogue Number (UK): SNY66127.2
Track Listing: Into The Pit (Live)/Nailed To The Gun (Live)/Freewheel Burning (Live)/Little Crazy (Live)/War Of Words (Bloody Tongue Mix)/Kill It (Dutch Death Mix)/Vicious (Middle Finger Mix)/Immortal Sin (Tolerance Mix)/Little Crazy (Straight Jacket Mix)

FIGHT
A Small Deadly Space
Year of Release: 1995
Label: Epic
Catalogue Number (UK): EK66649
Track Listing: I Am Alive/Mouthpiece/Legacy Of Hate/Blowout In The
Radio Room/Never Again/Small Deadly Space/Gretna Greene/Beneath
The Violence/Human Crate/In A World Of My Own Making

LIVE ALBUMS, CDs

RACER X
Extreme Volume – Live
Year of Release: 1988
Label: Shrapnel
Catalogue Number (UK): SHR1038.2
Track Listing: Loud And Clear/Dangerous Love/Bruce's Solo/Gone Too
Far/John's Solo/ She Wants Control/ Scit Scat Wah/Into The Night/
Paul's Solo/Motorman/Scott's Solo/Set The World On Fire

RACER X
Extreme Volume II – Live
Year of Release: 1992
Label: Shrapnel
Catalogue Number (UK): SHR1059.2
Track Listing: Hammer Away/Poison Eyes/Heart Of A Lion/Moonage
Daydream/Sunlit Nights/Give It To Me/On The Loose/Rock It/Detroit
Rock City

RACER X
Live At The Whiskey: Snowball Of Doom
Year of Release: 2001
Label: Mascot
Catalogue Number (UK): M7064CD
Track Listing: 17th Moon/Into The Night/Let The Spirit Fly/Street
Lethal/Dead Man's Shoes/Scarified/Get Away/Snakebite/Hammer
Away/Evil Joe/Phallic Tractor/ Fire Of Rock/O.H.B./Godzilla

RACER X
Snowball Of Doom 2 (Official Bootleg, recorded in Yokohama)
Year of Release: 2003
Label: Rock Empire
Catalogue Number (UK): *Unknown*
Track Listing: Superheroes/Phallic Tractor/ Fire Of Rock/ The
Executioner's Song/ King Of The Monsters/Dead Man's Shoes/Sunlit
Nights/Into The Night/Y.R.O. + Paul Solo/Let The Spirit Fly/Waiting/
Hammer Away/John's Solo/ Miss Mistreater/ That Hormone Thing/
Scarified/Scott's Solo/Motorman

AL ATKINS

STUDIO ALBUMS, CDs

*Since his departure from Judas Priest over 30 years ago, Al Atkins has recorded
several solo albums over the years, although most of these releases can be difficult to
get hold of.*

Judgement Day
Year of Release: 1989
Label: SPM
Catalogue Number (UK): SPM-WWR-CD-0008
Track Listing: Good Lovin' Runs Deep/Every Dream/Time After Time/
Go/Judgement Day/I Got Your Letter/Victim Of Changes

Dreams Of Avalon
Year of Release: 1991
Label: Green Tree
Catalogue Number (UK): TRC-GTR003
Track Listing: Dreams Of Avalon/Eastern Promise/If You Should Leave
Me/Coming Thick And Fast/Run River Run/Victim Of Love/Sacrifice/
Left Out In The Cold

Victim Of Changes
Year of Release: 1998
Label: Neat Metal
Catalogue Number (UK): NM027

Track Listing: Victim Of Changes/Never Satisfied/Black Sheep Of The Family/The Meltdown/Winter/Metanoia/Mind Conception/Holy Is The Man/Caviar And Meths

Heavy Thoughts
Year of Release: 2003
Label: Market Square
Catalogue Number (UK): MSMCD120
Track Listing: Heavy Thoughts/Turn Around/Price Of Love/When Love Steals The Night/Void To Avoid/Deepest Blue/Little Wild Child/Caviar And Meths/Cradle To The Grave★/Sentenced★

★*Bonus tracks*

(This album was originally planned to be released in 1995 by Gull Records but was shelved and eventually issued in 2003 on the London-based label Market Square Records. Two bonus tracks are included.)

Demon Deceiver (The Sin Sessions)
Year of Release: 2006
Label: Diesel And Glory
Catalogue Number (UK): DG 003
Track Listing: Demon Deceiver/Money Talks/Blood, Demons And Whiskey/Drown/Sentenced/Victim Of Changes/Bleeding/God Help Me/Cradle To The Grave/Dreamer Deceiver

BIBLIOGRAPHY

There is a bewildering amount of information available on Judas Priest in books, magazines and on the internet. In addition to the author's own personal interviews with various artists, music business people, former band members, and childhood friends and acquaintances, the following sources have been invaluable in constructing and refining this book. The author is openly indebted to all of them.

Music-Related Books:

Baddeley, Gavin. *Lucifer Rising: Sin, Devil Worshipping & Rock 'N' Roll*. London: Plexus, 1999.

Barker, Derek (Ed.) *20 Years Of Isis: Bob Dylan Anthology, Volume 2*. Surrey: Chrome Dreams, 2005.

Christe, Ian. *Sound Of The Beast: The Complete Headbanging History Of Heavy Metal*. London: Allison & Busby Limited, 2004.

Gett, Steve. *Heavy Duty: The Official Judas Priest Biography*. New York: Cherry Lane Music. Co., Inc. 1984

Larkin, Colin. *The Virgin Encyclopaedia Of Rock*. London: Virgin Books, 1999.

McIver, Joel. *Sabbath Bloody Sabbath*. London: Omnibus Press, 2006.

Roberts, David (Ed.) *British Hit Singles & Albums (19th Edition.)* London: Guinness World Records Ltd, 2006.

Tucker, John. *Suzie Smiled . . . The New Wave Of British Heavy Metal*. Shropshire: Independent Music Press, 2006.

Wall, Mick. *Run To The Hills: The Authorised Biography Of Iron Maiden (Revised Edition)*. London: Sanctuary Publishing, 2001.

Non-Music Related Books:

Hopkins, Eric. *The Rise And Decline Of The English Working Classes. 1918–1990: A Social History*. London: George Weidenfeld & Nicolson Ltd, 1991.

Hoskins, W.G. *Local History In England (3rd Edition)*. Essex: Addison Wesley Longman Ltd, 1984.

James, Clive. *North Face Of Soho*. London: Picador. 2006.

Lee, J. Stephen. *Aspects Of British Political History: 1914–1995*. London: Routledge, 1996.

Moorhouse, Frank. *Satanic Killings*. London: Allison & Busby Limited, 2006.

Pearce, Malcolm and Stewart, Geoffrey. *British Political History 1867–1995: Democracy And Decline (2nd Edition)*. London: Routledge, 1996.

Tiller, Kate. *English Local History: An Introduction (2nd Edition)*. Gloucestershire: Sutton Publishing, 2002.

Music Papers/Magazines/Fanzines:

Sounds & Sounds: Guitar Heroes, Kerrang! & Kerrang! Mega Metal, Metal Hammer, Hard Rock, Metal Forces, Raw, Classic Rock, Record Collector, Fireworks Melodic Rock, Metal Edge, Rock Hard, Zero Tolerance, Hard Roxx and Powerplay.

Music Features/Articles:

Reesman, Bryan. *Hell Bent For Leather: The Story Of Judas Priest*. Goldmine Magazine, June 5, 1998, Vol. 24, No.12, Issue 466. Krause Publications, 1998.

Reesman, Bryan. *The State Of Metal 1999: Rocking Hard, Riding Free*. Goldmine Magazine, May 21, 1999, Vol. 25, No.11, Issue 491. Krause Publications, 1999.

Online Articles

http://www.thenervemagazine.com/article_template.php?id=2

Judas Priest-Related Websites:

http://www.judaspriest.com/
http://www.robhalford.com/

http://www.alatkins.com/
http://www.glenntipton.co.uk/default.asp
http://www.thecadence.co.uk/ *(this site belongs to ex-Priest bassist and founding member Bruno Stapenhill and has some little anecdotes from the early days with Al Atkins)*

Judas Priest Fan Sites:

http://home.earthlink.net/~judas_priest_bootlegs/ *('Return Of The Metal Gods: Judas Priest Bootlegs' has a comprehensive list of Priest bootlegs from throughout their history – interesting)*
http://members.firstinter.net/markster/MENU.html *('Judas Priest Info Pages' offers information of K.K. Downing and Glenn Tipton)*
http://www.judas-priest.com/ *('The Judas Priest Shrine' is an excellent website)*
http://judaspriest.free.fr/ *(Every Priest fan must pay a visit to 'The French Metallian' – outstanding!)*

Other Artists' Websites:

http://www.savatage.com/
http://www.jonathanvalen.com/index.html

Music-Related Websites:

http://www.mvdbase.com/
http://www.rockdetector.com/index.sm
http://www.vh1.com/
http://www.mp3.com/
http://uk.launch.yahoo.com/

Non-Music Websites:

http://en.wikipedia.org/wiki/Wikipedia
http://www.youtube.com/
http://www.imdb.com/

http://news.bbc.co.uk/onthisday/default.stm
http://encyclopedia.jrank.org/
http://www.reversespeech.com/Simple_Examples.htm
http://www.skepticfiles.org/
http://www.meta-religion.com/
www.localhistory.scit.wlv.ac.uk/home.htm
http://www.cnn.com/

Multimedia Resources:

John Hinch interview on the American release of *The Best Of Judas Priest* (Transluxe Records. Catalogue Number: 57800–2)

Classic Albums: British Steel (Eagle Vision/Isis Productions: 2001. Catalogue Number: EREDV163)

Metal Works: '73–'93 (SMV Enterprises: 1993. Catalogue Number: 2004962 – VHS)

National Newspapers:

The Advocate, May 12, 1998
The New York Times, July 17, 1990
The New York Tines, August 14, 1997
Metro, March 29, 2006
The Sun, February 8, 2003
The Times, October 11, 1947
_____, April 5, 1948
_____, October 25, 1948
_____, January 20, 1951
_____, August 25, 1951
_____, October 27, 1951
_____, March 21, 2005

Provincial Newspapers:

Northampton Chronicle & Echo, August 9, 2003
_____, January 16, 2004

_____, January 17, 2004

_____, January 20, 2004

_____, January 21, 2004

_____, January 22, 2004

_____, January 24, 2004

_____, January 26, 2004

_____, February14, 2004

ACKNOWLEDGEMENTS

Writing a book is not a solo effort. There have been innumerable people who have helped me along the way. First and foremost, I'd like to thank Chris Charlesworth for his guidance, patience and, primarily, for giving me such a big opportunity in the first place. I'd also like to pass on my thanks to the staff at Omnibus Press.

I was not given access to the members of Judas Priest or their close circle of friends and colleagues; however, that did not prevent me from speaking to their former bandmates. In alphabetical order, I'd like to thank: Al Atkins, Ernie Chataway, John Ellis, John Hinch, Dave Holland, Tim 'Ripper' Owens, Simon Phillips, and Brian 'Bruno' Stapenhill. It is worth mentioning here that artist John Pasche was very kind, offering his memories from working with Priest during their Gull Records years. Eighties Priest biographer Steve Gett was also generous with his time.

I'd also like to thank the following artists for their first-hand accounts of working with Priest, or simply for being fans and admirers. In alphabetical order, they are: Pete Boot, Cronos (Venom), Don Dokken, Kevin DuBrow (Quiet Riot), Roger Glover (Deep Purple), Frank Harthoorn (Gorefest), Wolf Hoffmann (Accept), Adrian Ingram, Scott Ian (Anthrax), Chris Jericho (Fozzy), Christopher Kinder (Jon Oliva's Pain), Claus Lessmann (Bonfire), Michael McKeegan (Therapy?), Jason McMaster (Dangerous Toys), Jon Oliva (Savatage and Jon Oliva's Pain), Doane Perry (Jethro Tull), Doro Pesch, John Ricci (Exciter), Brian Ross (Blitzkrieg), Ralf Scheepers (Primal Fear), Marc Storace (Krokus), Joe Lynn Turner, Martin Turner (Wishbone Ash), Jonathan Valen and, finally, Jeff Waters (Annihilator).

The following record company personnel and producers have been incredibly helpful. In alphabetical order, they are: David Howells (Darah), Geraint Hughes, Gerardo Martinez (Nuclear Blast Records), Derek Oliver (Roadrunner and Rock Candy Records), Manuel Schoenfied and the staff at SPV, Jim Simpson (Big Bear Music), Michael Wagener and Pete Waterman.

I'd also like to thank the following PR people for their help and patience. In alphabetical order, they are: Sharon Chevin (Publicity

Connection), Alison Edwards (Pure Press), Maria Ferrero (Adrenaline PR) and Louise Molloy-Harris (Quite Great PR).

The following journalists and writers have been very generous with their time: Phil & Sue Ashcroft (*Fireworks Melodic Rock*), Jason Draper (*Record Collector*), Mark Hoaksey (*Powerplay*), Tim Jones (*Record Collector*), Joel McIver (freelance writer/author) and Daniela Pilic (*Sweden Rock Magazine*.) Special thanks must also go to author/journalists John Tucker, for boosting my confidence; and Bruce Mee of *Fireworks Melodic Rock* for letting me use his extensive collection of rock magazines from the Eighties to the present day; and Jeff Apter for offering me tips and for editing selected chapters when he really didn't have to.

In no particular order, I'd like to thank the staff of the Northampton-shire Central Library and other libraries situated in and around the Midlands; *The Northampton Chronicle & Echo*, and various other Midlands/ Northamptonshire-based papers that published my letters of inquiry, Helena Denham and the staff of Walsall Reference Library; Janine Graeme and the staff of the Grand Theatre in Wolverhampton; Brian Ench and John Williams.

Several former friends of the band made contact, offering their thoughts and memories. They are: Alan Dunckley, Michael Gadsden, David Lucas, Colin 'Cobbies' Roberts, Beverley Stone, Graham Walker and Morris Walker. Thanks to all those generous people who replied to my letters/ e-mails when I was digging into the early years of the band – much appreciated.

Also, I'd like to apologise to all those whom I annoyed with my continuous pestering – I think that's everybody on this list!

A number of interviews were done by e-mail and whenever required I corrected/amended any spelling, grammatical and punctuation errors, although this did not alter the meanings, content or opinions.

On a personal note, I'd like to thank my partner Emma Kilgannon for, well, putting up with my tantrums, for making me many cups of coffee and for allowing me to spend many late nights in our office working on this book. Thanks also to Scott, Rob and Graeme for being good friends and, of course, to my parents Ann and Andrew and the rest of my family.

I apologise in advance if I have forgotten anyone – humans cannot think straight with such little sleep. Now if you don't mind I'd like to give *British Steel* another spin!